THOMAS FRANCIS MEAGHER

To George,

If not often seen these days, hardly forgotten!

Greetings from South Carolina,

As Ever,

Ron

December 2005.

THE IRISH ABROAD

General Editor: Ruan O'Donnell, University of Limerick

This new series aims to publish short biographies of Irish men and women who made their mark outside their native country. Accounts of those who settled permanently overseas will be published along with the life stories of temporary residents and involuntary emigrants. Expatriates of all types will be considered whether explorers, travellers, military personnel, colonial pioneers, members of religious orders, professionals, politicians, revolutionaries, exiles or convicts. While it is envisaged that the majority of the subjects would have gone overseas during the early modern and modern period, persons from different times may also be deemed appropriate for inclusion. Most titles will concern the Irish in North America, the former territories of the British Empire (including Australasia) and Great Britain, although it is intended that biographies of those who journeyed to Spanish America, the West Indies, Africa, Continental Europe and other non-English speaking sectors will form part of the series. Men and women of Irish extraction will also merit inclusion if it is evident that their perceived ethnicity and family origins played a significant part in their careers. A number of autobiographies will be selected for republication with critical introductions by leading scholars.

Also in the Irish Abroad series from Irish Academic Press:

Thomas Francis Meagher
The Making of an Irish American
John M. Hearne and Rory T. Cornish (eds)

Through American and Irish Wars
The Life and Times of General Thomas W. Sweeny
Jack Morgan

Bishop in the Dock
The Sedition Trial of James Liston
Rory Sweetman

Equestrian sculpture of Thomas Francis Meagher, The Mall, Waterford, Ireland.
(Sculpture by Catherine Green, photograph by Terry Murphy Media)

THOMAS FRANCIS MEAGHER
The Making of an Irish American

Editors
JOHN M. HEARNE
Waterford Institute of Technology

RORY T. CORNISH
Winthrop University, South Carolina

Foreword by
ROY FOSTER

IRISH ACADEMIC PRESS
DUBLIN • PORTLAND, OR

First published in Great Britain in 2006 by
IRISH ACADEMIC PRESS
44 Northumberland Road, Dublin 4, Ireland

and in the United States of America by
IRISH ACADEMIC PRESS
c/o ISBS, Suite 300, 920 NE 58th Avenue
Portland, Oregon 97213-3644

Website: iap.ie

British Library Cataloguing in Publication Data
An entry can be found on request

ISBN 0-7165-2812 6 (cloth)
ISBN 0-7165-2813 4 (paper)

Library of Congress Cataloging-in-Publication Data
An entry can be found on request

Typeset by FiSH Books, Enfield, Middx.
Printed by MPG Books Ltd, Bodmin, Cornwall

CONTENTS

List of Contributors

Jon Axline is currently the historian at the Montana Department of Transportation in Helena. He has an MA from Montana State University (Bozeman) and specializes in the history of the American West. Jon has published extensively on socio-economic issues pertaining to Montana and the wider American West. He is author of a forthcoming publication which details the historic highways and bridges of Montana.

Eugene Broderick teaches history and English at Our Lady of Mercy Secondary School in Waterford City and lectures in History at Waterford Institute of Technology. He is a graduate of the National University of Ireland, Cork. Dr Broderick has contributed many articles to national and international publications on various aspects of nineteenth- and twentieth-century Irish history. He was a contributor to the widely acclaimed *Waterford Treasures: A guide to the historical and archaeological treasures of Waterford City* (2004).

Rory T. Cornish was educated at the University of East Anglia, Davidson College, North Carolina and University College London. Having taught at Gonzaga University, Whitman College and the University of Louisiana at Monroe, he was appointed Chair of the Department of History at Winthrop University, South Carolina in 2002. The author of a book on George Grenville and contributor to seven other joint publications, he wrote the new entry on Thomas Francis Meagher in the *Oxford Dictionary of National Biography*, (2004).

David Emmons is Professor Emeritus at the University of Montana, Missoula. He has written extensively on the Irish in America and on the Irish in Montana. Professor Emmons is author of the critically acclaimed *The Butte Irish: Class and ethnicity in an American mining town* (1989) and is a frequent broadcaster and critic.

Roy Foster was born in Waterford in 1949 and educated at Newtown School, and subsequently at St Andrew's School, Delaware, USA, and at Trinity College Dublin, where he was a foundation scholar in history. He is currently Carroll Professor of Irish History at Oxford, having previously been Professor of Modern British History at Birkbeck College, University of London. He has been awarded honorary degrees from University of Aberdeen, Queen's University, Belfast, Trinity College, Dublin and the National University of Ireland; he has been a fellow of the British Academy since 1989 and has held visiting fellowships at the Institute of Advanced Study, Princeton, and Princeton University. He is also a frequent broadcaster and critic. His books include *Charles Stewart Parnell: The man and his family* (1976), *Lord Randolph Churchill: A political life* (1981), *Modern Ireland 1600–1972* (1988), *The Oxford Illustrated History of Ireland* (1989), *The Sub-Perfect Should Have Held His Tongue: Selected essays by Hubert Butler* (1990), *Paddy and Mr Punch: Connections in Irish and English History* (1993), *The Irish Story: Telling tales and making it up in Ireland* (2001), and *W.B. Yeats, A Life, 1: The apprentice mage, 1865–1914* (1997) and *11: The arch-poet, 1915–1939* (2003).

John M. Hearne was born in Waterford and is a graduate of the National University of Ireland, Cork, where he worked between 1992–98. He is former editor of *Decies*, Journal of the Waterford Archaeological and Historical Society and has published widely in national and international journals. Dr Hearne, a contributor to five joint publications is currently working on a full biography of Thomas Francis Meagher. He currently lectures in economic and social history at Waterford Institute of Technology.

Pat McCarthy was born in Waterford City where he was educated at Mount Sion Secondary School. He holds a Ph.D. in Chemistry and MBA from the National University of Ireland, Dublin, where he currently lives. He is employed in the pharmaceutical industry and is currently Correspondence Secretary of the Military History Society of Ireland and is a frequent contributor to national and international publications.

John Mannion holds a BA (1963) and MA (1965) in geography from the National University of Ireland, Dublin and a Ph.D. (1971) from the University of Toronto (Canada). He has been teaching cultural and historical geography at Memorial University of Newfoundland since 1969. Professor Mannion was recently (2004) awarded an Hon. D.Litt. from the National University of Ireland, Galway, for his work on Irish migrations and settlement in Newfoundland.

Eamonn McEneaney is a graduate of Trinity College, Dublin and has published widely on the history of medieval Waterford. He is editor of *Waterford Treasures: A guide to the historical and archaeological treasures of Waterford City* (2004) and author of *Discover Waterford* (2001) and *A History of Waterford and its Mayors* (1995). He is currently Director of Waterford Museum of Treasures and Curator of Reginald's Tower.

William Nolan is senior lecturer in geography at the National University of Ireland, Dublin. A native of Tipperary, he was born within sight of the Widow McCormack's house where the confrontation between the Young Irelanders and police occurred on 29 July 1848. In recent years he was involved in the campaign to have the 'Warhouse' declared a national monument and taken into state care. In 2004, the house was officially opened as a heritage centre dedicated to the history of the Young Irelanders. Dr Nolan is editor and originator of the *Irish County – History & Society* series.

David Smith is a retired civil servant and native of Waterford City. He has had a life-long interest in local history, both civil and ecclesiastical. He has published widely in journals, anthologies and in magazines.

Elaine Sullivan was born and educated in Melbourne, Australia and was educated at Deakin University (Melbourne), University of Bristol (UK) and Hawthorn Institute of Education (now University of Melbourne). She has had a life-long interest in the Young Irelanders and has researched and photographed where the seven lived and were imprisoned, both in Ireland and Australia.

Michael Toomey is currently staff historian at the East Tennessee Historical Society having previously been Associate Professor at Knoxville College (1991–99). Educated at the University of Tennessee (Knoxville) Dr Toomey has published extensively on various aspects of American History. He currently lives in Anderson County, not far from the home site John Mitchel first considered, then rejected, in favour of Tuckaleechee Cove

List of illustrations

Acknowledgements

The completion of this book is due in no small part to the dedication and expertise of a small group of contributors across three continents; and to the wonders of modern technology. In the process, this project has consumed the last two years of my life and, in so doing, has led to the accumulation of debts of generosity that I can never hope to repay. From the very moment that the idea of revisiting the enigma that is Thomas Francis Meagher was conceived, the encouragement for the undertaking has been overwhelming. My wife, Corinne has had to endure my long periods of self-imposed exile while my daughter, Aoife, in the midst of her studies, acted as conduit in Knoxville and Boston and also accessed much important material unavailable in Ireland. To both I extend my thanks and gratitude.

I would like to extend special thanks to Professor Joseph Lee, New York University and Professor Dermot Keogh, National University of Ireland, Cork for their encouragement, and to Professor Roy Foster, Oxford University, for undertaking to write the Foreword during a hectic schedule on the basis of a rough (very rough) draft. To the editorial staff at Irish Academic Press, Lisa Hyde, Rachel Milotte and Sarah Clarke (and Dr Ruan O'Donnell) for believing in the project, I extend my heartfelt gratitude.

In 2003, I was invited to deliver a lecture on Thomas Francis Meagher in Helena, Montana. This provided the stimulus to embark on this publication. Support for the venture was provided by Minister Martin Cullen and was grant-aided by the Cultural Affairs Committee of the Department of Foreign Affairs. I would like to take this opportunity to thank all concerned for their assistance.

Dr Cornish and I would like to especially acknowledge and thank the Heritage Council for its generous support for this publication.

The Montana Historical Society was generous in providing original documents and photographs at very short notice and, in this regard, I would like to acknowledge the assistance of Dr Clark Whitehorn and Rebecca Kohl. The National Library of Ireland also supplied unique photographs and I would like to acknowledge the assistance of Colette O'Flaherty, Siobhan O'Donovan and Sara Smyth. The staffs at Waterford Municipal Library, Boole Library, National University of Ireland, Cork and Waterford Museum of Treasures were always generous with their time and expertise and helped expedite my research in a friendly and understanding atmosphere. I would also like to extend my appreciation to Professor Catherine O'Brien, Dr Gillian Doherty, Clodagh Wall, Denis Naughton, Ailbe O'Donoghue, Eamonn McEneaney, Joan Johnston and Terry Murphy for their assistance during the past three years.

Finally, it would be remiss of me not to acknowledge the enormous academic debt I owe to the vibrant Department of History at National University of Ireland, Cork, and, in particular, to the late Dr John B. O'Brien, my former lecturer, supervisor and friend. John was an exceptional historian and his exacting standards have left an indelible mark on my academic career. He would have liked this.

Dr John M. Hearne
Waterford Institute of Technology
January 2005

In completing this project I owe thanks to a number of people. My wife Rachael Theodorakaki-Cornish first took me to Waterford in a personal quest to find her great-grandfather's grave. It was this visit in 1996 which first sparked my interest in Meagher. During the last two years she has tolerated my long absences, both physical and mental, while I concerned myself with Meagher's career. Rachael has learnt more about Meagher's career than, I suspect, she had ever wanted to. I would also like to thank Serena Kelly, Head of Corporate Information Management at the British Library, for her generous hospitality which made my numerous research trips to London possible. Carol Hanlon, the administrative assistant in the Department of History at Winthrop University, typed my numerous editorial re-writes with professional expertise while displaying the patience of a saint.

Over the years the professional and academic debt a practicing historian owes to his colleagues continually grows. I would like to thank four colleagues in particular that have helped shape my career, its direction and its development. Dr Roderick Von Stackleberg, a direct descendant of Thomas Addis Emmet, welcomed me to my first academic appointment in the United States at Gonzaga University with unfailing humour and support. Dr George McCowan of Willamette University revived my interest in Irish history by inviting me to deliver the 1999 Whipple Lecture on the contribution the Irish made to the antebellum American republic. My own interest in the American Civil War was rejuvenated by my former colleague at the University of Louisiana at Monroe, Dr Terry L. Jones, one of the finest historians it has been my pleasure to meet. Finally, I would like to thank Professor Roger F. Thompson of the University of East Anglia for transforming an unruly undergraduate into the transatlantic historian and teacher I am today.

Dr Rory T. Cornish
Winthrop University
January 2005

Foreword

The life of Thomas Francis Meagher suggests a fiction from the quintessential era of European Romanticism, perhaps a novel by Victor Hugo, or even an opera by Berlioz. The hero's headlong life combines the themes of youth, idealism, conflict with a powerful father, failed revolution, transportation to and escape from an exotic location, impulsive marriage, exile and war, and the climax comes with a sudden and mysterious death. But it also closely reflects the key social and political realities of early nineteenth-century Ireland, and Meagher's world is intimately linked with the history of his native Waterford. No one who walks past the substantial Granville Hotel on the Quay can fail to be reminded that this was the family home of Meagher's mother, and subsequently his parents; the fact that it was subsequently owned by the transport supremo, Charles Bianconi underlines the connection with the modernizing world of Daniel O'Connell, a figure who shaped the careers of both Meagher and his father, in different and antagonistic ways. But there are other patterns of relationship too, which make it highly apposite that this collection of essays about one of Waterford's most famous citizens is co-edited by a scholar of Waterford's history. The book adds greatly to our understanding of life in this corner of Ireland in the 1820s and 1830s, as well as the politics of the Irish Confederation, the fate of rebels transported to Van Diemen's Land, American fenianism, and the politics of the American Civil War.

The background to Meagher's family and their local connections is emblematic of Waterford's commercial culture; they represent the establishment of the prosperous Catholic bourgeoisie, whose lives would be later memorably anatomised in Katharine Cecil Thurston's 1908 novel, *The Fly on the Wheel.* John Mannion shows here how Meagher's grandfather emigrated to Newfoundland, and made a fortune in the cod trade, sending fish products back to Waterford and importing necessities back to St John's in return (as well as following that other classic route to riches, marrying his employer's widow). Waterford would be the hub of the family's prosperity: by a fitting irony, their main trading vessel was called the *Berisford*, echoing the name of the local Ascendancy grandees, whose political dominance was ended by O'Connell's movement. Meagher's father, Thomas, succeeded to a substantial role in the city's life, linked by politics and business to those family names familiar to Waterford historians, and still often to be found there today – Wyses, Aylwards, Meades, Sweetmans, Morrises. The locations of the family's property are also significant – not only the Quay but the

Mall, and Ballycanvan on the Suir a few miles outside the town. Meagher's father, a devout O'Connellite, was secretary of the local Catholic Association, and later the first Catholic Mayor of Waterford, as well as an MP at Westminster; as Eugene Broderick shows, he represents exactly the *couche sociale* politically empowered by the O'Connellite revolution, and the classes who took up Father Mathew's temperance crusade – an interest in marked contrast to the convivial tastes of his famous son.

More profoundly, Thomas Francis chose to embrace another kind of political revolution, and the early chapters of this book trace a relationship which, in terms of family politics, might come out of Turgenev's *Fathers and Sons*. The impulsive young man returns from education in England and launches himself into Young Ireland romanticism rather than moderate Repeal; the Young Turks confront the ageing magus-politician, the Famine advances, the political situation radicalizes, and Thomas Francis becomes briefly famous for a classic piece of revolutionary rhetoric – though, as John Hearne points out here, his basic beliefs may have been closer to his father's constitutionalism than was seen at the time, or remembered since. Meagher's own description of his leavetaking from his father's house is again, as concrete and vivid as a scene from a novel:

> I ran up to the drawing-room, where my father and aunt were sitting at the time, to wish them good-bye. I put on my tri-colour sash – green, white and orange – buckled on my sword-belt, cross-belt, cartouche box, and flourishing a very handsome old sword, which belonged to a granduncle of mine in the days of the Merchant Corps of the Waterford Volunteers…gave myself up to the gay illusion of a gallant fight, a triumphal entry, at the head of thousands, into Dublin before long. I was full of liveliness and hope at that moment, and welcomed the struggle with a laughing heart. But, I recollect it well, my father was far otherwise. He seemed to me mournfully serious, and impressed with the saddest anticipation.

After the debacle, the ship taking him to transportation slips past Waterford Harbour, and he says goodbye to the lights of Dunmore, like so many emigrants before him. 'I pass by, and my own people know nothing of it.'

He had thrown the dice, and one of his attractive characteristics is his lack of complaint at the ill luck that his youthful rashness often brought him. His revolutionary career would bring him into contact with the next phase of activism, fenianism – a relationship interestingly prospected here by Pat McCarthy. Meagher's ambiguity on the subject could be read as reservations about James Stephens rather than about fenianism per se; while his eventual career in America provides an illuminating contrast to that of his Irish Confederation comrade, John Mitchel, whose stance on slavery, the Civil War and Irish-American politics is suggestively delineated by Michael Toomey. Though France, and its 1848 Revolution, repeatedly features as an inspiration in

Meagher's early career, Hearne convincingly suggests that we might see his idea of democracy as Jacksonian; here, again, he is a man of his time. His career as a commander in the American Civil War has been much argued over, and is judiciously explored here by Rory Cornish, while Jon Axline establishes more clearly than ever before the context of Meagher's irruption into Montana politics – already subject to multiple kinds of unrest and insurgency. It is worth remembering just how young he still was at the time of his death – only 43. He had been 23 when he delivered the famous oration against O'Connell's peace resolutions, 26 at the time of his transportation, 29 when he arrived in America. Though much had gone wrong for him, it was a life cut short. David Emmons hypothesizes entertainingly about the dramatic and mysterious nature of Meagher's disappearance off a steamboat at Fort Benton on the Missouri River, suggesting several levels of skulduggery and the presence of a sinister enemy. Thus the opera ends on a resoundingly tragic note, with a wife haunting the river-bank in search of a body that will never be found.

But the reputation goes marching on. Thomas Francis Meagher's continuing resonance was assured, not just by his glamorous career, controversially cut short, nor even by the 'Sword' speech, which passed into the apostolic tradition of Irish revolutionary rhetoric, but by the use made of his reputation by Arthur Griffith and others determined to establish an unbroken chain of violent resistance to British rule. Much of the work in this book suggests a more nuanced, discontinuous and paradoxical process than that, and the disillusionments, miscalculations and failures which were prominent in Meagher's later life are squarely faced. But he remains a charismatic figure nonetheless, and his mark on Irish history is there to be seen. It has just been emblematized by a new equestrian statue of him in his native city – the classic way of memorializing a Romantic hero, which echoes the similar statue raised a century ago in Helena, Montana. Just as fittingly, the impressive Granary Museum in Waterford, commemorating the city's history, is established in a building that belonged to the Meagher family. Not only Meagher's unique career but the Irish and emigrant worlds he reflected, symbolize a continuous engagement with Irish history and its interpretation. This book constitutes an important intervention in the process of understanding the man, his world and his times.

Roy Foster
January 2005

1

An Introduction

Rory T. Cornish and John M. Hearne

On 1 January 1801, the independent Irish Parliament in Dublin was abolished by the terms of the Act of Union creating the United Kingdom of Great Britain and Ireland. The resulting struggle to regain Irish self-determination, from the abortive rebellion of Robert Emmet in 1803 to the Easter Rebellion of 1916 and beyond, created an enduring republican tradition in lreland.

This struggle has recently been masterfully reconstructed by Alvin Jackson in his *Home Rule: An Irish History, 1800–2000* (Oxford: Oxford University Press, 2003). While Professor Jackson links the multiple incarnations the Home Rule Movement would take, including the Young Ireland Movement, the name Thomas Francis Meagher does not appear in his text. This is not an unusual omission. In his 1966 O'Donnell Lecture, Dennis Gwynn, Meagher's only Irish biographer to date, noted that while few nineteenth-century historians achieved 'such heights of hero worship among their contemporaries as did Thomas Francis Meagher', few nationalist spokesman have equally 'left so little permanent mark upon the age'.[1]

Born in Waterford, Ireland, in 1823 to a wealthy mercantile family, he was the eldest son of Thomas Meagher Jr, the son of an Irish immigrant to Newfoundland. Thomas Meagher Jr was born in Newfoundland in 1789 and returned to Waterford in 1819 where he became a prominent civic leader. In 1843, he became the first Catholic Mayor of Waterford City in almost 200 years, was an important ally of Daniel O'Connell and a member of the British House of Commons, 1847–57. Educated by the Jesuits at Clongowes Wood and later at their famous academy at Stonyhurst, Lancashire, England, the young Thomas Francis Meagher returned to Waterford in 1843. In 1844, he was sent to Queen's Inns, Dublin, to study law but abandoned his legal studies to embrace the politics of the Repeal Association led by O'Connell.

Thomas Davis, however, was Meagher's real political mentor during these years. Following Davis' premature death in 1845, Meagher paid homage to the leader of Young Ireland in his first publication, *Letters of a Protestant on Repeal. By the Late Thomas Davis* (Dublin: Publications of the Irish Confederation No. 2, William Holden, 1847). Similarly, in his first publication in exile in the United States, *Speeches on the Legislative Independence of Ireland*, Meagher again lamented the premature death of Davis: the death of Davis, Meagher wrote 'was an unspeakable calamity. Never did a heavier one full upon a doom nation.'[2] The co-founder of the nationalistic paper the *Nation*,

Davis was unwilling to follow O'Connell's lead within the Repeal Association regarding O'Connell's preference for denominational education in Ireland. Meagher would follow a similar path in opposing O'Connell's rejection of the moral right of physical force against British rule at the height of the Irish Famine. Meagher's speech during an emotional meeting in Conciliation Hall, Dublin, 28 July 1846, 'Freedom of Opinion–Morality of War' not only split the Repeal Association, it made Meagher something of a celebrity.[3] A reluctant revolutionary, Meagher's fiery orations and membership of the radical Irish Confederation heightened political tensions during 1847 and 1848.

During February 1848, Meagher again attracted attention by unsuccessfully contesting a by-election for a vacant parliamentary seat in Waterford City, and by his visit to the new republican government in France seeking support for the Irish Confederation. Returning to Ireland, he unfurled the Irish tricolour flag with the intention of it becoming the national flag, and was involved in the failed attempt at rebellion at Ballingarry, County Tipperary, 1848. Perhaps the best account of this failed 'rebellion' is found in Richard Davis, *The Young Ireland Movement* (Dublin: Gill and Macmillan, 1987). Arrested and tried for treason in October 1848, Meagher's speech from the dock has been favourably compared to that of Robert Emmet and in the preface to his edited collection of Meagher's speeches, *Meagher of the Sword. Speeches of Thomas Francis Meagher in Ireland 1846–1848* (Dublin: M.H. Gill and Son, 1915) Arthur Griffith, the founder of Sinn Fein, saw Meagher's oratory as the embodiment of Irish nationalism. While Griffith included a useful list of Meagher's contemporaries at the end of his book, in his preface he concluded that while Meagher had not been the most influential member of the Young Ireland movement, his oratory had made him the most popular 'Irish patriot of the nineteenth century except for Robert Emmet'. Meagher, among all his contemporaries in the nineteenth century, deserved the title of 'National Orator' according to Griffith.[4] Found guilty of treason and initially sentenced to death, Meagher's sentence was later commuted to transportation for life to the penal colony of Van Diemen's Land, present day Tasmania. In 1852, like many other exiled members of the Irish Confederation, such as Terence Bellew MacManus and John Mitchel, Meagher escaped to the political sanctuary of the United States.

While Meagher's later career in the United States has been the subject of uneven scholarship, Irish historians have been slow in recognizing his importance to both Irish history and the development of a transatlantic community. In his study of the 1849 rebellion at Cappoquin, County Waterford, *The Waterford Rebels of 1849* (Dublin: Geography Publications, 1992), the author, Brendan Kiely, lamented the fact that the careers of the Young Ireland Movement had not generated more interest amongst the Irish academic community. Most recent scholarship, he added, seems to be 'Australian and United States based'.[5] However, in one of the first studies on the transported Young Irelanders, *Young Ireland in Exile* (Dublin and Cork: The Talbot Press), the author, Rev. J.H. Cullen, outlined his reason for undertaking this task as merely 'collecting into one volume information about the Tasmanian careers of the Irish state prisoners'. When concluded however, Cullen had, in effect, completed seven separate biographies of the exiled Young Irelanders, based mainly on primary source material and 'As far as possible the story is told by the exiles themselves.'[6] In this unique way, Cullen highlighted the powerlessness felt by each of seven exiles and their attempts to bring meaning to their lives. In so doing, he provided an invaluable reservoir of material for future historians.

This theme was also explored in T.J. Kiernan's *The Irish Exiles in Australia* (Dublin: Clonmore and Reynolds, 1954). A former Irish ambassador to Australia, Kiernan based his account on previously unpublished primary sources regarding the Irish political exiles. Concluding his history of transportation with the arrival of the *Hougoumont* in 1868, Kiernan ably illustrated the disorientation and sense of loss Meagher, and his fellow political prisoners, many of whom were from educated, middle-class backgrounds, felt. This sense of otherness was well illustrated by Kiernan's use of Mitchel's eulogy of Meagher in the *Shamrock*. There, Mitchel stated that the political Irish exiles 'were all misplaced in the world and that Meagher and his friends had been suddenly thrown into this anomalous state of society' and between these widely differing elements the honest colonists and the felonious population, 'yet belonging to neither'.[7] Two more recent biographies of Meagher's fellow exiles have shed further light on Meagher's early career in Ireland. Robert Sloan's *William Smith O'Brien and the Young Ireland Rebellion of 1848* (Dublin: Four Courts Press, 2000) illustrates Meagher's involvement in the movement during the year preceding the ill-fated rising at Ballingary, while Helen F. Mulvey's *Thomas Davis and Ireland. A Biographical Study* (Washington, D.C.: Catholic University of America Press, 2002) outlines the ideological foundations of the Young Ireland movement itself. This latter work explains why Meagher, and other middle-class, educated Irishmen, found Davis, and the philosophical influences which shaped his career, attractive.

The most important phase of Meagher's political career, however, developed following his escape to the United States in 1852. It was in the young American republic, a new nation finally granted independence from Britain in 1783 – only forty years before Meagher's own birth, that his career finally flourished. Welcomed by fellow Irish exiles and the young republic's political establishment, Meagher became the most successful and the most culturally assimilated of all the Irish Confederation's escapees. As a republican spokesman, lecturer, newspaperman, Democrat Party activist and, finally, soldier, Meagher established himself as one of the most important Irish ethnic spokesmen and leaders in the antebellum American republic. The publication of his *Speeches on the Legislative Independence of Ireland* (New York: Redfield, 1853), established his republican credentials in the United States and his marriage to the socially prominent Elizabeth Townsend equally established his membership, if only peripherally, of New York City's elite. In 1857 Meagher became a United States citizen.

At the outbreak of the American Civil War, April 1861, Meagher volunteered for military service to preserve the Union. As an officer in the 69th New York Militia, he fought at the first battle of Bull Run. His account of his regiment's record during this action, *The Last Days of the 69th in Virginia*

(New York: Lynch and Cole, 1861) quickly enhanced his reputation as a republican patriot in arms. Commissioned a captain in the regular United States Army, Meagher became, briefly, colonel of the reformed 69th New York Infantry and later founder of the New York Irish Brigade. Appointed its first commander by President Abraham Lincoln, he was commissioned a brigadier general in October 1861. It was his command of one of the finest combat units in the Army of the Potomac that has largely kept Meagher's name alive in the annals of history.

The American Civil War became the first modern war of attrition and, as the casualty rate of the Irish Brigade mounted, Meagher's continued dedication to the Union made him not only an increasingly controversial figure within the Irish community in the North, but also in Ireland itself. During the latter years of the war the increased suffering and war weariness of Irish-Americans tended to tarnish his reputation. In the post-war period, however, Meagher's name was kept alive and celebrated by the publication of a number of memoirs by Irish Brigade veterans. This veneration of Meagher's memory has been recently attacked by Kelly O'Grady in *Clear the Confederate Way! The Irish in the Army of Northern Virginia* (Mason City, IA: Savas Publications, 2000). Dismissing these post-war memorials as 'little more than emeralds in the crown of Civil War legends' they were published, he believes, to further a cause close to Meagher's own heart, the assimilation of the Irish into mainstream American society.[8] If many of these post-war books were uncritical of Meagher's military reputation it should be remembered that this tended to be a feature of most Victorian histories and biographies.

In the year of his death, 1867, two accounts of Meagher were published by former colleagues. His old school friend from Clongowes, P.J. Smyth, published *The Life and Times of Thomas Francis Meagher* (Dublin: The Irishman, 1867). Useful for Meagher's school days at Stonyhurst, this work illustrates how Meagher came to the attention of Daniel O'Connell. Evidently, Meagher's essay on the history of the Jesuit College so impressed O'Connell, whose son also attended this famous Jesuit school, that he remarked 'the genius that could produce such a work is not destined to remain long in obscurity'. The work is also useful for its reflections upon Meagher's tour of the Rhine and his impressions of the fortifications at Antwerp, experiences that influenced the imagery in his famous 'Sword Speech'.[9] Smyth was also a strong supporter of the cause of the Union during the American Civil War and this contemporary work is, naturally, supportive of Meagher's own decision to volunteer to fight for the North; a decision equally supported by D.P. Conyngham in *The Irish Brigade and its Campaigns* (New York: McSorley, 1867).[10]

A native of Crohane, County Tipperary, Conyngham had studied at Queens College, Cork, and became a member of Young Ireland. A successful novelist and newspaperman before the American Civil War, he came to the United States in 1861 as a war correspondent. Armed with letters of introduction from both Smith O'Brien and P.J. Smyth, Meagher appointed Conyngham to his staff in

1862 with the rank of captain. His history of the Irish Brigade was published to rescue from 'oblivion the glorious military record we (the Irish) have earned in America' as well as to counter the charge that Meagher and the Irish Brigade had been little more than Union mercenaries during the war.[11] Consequently, it should not be surprising that the ordinary soldiers of the brigade emerge as patriots who were motivated by 'the great principle of democracy' and Meagher is portrayed as a glorious figure who reminded Conyngham of 'one of the Old Irish princes of medieval times'.[12] The work remains useful to the historian for the eyewitness accounts of the activities of the brigade between 1862 to 1863, and the brief biographies of its more colourful officers. Similar heroic themes are also evident in a book published by Captain W.F. Lyons just three years after Meagher's death, *Brigadier General Thomas Francis Meagher. His Political and Military Career* (New York: D.J. Sadlier and Company, 1870).

Lyons compiled this work in response to Meagher's own wish that his speeches be recorded in a permanent form. A life-long follower of Meagher, Lyons had served in the Irish Brigade and his work, if somewhat unreliable about the dates and context of Meagher's speeches, remains a valuable storehouse of Meagher's views on republican government and the need to preserve the American Union. If Lyons tended to inflate the importance of Meagher's later career as commander of the Etowah District, Tennessee, he was the first author to try and explain Meagher's mysterious death. Meagher had a reputation for hard drinking. To counter persistent rumours that this had led to Meagher's death by drowning when he fell from the *G.A. Thompson* into the Missouri River, Lyons published a letter from John T. Doran, the pilot of the vessel, who was with Meagher on the night of his death. In Doran's account Meagher's fall from the *G.A. Thompson* was the result of delirium brought on by the general's weakened state due to illness.[13]

As the twenty-fifth anniversary of the American Civil War approached four other books written by former colleagues kept Meagher's name alive. These books were clearly the result of the pride some of the authors felt in being attached to the Irish Brigade and their publications coincided with the first wave of monument building to the brigade itself. In 1888, the Irish Brigade Monument was erected on the Gettysburg battlefield and it was followed, in 1889, by a monument to the 116th Pennsylvania, one of the brigade's regiments. Another later monument to the Rev. William Corby, chaplain to the 88th New York Volunteer Infantry, was also erected. St Clair Mulholland, a former lieutenant colonel of the 116th Pennsylvania and a recipient of the Congressional Medal of Honor, was one of the driving forces behind these Gettysburg monuments. He was also the author of one of the first regimental histories of a unit in the brigade, *The Story of the 116th Regiment, Pennsylvania Volunteers, in the War of the Rebellion* (Philadelphia: McManus, 1889).

Written to preserve the heroic record of his fellow soldiers, Mulholland portrayed Meagher as a stately, courteous and brave man, the 'orator-soldier from the Emerald Isle', a commander whose demeanour, however, could become quite 'animated' when 'the canteen had been passed around'.[14] William Corby's work, *Memoirs of Chaplain Life* (Chicago, IL: Lamonte, O'Donnell and Co., 1893), was partially written to deflect continued nativist attacks on the bravery of the Irish as well as defend Meagher's reputation. Not only were the soldiers of the Irish Brigade saints and gentlemen, but Meagher was a true Irish patriot who only drank to excess occasionally when motivated by the enjoyment of the moment and good company. As a commander, Meagher, Corby recollected, constantly looked after the physical and spiritual needs of his men and often attended confession before upcoming engagements.[15]

Meagher's own family background was the theme of Joseph Casimer O'Meagher's book, *Some Historical Notices of the Meagher's of Ikerrin* (New York: privately published, 1890). Dedicated to Meagher's second wife, Elizabeth Townsend Meagher, the work celebrates the history of the Meagher, O'Meagher, Marr and Maher extended family and a great deal of emphasis was placed upon Meagher's own ancestors who had left Ireland to fight in the Irish brigades of both France and Spain in previous centuries. Clearly, the impression is given that 'Meagher of the Sword' had sprung from a knightly and military family tradition and, if the book is somewhat disorganized, it remains useful as Joseph O'Meagher notes the names and experiences of over 300 Meagher, Marr and Maher soldiers who had fought for the Union during the American Civil War. Meagher as knight errant and Irish patriot was also the theme of Michael Cavanagh's, *Memoirs of Gen. Thomas Francis Meagher. Comprising The Leading Events of His Career* (Worcester, MA: Messenger Press, 1892).

A fellow Young Irelander who first met Meagher in 1848, Cavanagh became a leading Fenian in the United States. Having been the secretary to John O'Mahony, a founding member of the Fenians who had fought in the American Civil War as a Union colonel, it is not surprising that Cavanagh's book tends to re-cast Meagher as a fervent nationalist long dedicated to the principles of 'National Liberty'. In a virtual storehouse of laudatory addresses, speeches, documents and uncritical narrative regarding the hero, Cavanagh hoped to keep alive in the minds of a younger generation of Irishmen the memory of 'Ireland's soldier-orator'.[16] A continually cited work, Cavanagh's book is the main source of the myth that Meagher was, and remained, a dedicated Fenian. Nonetheless, it remains a valuable source of information on the Irish Confederation by supplying a membership list of its council and describing the prevailing tensions within the leadership prior to the rising at Ballingarry.[17]

Meagher's only modern full-length biography was completed by Robert G. Athearn, *Thomas Francis Meagher: An Irish Revolutionary in America* (Boulder, CO: University of Colorado Press, 1949). Based largely upon previously unpublished documents, official archives and extracts from American newspapers, Athearn's Meagher is a mercurial, ambitious and self-seeking individual whose career in America was something of an anti-climax. As the title suggests, Athearn added little to Meagher's Irish career and Denis Gwynn, in his short corrective work, *Thomas Francis Meagher* (Cork: National University of Ireland Press,

1966), pondered the question as to whether or not American historians would henceforth ask whether Meagher had ever really justified his contemporary reputation?[18]

Since the centenary of the American Civil War a virtual torrent of books, still unabated, has been published on every aspect of the war. Meagher's reputation has not benefited from this increased scrutiny. At best he has been simply ignored; while at worst he has been denigrated as an incompetent political general. For example, in his widely popular trilogy, *The Civil War. A Narrative* (New York: Random House, 1958–74), Shelby Foote managed to write an account of both the battles of Antietam and Fredericksburg without mentioning either Meagher or the Irish Brigade once. Similarly, one of the most prolific authors on the eastern theatre during the American Civil War, Stephen W. Sears, only briefly mentions the brigade and when Meagher is referred to, it is in the context of a 'whiskey general', a commander who gained his courage from a bottle.[19]

Of course, Meagher has featured prominently in modern works on foreigners in the American Civil War and works on ethnic regiments, but, once again, this has not usually been to his benefit. In his *Melting Pot Soldiers* (New York: Fordham University Press, 1998), William L. Burton concluded that Meagher was a familiar figure in the antebellum republic; if a symbol of Irish nationalism, he was prepared to use his popularity to escape his ethnic background while transforming himself into something more suitable for a gentleman of his class, an American congressman.[20] The outbreak of the Civil War naturally aroused great interest in Ireland itself, and Meagher's position in the then ongoing debate as to where its loyalties ought to lie has been treated well in Joseph M. Hernon's, *Celts, Catholics and Copperheads* (Columbus, OH: Ohio State University Press, 1968). Unfortunately for Meagher's reputation, Hernon suggests that his opponents, such as the fellow Young Irelanders John Mitchel and Smith O'Brien, were more logical in their support for the South.[21] This is also a reminder that not all Irishmen fought for the Union. Indeed a significant minority supported the South and one of the most important proponents of southern nationalism was Meagher's closest friend, John Mitchel.

Clearly then, it has been Meagher's association with the Irish Brigade that has largely kept his name alive. The unveiling of a monument to him on the Antietam battlefield, in October 1997, resulted in the reissuing of Joseph G. Bilby's, *The Irish Brigade in the Civil War* (Conshohaken, PA: Combined Publishing, 1998).[22] A virtual celebration of the achievements of the Irish Brigade, as well as being a useful source of excellent contemporary photographs, the work is interesting for its more realistic assessment of Meagher, the soldier and man. This less than flattering, but equally sympathetic, treatment of Meagher's military record can also be found in Pia Seija Seagrove (ed.) *The History of the Irish Brigade. A Collection of Historical Essays* (Fredericksburg, Virginia: Sergeant Kirkland's Museum and Historical Society, 1995). In his essay the 'Sprig of Green: The Irish Brigade', Kevin E. O'Brien pays tribute to both Meagher's and the Irish Brigade's bravery at Antietam and Fredericksburg. O'Brien was also responsible for bringing to light perhaps the most personal and accurate contemporary account of Meagher during the Fredericksburg campaign, *My Life in The Irish Brigade. The Civil War Memoirs of Private William McCarter, 116th Pennsylvania Infantry* (Campbell, CA: Savas Publishing, 1996). A Derry-born Protestant, McCarter acted for a while as Meagher's orderly and although he was critical of his general, especially his drinking, his diary is a testament to the personal loyalty Meagher could engineer amongst his contemporaries.[23]

If somewhat diminished, it is clear that the name of Thomas Francis Meagher is alive and well, especially in the United States. A brief, cursory visit to the Internet will turn up over 5,000 hits on his name alone; the Irish Brigade reveals a staggering 50,000 hits. The popular military painters Mort Kunstler and Don Troiana have immortalized the bravery of the Irish Brigade; both the brigade and Meagher have also been the subject of novels.[24] A recent film 'Gods and Generals', based upon Jeffrey M. Shaara's bestseller, celebrated the Irish Brigade's valour at Fredericksburg with an actor/Meagher making a somewhat unflattering appearance. Recently a real rollercoaster of a book on the Irish abroad which also features Meagher has been published: Thomas Keneally's *The Great Shame and the Triumph of the Irish in The English Speaking World* (New York: Doubleday, 1998). From its pages we once again return to the patriotic, nationalistic vision of Meagher evident in his nineteenth-century biographies. If Keneally's book turns us full circle, it has not gone unchallenged. In his *Clear the Confederate Way!*, Kelly J. O'Grady has championed the Irish who fought for the Confederacy. In doing so, he has found it necessary to further denigrate Meagher's reputation; he was, O'Grady's assures us, a drunken incompetent whose support of the Union was a betrayal of his previous championship of Irish nationalism and support for the struggles of smaller European nations.[25]

Meagher's public career in the United States did not end with the victory of the Union over the Confederacy in April 1865. Following the assassination of Abraham Lincoln his successor, President Andrew Johnson, rewarded Meagher for his support of Lincoln's re-election in 1864, by appointing him to the position of Secretary of the Montana Territory in July 1865. Due to Governor Edgerton's resignation, Meagher was, until his death, acting governor of the territory and, true to form, his twenty-one-month residency in Montana proved as controversial as had his service in the war. If his influence upon Montana's development proved minimal, the memory of Meagher, as Elliot West, Clark C. Spence, James L. Thane Jr and Jon Axline have recently indicated, still excites passion within the state.[26] Indeed, Thane in his 1967 MA thesis has argued that while Meagher 'may justly be criticized for compounding the confusion in which he found Montana' he, nonetheless, deserves some credit for getting the Territory back on the road to recovery'. Meagher was, Thane suggests, 'one of the Territory's most conscientious executives'. Thane was also critical of Meagher's American biographer, Robert G. Athearn, whom he declared was more willing to 'accept the stock interpretations of Meagher than do him justice' for his achievements.[27]

On 4 July 1905, Meagher's supporters unveiled a fine equestrian statue to him outside the Montana State Capitol building, Helena. In June 1963, President

John F. Kennedy addressed the Oireachtas (Houses of Parliament) Dublin. There, he praised Meagher and the Irish Brigade and presented to the people of Ireland the restored flag of the 69th New York. In September 2004, the memory of Thomas Francis Meagher was finally commemorated by the city of his birth, Waterford, Ireland, where another fine equestrian statue was erected to his memory. Funded by the Department of the Environment, Heritage and Local Government, to mark a meeting of the twenty-five EU Environment Ministers in Waterford, an impressive pageant accompanied the dedication that reflected Meagher's role as an international republican.

While the career of Thomas Francis Meagher awaits a modern biographer who will do justice to the entirety of his colourful career, this present volume, consisting of articles on Meagher completed by scholars from three continents, hopes to present a more balanced assessment of this nineteenth-century republican. From this new work Thomas Francis Meagher emerges as a complex individual; a highly intelligent and passionate man whose memory and reputation has been as much revered as it has been reviled. The contributors also hope this volume will enhance our understanding of Meagher the man as well as add to the growing corpus of knowledge regarding the transatlantic nineteenth-century community and the Irish abroad.

NOTES

1. D. Gwynn, *Thomas Francis Meagher* (Cork: National University of Ireland Press, 1966) p. 58. This is Gwynn's full O'Donnell lecture in print. To date, Gwynn is Meagher's only Irish biographer. A very useful overview of the Young Ireland movement, and brief biographies of its leaders, can be found in R.F. Foster, *Modern Ireland 1600–1972* (London: Allen Lane, 1988) pp.310–17.
2. Thomas Francis Meagher (ed.), *Speeches on the Legislative Independence of Ireland. With Introductory Notes by Thomas Francis Meagher* (New York: Redfield, 1853) p.xxii.
3. The best edited version of this speech, often referred to as the 'Sword Speech', can be found in Meagher's own work, *Speeches*, pp.85–90.
4. Arthur Griffith, *Meagher of the Sword. Speeches of Thomas Francis Meagher in Ireland 1846–1848* (Dublin: M.H. Gill & Son, 1915) pp.xvii–xviii.
5. Brendan Kiely, *The Waterford Rebels of 1849. The Last Young Irelanders and their Lives in America, Bermuda and Van Diemen's Land* (Dublin: Geography Publications, 1999) p.96.
6. Rev. J.H. Cullen, *Young Ireland in Exile* (Dublin and Cork: The Talbot Press, 1928), p.5.
7. Quoted in T.J. Kiernan, *Irish Exiles in Australia* (Dublin: Clonmore and Reynolds, 1954), p.51.
8. Kelly O'Grady, *Clear the Confederate Way! The Irish in the Army of Northern Virginia* (Mason City, Iowa: Savas Publishing, 2000), pp.118–19.
9. P.J. Smyth, *The Life and Times of Thomas Francis Meagher* (Dublin: The Irishman, 1867), pp.5–6.
10. D.P. Conyngham, *The Irish Brigade and its Campaigns: With Some Account of the Corcoran Legion and Sketches of the Principal Officers* (New York: Willam McSorley, 1867). Conyngham's book was also printed by P. Donohoe in Boston, 1869. Other editions were also published in a slightly different form in Glasgow, Scotland, by R.T. Washbourne, 1866 and 1868, and by Cameron Ferguson, no date. The most reliable edition has been edited by Lawrence F. Kohl, *The Irish Brigade and its Campaigns* (New York: Fordham University Press, 1996). Kohl's edition contains a useful introduction and biography of Conyngham, pp.xviii–xxiii.
11. Kohl, *Irish Brigade*, p.xxii.

12. *Ibid.*, pp.75–6.
13. W.F. Lyons, *Brigadier General Thomas Francis Meagher. His Political and Military Career* (New York: D.J. Sadlier and Company, 1870), pp.351–7. Lyons had been brought as a child to meet Meagher in his cell at Clonmel. He would cross the Atlantic to volunteer to fight under Meagher in 1861.
14. Lawrence F. Kohl (ed.), *The Story of the 116th Regiment* (New York: Fordham University Press, 1996), pp.12, 24.
15. William Corby, *Memoirs of Chaplin Life* (Chicago, IL: LaMonte, O'Donnell Co., 1893), pp.28–30.
16. Michael Cavanagh, *Memoirs of General Thomas Francis Meagher. Comprising The Leading Events of His Career* (Worcester, MA: Messanger Press, 1892), p.5.
17. *Ibid.*, pp.488–90, Appendix, pp.1–2.
18. Denis Gwynn, *Thomas Francis Meagher* (Cork: National University of Ireland Press, 1966), p.60.
19. See, Stephen W. Sears, *To The Gates of Richmond, The Peninsula Campaign* (New York: Tichnor and Fields, 1992) p.248, and his account of Meagher at Antietam, *Landscape Turned Red. The Battle of Antietam* (New York: Tichnor and Fields, 1983) pp.244 and 394.
20. William L. Burton, *Melting Pot Soldiers. The Union's Ethnic Regiments* (New York: Fordham University Press, 1998), pp.9, 209–10. Meagher's role in mobilizing Irish support in the North is also somewhat unflatteringly portrayed in Ella Lonn, *Foreigners in the Union Army and Navy* (Baton Rouge: Louisiana State University Press, 1951) pp.68–79 and more recently in Dean B. Martin, *The Blessed Place of Freedom. Europeans in Civil War America* (Dulles, Virginia: Brassey's, 2002) pp.21–8.
21. Joseph M. Hernon, *Celts, Catholics and Copperheads. Ireland Views the American Civil War* (Columbus, OH: Ohio State University Press, 1968), pp.81–113.
22. This book was originally published as *Remember Fontenoy! The 69th New York and the Irish Brigade in the Civil War* (New Jersey: Longstreet House, 1995). For Joseph G. Bilby's useful modern assessment of Meagher, see *The Irish Brigade in the Civil War. The 69th New York and Other Irish Regiments of the Army of the Potomac* (Conshohacken, PA: Combined Publishing, 1998), pp.135–43. A more traditional assessment of Meagher's career in the Irish brigade can be found in Paul Jones, *The Irish Brigade* (London: New English Library, 1969).
23. For McCarter's assessment of Meagher see *My Life in the Irish Brigade. The Civil War Memoirs of Private William McCarter, 116th Pennsylvania Infantry* (Campbell, CA: Savas Publishing, 1996), pp.15–16, 69–71. For another account of experiences in the Irish Brigade written by an ordinary soldier also see Lawrence F. Kohl and Margaret Cosse Richard (eds), *Irish Green and Union Blue: The Civil War Letters of Peter Welsh* (New York: Fordham University Press, 1986).
24. For an account of the almost mystical clash between the Irish Brigade and the Irish Confederates in the Georgian brigade of General Thomas R.R. Cobb at Marye's Heights, Fredericksburg, see Kirk Mitchell, *Fredericksburg: A Novel of the Irish at Marye's Heights* (New York: St Martin's Press, 1996). Richard Wheeler has recently published a novel on Meagher, *The Exile* (New York: Tom Docherty Associates, 2003). Another fictional account of Meagher's career is Christian Stevens, *Meagher of the Sword: A Dramatization of the Life of Thomas Francis Meagher* (New York: Dodd & Mead, 1967).
25. O'Grady, *Clear the Confederate Way!*, pp.121–30.
26. For Meagher in Montana see; John B. Bruce (comp.), *Lectures of Governor Thomas Francis Meagher in Montana* (Virginia City MT, Bruce and Wright, 1867); Elliot West, 'Thomas Francis Meagher's Bar Bill', *Montana. The Magazine of Western History*, 35, (1985), pp.16–23; Clark Spence, *Territorial Politics and the Government in Montana, 1864–1889* (Urbana, University of Illinois Press, 1975) and Jon Axline, 'In a Fierce and Frightful Region: Thomas Francis Meagher's Montana Adventure, 1865–1867', *Decies*, 59, (2003), pp.119–38.
27. James L. Thane, Jr, 'Thomas Francis Meagher "The Acting One",' (unpublished MA thesis, University of Montana, 1967), pp.3–4, 87.

2

Genealogy, Geography and Social Mobility: The Family Background of Thomas Francis Meagher

John Mannion

Amongst the more poignant passages in Meagher's *Personal Reminiscences* of 1848 is an account of his return home to Waterford following a political tour of south-east Tipperary. He did not know it, but it was to be his final farewell.

> On Sunday evening, July the 16th, I came down from Slievnamon, and remained at home until the following Thursday, superintending the organization of the Waterford Confederates.
> ...Thursday brought us the proclamation of the Arms Act; copies of which, during the early part of the day, were posted upon the walls of my native city...I resolved to leave at once for Dublin, with a view to ascertain there the intentions of the principal Confederates...
> In the evening...I ordered a covered car...Whilst the car was getting ready, I ran up to the drawing room, where my father (Thomas Jr) and aunt (Johanna Quan) were sitting...to wish them good bye. I put on my tricolour sash – green, white and orange – buckled on my sword belt, cross-belt, cartouche box, and flourishing a very handsome old sword, which belonged to a granduncle of mine [James Quan] in the days of the Merchant Corps of the Waterford Volunteers [1782]...That evening...I saw my home for the last time.[1]

From the perspective of family and kindred, it was a lonely parting. His father, aunt and the Sweetmans of Blenheim excepted, all of Meagher's near relatives were dead or lived elsewhere. His only brother Henry, a graduate of the University of Frieburg, was in Rome with a papal regiment, his only surviving sister a nun in Taunton, Devon. Meagher's aunt and godmother, Christina Quan, had died in 1847 at the Mall; another aunt, Mary Quan, was also a nun. There is no mention of his uncles, Edmund or Thomas Quan. Edmund Forstall was the only surviving member of his maternal grandmother's family in their old home at Rochestown in the parish of Glenmore, Kilkenny. Forstall's sister, Letitia, was a nun and his uncle Patrick Meagher a Jesuit, both in Dublin. As far as can be determined, Meagher's next nearest kin in Waterford and environs would be third cousins from the ranks of the Wyses, Cashins, Hayes, Ducketts and Flemings.

Ancestry, kinship, community, locality, commerce and social class were important in shaping the personality and culture of Thomas Francis Meagher: so were language, religion and ethnicity. His turbulent political career was the focus of an enormous popular interest even as it evolved on three continents over the relatively short span of two decades. It has been the subject of much scholarly writing for more than a century. This chapter does not attempt to add to that particular literature. It focuses instead on Meagher's roots, on his social, cultural and economic background. It traces the evolution of his extended family over three or more generations. It examines issues of geography, migration, social mobility and cultural change.

Growing up in his native Waterford Thomas Francis Meagher belonged to an extended family and social group in political and cultural transition. They were mainly urban, mercantile and middle-class. All were Catholic and, at least in Waterford City, English was the language of public discourse. For more than a generation the various leaders of this upwardly mobile group were engaged in a constitutional campaign for civil and religious rights. Meagher was only 6 years old when O'Connell and his party secured Catholic Emancipation and witnessed the subsequent struggle for repeal of the union and the fight for local municipal reform. His own father, Thomas Jr, born and raised in St John's, Newfoundland, but a prominent merchant in Waterford from 1820, played a leading role in the battle for reform. A talented orator and political organizer, a champion of the poor and disadvantaged, his politically moderate course earned the respect and support of emerging liberal Protestants in the city and environs. One measure of Thomas Meagher's progress was his election as Mayor of Waterford in 1842, the first Catholic to hold that position in more than one hundred and fifty years. He was also chief magistrate and chair of the city council. In 1847 Thomas Meagher was elected member of the House of Commons for his adopted city and served in that capacity for a decade.

Thomas Francis Meagher chose a very different political path. He joined Young Ireland in Dublin in 1844, rejected the O'Connellite policy of peaceful reform and became instead one of the leading spokesmen for radical political change and physical force. His father refused to support him as an election candidate for Waterford. The differences were highlighted in 1848 when 'Meagher of the Sword' was arrested, convicted of treason and sentenced to death. His father was then serving his second year as MP for Waterford City in London. Despite novel influences and radical departures in the mid-1840s, much of Meagher's character remained rooted in a rich family heritage. His formal education, for example, followed some family precedent. An uncle, Patrick Meagher, born in St John's, attended the Jesuit college at Stonyhurst, in Lancashire, between 1813–20, and thence to Dublin to study law. So did his more illustrious nephew. Patrick abandoned law and joined the Jesuits in Dublin in 1829. He was influential in the decision to send Thomas Francis and his brother Henry to Clongowes Wood to begin their secondary education. And, following his expulsion from Clongowes, Fr Patrick Meagher was instrumental in arranging Thomas Francis' transfer to Stonyhurst.[2]

Meagher's boyhood in Waterford is not as well documented. His mother Alicia, daughter of Thomas Quan, a wealthy Waterford merchant, died at her home – site of the present Granville Hotel on the quay of Waterford – when he was only a child. Meagher and his three surviving siblings were raised by their father and their grandparents, Thomas Meagher Sr and Mary Meagher. Following Mary's death the young Meaghers were cared for largely by their unmarried aunts, Christina and Johanna Quan. Christina, as noted above, was Thomas Francis' godmother; Johanna was later to stand as sponsor to his son. The Quan sisters ran an 'academy' on the Mall where the Meagher children probably first went to school. Mention of the Quans' nurturing role is a reminder of the importance of kinship connections in the early life of Thomas Francis Meagher. Extended family links were equally important in the economic sphere where marriage settlements, for example, brought landed property and merchant capital together to propel families such as the Meaghers, Quans and Sweetmans to a prominent position in Waterford society.

RURAL ROOTS

Most of Thomas Francis Meagher's ancestry can be traced back to Catholic tenant farms in the hinterland of Waterford, specifically in south-east Kilkenny, south-east Tipperary, and east Waterford in the eighteenth century. One line hailed from Morristown, in distant Kildare. Some of these families were substantial farmers, operating holdings of 200 acres or more. One of Meagher's great-great-grandfathers was Thomas Wyse, a farmer in Tycor, just west of Waterford City. He was kin to the Wyses of the manor of St John's, amongst Waterford's most prominent Catholic families since the Reformation. The Tycor branch typified the large farmer class whence the mercantile Meaghers had sprung. Thomas Wyse and his wife, Ellen Connor had three sons. Thomas Wyse Jr inherited the ancestral farm at Tycor. His brother Stephen moved to a large farm in Ballygunner, a few miles east of the city, while their third son, James, entered trade in Waterford around 1740. Two decades later James Wyse was one of Waterford's principal Catholic merchants in the salt provisions trade, particularly in butter, with extensive urban commercial and residential property. He also retained or expanded his interests in his brothers' farms and lands adjoining, notably at Ballygunner.[3] Arthur Young, who stayed at the Bolton residence in nearby Ballycanvan (later the home of Thomas Meagher Sr), described in detail the improved farming of James Wyse in 1774 and 1775.[4] Wyses' lands in Ballygunnermore, comprising 271 Irish acres at £260 rental a year were shared by William Quan who was married to the sister of James and Stephen Wyse. The Quans were big farmers in Islandkeane, near Tramore, and tenants of Thomas Wyse of the manor of St John's. Thomas Quan was raised in Ballygunner with his brother James and their four sisters. The Quan brothers were taken as apprentices by James Wyse in Waterford, and by 1775 had graduated to partnership status with another Wyse in-law, Roger Cashin. Thomas Quan was pivotal in establishing the Meaghers' Waterford enterprise through the marriage of his daughter Alicia to Thomas Meagher Jr in 1820.[5]

Amongst Meagher's most distinguished ancestors were the Forstalls of Ringville and Rochestown in the modern Catholic parish of Glenmore in south-east Kilkenny. They were, like the Wyses, of Anglo-Norman origins with a keen sense of genealogy and sub-gentry status. Meagher's maternal grandmother, Christina Forstall could trace her lineage back six generations to the castle at Carrickcloney, by the river Barrow. It was one of four or more Forstall castles spread over a medieval manorial estate of perhaps a dozen townlands. Much of this patrimony was lost in the conquest and confiscation's of the seventeenth century, but some Forstall branches managed to retain leasehold interests in large farms.[6] Thomas Francis Meagher's great-grandfather's great-grandfather, Edmund Forstall, was established at Rinn, just north of the Butler castle at Ballinlaw, in the mid-seventeenth century. His wife, Eleanor Butler of Dangan, was related to the Ormond Butlers, Kilkenny's premier Norman clan. This was noted with some pride by Letitia Forstall of Rochestown (Meagher's first cousin, once removed) in her letters to a distant Forstall cousin in New Orleans as late as 1860. Meagher's ancestors included Nicholas Aylward of Shankill, Henry Meade of Ballyhale, Michael Keating of Shanballyduff, all prominent Kilkenny families, and the Lattins and Kennedys of Morristown in Kildare. To what extent Meagher was aware of the depth of his middle-class roots in rural Kilkenny and Kildare is unclear, but his grand-aunt Juliet Forstall and her son Roger Forstall Sweetman, close friends of the Meaghers in Waterford, were familiar with their distinguished Forstall ancestry, as were the Quans. Both the Quans and the Sweetmans had extensive interests in the Forstall estate largely through marriage settlements in 1791, but the Meaghers did not. When Alicia Quan married Thomas Meagher Jr in 1820 she released her one-quarter share in the Forstall lands at Ballinlaw to her three sisters Christina, Johanna and Mary Anne.[7]

MIGRATION TO NEWFOUNDLAND

The Meaghers themselves are more difficult to trace. In notes prepared on the family by Thomas Francis Meagher, his grandfather Thomas Sr was described as a 'respectable farmer born at Nine Mile Hill, County Tipperary, who early in life emigrated from this country and settled in St John's Newfoundland where he amassed a large fortune'.[8] Nine Mile Hill may refer to the village of Ninemilehouse in the civil parish of Grangemockler on the old turnpike between Clonmel and Kilkenny. Maurice Lenihan, born in Waterford in 1811 and a friend of the Meaghers, stated that Thomas Sr was a farmer near Fethard, a large town west of Grangemockler.[9] A friend of Meagher in Ireland and America, Michael Cavanagh of Cappoquin followed Linehan in stating that Thomas Sr came from Tipperary, 'had been a farmer in early manhood, but preferred seeking his fortune in another and more independent sphere. He emigrated to Newfoundland and became in turn a trader, a merchant, and a shipowner.'[10]

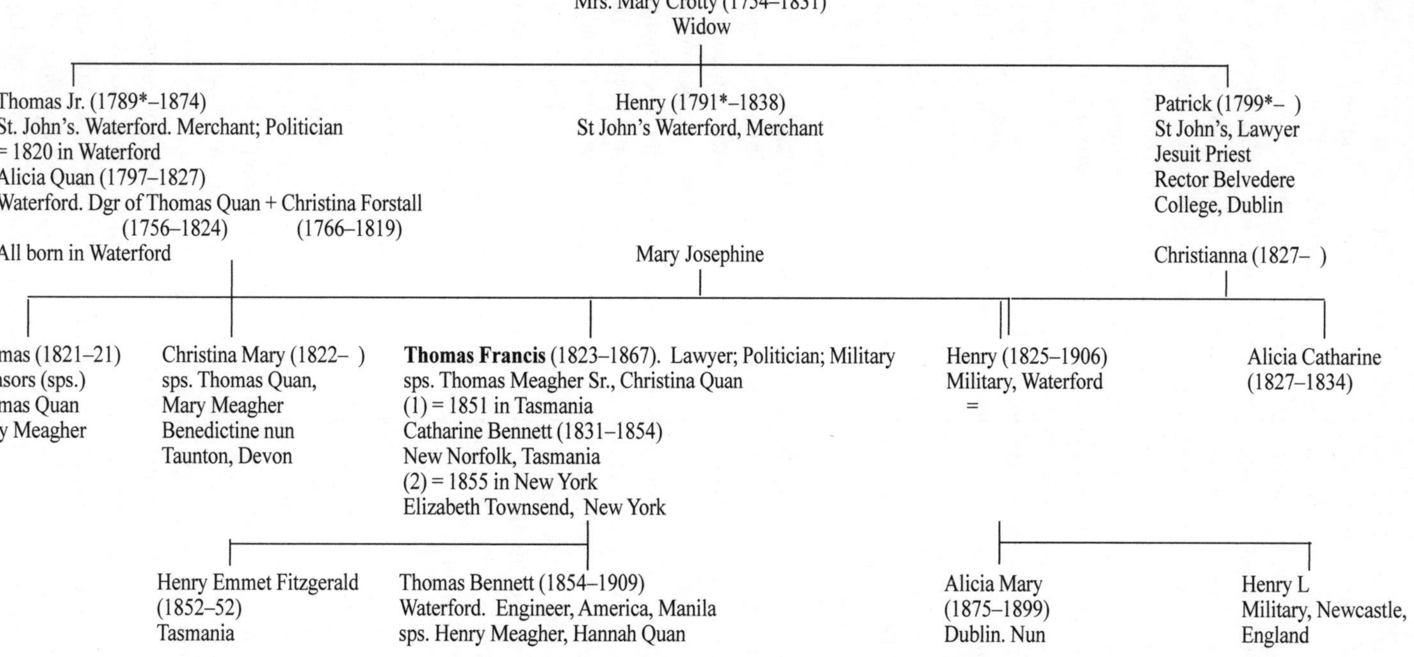

*Year of birth uncertain. The main sources for this genealogy are noted through the text. My thanks to David Smith for information on Henry, Generation 3, 4.

Meagher's achievements as a merchant in St John's, his outstanding record of public service there, and the political careers of his son and grandson generated a keen interest in the family in Newfoundland. One of the most interesting accounts of the commercial career of Thomas Sr comes from Michael Howley, a member of another talented family of south-east Tipperary origins in St John's. Trained at All Hallows, in Dublin, Howley was the first native Newfoundlander to be appointed an archbishop. While in Ireland he visited his Howley kin at Clonmel, compiled a detailed genealogy, tracing his ancestry to Glangoole, New Bermingham, where the family operated a large farm through the eighteenth century. His grandfather moved to Fethard to farm, and thence to Cheekpoint, near Passage East, Waterford, where they managed the local inn. Howley's father and two uncles emigrated to St John's and became prominent merchants. Because of their common geographical origins, migrations and mercantile pursuits, the Howley and Meagher families were close. Mary Meagher was godmother to an aunt of Archbishop Howley's in St John's. Mary O'Neill of Clonmel, first cousin of the archbishop, was engaged to marry Meagher prior to his deportation, and amongst the extensive Howley family papers in St John's is Meagher's copy of the poems of Thomas Davis, published in Dublin in 1846.[11]

Howley differs from other authors in stating Meagher Sr came from Clonmel. He is also the only one to note Meagher's rather humble beginnings as an apprentice to a tailor, Mr Crotty, in St John's.[12] Crotty died and Meagher married his widow, Mary, whose birthplace and maiden name are not known. Howley's account of Meagher's start in St John's is supported in the documents. In 1795 the family is recorded in the centre of town, between 'the Engine House and the Kings Beach'. They are the only Meaghers amongst over 600 heads of household recorded that winter, one of several tenants of William Thomas, member of a prominent and long-established merchant family of Dartmouth origins in St John's. The precise location cannot be pinpointed but the Meagher home was around 100 metres east of Church Hill and Clift's Cove. They were almost certainly on the Lower Path (later Water Street) or on a lane leading off it. Meagher is described as a tailor in 1795.[13] The household consisted of only his wife, son, and daughter. Meagher himself was actually absent, as were a number of male heads of household during the winter of 1795. Some were merchants and traders in Britain on business. Amongst notes on his grandfather, T.F. Meagher reported that 'in 1795 in the course of one of his many passages to and from St John's he [Thomas Sr] was captured by a French privateer and brought into [Le] Havre where for several months he was detained a prisoner by order of the French Repubic'. Howley's claim that Meagher succeeded Crotty through a strategic marriage to an older woman is reinforced by birth dates, and by the fact that the Meaghers were on or near the same site as was Crotty a decade before.[14]

The last decade of the eighteenth century was a period of considerable transition in St John's, with the collapse of the old migratory ship fishery and the rise of family settlement. Crafts such as tailoring expanded and were dominated by the Irish. All but one of the nineteen tailors recorded in 1795, for example, were of Irish birth or descent. Like most trades popular amongst the Irish in the town, tailoring required little start-up capital for premises, equipment or materials. Success depended more on individual skill, reputation and cultural connections. It could be a profitable trade. Meagher was one of a number of Irish tailors in St John's who advanced to mercantile status. Progress, however, was usually slow. Meagher was still listed as a tailor as late as May 1808, but as a chapman that July. By then he was close to fifty and had spent more than twenty years in St John's.[15] The transition from tailor trader to fully-fledged merchant was expedited in 1808 with the acquisition of a sixty-ton brig for deep-sea trade. It was replaced by a much larger vessel the following year.[16] A pattern of trading quickly emerged that was typical of the nascent Irish merchant in St John's. In the autumn of 1809 Meagher shipped over 1,300 quintals (67,500 kilograms) of dried cod from St John's to Waterford. The vessel arrived back the following spring with salt pork, beef, butter, bread, oatmeal and sixty-two passengers. It was then sent to Boston in ballast on the first of three round trips that summer, bringing back butter, bread, flour, livestock and other produce. In December the ship was again loaded at St John's for Waterford to commence another circuit of voyages.[17]

Meagher entered maritime trade on the crest of a boom in the cod economy. The final years of the Napoleonic wars witnessed a rising demand for Newfoundland fish in Europe. This was especially the case in Spain where a lowering of tariffs on cod imports from the island in 1808 resulted in a virtual monopoly by Newfoundland merchants. Prices soared, as did servants' wages in the fishery. Traffic in passengers and provisions from the port and harbour of Waterford to St John's increased dramatically between 1809 and 1815. The demand for cod in Waterford and its hinterland also expanded, a reflection of rapid population growth there, particularly amongst the poor.

Much of Meagher's trade at Waterford can be re-constructed from the ledgers of his agent and principal supplier Richard Fogarty.[18] Although Fogarty's ledger survived for only three years, it remains one of the best sources on the structure of Waterford's commerce with Newfoundland for the early nineteenth century. Fogarty supplied close to fifty merchants and traders; almost all were based in St John's. Thomas Meagher was Fogarty's leading customer accounting for £12,000 or 20 per cent of the firm's total trade over three years. Each autumn Fogarty received Meagher's produce that he disposed of locally on Meagher's account. Cod dominated this commerce, but cod and seal oil, sealskins, salmon, herring, capelin, ox hides and barrel staves, plank, board and other small timber were also imported. A single shipment fetched up to £2,000 in the Waterford market. It was usually accompanied by orders for the following season: passengers to serve specific planters and artisans in Newfoundland, and provisions. Bills of exchange drawn in St John's on British and Irish houses engaged in the fishery were sent with these orders and were deposited by Fogarty in Newport's bank or other discounting houses in Waterford. During the winter and early spring Fogarty assembled supplies from local artisans, retailers and merchants, arranged for their payment through the private banks, and organized local transportation, packing, warehousing and eventually loading on to Meagher's or some other vessel bound for St John's. Fogarty also recruited suitable servants who were usually charged six guineas for their passage. Apart from specialized contract or indentured labour, Meagher also transported ordinary emigrants. Finally, Fogarty arranged insurance for the voyage, paid local port charges, paid off Meagher's mariners, hired replacements, and deducted his own commission charges.

Some Waterford merchants and artisans dealt directly with Meagher. Davis and Strangman, a Quaker brewing firm and located in the far west end of the city, sent out beer and porter. Cordwainers John Burke and John Farrell sent boots specially made for the fishery and Thomas Fogarty, who returned from St John's to set up business on his own account, sent feather beds and leather. Almost all transactions were paid for in bills but there were occasional examples of barter, an indication of the intimacy of commercial links across a vast ocean. Thomas Fogarty took ox hides from St John's for his tannery and, with Burke and Farrell, cod and seal oil for softening leather.

Meagher did not depend solely on his own ship for transatlantic trade. Waterford shipowners carried goods for him, as did sea captains from south-west England. Meagher, moreover, rented space on his own vessel to traders on both sides of the Atlantic or took goods on freight. Flexibility in shipping and the diversification of imports were important. Meagher imported a wide range of supplies from British ports, particularly from Liverpool, where he registered his third ship in 1813.

Traffic between Newfoundland and America, prosecuted only under special license when Meagher began trading overseas, was halted by the war of 1812. It was trifling for a decade thereafter. Commerce with the Maritimes intensified instead. Meagher adapted to this change. Irish emigrants and some British manufacturers were re-shipped from St John's and staples like fresh farm produce and livestock from Charlottetown, Prince Edward Island, coal from Sydney, Cape Breton, West Indies and other goods from Halifax, Nova Scotia, and timber from St Andrews and St John, New Brunswick, were collected.

The Newfoundland cod fishery entered a recession in the wake of the Napoleonic wars. Trade with Spain dropped dramatically in the face of high tariffs and increasing competition from Norwegian fish. A number of important merchant houses in St John's collapsed or quickly withdrew. Merchants such as Meagher, smaller in scale, were less affected by the problems besetting the south European markets because, unlike the Wexford firms of Elmes, Koughs and Sweetmans, for example, they did not deal directly there. By contrast, the demand for fish in Waterford continued to increase. Imports had trebled between 1794 and 1813 and doubled over the next decade.[19] The rapid expansion of permanent settlement in south-eastern Newfoundland ensured a continuing demand there for imported supplies.

Late in 1815 Meagher admitted his two sons, Thomas Jr and Henry, as full partners.[20] The company invested in landed property, particularly in waterfront premises and dwellings. Profits derived from leases helped finance maritime trade. Alternatively, the profits from ocean commerce were invested in the local land market. In 1809 Meagher paid £2,000 insurance for two contiguous premises.

Meagher's house and shop were by Scanlon's Lane on the north side of Water Street (the lower path), with his store and counting house on the south side. Jones reported in 1809 that warehouses still dominated the south side, leading down to the wharves. In 1816 Meaghers relocated their premises to the west at Codner's Cove, and William B. Thomas advertised for rent 'that well known valuable premises formerly occupied by Mr Thomas Meagher'. It contained a house, shop, counting house and store located 'in the most eligible part of town for business' and was 'also well calculated for retail trade'.[21]

Apart from the space reserved for formal trade, Meagher acquired considerable interests in property on the waterfront. He ranked twelfth of twenty-six merchants recorded by Jones in 1809. James Murphy of Kilcash and his merchant partner Matthew Gleeson of Nenagh rented Meagher's interest in a room (waterfront space and structures) owned by a Greenock firm and insured by Meagher for £500 a year.[22] It is amongst the first records of Tipperary links that characterized Meagher's dealings, both commercial and social, during his sojourn in St John's.

The migratory ship fishery, based largely in south Devon, collapsed around 1790 but the laws protecting ships' rooms in St John's remained, frustrating private development. In 1811 a concerted effort was made by merchants, traders and other leading inhabitants resident in the town to have these restrictions repealed. The government in London finally yielded freeing prime waterfront property for entrepreneurs. Meagher, who was involved in the public protest, rented two properties, one in the Admiral's Room, the other in Church Hill, for £120 a year. These were re-let to under-tenants at a substantial profit.[23]

Meagher also acquired farmland on the edges of town, connecting him conceptually with his cultural background in Tipperary. In 1809 he held a field of six acres south of Fort Townshend which was still in the hands of his son, Thomas Jr, as late as 1849.[24] He is also recorded leasing a garden on the Newman estate, south of the Catholic chapel, which he sublet to the Benevolent Irish Society in 1811 for ten guineas a year.[25] Agricultural land on the fringes of St John's had become more valuable than much of the farmland in south-east Tipperary. Many leading citizens in the town operated gardens and pastures and even farms, either for their personal use as a source of fresh food, as commercial units, or for rent. Meagher and Sons, for example, leased a house and eight acres to an Irish farmer on the south side of Quidi Vidi pond.[26]

SOCIETY AND CULTURE IN A COLONIAL PORT

Migration to Newfoundland resulted in a mingling of people to a degree without precedent in their homelands. For a migrant from south Tipperary, where Catholics composed the vast majority of inhabitants, the presence of so many people of Protestant English birth or descent in St John's represented a sudden and dramatic cultural change. Some of Meagher's commercial dealings involved his new English neighbours. This was particularly the case at the mercantile level. He carried on a lively trade with English and Scottish houses. British shipowners transported goods to and from his wharf, bills of exchange were drawn on British firms, and he leased his properties primarily from British proprietors. Formal trading partnerships between the two dominant cultural groups in St John's, however, were rare. Meagher did supply English families and rented houses to them, but his clientele remained predominantly Irish.

One of the central experiences of Irish immigrants and migrants in St John's was the gradual assimilation into a new sense of Irishness, a merging or discarding of highly localized homeland traditions. Prior to migration, Meagher's life was almost certainly confined to his home place in south Tipperary. In St John's he worked with migrants and immigrants from five other south-eastern Irish counties and with native Newfoundlanders of Irish or mixed ancestry. St John's was a melting pot where religion outstripped language as the salient symbol of ethnic identity. Although there is no reference to it in the documents, Thomas Meagher almost certainly spoke Irish in his native Tipperary; English, however, was the language of commerce in Newfoundland. His close friend Timothy Flannery, a fellow tailor-trader from Stradbally, County Waterford, was a fluent Gaelic speaker, acting as translator in court for Irish migrants with no English. But however widely Irish may have been spoken in St John's, there is no evidence of generational transmission. It is highly unlikely that any of Meagher's three sons, for example, could speak it.

Migration from Ireland accelerated cultural change. Yet some sense of identification or attachment to home places persisted. Surviving data on Meagher suggest considerable social interaction and commercial clannishness amongst immigrants from his native Tipperary. Apart from those Tipperary immigrants already noted – Murphy, Gleeson and Howleys – they included several mercantile families: Timothy Ryan and Sons, Henry Shea and Geoffrey Morris of Carrick-on-Suir, Cornelius Quirk and the O'Donnells of Kilcash, and Timothy Hogan of Clonmel. His closest ties were with Ryan and Co., Tipperary's foremost traders in early nineteenth-century Newfoundland. It was headed by Timothy Ryan and included his two sons, Patrick and Joseph and two sons-in-law, Henry Shea and Geoffrey Morris. Joseph Ryan was company agent in Liverpool, Timothy operated in St John's with Shea, and Patrick Ryan was based in Burin on the south coast, with Morris. Their ledger and letter books survive for Burin and give a detailed picture of the patterns of trade. Joseph Ryan also acted as Meagher's agent in Liverpool, shipping a wide variety of manufactured goods each season on commission, and sometimes on Meagher's vessel. Some of these goods were sent to Burin in exchange for fish.[27] Meagher and Shea were appointed administrators of Patrick Ryan's considerable property following his sudden death in 1814, and Meagher later acted as trustee for the insolvent estates of both Timothy Ryan and Henry Shea.[28]

Social and economic links amongst the immigrant Irish were reinforced and articulated through the Catholic Church. It was formally established in 1784 by Dr James Louis O'Donel of Knocklofty in south Tipperary, with financial support and stimulus coming from the emerging Irish middle class, primarily in St John's. The Catholic Church was an overwhelmingly Irish institution and was central in sustaining an ethnic consciousness in Newfoundland. Meagher witnessed its beginnings, having arrived about the same time as O'Donel, and was most likely married by him. Once established as a merchant, Thomas Meagher played a prominent role in parish affairs. He provided a 'very liberal gift of books' to a newly established Sunday School in St John's in 1812, for example, and chaired a committee in charge of construction of a new house for the Catholic clergy there two years later.[29]

Comprehensive data on Roman Catholic marriages and baptisms for the parish of St John's survive from 1802. It is too late for any record of their own children's baptisms, but both Thomas and Mary Meagher appear as witnesses to marriages and as godparents between 1803 and 1817.[30] Choice of witnesses and sponsors reflected residential location in St John's: near neighbours, ethnicity, occupations and commercial connections, social status and sometimes even regional origins in south-east Ireland. Thomas Meagher is recorded as godfather to seventeen children, his wife to at least six. All parents were Catholic Irish by birth or descent. Around one-third had Tipperary connections, some of them were well established merchants. They included Henry Shea, James Murphy, John Wall and Timothy Hogan who married Mary O'Donnell of Kilcash. Meagher witnessed Hogan's marriage and was godfather to one of their children. An immigrant from Thurles chose young Henry Meagher as a sponsor. Memories of home were sustained through these relationships. More impressive were Meagher's social links with immigrants from places in south-east Ireland that a south Tipperary native would normally not know: Limerick, south-east Cork, south Waterford, south-east Kilkenny, Wexford and Enniskillen. Most families were well established, upwardly mobile, or already middle-class. Meagher was godfather in 1815 to the daughter of Patrick Morris, a native of Waterford and by now a leading merchant and emerging politician in St John's. Both Thomas and Mary were sponsors for John Dowsley, another Waterford merchant trading with Meagher. Most of their godchildren came from established retailing families and artisans in the town. They included a master carpenter, a master cooper, a baker, a block-maker, a publican, a shopkeeper, a farmer, and a group of tailors largely from south and west Waterford. Amongst the latter was William Slator of Clashmore. Slator and Meagher established a partnership in the cloth trade, which was dissolved late in 1811.[31] Meagher also established close links with Thomas Foley from the parish of Whitechurch, beside Clashmore, who began his career in Harbour Grace as a tailor. He became a leading merchant there. Foley's daughter married Patrick Morris in 1814. These links suggest a close-knit network woven around religion, occupations and place origins. It typified the social geography of the more established Irish in St John's.

Meagher's long residence in Newfoundland and consequent knowledge of its economic and cultural character, meant that he was frequently called upon for public duty. He served as a petty juror from 1804 and in 1811 was appointed to the Grand Jury. With Henry Shea, he was one of only a dozen Catholic Irish thus honoured in the early nineteenth century.[32] His talents were sought as an assessor of property, as an arbitrator over boundary disputes, litigation over payments for goods and services and in cases related to the passenger and supply trades, theft, assault and murder.

The family's most notable public service in Newfoundland was to the Benevolent Irish Society. Established early in 1806 to alleviate distress amongst the Irish poor in St John's, particularly newcomers, membership of the society was restricted to men of Irish birth or descent. Although over 90 per cent of the original 286 members were Catholics, the founding executive was exclusively Protestant apart from Henry Shea. They were drawn from the military, the professional class and the small Irish Anglican trading community in the town. Thomas Meagher was one of a handful of Catholics chosen in 1806 to serve on a committee.[33] Within a decade, however, Irish Catholics had come to dominate the running of the society. Meagher succeeded his deceased friend Patrick Ryan as treasurer in 1814. Following his final departure for Waterford four years later his son, Thomas Meagher Jr, was appointed treasurer. It was a seminal appointment in a public career that spanned almost half a century of Waterford politics. He relinquished his position on his move to Waterford but the family remained active in the society. Patrick Morris reported that the Benevolent Irish Society had collected and disbursed £8,000 between 1806 and 1827, and had £1,500 in deposits in Waterford, probably in Newport's bank. Morris and Meagher Jr, both resident in Waterford, were trustees. At the annual banquet in St John's in 1819 the Meaghers were toasted as 'staunch friends and able supporters of the Society'.[34] It is a reminder of the close cultural ties between the two ports, ties that were sustained by ethnic institutions such as the Benevolent Irish Society and the Catholic Church and in which Thomas Meagher Jr, in particular, played a prominent role.

RETURN TO IRELAND

Of the vast numbers of Irish moving to North America only a tiny minority ever returned permanently. Newfoundland's transatlantic migratory cod fishery was an exception. In the eighteenth century most Irish migrants were seasonal workers or temporary residents who eventually came home. This annual autumnal migration declined dramatically with the advent of the Napoleonic Wars and the recession that ensued. Increasingly, Irish servants settled in Newfoundland, married and formed families. Successful merchants such as the Meaghers, by contrast, could afford to return. Some did so to establish mercantile bases and expand their commerce through a more vertically organized company structure. Others abandoned the cod fishery altogether, investing instead in the local land market. Still others retired from trade to enjoy the fruits of colonial endeavour.

The progression from apprentice tailor to mercantile status was an impressive accomplishment and illustrates the links between migration and upward social mobility. Meagher's decision to leave south-east Tipperary with its rising population and unpromising prospects for sons of farmers, and settle in an expanding colonial port, ultimately brought its reward. Between 1780 and 1820 more than fifty Irish migrants like Meagher advanced from relatively humble beginnings to merchant status. Some began as apprentices to artisans, others as clerks in the counting houses, or as agents. Henry Shea began as a clerk to a New England merchant, Patrick Morris to a merchant kinsman from Waterford. Almost all young Irishmen destined for mercantile careers were literate and numerate, were fluent in English and were not the sons of labourers. Some may even have had a small amount of capital to begin with, or hoarded meagre wages and profits to make a start on their own account. A strategic marriage such as Meagher's accelerated the process.

In 1817 James MacBraire, president of the Benevolent Irish Society and one of Ireland's most successful merchants in St John's, decided to relocate company headquarters in Greenock. As treasurer of the society, Meagher Sr was involved in procuring 'a piece of plate, suitably inscribed' from Dublin as a gift for the departing and highly popular president. Meagher Sr and Jr attended a society banquet for him that June. Like MacBraire, Meagher had also decided to leave. He did so in the autumn, taking his wife and perhaps his son Henry to Waterford, long the focus of their transatlantic trade. Thomas Jr remained in St John's to continue company operations. In December he advertized the family's horse, gig and sleigh for sale.[35] He was single, and probably without kin in Newfoundland.

Meaghers typified the social structure of an Irish firm engaged in the fishery: patriarchal, small in scale, and centred on the nuclear family. Formal partnerships involving non-kin or even extended family members were relatively rare. Commerce in the fishery did not require the extensive capital associated with other colonial staples such as timber, tobacco or sugar. Although there were some large vertically integrated houses, particularly amongst shipowning firms negotiating the south European markets, the cod trade was dominated by small family firms not unlike the commission houses in Irish provisions ports such as Waterford. Meagher's move represented more a continuation and extension of a mercantile and shipping system in place than a new beginning. He simply assumed the duties of his agent Richard Fogarty and used his own expertise and connections to continue the traditions of Waterford – St John's commerce.

A crucial factor in Meagher's successful relocation was the considerable capital he had accumulated in St John's and had transferred to Waterford. It exceeded £20,000 and was deposited in Newport's bank. Shortage of working capital was the bane of Irish merchants and Meagher's windfall profits from the fishery were invested in acquiring an extensive trading premises on the quay in Waterford City to match those in place in St John's, and impressive accommodation for his family. Within a year of his return Meagher leased an imposing Georgian villa at Ballycanvan. Formerly the residence of the Boltons, a landed family of Cromwellian origins and sub-gentry status, the estate was rented to Samuel Roberts, a city banker, for £183 a year plus a lease fine of £1,600.[36] Roberts invested a further £5,000 in renovations and improvements. Located four miles downstream from Waterford City, on the south bank of the River Suir with a commanding view of the river and its traffic, it was the ideal location for a shipowning merchant. The estate comprised sixty Irish acres, with an elegant tree-lined avenue, walled gardens, a coach house and outbuildings. The Meaghers had been living in some style in St John's, as an advertizement for their furniture there reveals,[37] but there was nothing in St John's or elsewhere in Newfoundland in 1818 to equal the elegance of Ballycanvan.

In the spring of 1818 Thomas Meagher assembled his first cargo in Waterford for his son in St John's. It included traditional salt provisions, salt and passengers. Meagher used his own ship, the *Berisford*, under the command of Captain Sinnott. The *Berisford* had been plying this route for Meagher since 1813, making two round trips most years. It did so in 1818. A more detailed inventory of the second shipment, in September, survives. It included '66 barrels of pork, 18 barrels of beef, 189 cwts of butter, 389 bags of bread, 249 barrels of oatmeal, 6 cwts of lard, 5 feather beds, and 5 casks of glass'.[38] It was a typical Waterford cargo both in range and quantities, and one Meagher had become thoroughly familiar with in over a decade of trading. Most Waterford merchants in the Newfoundland trade operated on a commission basis, assembling cargoes for south-west English shipowners. Meagher, by contrast, worked from the outset on his own account, initially as an importer in St John's, subsequently as an exporter based in Waterford.

In the summer of 1818 the Meaghers recruited Thomas Beck as a partner to assist Thomas Jr in St John's. A native of Thomastown, County Kilkenny, Beck was an established merchant focusing on the Irish passenger and provisions trades. He already had links with the Meaghers through his marriage to the daughter of Henry Duggan, a baker and close associate of Thomas Sr in St John's.[39] The company's activities in St John's are well documented over the next year. Thomas Jr continued his father's dealings in the St John's land market, paying rents and collecting rents from under-tenants, acting as an administrator or trustee for clients' estates, issuing writs and settling accounts.

Advertizements were placed regularly in the St John's newspapers detailing a wide range of supplies for sale at their wharf, warehouse or shop on Water Street.[40] The company had a schooner delivering supplies and collecting fish and oil in outharbours along the east coast and another engaged in catching cod. Waterford remained the main market for their Newfoundland produce and the principal source of supply. Apart from company commerce there, they acted as agents for Thomas Fogarty of Waterford who had a vessel in the St John's trade.

In August 1819 the three Meaghers leased an extensive premises on the quay of Waterford City from Thomas and James Quan for £100 a year. It extended 129 feet along the quay, west of Hanover Street and 154 feet south to King Street on the west side. The property included 'The Singeing Bed', a store on the corner of Hanover West and the quay (site of the modern Granary Museum), and 'The Long Bacon Cellar'.[41] Thomas Jr joined his family in Waterford that summer leaving Thomas Beck in sole charge of company business in St John's. A fire destroyed the premises at Codner's Cove in July but the company rebuilt that autumn.[42] The departure of Thomas Jr marked the end of a family presence in St John's. None of them ever returned. It is possible that the Meaghers had already decided to cut back or wind down their Newfoundland ventures and focus instead on the burgeoning bacon trade between Waterford and England. By 1820 bacon exports had supplanted salt pork in the meat industry and Waterford's Newfoundland trade was in rapid decline.

In October 1820, Thomas Meagher Jr married Alicia Quan. The marriage settlement reveals two families with substantial wealth. In return for a bond of £4,000 from the Meaghers, the Quans assigned Thomas Jr their leasehold interests in three properties: the premises on the quay, the 'Poor House Lot' on south King Street, and 'Samuel Fowkes Garden' located close by. The 'Poor House Lot' had been developed by James Wyse in the late eighteenth century, and contained warehouses, granaries, stores and stables leased to under-tenants for £75 for a year.[43] Thomas Jr took up residence on north King Street where he is recorded with his wife and brother Henry in 1821. He quickly emerged as the most active member of the firm. Meaghers had £7,600 in Newport's bank at the time of its crash in June 1820 and Thomas Jr was appointed principal assignee with the bacon merchant John Harris. As Waterford's leading bank, Newport's has a large clientele that included landowners, substantial tenant farmers, merchants, retailers and artisans. Meetings with creditors extended over two years, exposing Thomas Jr not only to the local commercial community but also to the complexities of financial exchange in an Old World port.

Thomas Meagher Sr was himself called as an expert witness in a landmark case on Newport's collapse. It focused on commercial practices surrounding the conduct of the Waterford–Newfoundland trade. In January 1820 Thomas Foley arrived in Waterford with the intention of investing in the local land market. When Foley entered merchant commerce shortly after 1800, Meagher recommended Richard Fogarty as his Waterford factor. Each autumn thereafter Foley remitted bills of exchange from Harbour Grace, usually drawn in 'the most respectable of

English houses' notably in Bristol, an important centre for Harbour Grace commerce. Fogarty used these bills as payment for provisions assembled and dispatched to Newfoundland in the spring. On arrival in Waterford, Foley first sought out Meagher, 'a very old and highly respected friend' for advice on investment. Meagher recommended he speak to Fogarty and their attorney, George Ivie. The latter recommended land in the Bessborough estate at Piltown in nearby Kilkenny. The leasehold interest there was assessed at £6,000, double what Foley had delivered in bills of exchange to Fogarty. Meagher agreed to invest £3,000 of his own capital jointly with Foley provided the estate was free of all 'charges' and 'encumbrances' and clear title secured. Fogarty deposited Foley's bills in Newport's bank while negotiations proceeded.

Foley was unusual in merchant circles in that he was illiterate and innumerate with little understanding of banks or the complexities of the Irish land market. In Newfoundland he relied for guidance on Patrick Morris, his son-in-law. Morris' wife died in childbirth in 1815 leaving a daughter who was sent to the Morrises in Waterford to be raised. Thomas Meagher Sr was her godfather. Patrick Morris was supplied by his brother, James, in Waterford and, partly out of family loyalty or pressure, Foley decided to replace Fogarty with James Morris as his factor and Joseph Fanning, the latter's attorney and a relative, for George Ivie. Meagher disapproved and refused to deal with Fanning claiming Ivie was a much more experienced agent. Should Foley abandon the Bessborough search, Meagher proposed investing the entire £6,000 required and advised Foley on some other landed security. It is another example of the considerable capital at Meagher's disposal.

Foley decided to return to Harbour Grace in April. He got a statement of his current account with Fogarty and receipts for the bills of exchange. The latter he left with Meagher at Ballycanvan 'a gentleman who, amongst the many respectable merchants concerned with the trade in Newfoundland stands in the foremost class'. Foley had instructed his new agents that no investments should be made unless approved by Meagher.

In June 1820 the bank collapsed and Foley subsequently sued Fogarty for £3,000. He alleged that Fogarty, and not the bank, was responsible for the bills of exchange. The trial 'caused much excitement amongst commercial interests in Waterford City' and was reported in detail in the local newspapers.[44] It was held in Clonmel at Foley's request, claiming he would not get an impartial jury in Waterford because of Fogarty's status and influence there. Meagher was the key witness; his detailed and balanced testimony was instrumental in exonerating Fogarty. Foley did succeed in recovering £900 from the bankrupt Newport estate. The case yields important information on four prominent Catholic Irish houses engaged in Waterford–Newfoundland commerce, the relationship between principal and factors, credit arrangements, bills of exchange, banking, the role of overseas mercantile capital in the rural land market and the importance of social and kinship connections in the conduct of trade.

COMMERCIAL RE-ORIENTATION AT WATERFORD, 1820–30

Just as the Meaghers seemed poised to expand their Newfoundland trade, they decided to abandon it. By 1820 the transatlantic provisions trade out of Waterford was in rapid decline. Unprocessed or semi-processed foodstuffs – livestock, grain, flour – had dislodged salt meat and breadstuffs. Bacon and pigs replaced salt pork, cattle replaced salt beef and the English market for butter intensified, resulting in a contraction in Waterford's continental and colonial exports. Increasingly, merchants in the Newfoundland trade looked elsewhere for provisions. The growth of agriculture in the Maritimes and Quebec and the resumption of food imports from America, reduced Irish commerce. Fewer than a dozen Waterford houses remained active in the trade in 1820, one-quarter the number in 1770. By the end of the 1820s ports in northern Europe – Hamburg, Bremen, Danzig – had emerged as important centres for victualling Newfoundland. Merchants such as Patrick Morris and Pierce Sweetman sent their ships to those distant ports for supplies. Finally, a recession in the cod fishery – which Thomas Foley had identified as a reason for his plan to return to Waterford – was a serious concern for the Meaghers.

In August 1820 the family announced the dissolution of their partnership with Thomas Beck in St John's, effective at the end of the year. The company had advertized their main vessel, the *Berisford*, for sale that June and their premises in July.[45] Their premises were advertized again in December with an explicit statement by the Meaghers that they were withdrawing from the Newfoundland trade. It did not happen right away. The *Berisford* continued to sail, making two round transatlantic trips in 1821 and 1822 with winter voyages from Waterford to Liverpool. It sank in the Atlantic in December 1822. The Meaghers and Beck had lost a second vessel off Kinsale in May, and a third the following year. There is no record of shipowning thereafter, or of exports to Newfoundland. The company did retain some leasehold interests in property in St John's; the rents were collected by Thomas Beck and remitted to Waterford.

Meaghers switched to the English trade but it did not flourish. In 1827 they shipped only £3,235-worth of provisions, primarily bacon, placing them seventy-first out of ninety-seven merchant firms in Waterford.[46] They are listed as Newfoundland merchants in *Pigot's Directory* in 1824 and as late as 1831 received a cargo of cod oil from St John's.[47] Thomas Sr served on a committee of merchants, shipowners, shipmasters and traders seeking improvements to Waterford harbour the previous spring; it was more a reflection of his expertise than activity as a merchant.

Meagher's return migration led to the socially more prestigious pursuit of profit in the urban property market and careers for his sons in politics, law, the military and the Church. As one of the leading creditors of Newport's bankrupt estate, the Meaghers acquired further leasehold interests in city lands and buildings. The most strategic was on old lot three of the New Quay, west of

Barronstrand Street. It was originally demised by Waterford Corporation to Simon Newport, a merchant, in 1731. The lease was renewed to Newports as head tenants in 1789. They had probably built the impressive Georgian house that preceded the Granville Hotel. Around 1760 Newports sublet the premises to Philip Long, one of Waterford's foremost Catholic provisions merchants. The Quans succeeded the Longs. Thomas Quan is recorded there in 1789, and may have taken up residence in 1783 on his marriage to Anne Wyse. In 1794 Simon Newport leased the premises to Thomas and James Quan for 130 years at £70 a year. It measured 40 feet on the quay and, as in 1731, was 205 feet deep, widening beyond the remnants of the old city wall to 92 feet, with an exit to Little Barronstrand Street/George Street at the rear, along Rogers Lane.[48] Located in the mercantile heart of Waterford the property straddled the boundary between St Patrick's parish and Trinity Within.

Thomas Quan's six surviving children by his second wife, Christina Forstall, were born and raised here. They included Edmund Pierce, born in 1795 and Alicia born in 1797. She married Thomas Meagher Jr in 1820 and initially they lived on King Street. Precisely when they moved to her home on the quay is not clear. Thomas and James Quan, both widowers, and three children of Thomas were recorded there in 1821. The house had four storeys and faced the quay. In June 1822 Sir John Newport assigned to Thomas Meagher Sr of Ballycanvan, Newport's interest in Quans' premises.[49] Quans themselves declared bankruptcy in 1823; Francis Wyse, a kinsman, was appointed assignee. Meaghers paid over £2,000 for Quans' holdings. Thomas Quan 'died at his house on the quay' that December and his brother James left Waterford, clearing the way for the Meaghers' occupancy.[50]

In spring 1825 the Meaghers advertized their provisions and corn stores on the quay west of Hanover Street. They were leased to Edward Lynch, a merchant, and the Quaker, Samuel White for £185 a year.[51] Whites had occupied the southern section of this block along King Street north, since the 1770s. They were still there leasing part of their premises from the Meaghers a century later. It is an example of tenurial and residential continuity relatively rare amongst merchant families in an urban economy characterized by rapid change. It was also a clear indication that the Meaghers did not plan to expand their overseas provisions trade.

Early in 1827 Alicia Meagher died in the house she was raised in on the quay. Her death left Thomas Jr with four young children, and his brother Henry. Two years later Thomas Sr and his wife sold their interests in Ballycanvan for £1,400 to Richard Morris of Waterford and joined Thomas Jr on the quay.[52] Mary Meagher died there late in 1831 and the family finally withdrew from maritime trade. They advertized their house, furniture and premises, including extensive pork and bacon-curing and packing equipment. Charles Bianconi, the carriage entrepreneur, rented the property for £120 a year plus a payment of £600 to the Meaghers. It was converted to a stagecoach station, with Edward Commins establishing a hotel in Meaghers' house on the quay.[53]

FROM NEWFOUNDLAND TO IRELAND: CULTURAL POLITICS AND THE CATHOLIC MIDDLE CLASS

The Meaghers departed St John's just before the emergence of organized public protest and the politicization of the general population, particularly the Catholic Irish, in the town. For more than two centuries Newfoundland had been ruled directly from London. It was normally headed by a governor who, until 1817, was present for the summer only. There were no elections or formal political parties. Protestants held most of the positions in the colonial administration. In 1820 a Committee of Inhabitants, under the chairmanship of Patrick Morris, was established in St John's to pursue political and legal reform. Initially dominated by the growing Irish Catholic middle class, it expanded rapidly to include leading Protestants. Important changes to the legal structure were instituted in 1824, Catholic Emancipation established in 1830 and a local legislature formed in 1832. Roger Forstall Sweetman was elected as a member for Placentia.

Waterford's political culture had some parallels with St John's. By 1820 the Catholic middle class had begun to challenge Protestant hegemony in municipal government. The Meaghers, relatively rare in Irish municipal politics in that their experience was colonial, were quickly drawn into what was defined as the 'struggle for civil and religious liberty'. Their introduction was facilitated through the influence and expertise of Thomas Quan. As far back as 1792 Quan was one of six delegates representing Waterford at the Catholic convention in Dublin. Edmund Forstall of Rochestown was also a delegate. The convention resulted in a limited franchise, the right to bear arms, commissions for Catholics in the army and navy and the right to sit on grand and petty juries. Thomas Quan was the first Catholic, with fellow merchants John Blackney and John Archbold, to be appointed a grand juror for Waterford. Thomas Meagher Sr, as noted above, held a similar position in St John's.

In a little over a year after his marriage to Alicia Quan, and only two years' resident in Waterford, Thomas Meagher Jr was reported speaking 'at great length, and with great ability' on the unfair dismissal of the Recorder of Waterford. He put forward several resolutions, which were passed.[54] It marked the beginning of a long career in Waterford municipal politics. Two years later Thomas Jr was admitted to the Chamber of Commerce and appointed treasurer.[55] Originally almost exclusively a Protestant preserve, the composition of the chamber was in transition as the Catholic merchant community expanded and became more politically engaged.

The Meaghers' relocation at Waterford also coincided with the emergence of the city as a major centre in Daniel O'Connell's campaign for Catholic Emancipation. In April 1823, O'Connell established the Catholic Association. Membership was set at a guinea per annum. All three male Meaghers were members, but the association was largely middle-class. A year later O'Connell made the momentous decision to expand membership for a subscription of one penny per month. It had the effect of introducing, for the first time, the great mass of ordinary Irish Catholics into the political process. Committees were formed initially in the cities and towns, then in the rural parishes. Priests were members *ex officio*.

Thomas Meagher Jr was appointed secretary to the Waterford Association. In April 1824, just prior to the opening up of the Association to mass membership, Thomas Jr spoke on behalf of 150 'of the most respectable Catholics in the city' in a vote of thanks to Sir John Newport MP, for his support.[56] It was a pivotal appointment in the evolution of Meagher's political career. Thomas Meagher & Sons was a generous donor to O'Connell's campaign for Catholic Emancipation and, from 1830 onwards, for repeal. Both Thomas Sr and Jr served on committees, acted as stewards at repeal dinners and supervised the collection of the repeal rent for the parishes of Trinity Within, St Patrick's and St John's.[57] O'Connell became a personal friend. Three of his sons went to Clongowes; John O'Connell was a contemporary of Thomas Francis Meagher there. A decade later Daniel O'Connell recommended Meagher be admitted to study law at the Queen's Inns in Dublin.

Emancipation and repeal attracted more interest and financial support from the Irish abroad than any other political movement in Ireland up to that time. They played a major role in sustaining expatriate Irish consciousness and identity. Half of Newfoundland's population was of Irish birth or descent and the close ties of their leaders, both lay and clerical, particularly with Waterford, meant that the Newfoundland-Irish played a role disproportionate to their numbers in the context of a broad American diaspora. Subscriptions in Newfoundland were organized by Irish merchants and traders there, and forwarded to a committee in Waterford that included Newfoundland merchants such as Patrick Morris, Pierce Sweetman, Richard Fogarty and Thomas Meagher Jr.[58] Amongst the last donations recorded was from Placentia, where Roger Forstall Sweetman was the leading merchant. It was sent to Thomas Francis Meagher, then in Dublin.[59] The process reflects the intimacy and tenacity of transatlantic links between the two islands and the importance of kinship, migration and commercial connections in cultural politics.

In St John's the Meaghers had been prominent supporters of charitable institutions and causes. Most of their subscriptions were channelled through the Benevolent Irish Society or the Catholic Church, but they also contributed money and meals informally as crises occurred. Mercantile altruism was an aspect of community life familiar to the Meaghers in their new Waterford home. Several of their Quan kin and business associates were noted supporters of local charities. James Wyse, for example, established a Poor House on King Street in the late eighteenth century and left property and capital to the poor of Waterford, both Catholic and Protestant. The Quans in turn were regular and generous donors. Christine Quan acted as hostess in her house on the quay at meetings of the ladies' committee for the 'Friends of Poor Room Keepers'.[60] It was one of a number of charities run by women for women in distress.

Thomas Meagher Jr was widely acclaimed for his humanitarian work in

Waterford throughout his lengthy residency there. It was a continuation of established family tradition on both sides of the Atlantic. In 1824 Thomas Jr was appointed treasurer of the Trinitarian Orphan Society, a charitable organization founded in 1811 to feed, clothe and accommodate young boys without means to apprentice as artisans. The 'Orphan Asylum' was located on John Street and cared for some sixty-five inmates at a cost of around £1,400 a year. Like the Benevolent Irish Society in St John's, the 'orphan society' was nondenominational but only a handful of Protestants were involved. It was essentially a Catholic charity; a dozen priests served on the committee. The 'orphan society' was strongly supported in the 1820s by the Fogartys, the Meaghers and by Patrick Morris who was elected president in 1830.[61] Details of annual Trinitarian Orphan Society dinners were printed in the St John's newspapers, again an indication of the active participation amongst merchants in the Waterford–Newfoundland trade. Both Richard Fogarty and Thomas Meagher Jr served as vice presidents and as trustees. It is likely that the Orphan Asylum School established by the Benevolent Irish Society in St John's in 1827 was in part modelled on the Waterford Orphan Asylum.

The most familiar and certainly the most pervasive institution in the everyday life of the Meaghers in St John's and in Waterford was the Catholic Church. Increasingly, community life in St John's town was church-centred, its structure essentially a reproduction of the Irish Catholic parish system. Waterford was the ecclesiastical capital of Catholic St John's, and indeed of Newfoundland. The links are commemorated in the permanent display on the Newfoundland connection in the Granary Museum on the quay, once the premises of the Quans and the Meaghers. It is appropriate that Thomas Francis Meagher and his father share the floor space there with the excellent exhibition on the historic ties between the two islands.

Following the death of Mary Meagher and withdrawal from overseas trade, the family moved to a house on William Street in the fashionable east-end. Here Thomas Sr made his will, leaving 'all my property, whether in Ireland or in Newfoundland or elsewhere to my son Thomas in trust for his children Thomas Francis, Henry, Christianna and Alicia'.[62] It included the leasehold interests in all the property demised by the Quans on the marriage of Thomas Jr and Alicia in 1820. The Meaghers retained these interests until at least the 1870s when Henry, brother of Thomas Francis, is recorded as heir.[63]

MIGRATION AND THE SUNDERING OF FAMILY TIES

Thomas Francis Meagher makes little mention in his speeches, reminiscences or other writings of his ancestry or extended family. Perhaps it was that, by 1843, there were so few kin around him and his career led to social interaction primarily with colleagues away from home. Details on personal family background rarely entered public discourse. It was a coincidence that Meagher's political tour of 1848 should focus on his grandfather's homeland district in south-east Tipperary

– Ninemilehouse, Grangemockler, Carrick-on-Suir, Kilcash and Slievenamon. There is no reference to his Tipperary roots during this highly publicized campaign, despite Young Ireland's emphasis on Gaelic symbolism and heritage. His friend Michael Cavanagh's '*Memoirs*', written more than forty years later, began with the observation 'that the boy's first glance at the outer world lighted on the estuary of the noble river (the Suir) whose fountain-springs are situated in the ancestral patrimony of his father's race . . . the scion of a stock [the Meaghers] that kept possession of their ancient patrimony against all corners for fifteen hundred years'.[64] There is little, however, on the immediate background or social origins of Thomas Meagher Sr. It is possible that he never reconnected with kin or neighbours since his departure for Newfoundland; if true, then it is likely that by 1848 the links were lost.

Social and geographical mobility could be powerful solvents of traditional family ties and links to ancestral places. A general lack of knowledge, interest or deliberate obscuring of ordinary origins was evident in Irish Catholic mercantile society. The immediate challenge of commerce, a focus on the accumulation of wealth and a concern with social advancement, left little time for ancestry and an examination of tradition. If that tradition was largely undocumented, and was one of humble beginnings, genealogy and a search for social origins were not a priority for *arriviste* middle-class merchants or others of that status. 'The bitterest thing that could be said about a public man' Arthur Griffith wrote of Waterford snobbery 'was that his father made boots, was successful as a tailor, or tanned the best leather'.[65]

Families of middle-class or sub-gentry status like the Forstalls, Sweetmans and Wyses displayed an interest in heraldry and pedigree not as manifest amongst the Gaelic Meaghers and Quans.[66] Yet some tradition endured. Hereditary first names, for example, were part of the Meagher lineage. The name Thomas existed over at least four generations and Henry over three. Both Alicia and Christine go back to the Kennedys and Lattins in eighteenth-century Kildare. The names appear in the genealogies of the Forstalls, Quans, Sweetmans and Meaghers.

Despite the serious political rift, Thomas Meagher Jr stood by his son in 1848. While visiting him in Kilmainham gaol Thomas Jr wrote a letter of condolence to Roger Forstall Sweetman on the death of his mother, Juliet, at Blenheim. Born in 1771, she was aunt and godmother to Alicia Meagher, mother of Thomas Francis, and, as already noted, a custodian of much family tradition. Roger Sweetman rode through Waterford with Meagher following his arrest at the Mall in 1848 and helped calm the crowd in what was a tense situation. Indeed the Meagher and Quan homes on the Mall had been acquired through the Sweetmans.[67] Thomas Jr also paid the debts incurred by his son during his incarceration and trial. It is likely that Thomas Francis depended on his father for money since his return from Stonyhurst. It came from wealth largely accumulated by Thomas Meagher Sr, largely through the Newfoundland trade.

NOTES

1. Thomas Francis Meagher, 'A Personal Narrative of 1848', in A. Griffith (ed.), *Meagher of the Sword. Speeches of Thomas Francis Meagher in Ireland 1846–1848* (Dublin: M.H. Gill & Son, 1915), p.173. This chapter is a revision of 'From Comfortable Farms to Mercantile Commerce and Cultural Politics: The social origins and family connections of Thomas Francis Meagher', *Decies, Journal of the Waterford Archaeological and Historical Society*, 59, (2003), pp.1–29.
2. A. Pierce, 'The Clongowes of Thomas Francis Meagher', *Decies* 59, (2003), pp.31–9. My thanks to F.J. Turner, SJ, archivist, Stonyhurst College, for details on Patrick Meagher.
3. Registry of Deeds (hereafter Deeds) Dublin, 178280 (1755) to 807 237-8 (1825); *Minute Book*, Waterford Corporation, Admission of Freemen, 29 June 1747, National Library of Ireland (hereafter, NLI); *Abstracts, Jennings' Wills*, Public Record Office (hereafter, PRO), Dublin, Stephen Wyse, Ballygunnermore, farmer, 3 Feb. 1774; William Quan, Ballygunner, 9 Feb. 1784; James Wyse, Waterford, merchant, 1794, proved 1799. For a summary of the Wyse family in Waterford see Eamonn McEneaney (ed.), *A History of Waterford and its Mayors* (Waterford: Waterford Corporation, 1995), pp.104–10; see also E. McEneaney, *Discover Waterford* (Dublin: O'Brien Press, 2001), pp.52–4.
4. Arthur Young, *A Tour of Ireland, 1776–1779* (Shannon: Irish University Press, 1970), pp.406–15. The integration of farming and mercantile trade by James Wyse is outlined in John Mannion 'Waterford and the South of England: Spatial Patterns in Shipping Commerce, 1766–1776', *International Journal of Maritime History*, 6, 2 (1994), pp.115–53.
5. Roman Catholic Cathedral Parish, City of Waterford, Register of Marriages, 12 Oct. 1820; Deeds, 714229 (1817) to 803264 (1825).
6. Deeds, 13111(1714) to 395 387 (1788). My thanks to Richard Forstall of Virginia for detailed letters on the family, 1770–74, 1844 and 1856–61. They reveal the importance of primogeniture over six generations of Forstall inheritance in Glenmore. They also show knowledge of kinship links extending to third cousins, including Thomas Meagher Jr, Thomas Francis Meagher and the Forstalls of New Orleans. The latter were descendants of Nicholas Forstall of Gurteens Castle, Slieveroe parish, who established first at Nantes as a merchant, then at Martinique in the West Indies. His son Nicholas was commander of Louisiana under the Spanish. See Irene Neu, 'From Kilkenny to Louisiana: Notes on Eighteenth-Century Irish Emigration', *Mid-America*, 49, (1967), pp.101–114.
7. Deeds, 74297 (1819); 606141 (1808). The lands comprising 162 acres at £146 a year in 1812, were in the possession of Edmund Forstall and his wife, Alicia Kennedy of Ringville and then of Rochestown, parents of Christina and Juliet. They married in 1791 Thomas Quan and Pierce Sweetman respectively. The Sweetmans lived at Blenheim Lodge, beside Ballycanvan, 1810–55.
8. Meagher Papers, Royal Irish Academy (hereafter RIA) Dublin. Written on or after 1847, they contain a short account of the careers of Thomas Sr and his three sons Thomas Jr, Henry and Patrick, and of Henry, son of Thomas Jr, and brother of Thomas Francis. My thanks to Dr William Nolan, Department of Geography, NUI (Dublin) for a copy of the RIA Meagher Papers and to the Meaghers of Tullowhea, near Ninemilehouse, who claim kinship to Thomas Francis Meagher.
9. *Limerick Reporter*, 3 March 1847.
10. Michael Cavanagh, *Memoirs of Gen. Thomas Francis Meagher. Comprising the Leading Events in his Career* (Worcester, MA: The Messenger Press, 1892), p.12.
11. The book is signed 'Thomas Francis Meagher Clonmel Gaol Oct. 23rd 1848, the day upon which I was sentenced to death for High Treason'. My thanks to Michael and John Howley of St John's for this item and a copy of the Howley Papers.
12. Rev. M.F. Howley, 'How Meagher became a Millionaire: A true story of Old St John's', *The Newfoundland Quarterly*, 4, 3, (1904), pp.2–3.
13. Government of Newfoundland (hereafter GN), 2/39/A – 1795, *Census, District of St John's*. All Newfoundland references are at the Provincial Archives in St John's (PANL), unless otherwise noted.

14. GN 5/2/A/10,66 'Petition of Michael Crotty, Stephen Woolcock et al. V Elliott Elmes', 28 September 1784.
15. GN, 5/2/A/9, Administrative Bonds, Supreme Court, Central District, St John's, 1 May and 1 July 1808. Meagher acted as executor for the estates of a Tipperary shoemaker and two sailors, one from Waterford and the other from Prince Edward Island.
16. *Lloyds Register of Shipping*, (Holland: Gregg Press, 1808), p.504. Governor Duckworth Papers, (hereafter Duckworth Papers) 1/5, 18 Dec. 1809. Colonial Office 194, Public Records Office, London.
17. *Lloyds List*, (Farnborough: Gregg Press, 1969), 20 Feb. 1810; *Waterford Mirror* (hereafter *Mirror*), 24 April 1810; see also Duckworth Papers, 1/5/28, 11 June 1810, 1/5/25, 21 July and 2 Sept. 1810; 1/5/68, 17 Dec. 1810; *Royal Gazette and Newfoundland Advertiser* (hereafter *Gazette*), 22 Sept. 1810 and 14 January 1811.
18. Ledgers of Richard Fogarty, Waterford, (Maritime History Archive R 95/40: Memorial University, St John's), 1 Nov. 1810–1 Nov. 1813
19. Ledgers of Imports and Exports, Waterford, Customs 15, Ms. 353, NLI. On 17 December 1817, the *Waterford Chronicle* (hereafter *Chronicle*) reported that 6,800 quintals of Newfoundland fish had already arrived, 'the greatest in many years'.
20. *Gazette*, 21 Dec. 1815.
21. Jenkins Jones, policy 303748, 303768, 'In Lower Street opposite this wharf all Meagher's property' 6 June 1809, Phoenix Fire Insurance P7/B/18; Lionel Chancey, surveyor, 'Plan of Carwithin's Thomas & Flood's Wharfs, taken 1810'; Plan of Town of St John's destroyed by fire on the 21st November 1817', Map Collection, Public Archives, St John's, Newfoundland (hereafter PANL). *Gazette*, 15 Oct. 1812 and 20 May 1813. *Mercantile Journal* (hereafter, *Journal*), 9 Oct. 1816 to 14 Feb. 1822; *Chronicle*, 19 Aug. 1819.
22. GN, 5/2A/1, 28 Dec. 1808 and 2 Jan. 1809; GN, 5/2A/4, 146, 1809; Jones, Insurance Policy 303768. The rent for this room was set at £83 a year.
23. GN, 5/2/A/16–25; 1 Sept. and 12 Oct. 1811; Duckworth Papers, 1/5/22, 22 Nov. 1811; Colonial Office (hereafter CO), 194/52, 51–67.
24. GN, 5/2/A/1/20, 29 July 1809; *Gazette*, 31 Jan. and 20 Dec. 1811; *Morning Post*, 22 Nov. 1849; *Public Ledger*, St John's, 29 Oct. 1858.
25. Duckworth Papers, 22/28, 22/66, 12, 14 Oct. 1811.
26. *Journal*, 1 May 1818.
27. Ryan and Morris Ledger, PANL, 13 Oct. 1813 to 30 May 1818; *Gazette*, 10 Feb. 1814; *Journal*, 29 May and 16 Dec. 1817.
28. A broader context is provided in John Mannion, 'Henry Shea (1767–1830) – A Tipperary Trader in Newfoundland', *Tipperary Historical Journal*, 1, (1988), pp.182–91.
29. *Gazette*, 27 Feb. 1812 and 22 Dec. 1814. The school opened on 23 Feb. 1812 and despite severe weather, ninety-nine boys and eighty-four girls attended. It was probably nondenominational.
30. Roman Catholic Register, St John's, marriages and baptisms, 1808–17.
31. *Gazette*, 26 Dec. 1811.
32. GN, 5/2/A/1, 21 Aug. 1804 to 13 June 1816.
33. 'List of Original Members of the Newfoundland Irish Society,' *Centenary Volume of the Benevolent Irish Society, 1806–1906* (Cork: Guy & Co., 1907), pp.195–6; GN, 2/1/19 (1806), 7–8, 17.
34. *Gazette*, 25 Feb. 1813 to 21 March 1828. See also CO, 194/75 (1827), pp.172–4.
35. *Journal*, 8 June to 23 Nov. 1817; *Gazette*, 1 July and 2 Dec. 1817.
36. Deeds, 737579 (1818); *Mirror*, 3 April 1805. See also, William Wilson, *Traveller's Directory through Ireland* (Dublin: J. Fleming, 1815), p.456.
37. *Journal*, 3 July 1818. Meagher's furniture and other possessions in St John's included a dining table, chairs and card tables, all of mahogany; oak chairs, chests of drawers, dinner ware, china and glass ware, silver ware, poll lamps, an eight-day clock, a register stove, a bookcase, a pleasure boat, and a gig and sleigh with full harness.
38. *Chronicle*, 4 April to 12 Sept. 1818; *Journal*, 15 May to 12 Nov. 1818.
39. *Journal*, 19 July 1818; GN, 5/2/A/9, 2 July 1818. In November 1817, Thomas Meagher Jr

stood as godfather for Beck's son. The firm was renamed Thomas Meagher, Sons & Co.

40. *Journal*, 19 July and 10 Sept. 1819; GN, 5/2/A/30, 10 Sept. 1819. Meagher escaped the two fires of November 1817, prompting Thomas Jr, with Patrick Morris, to publish a note of 'thanks to the many people who helped in the preservation of their properties... the greater number of whom, though classed amongst the lower orders of this community, yet their conduct on both occasions was marked with the strictest integrity', *Journal*, 25 Nov. 1817.
41. Deeds, 74736, 18 Aug. 1819.
42. *Journal*, 19 July and 10 Sept. 1819. The last reference to Thomas Jr in St John's is 9 July 1819, when he acted as administrator of the Maddock estate with Patrick Morris. He appears at Ballycanvan in August with his father and brother.
43. Pierce Kelly, attorney, 'Deeds relating to the families of Meagher and Quan', 1794–1875, Ms. 8142, D 10041–61, NLI. The trustees for the marriage settlement were Patrick Meagher, son of Thomas Sr and Edmund Pierce Quan, son of Thomas.
44. *Chronicle*, 30 March to 6 April 1822.
45. *Journal*, 1 June to 8 Dec. 1820.
46. 'Value of the Export of Provisions from the Port of Waterford for the year ending 30th of April 1828'. Monteagle Papers, Ms. 13,370 (10), NLI.
47. *City of Dublin and Hibernian Provincial Directory* (London: Hibernian Press, 1824), p.316. *Chronicle*, 23 March 1830. Kough Letter Book, New Ross, P3B16, 5 Feb. 1831, Public Records Office, Northern Ireland, Belfast.
48. Kelly, 'Deeds... Meagher and Quan', 24 Oct. 1794; Deeds, 3280 (1872). See also, Probate, last will of Thomas Meagher Jr, Ms. 8142, DIO, 041–61, NLI.
49. Deeds, 775251 (1822).
50. Deeds, 790573 (1824); 803264 (1825). *Chronicle*, 13 Dec. 1824. *Waterford Mirror*, 18 Dec. 1824. A week after Thomas Quan's death the 'house and stores on the quay, lately occupied by the Quans', were advertized for sale. In 1848 T.F. Meagher was told at Ninemilehouse, Tipperary, that his (maternal) grandfather's funeral 'covered the length of the quay'.
51. *Waterford Mirror*, 30 March 1825; Deeds, 801277 to 876401 (1825).
52. Estate of Cornelius Henry Bolton, Land Estates Court 4635, 1857, PRO, Dublin. *Waterford Chronicle*, 24 Aug. 1829. Thomas Maher, Esq. is recorded at Ballcanvan with ninety-four acres leased from Mrs Bolton in 1826. Tithe Applotment Book, 29/52, 1826, p. 5, Parish of Kill St Nicholas. Over sixty-five acres were described as first-class land, the rest mainly marsh. He paid £7.14s.8d in tithes.
53. *Waterford Chronicle*, 12 and 15 Nov. 1831; 18 Feb. to 2 June 1832. *Mirror*, 15 Feb. 1832. Kelly, 'Deeds... Meagher and Quan', 24 March 1832. Deeds, 1338 (1833).
54. *Chronicle*, 18 Dec. 1821.
55. *Mirror*, 29 Nov. 1833. Only eight of the eighty-seven members of the chamber in 1815 were Catholic, Charter of Incorporation (Waterford, 1815).
56. *Mirror*, 27 April 1824.
57. *Mirror*, 3 Jan 1828 to 4 Jan. 1833. *Chronicle*, 7 Feb. 1829 to 24 April 1832.
58. *Mirror*, 25 Jan. 1829. *Chronicle*, 21 Jan. 1829; 24 April 1832; *Newfoundlander*, 16 April 1829 to 12 Jan. 1832; *Public Ledger*, 7 Feb. 1832. See also John Mannion, 'Patrick Morris and Newfoundland Irish Immigration' in C.J. Byrne and M. Harry (eds), *Talamh an Eisc: Canadian and Irish Essays* (Halifax: Nimbus Press, 1986), pp.180–202.
59. *Nation*, 20 Jan. 1844.
60. *Chronicle*, 20 Feb. 1814 to 30 Jan. 1819. *Mirror*, 24 February 1817.
61. *Mirror*, 10 Jan. 1824 to 5 Jan. 1830. *Chronicle*, 9 Jan. 1829. *Public Ledger*, 23 April 1830.
62. Kelly, 'Deeds... Meagher and Quan...'. Will of Thomas Meagher Sr, 3 Oct. 1833, probate, 1837, Ms. 8142, NLI. See also, Thomas Hanton, *A Complete List of the Poll... City of Waterford, 1835* (Waterford: Hanton, 1835), p.18. *Deeds*, 3280 (1872). *Chronicle*, 28 Jan. 1837.
63. Deeds, 3280 (1872) to 38111 (1876).
64. Cavanagh, *Memoirs*, p.13.
65. Griffith, *Meagher of the Sword*, p.215.
66. John Mannion, 'A Transatlantic Merchant Fishery: Richard Welch of New Ross and the

Sweetmans of Newbawn in Newfoundland, 1744-1862', in Kevin Whelan and William Nolan (eds), *Wexford History & Society* (Dublin: Geography Publications, 1987), pp.373–421.

67. Deeds, 626513 (1811) to 20273 (1863). See also, T. Shearman, *The New Commercial Directory* (Kilkenny, 1839).

My thanks to the late Randell Verran of Placentia, great-great grandson of R. F. Sweetman, who first showed me the Meagher correspondence in January 1968, and stimulated my interest in both families.

3

From the Shadow of his Son: 'Honest Thomas Meagher'– The Father of an Irish Patriot

Eugene Broderick

One historian has written that 'the only claim of Thomas Meagher to remembrance is that he was the father and active opponent of Thomas Francis Meagher'.[1] This assessment is in stark contrast to that of his son by the Waterford historian, Patrick Egan, who lauded him in almost hagiographical terms as 'the pride of Waterford, the day-star of its political heaven . . . bringing fame and glory upon the Irish sword and Irish heroism'.[2] It is understandable that Thomas Meagher has been overshadowed by his son. Yet, he was a figure of some substance in his own right, not least because he became the first Catholic Mayor of Waterford since 1688 and represented the city in Parliament for a decade. Thomas Meagher was a member of the Catholic middle class that gradually came to dominate Irish politics and society in the nineteenth century. He was an ardent champion of the nationalism of Daniel O'Connell and played a significant role in the Independent Irish Party of the 1850s.

BUSINESSMAN

By the 1820s, Thomas Meagher was one of the most prominent and wealthy businessmen in Waterford. He was born in Newfoundland in 1789,[3] his father, who bore the same name, having emigrated from County Tipperary in the 1780s. Meagher Sr was a tailor who advanced to mercantile status and amassed a considerable fortune by engaging in commerce on the lucrative Waterford–Newfoundland trade route. In 1815 he admitted his two sons, Thomas and Henry, as full partners in his enterprises. When Meagher Sr decided to return to Ireland in 1817, it was no surprise that he settled in Waterford, a place with which he had many business connections. Joined by his son, Thomas, in 1819, Waterford now became the centre of their business ventures. They began the more socially prestigious activity of investing in property, acquiring interests in land and buildings in the city. The marriage of Thomas Jr to Alicia Quan in 1820 united families of wealth and substance, contributing significantly to establishing his status in the commercial life of the city. This position was recognised by his admission to the Chamber of Commerce and his appointment as its treasurer in 1823.

CATHOLIC EMANCIPATION

The 1820s was a decade of social and political transition in Ireland, as Catholics challenged the political hegemony of Protestants. In 1823 Daniel O'Connell founded the Catholic Association to campaign for emancipation. Thomas Meagher Jr became a member and was appointed secretary of the Waterford Association,[4] the city and county emerging as a major centre of political activism in the struggle.[5] In April 1824 he attended a meeting of the friends and supporters of Sir John Newport, MP for the City of Waterford and an advocate of emancipation. Speaking on behalf of the Waterford Catholic Association, Meagher addressed the gathering at some length on the concerns of his co-religionists. He expressed their feelings of gratitude towards Newport and conveyed the terms of a resolution adopted at a meeting of over 150 of the city's leading Catholics, which described the MP as 'a true friend of Ireland' and promised him their support in the upcoming general election.[6] Newport's subsequent public reply was an acknowledgement by him of the importance he attached to this promise of support.[7]

At first the Catholic Association was largely a middle-class organisation, the one guinea membership fee being a deterrent to the Catholic population at large. Early in April 1824 O'Connell proposed the admission of associate members at a subscription of a penny a month. This had the effect of transforming the Association into a mass movement which 'became a colossus of democratic power unprecedented in the annals of political organisation in the British Isles'.[8] This power was given dramatic expression during the general election of 1826, when the Catholic Association supported Henry Villiers Stuart in his successful challenge to Lord George Beresford, a staunch opponent of emancipation and a member of a very powerful Ascendancy family.[9] Thomas Meagher, as secretary of the Waterford Catholic Association, played a very important role in the campaign. Victory required an appeal to the predominantly Catholic electorate to vote for Stuart. That this was a truly radical tactic is apparent when one considers that the forty-shilling freeholders were seen as having no political independence. Thomas Wyse, the architect of the strategy, described them as 'mere serfs' when it came to the exercise of the franchise.[10]

It was these 'mere serfs', however, who had to suffer the retribution of the Beresfords and their supporters in the aftermath of Stuart's victory. The immediate reaction of some of the landlords, whose authority had been challenged, was to evict tenants. At a meeting in Waterford City in September 1826 it was claimed that 500 ejectment notices had been served on the Beresford estates.[11] O'Connell was informed by a correspondent in the city that 'the gentry and the aristocracy here have resolved to wage war *usque ad internecionem* against the forty-shilling freeholders who overturned their power at the last election'.[12] In response to the plight of the evicted tenants a Protecting Association was formed on 7 August 1826. Thomas Meagher was appointed secretary.[13] Almost a year after the election most of the letters to the Catholic

Association in Dublin seeking aid for freeholders came from Waterford,[14] prompting O'Connell to describe the county as 'screaming for relief from one end to the other'.[15]

REFORM OF WATERFORD CORPORATION

Daniel O'Connell regarded municipal reform as a crucial step in completing the process initiated by the granting of Catholic emancipation in 1829:

> There remains this corporate monopoly and it is the only thing remaining that prevents justice being done to the people. This, and this alone, shuts the inhabitants out from participation in the advantages of British institutions.[16]

Irish corporations were under Anglican control. They had long used their energies in protecting the position of a narrow political and sectarian class.[17] For the middle-class Catholics of Waterford, as elsewhere, there was the galling fact that they were at least the financial equals of their Protestant counterparts who enjoyed the privileges and advantages of this system of corporate monopoly. In fact, the economic and social position of Anglicans was in decline in the city in the 1820s, and they were being supplanted by Catholic merchants. This reality was given a graphic representation when Newport's Bank, one of Waterford's most venerable business institutions, headed by one of the city's most powerful and prestigious Anglican families, crashed in June 1820.[18] Thomas Meagher was appointed a principal assignee.[19] Thus was new money, with a Catholic hue, subsuming old money, with its Protestant one.

Notwithstanding wealth and success, Catholics were denied any official voice in the regulation of municipal affairs. Moreover, they were denied access to corporate patronage, which was not inconsiderable. During the 1820s the affairs of Waterford Corporation were governed by the terms of a secret compact, drawn up in 1818, between two Anglican families, the Alcocks and the Newports.[20] Both parties to the agreement secured control and leadership of the corporation.[21] They decided on all appointments to corporate offices and regulated admissions to the freedom of the city, which carried with it the right to vote at parliamentary elections.

What middle-class Catholics wanted was a status in municipal politics commensurate with their economic power. In March 1822 Thomas Meagher spoke at a public meeting convened to call on Waterford Corporation to initiate reforms in the manner it conducted public affairs, so as to benefit the citizens of the city at large.[22] The Protestant corporate monopoly was even more objectionable when it was considered that these citizens were overwhelmingly Catholic. An enumeration of denominational affiliations in 1834 revealed that members of the Church of Ireland constituted only 15.5 per cent of the city's population. When the county was taken into account this percentage was reduced to a mere 4.7 per cent.[23]

The compact ended in 1830,[24] but by then Irish corporations were under the scrutiny of Parliament. A royal commission was appointed to examine the manner in which they discharged their municipal functions and it reported in 1835. It concluded that 'corporations were in many instances, of no service to the community; in others injurious; in all, insufficient and inadequate to the proper purposes and ends of such institutions'.[25] Waterford Corporation was exposed as a bastion of Anglican privilege, only two Catholics having been elected to that body: Thomas Wyse[26] and John Archbold.[27] In 1840 a municipal reform bill was enacted, O'Connell hailing the new law as 'the commencement of the reign of justice'.[28]

ELECTION AS MAYOR OF WATERFORD

Waterford's middle-class Catholics embraced the potential offered by the reformed corporation to realize what they regarded as their rightful leadership role at the head of the city's government. Thomas Meagher's candidature in the municipal elections of October 1842 was a logical and natural step for a man who was active in local politics. Meagher successfully contested the Tower Ward, being returned as an alderman.[29] Reflecting the religious profile of the electorate, the majority of those elected were Catholics.[30]

The first duty of the new corporation was the election of a mayor. According to the *Waterford Chronicle*, this caused great excitement in the city 'because of the extraordinary change about to take place, in having a Roman Catholic mayor placed over them'.[31] It had been expected that Alexander Sherlock would have the honour of being the first Catholic mayor of the reformed corporation. He was proposed but declined the nomination due to the pressure of other commitments. He then proposed Thomas Meagher, the motion being seconded by an Anglican, Sir Benjamin Morris. Meagher was duly elected,[32] the *Waterford Chronicle* rejoicing in the council's choice of 'a gentleman proverbial for his consistent integrity as a patriot'.[33]

One of the first official duties undertaken by the new mayor was to attend Mass on the Sunday after his election. The occasion resonated with symbolism and was a public expression of the significant changes which Meagher's election presaged. It was a tangible and visible manifestation of a new political dispensation, a demonstration of the fact that Catholics were progressing towards the achievement of religious equality. The mayor's attendance at Mass was an event which captured the popular imagination; the city's Catholic citizenry could identify with this act as a clear signal that the old order had been swept away. Accordingly, thousands of people assembled opposite the city hall, in festive mood. Shortly before noon, Meagher, accompanied by all the civic officers and members of the corporation, including the Protestant ones, walked in a dignified and impressive procession to the Cathedral of the Holy Trinity, in Barronstrand Street. The preacher at the Mass alluded to the extraordinary events taking place in the city's social and political life. After the ceremony, Meagher once again processed to the city hall, accompanied by a crowd of at least 10,000.[34]

REPEAL

Meagher, like the majority of the members of Waterford Corporation, was a confirmed repealer. He was one of Daniel O'Connell's most loyal supporters, joining the Society for the Repeal of the Union shortly after its foundation in July 1830. Meagher and his father served on committees and acted as stewards at repeal dinners in Waterford. They supervised the collection of the repeal rent in the parishes of Trinity Within, St Patrick's and St John's.[35] The cause, however, failed to capture a significant degree of popular support. Unlike Meagher, most middle-class Catholics, whose involvement in the campaign for emancipation had been crucial to its success, were now more concerned that their newly achieved political status be translated into practical benefits. The breaking down of entrenched Protestant privilege was their principal objective and accordingly, it was believed that reform in areas such as local government was more urgent. In the circumstances, O'Connell was forced to adopt a different political strategy and in the spring of 1835 he formed a parliamentary alliance with the Whigs. He concentrated on extracting reforms for Ireland. This alliance endured until 1841, when the Tories returned to power.[36] In anticipation of this development O'Connell had formed the Loyal National Repeal Association in 1840.

O'Connell never defined precisely what he meant by repeal.[37] In theory it meant the restoration of the pre-1800 Irish Parliament. In practice, O'Connell probably realized that no British government would return to such a loose and undefined constitutional arrangement. Repeal, therefore, was not regarded by him as a specific proposal or demand; rather, it was the opening bid in a process of negotiation that might lead to some form of limited self-government.[38] Clearly, his objective was not separatist in intent. Moreover, the organization for the promotion of his ideas, the Repeal Association, was loyal to the Crown and committed to the total disavowal of physical force and illegal activity. Like the Catholic Association, it relied on the force of organized public opinion. At popular level, repeal became the focus of extravagant expectations, the abstractions of the constitution being ignored in favour of the notion that it somehow represented the prospect of the amelioration of Ireland's many ills.

It was not until the winter of 1842–43 that the repeal cause began to gather popular momentum, being at its most intense during the period of Meagher's mayoralty. His terms of office in 1843 and 1844 were dominated by O'Connell and his repeal campaign. The reformed corporation played a central part in the struggle, becoming a focus of local support in Waterford and a vehicle for the articulation of the city's adherence to O'Connell's crusade. By virtue of his position, Meagher became, in many ways, the public face of the movement in the city. At various times, he had to offer decisive leadership, as the political reverberations of the repeal campaign convulsed Waterford.

The importance accorded to repeal by Waterford Corporation was apparent at its first meeting on 1 November 1842. It resolved that Thomas Meagher, as mayor, write to O'Connell and invite him to visit the city, at his earliest convenience.[39] The invitation was accepted and he visited Waterford on 10 November. O'Connell's prompt response was indicative of the significance he attached to the support he was receiving in the city and county. Doubtless, he was mindful of the key part Waterford had played in the emancipation campaign, and the memory of this he hoped to exploit. Meagher and fellow corporation members met O'Connell at the outskirts of the city and walked in procession, together with a huge crowd, behind his carriage. The place was in festive mood.[40] A contemporary account recognized the pivotal role the corporation would play in the forthcoming political struggle: 'the cortege moved onwards to the town hall, thus consecrating to purposes of national independence a spot hitherto sacred to public rapine, plundering monopoly, and the withering influence of a foul, corrupt, and bigoted ascendancy'.[41] O'Connell addressed a public meeting of nearly 50,000 from the building. That evening he was the chief guest at a dinner, presided over by Meagher. In his speech of welcome, the mayor reminded his audience of O'Connell's past successes, especially emancipation. It was due to his part in securing municipal reform that he enjoyed the honour of being Mayor of Waterford.[42]

A repeal meeting was held in the city hall in February 1843, presided over by Meagher. A resolution was passed which declared that 'the destruction of the trade, the ruin of commerce and the annihilation of the manufactures of Ireland was due to the Act of Union and the country must remain plundered, degraded and impoverished until its repeal'.[43] On 21 March there was a meeting of the corporation to petition Parliament for repeal, an occasion probably inspired by one held by Dublin Corporation the previous month. In the course of his address Meagher asserted that due to the economic circumstances of the country, millions of people were in distress. He rejected the notion that such conditions would prevail under a legislature devoted to improving the state of the country. Ireland's prosperity depended 'on her being legislated for by men who understood her wants and feel for her people'.[44] The petition adopted by the corporation claimed 'the indisputable right' of the Irish nation to an 'independent' parliament. The absence of a native legislature had resulted in the country suffering 'helpless misery and unavoidable ruin'. According to the petition, it had been 'authoritatively ascertained' that 2,300,000 people were living in conditions of 'appalling want', while 'multitudes' had been forced to emigrate. The only solution to these problems was the restoration of the Irish Parliament by the repeal of the Act of Union.[45]

Daniel O'Connell declared that 1843 would be the year of repeal. In order to exert pressure on Parliament, he began organizing a series of huge gatherings around the country. These usually took place on Sundays or holy days, and quickly became known as 'monster meetings', such were the crowds in attendance. Intended to be 'demonstrations of the massiveness of organized democracy', they were 'the hedge schools in which the masses were educated in the nationalist politics of repeal'.[46]

Waterford City was the venue for a monster meeting on 9 July and this gathering was probably the largest that has ever been witnessed in its long history. The event attracted over 300,000 people, the occasion capturing the popular imagination, especially the dramatic procession which preceded the meeting. This left the city, early in the morning, to meet O'Connell. The vast concourse was led by groups of tradesmen, each marching behind a banner with an inscription supporting repeal. On meeting O'Connell, the concourse returned, accompanied by over thirty bands. It was not until 5.00 p.m. that the meeting began, such was the throng on the route. The first speaker was Thomas Meagher, who spoke very briefly. He reiterated the often repeated theme of repealers – such was the degradation to which Ireland had been reduced that the only solution lay in a restored native parliament. That evening a banquet was held in the city hall with 800 in attendance. It was Meagher who once again commenced the official proceedings by proposing a toast to O'Connell and repeal.[47]

By means of monster meetings O'Connell had worked the country into a fever pitch of excitement by the autumn of 1843. The repeal cause, however, suffered a severe setback when the government banned the monster meeting scheduled for Clontarf on 8 October. O'Connell was arrested on 14 October and charged with conspiring to cause disaffection. His supporters in Waterford expressed their full confidence in him at a meeting in the city hall a few days after his arrest. The building was thronged and thousands failed to gain admission. Thomas Meagher, addressing the audience, declared that he was not surprised to see such a gathering,

> knowing that nothing has occurred to change your opinion upon the subject which has brought you together... to change your mind... and disturb your confidence, or weaken your affection towards the illustrious man who is leading on the peaceful warfare for the restoration of your liberties.[48]

A meeting of the corporation on 20 October passed a resolution expressing 'its unalterable confidence in Mr. O'Connell and a firm determination to support him'.[49]

In the midst of the crisis that had befallen the repeal movement, Meagher was re-elected mayor. A resolution of the corporation stated that one of the reasons for this honour was 'his zealous support of the vital question to Ireland of repeal'.[50] His second term, like the first, was dominated by the issue. The year 1844 was a very difficult one for O'Connell but Meagher never faltered in his unwavering support.

On 15 January O'Connell was put on trial for conspiracy and found guilty a month later, sentencing being deferred until May. In April a dinner in Cork in honour of O'Connell was seen by the corporation as 'a suitable occasion to manifest towards that distinguished individual our unabated confidence'. It was resolved that members would attend the function in their official capacity.[51] A steamer, *The Mermaid*, was chartered to carry a deputation of repeal supporters to Cork. Many councillors travelled on this vessel, while Meagher went by coach.[52]

On 30 May O'Connell was sentenced to twelve months' imprisonment. The next day, at a meeting of the corporation, it was resolved that a special session be convened to consider the best means of expressing 'its unalterable sentiments of respect, confidence and attachment' for O'Connell during what was described as his 'present unremitted suffering'.[53] This session took place on 4 June, when a resolution was adopted by the councillors declaring their 'imperative duty to renew in the most unqualified terms the expression of entire confidence in the great leader of the repeal cause'. An address was prepared deploring the 'indignity' to O'Connell's person and the Irish nation. It was decided that Meagher would present it in person to him in Richmond Prison.[54] When O'Connell's sentence was overturned by the House of Lords in September, the corporation met to express its delight.[55]

As mayor, Thomas Meagher promoted the cause of repeal in Waterford with vigour and was unfailingly loyal to O'Connell's beliefs. He was very much the Liberator's political acolyte. In keeping with his leader's deeply held convictions, Meagher repeated many times that only non-violent means were to be used in the campaign. At a repeal meeting in 1843 he called on his listeners to persevere in their 'judicious and temperate cause' and to exhibit to the English government 'the example of a people remarkable for their legal, constitutional and peaceable conduct'.[56] In June 1844 he repeated these sentiments while addressing citizens protesting at O'Connell's imprisonment:

> Let us therefore persevere but let it be in a strictly legal, peaceful and constitutional course. Let not a single crime, nor the least act of violence be committed, as it would stain the holy cause in which we are engaged. Let not even a word be uttered, or an expression used that would tend to excite bad feeling, or give the slightest offence to an enemy.[57]

Furthermore, Meagher emphasized that repeal did not mean separation from England. At the special corporation meeting convened to discuss the matter in March 1843, he explained that advocates of the measure did not seek 'to dim the jewel of Ireland in the crown of their beloved sovereign but that it should shine forth the brightest ornament of the imperial diadem'. His remarks were greeted with cheers.[58] Indeed, the corporation over which he presided gave several expressions of loyalty to the Crown. On 2 May 1843 an address of condolence was sent to Queen Victoria on the death of the Duke of Sussex. The same meeting also resolved to congratulate the queen on the birth of a daughter.[59]

In his service to the repeal cause Meagher played one very important role: he encouraged co-operation between the repeal and temperance movements in Waterford. In pursuit of his objectives, O'Connell enlisted Fr Theobald Mathew's temperance movement, convinced that it would provide the manpower and moral force that might transform his campaign into an irresistible crusade.[60] He succeeded in channelling the inherent political energy of the temperance movement in the direction of repeal agitation. Sobriety contributed to the discipline of monster meetings and this orderliness made them all the more intimidating for the government. Such was the appreciation by O'Connell of the political significance of Fr Mathew's activities that he told a meeting at Kilkenny that temperance would bring repeal.[61] Limerick and Waterford, vibrant centres of temperance, were also strongholds of support for O'Connell. It has been observed that practically every town had local leaders who endorsed both crusades and who bore witness to the cause argued by O'Connell that Temperance Societies and Repeal Associations were two sides of the same coin.[62] Meagher was one such leader. At a meeting in 1843 he addressed special words to the teetotallers in the audience:

> There is one class of repealers, in particular, the most important and influential, on whom depends in a great measure the success of the present movement, to whom I will address a few words, the teetotallers. On you depends the destiny of your country. Mr. O'Connell himself has declared that but for the influence of temperance he could not have advanced the cause to its present position.[63]

THOMAS MEAGHER, FR MATHEW AND TEMPERANCE

While Thomas Meagher was happy to associate the temperance movement with repeal for political reasons, he (unlike Daniel O'Connell) also appears to have had a genuine interest in promoting Fr Mathew's cause. The temperance crusade was the single most extraordinary social movement that occurred in pre-famine Ireland.[64] After O'Connell, the Cork-based Capuchin friar was the most popular figure in the country in the early 1840s, the *Waterford Chronicle* opining: 'No one has done more for his country than Fr Mathew – we scarcely except the Liberator himself. One has been the great moral regenerator, the other the political.'[65] Over the five years beginning in 1838, between 3 and 5 million people – at least half the population – took the pledge to abstain from alcoholic drink for life.[66] The movement's most striking feature was the enthusiasm, emotion and eagerness with which people embraced it,[67] and across most of

Ireland public life became marked by a fiercely determined temperance ethic.[68] One historian has observed that the crusade against intoxicating drink 'set its face not merely against private habit but against a very public and practically universal way of life'.[69] That it was successful for a time is beyond question. There is evidence which indicates a decline in drinking during the early 1840s approaching 60 per cent or more.[70]

Thomas Meagher's interest in temperance reflected the influence of Fr Mathew on Irish life, and his belief that he should support his activities in his capacity as mayor. He was also motivated by a real concern for the poorer classes of Waterford. On the occasion of his election as mayor, he was reported as saying that 'the industrious poor, although no sharers, directly or individually, in the proceedings of the day, shall be the peculiar objects of his solicitude'.[71] Meagher clearly realized that the abuse of alcohol had a debilitating effect on the city's economic and social life. In 1836 it was estimated that 6,000 gallons of legal whiskey were consumed in Waterford every year.[72] This would only account for a fraction of alcohol consumption, as poteen, at half the price, was widely available.[73] The problems caused by this scale of drinking were to be seen in the fact that 60 per cent of those tried before the mayor's court in September 1838 were charged with drunkenness.[74] The prosperity of the city was suffering: there was a leakage of at least £300,000 out of the circular flow of income of the local economy and one-third of this figure can be attributed to expenditure on drink.[75]

The Christian Brothers at Mount Sion in Waterford had, with the co-operation of the Catholic bishop, Dr Nicholas Foran, established teetotal societies in the summer of 1839 to cater for those who could not travel to Cork to take the pledge to abstain from alcoholic drink from Fr Mathew. The friar was invited to visit the city and did so in December 1839. This visit, and an earlier one to Limerick, marked a significant stage in the development of the Cork Total Abstinence Society as a national movement.[76] The December visit popularized the temperance cause in Waterford, with between 70,000 and 90,000 people from the city, county and adjoining areas taking the pledge.[77]

Thomas Meagher certainly identified himself very closely with Fr Mathew's crusade. In January 1843 when the friar visited the city the mayor's carriage met him. He was taken to Meagher's house where he was entertained. The next day, accompanied by the mayor, Fr Mathew administered the pledge to a large number of people.[78] In May of the same year Fr Mathew visited the Christian Brothers' School at Mount Sion. He was again accompanied by Meagher. The pledge was administered to over 1,000 children. That same evening there was a temperance meeting at the school and Meagher presided over the proceedings. In the course of a short address he referred to the orderly conduct of the city's teetotallers and the significant reduction in crime since the progress of teetotalism. The next day Fr Mathew went to the court-house to administer pledges in the company of Thomas Meagher, who delivered an address on behalf of the citizens of Waterford to the priest extolling his achievements.[79]

In September 1843 Meagher attended the general meeting of the city's Temperance Societies, once again at Mount Sion. In a speech he referred to the fact that he had been absent from Waterford for a number of months in 1839 and 1840, when Fr Mathew had first visited the city. When he left the country it was 'sunk to the lowest state of degradation, owing to the intemperance of the people'. On his return he noted what Meagher termed 'a happy and extraordinary change':

> His ears, as he walked the streets, were no longer assailed with horrid blasphemy – no longer the spectacles of drunkenness, which but a few months before were familiar to the public, presented their hideous forms in the public way – in their stead tranquillity, sobriety, and increased comfort, were manifest.

He stated that his object was to give 'permanence and consistency' to the temperance cause and 'his anxious wish was that it should extend, not only over the city, not only to the country but to the whole world'.[80]

The level of support for temperance offered by Thomas Meagher was appreciated by Fr Mathew. During his visit to the city in May 1843 he thanked the mayor, whom he described as 'his esteemed friend', for all the assistance and encouragement he had given his mission.[81] The association of a person of Meagher's social position with the temperance cause was especially valued because there was a general reluctance among the Catholic middle classes to involve themselves in the advocacy of the total abstinence movement.[82] Due to the fact that the temperance movement recruited from the nation at large and placed no financial barriers to membership, it possessed a decidedly plebeian profile which discouraged class-conscious persons from becoming members.[83] This was a matter of concern for the leadership and attempts were made to induce the wealthier elements of Catholic society to become involved. Indeed, during a visit to Dublin in March–April 1840 Fr Mathew concentrated much of his energy on trying to attract such support.[84] Even when some joined, they did not want to be associated with the mass pledge taking which was an important feature of Fr Mathew's crusade. During his first visit to Waterford in December 1839, 'respectable men above the working class' took the pledge at Bishop Foran's house in the evening, not wishing, it would appear, to join the masses assembled in front of the court-house during the day.[85]

The temperance movement, however, was in decline by 1843[86] and in the middle of that year there were reports of an increase nationally in public drunkenness.[87] Comments made by Meagher in his address at Mount Sion in September confirm this. He stated that he regretted to inform his audience of teetotallers that for the last month there were more cases of drunkenness brought before him 'than during all the rest of the time he had held office'. He feared that 'inebriety' was beginning to creep into the city once again. Deploring such behaviour, Meagher called on sober and decent people to assert themselves in the face of such developments.[88] He remained deeply committed to the temperance ideal. As late as July 1847, in the course of a speech in support of his parliamentary candidature in the general election, he declared:

> I am a teetotaller myself, and I do not like to see any man drunk. Oh! They are not my friends or supporters who would be drunk; I repudiate them . . . I ask you what greater crime can there be than drunkenness, for by it man lowers himself to the condition of the brute and, in that condition, not knowing what he does, he is capable of committing any crime.[89]

PHILANTHROPIST

A concern for his less fortunate fellow citizens was an important determinant in Meagher's support for temperance. This concern was manifested in other ways. In fact, he was widely acclaimed for his humanitarian work in Waterford during his lengthy residency there.[90] In 1824 Meagher was appointed treasurer of the Trinitarian Orphan Society, a charitable body founded in 1811 to feed, clothe and accommodate young boys without means to apprentice as artisans. An asylum for orphans was located on John Street and cared for sixty-five inmates a year. He also served as a vice president and trustee.[91] He contributed to the Fanning Institute which aided natives of the city, who through indigence, old age or infirmity, were unable to support themselves.[92] Meagher displayed a real civic mindedness when he declined to draw his salary of £276.18s.5d as mayor, bestowing it instead for the benefit of the city.[93] For a man of his wealth this was a small sacrifice; it was, nevertheless, a generous and constructive act. Certainly, at times Meagher displayed a paternalistic attitude towards the poorer classes, especially in some of his addresses on the subject of temperance. He was, nonetheless, a decent and sincere person, a fact recognized by the writer of the account in the *Waterford Chronicle* of his election as mayor, when he wrote of a man who 'so paternally and feelingly spoke of his less favoured fellow citizens'.[94]

MEMBER OF PARLIAMENT, 1847–57

An active supporter of repeal and one of Waterford's most prominent citizens, Thomas Meagher was selected as a candidate for the city constituency in the 1847 general election. A confluence of three circumstances gave this contest a peculiar character. The electoral drama, such as it was, had to be enacted against the backdrop of the Great Famine, with its attendant misery and suffering casting a shadow over events. The repeal cause had lost its leader in May 1847, when O'Connell died while en route to Rome. Finally, the Repeal Association was split.

After the cancellation of the Clontarf meeting in 1843 and his release from prison in 1844, O'Connell knew that no form of self-government for Ireland was realizable in the near future. Accordingly, the ever pragmatic politician sought to renew his alliance with the Whigs in order to secure whatever benefits were possible for Ireland.[95] His political overtures aroused the intense hostility of the Young Irelanders. They and O'Connell were on fundamentally different political wavelengths. While for him repeal was the opening bid in a process of negotiation, for them it was a non-negotiable great crusade. They believed that the maintenance of the political independence of the O'Connellite party was essential to success, and therefore discussion with the Whigs was anathema. Tensions came to a head over Sir Robert Peel's proposals for non-denominational university colleges. While these Queen's Colleges were denounced by O' Connell as 'godless', the Young Irelanders welcomed them as a means of uniting all Irish men. Determined to assert his authority and to quash dissent, in July 1846 O'Connell demanded acceptance of resolutions that no political objective justified the use of violence. Unable to accept them, the Young Irelanders were effectively driven out of the Repeal Association. They established the Irish Confederation in 1847.

At the general election of 1847 the Young Irelanders, not surprisingly, were blamed for hastening the death of the much loved Liberator.[96] Some hostility was directed at Thomas Meagher, whose son, Thomas Francis, had played a significant role in the rejection of the peace resolutions, he giving expression to his views in the famous 'Sword Speech'.[97] Initially, the *Chronicle* was unenthusiastic in endorsing Meagher as a prospective candidate. An editorial in June 1847 commented that he might be an acceptable candidate at some future time, 'when the remembrance of the Liberator in connexion with some insinuations of a member of Mr. Meagher's family will have passed away'. The journal continued:

> But oh! It is well to spare the feelings of the Liberator's family at present and not put a premium on the wretched attacks of wantonness on the kindly susceptible heart which now lies in eternal Rome and whose noble courage had triumphed over open and banded enemies, previous to its being pierced by the poignant swords of professed friends.[98]

A meeting of electors was held later in the same month in the city hall, for the stated purpose of selecting 'two undoubted and uncompromising repealers' to represent the city at Westminster. The occasion was charged with emotion and was used to re-dedicate people to the repeal cause as a means of honouring O'Connell's memory. The mayor, Councillor Owen Carroll, stated that those in attendance were there to 'do their duty to Old Ireland and to follow in the footsteps of O'Connell'. Another speaker asserted that though he was dead, 'his spirit lives to work out the independence of Ireland'. A resolution was adopted declaring that 'our opinions on the question of repeal are unaltered and unalterable' and that the struggle would continue using every 'peaceable, constitutional and legal means'. A Catholic priest, and a future bishop of Waterford, Rev. Dr Dominic O'Brien, proposed that Meagher and Sir Benjamin Morris Wall, a liberal Protestant, be invited to contest the two city seats. He reminded his listeners of the importance of choosing candidates who would oppose measures such as the Queen's Colleges which had been condemned by the Bishop of Waterford and other bishops.[99]

While Wall declined the invitation, Meagher accepted it. The sentiments he expressed during the campaign were consonant with those of the meeting which proposed his candidature and with those of a faithful O'Connellite repealer. His election address was an unequivocal statement of his commitment to repeal and to the view that it was attainable by the peaceful and constitutional means advocated by O'Connell.[100] On polling day Meagher asserted that nothing could save Ireland from absolute ruin but repeal.[101]

In his address Meagher also stated that as a Roman Catholic no parliamentary measure affecting the interests of the Catholic Church would have his support until it had received the approval of a majority of bishops. He was thus aligning himself with those in the Repeal Association, in particular O'Connell, who had rejected the Queen's Colleges. Such an opinion was in keeping with his loyalty towards the late Liberator. It was also politically expedient to express such a view given the sentiments expressed by Rev. Dr O'Brien. Meagher, however, was not acting primarily out of loyalty or expediency. Rather, as a faithful Catholic, he accepted the pronouncements of his Church's leaders. According to John Mannion, the most familiar and pervasive influence in the everyday life of Meagher was the Catholic Church.[102] Certainly, many of his philanthropic activities were associated with Catholic causes. In 1841 he was one of three Waterford citizens who took a lease of five and a half acres in the townland of Clowne, Lisduggan, for the building of a convent for the Presentation Sisters. Meagher became a generous benefactor of the order.[103] He was one of the governors and later treasurer of a Magdalen home, established in 1842 by Rev. Timothy Dowley, to address the social evils of prostitution.[104] In the same year Meagher helped the Irish Sisters of Charity establish a foundation in the city[105] and presented a silver chalice to the new convent.[106] Two years later, when Edmund Ignatius Rice, the founder of the Irish Christian Brothers died, he was active in a campaign to construct a memorial chapel.[107] He was a member of the committee to establish a Catholic university in Ireland and he donated the substantial sum of £100 to the project.[108] Thus Meagher's declaration that he would be guided by the bishops in relation to prospective legislation was entirely consistent with his fervent Catholicism.

Thomas Meagher headed the poll, being elected with 521 votes. The other repeal candidate was Daniel O'Connell Junior, the Liberator's youngest son, who received 499 votes.[109] The results showed, according to the *Chronicle*, that Waterford was committed to repeal and was bound by 'an eternal tie to Daniel O'Connell'.[110]

This comment, however, served to underscore the surreal quality of the election, both locally and nationally. An effectively dead cause, which had been championed by a now dead leader, was being promoted at a time when thousands were dying of disease throughout Ireland. The electoral contest witnessed the triumph of (understandable) emotion over political rationalism. The truth was that the repeal movement had been in terminal decline since the abortive Clontarf meeting, the final obsequies only being delayed by O'Connell's continuing leadership. With his death, it gave up the ghost and all semblance of viability began to disappear. The efforts by John O'Connell, the Liberator's son and political heir, in late 1849 and early 1850, to resume the indoor public meetings that had characterized the repeal movement under his father failed because of lack of support.

Most of the three dozen or so MPs elected as repealers in the 1847 election sat in Parliament during the 1850 session as Liberals.[111] By then land agitation had replaced the campaign for repeal and the movement for tenant reforms was the dominant feature of public life in Ireland.[112] This was a response to the level of rents and an increase in the number of evictions. A tenant protection society founded at Callan, County Kilkenny, in 1849 served as an example for other places. In August 1850 a national Irish Tenant League was established to achieve the three 'Fs' – fair rent, free sale and fixity of tenure. However, the appeal of the tenant cause had begun to evaporate by 1851, as agriculture returned to a modest level of prosperity. Moreover, it was overshadowed by bitter religious controversy.

In 1850 the Pope restored the Catholic hierarchy in England. There was an explosion of Protestant outrage. The government responded by introducing the Ecclesiastical Titles Bill, which made illegal the assumption by Catholic prelates of their diocesan titles. Irish Liberal MPs were trenchant in their opposition to the measure and to its author, the Liberal government of Lord John Russell. Some Irish Liberals began opposing the government on other issues in protest. Those members were soon being referred to as 'the Irish Brigade'. An alliance was formed between the brigade and the Tenant League.[113]

Meagher was vehement in his opposition to the Titles Bill. As a Catholic, he found reprehensible the prejudicial sentiments to his religion on which the bill was predicated. As a long time activist for civil and religious equality for members of his faith, the proposed legislation seemed to portend a reversion to an era when adherents of Catholicism were accorded an inferior status under the constitution. Such a development was contrary to the trends of previous decades, which had been towards the evolution of a society based on religious tolerance and the recognition of denominational equality.

John Whyte has analyzed the voting record and the political behaviour of Irish Liberal MPs during the 1851–52 parliamentary session. On the basis of the information he has compiled, Meagher emerges as one of the most loyal and dedicated of the brigadiers, and one of the most consistent in opposing the government.[114] This fact was recognized at a meeting in the Catholic cathedral in Waterford in March 1851. The object of the gathering was to protest at the

Titles Bill, the deliberations revealing that the proposed legislation 'produced as great an effect among the people of Ireland as it did on their representatives in the Commons'.[115] Meagher was lauded because 'on all occasions in Parliament he has done his duty to his religion and country' in opposing the attempted 'revival of the Penal Laws'.[116] With the enactment of the bill, a new body, the Catholic Defence Association of Great Britain and Ireland, was set up at a meeting in the Rotunda, Dublin, on 19 August 1851. Meagher played a significant role in the proceedings, he being one of the four MPs who drew up the resolutions adopted by those in attendance. The repeal of the Titles Act was the primary objective, and to attain this it was decided to maintain a distinct parliamentary party in the Commons.[117]

The religious issue animated the general election of July 1852. Meagher was re-elected. Speaking in reply to his nomination on polling day, he made clear his support for a policy of opposition to any government which failed to adopt the demands for repeal of the Titles Act and tenant right.[118] At a conference after the election, forty-two MPs formed the Independent Irish Party, pledging themselves to oppose any administration which did not undertake to rid the statute book of the Titles Act and to grant tenant right.[119] The failure of the party has been well documented, with many MPs reneging, totally or partially, on their pledges.[120] Meagher, however, honoured his pledge. On the basis of data compiled by Whyte for the years 1852–57, he was one of six MPs who remained fully committed to the concept of an Independent Irish Party.[121] Whyte has pronounced his independence as 'unquestionable'.[122]

The manner in which he honoured his pledges reflected important attributes of Meagher's character as a politician – his honesty and integrity. He was widely praised and regarded because of this. During the 1847 election, one of his supporters encouraged voters 'to approach the hustings with the firm tread of old grenadiers to record your votes for honest Thomas Meagher'.[123] In 1852, when he had announced his intention not to seek re-election, a speaker at a public meeting in the city delivered the following encomium: 'The poet had truly described the beautiful excellence of character in pronouncing an honest man God's noblest work: and Mr. Meagher is entitled to that designation.'[124] An editorial in the *Waterford Chronicle*, a journal which was sometimes critical of him, admitted that 'his sterling honesty places him above the shadow of suspicion'.[125]

Thomas Meagher, though an accomplished speaker, was not the most vocal of MPs; during the ten years he served in the House of Commons he is reported as speaking only seven times, one of these being to second a motion.[126] Some of his other contributions were short, amounting to no more than ten lines in the official record of proceedings. What contributions he did make to debates reflected concerns he had articulated and acted upon during his public life. Foremost was his belief in religious and civil liberty for all. He was a strident opponent, therefore, of a tax styled minister's money. This had been created by an act of the Irish Parliament during the reign of King Charles II, and under its provisions the householders of certain cities were taxed for the payment of Anglican clergy.[127] Meagher spoke twice on this matter. In February 1856 he called for its total abolition as it was a source of 'great annoyance' to the inhabitants of those places in which it was levied.[128] A few months later he asserted that he was anxious for its repeal 'precisely because it was a relic of the penal code'.[129] (Minister's money was abolished in 1857.) During a debate on the grant for Maynooth College in April 1856, Meagher expressed strong disapproval at the fact that one of the speakers had attached 'the name of idolaters to millions of his fellow subjects'.[130] As a sincere Catholic, he took grave exception to the remark. A social concern he had revealed as mayor and philanthropist was apparent in two brief speeches. He inquired about the government's intention to introduce bills to regulate sanitary arrangements[131] and spoke in a debate on dwellings for the labouring classes, expressing the view that the bill before the house was inadequate.[132] Finally, it was Meagher's experience as a successful businessman which probably motivated his call for the establishment of a select committee to inquire into postal arrangements in Waterford and other counties, with a view to improving them.[133] He subsequently chaired the committee.[134]

It was this relative silence by Meagher which probably prompted the *Waterford Chronicle* in late 1850 to engage in polite but firm criticism of his suitability as a parliamentary representative. Up to that time he had only a single utterance to his name. The journal suggested that Meagher was not a man suited 'to forward the interests of his constituency in this bustling age'; nor was he 'bold and strenuous exponent of our grievances and wrongs'.[135] How fair were these remarks?

In any examination of Meagher's parliamentary career one significant fact emerges – he was a very reluctant MP. Politicians often feign reluctance; in his case it was undoubtedly genuine, a fact attested to by Waterford's three newspapers. Before the 1847 election he stated that he was not interested in being a candidate.[136] As a result of considerable pressure, he was prevailed upon to allow his candidature. In his reply to the speech on his nomination on polling day, he told his audience that he found himself in a position that he had tried to resist in public and in private.[137] In December 1850 it was being reported that he would be standing down at the next election.[138] He confirmed this a few months before the 1852 general election when a letter from him was read at a meeting of electors.[139] However, efforts to find a replacement were hindered by bitter divisions among supporters of the Independent Irish Party.[140] Only with the prospect of certain defeat facing the cause of tenant right and independent opposition, and under pressure from electors, especially Bishop Foran and his clergy, did he relent in his decision.[141] So hurried was his candidature that he did not even produce an address to electors.

There was a consensus in the Waterford press that Meagher found a parliamentary career unpalatable. From its comments and observations there emerges a picture of a man who was essentially very private; in the words of the

Waterford Chronicle he had 'a love of retirement and self-communion.'[142] So impatient was the *Waterford Mail*, the organ of his political opponents, at the efforts to convince him to stand in the 1852 election, that it snapped: 'Let the recluse quietly enjoy his seclusion.'[143] Though unkind in expression, there was articulated an essential truth about his nature. Moreover, this same nature inclined him to reflect deeply on matters.

> In any matter in which patient investigation or the working out of details shall be found important – to deal with an involved subject, and quietly to unravel its incidents, and to decide what is right and just – in all these things we confidently assert that he will be found fully competent.[144]

However, these attributes do not always facilitate a career in politics. This certainly was the opinion of the *Waterford Chronicle*.[145]

Meagher also suffered from ill health. This was the reason he gave for not seeking re-election in 1852.[146] The *Waterford News* commented that 'he finds a parliamentary life neither suitable to his health nor his habits'.[147] That his health was delicate was accepted by the local press.

Notwithstanding his reluctance, temperament and poor health, Meagher made a real contribution to politics and Parliament. He did this by the diligence of his attendance in the House of Commons and by the use of his vote there. The latter was critical – the *raison d'être* of the Independent Irish Party was that it should continue independent of, and in opposition to, every government which failed to adopt its programme. The most effective means to give practical expression to this policy was in the exercise of negative votes against the ministry during divisions. Those who, unlike Meagher, failed to do this undermined, decisively and irreparably, the whole concept of independent opposition. His seconder at the 1852 election, James Delahunty, recognized and summarized his achievement thus: 'He is not the one to talk a great deal of nonsense; he has, by his votes and attendance in his place in parliament, assisted to organize an Irish Party.'[148]

Though quiet and self-effacing, the member for Waterford City was one of the most radical Irish representatives in Parliament. Even before the formation of the Irish Brigade, Meagher had voted against the Liberal government more often than supporting it. While ranking nominally as a Liberal, he was worse than useless to the party whips.[149] He supported the extension of the franchise, the secret ballot and shorter parliaments.[150] During the 1847 election, he declared himself for tenant right.[151] This must be one of the earliest declarations of support by a parliamentary candidate. In Parliament he voted for it. At the 1852 election he stated his intention of continuing to vote in favour of radical demands.[152]

While Meagher's parliamentary career contributed significantly to the notion of independent opposition and an Irish party dedicated to this objective, it lacked, nevertheless, exciting elements. This fact reflected his temperament and 'the lack of any widespread political excitement that characterized most of the decade'.[153] The cause of tenant right and independent opposition did not generate an intense political movement. The initial energy of the tenant right cause fizzled out when agricultural prosperity began to return. The interest in the campaign against the Ecclesiastical Titles Act raised the political temperature somewhat more but was of relatively short duration when it became apparent that it did not herald a return to the days of penal legislation. This legislation was never enforced.[154] The quiescent nature of the politics of the 1850s is understandable. The country was adjusting to the profound social and economic changes of the post-famine years. The preceding decade had witnessed the convulsions of repeal agitation, hunger, disease and failed revolution. Quite simply, people did not have the psychological and emotional reserves for any cause demanding a political engagement of prolonged duration and intensity. Notwithstanding Fenianism, Ireland was settling as never before, or after, into an accommodation with English power within the United Kingdom, a situation which lasted until the land war.[155] Thus the undramatic style of politics practised by Meagher accorded with the *zeitgeist* of the 1850s.

THOMAS MEAGHER AND HIS REBEL SON

On 24 July 1849 Thomas Francis Meagher boarded a ship in Dublin for transportation to Van Diemen's Land (Tasmania) for his part in the Young Ireland rising of 1848. By his revolutionary actions, he had engaged in a political course antithetical to his father's politics and which represented a rejection of Thomas Meagher's deeply held convictions. All his life the older Meagher was a constitutionalist, loyal to the Crown and dedicated to achieving political objectives by peaceful and lawful means. He was committed to repeal and later to independent opposition; the advocacy of, and participation in, an armed insurrection was anathema to his political canon.

Thomas Francis Meagher was born on 3 August 1823. With the death of his mother in 1827, his father became the sole parental influence. Thomas Meagher obtained for his son a privileged education which was intended to prepare this scion of a wealthy Catholic family for a role in society that reflected the increasing sense of importance of the members of Ireland's Catholic middle class. When 11 years old, Thomas Francis was sent to Clongowes Wood College, a Jesuit-run boarding school in County Kildare. An establishment for the sons of Catholic gentlemen,[156] its purpose was to satisfy the social and religious aspirations of parents by supplying young boys with the attainments and tastes of nineteenth-century Catholic gentlemen.[157] Sons of Daniel O'Connell had attended there; for a person of Thomas Meagher's wealth and position it was the educational establishment of choice. At the age of 16, in 1839, his son was to continue his education at Stonyhurst College, another Jesuit-run school, in England.[158] Here 'the sons of wealthy Irish, and even the children of Spaniards and French, were sent to receive a comprehensive British education'.[159]

When Thomas Francis Meagher returned to Waterford in 1843, his father was the city's mayor. He appreciated the importance of this achievement for the largely Catholic population, who thought it a 'glorious thing to see some of their sort in possession of the town hall' and 'to see the mayor going to mass'.[160] In the course of his famous 'Sword Speech' in July 1846, he again referred to his father's election as mayor, and the fact that he was the first Catholic to occupy the position in nearly two hundred years.[161] One senses that he was proud of his father's achievement. He sometimes accompanied him as he discharged his public duties. He was with him on a few occasions as he promoted temperance,[162] and it was Thomas Francis who composed an address presented to Father Mathew by the mayor during a visit to the city in May 1843.[163] At the banquet following the monster repeal meeting held in Waterford in July 1843, the young Meagher read out letters of apology to the assembled guests.[164]

In 1844 Thomas Francis Meagher went to Dublin with the intention of studying law but his studies were discarded as he immersed himself in the excitement of repeal politics. A political chasm was soon to open between father and son, when the latter associated himself with the Young Ireland faction in the Repeal Association, his 'Sword Speech' playing a significant part in the subsequent split. Thomas Meagher remained a committed repealer of the O'Connellite variety, though the consequences of what were regarded as the political sins of the son were visited on the father. As was noted earlier, his son's role in the divisions which afflicted the Repeal Association caused some doubts to be cast on Thomas Meagher's suitability as a candidate in the 1847 general election. The tensions between Young and 'Old' Ireland manifested themselves in a very personal way for the older Meagher on the day of the election. Speeches were interrupted by various calls on Thomas Francis, who was present, to speak on behalf of the Irish Confederation. He replied that he did not wish to be associated with anything which might disturb the proceedings, a response likely motivated by a desire not to embarrass his father.[165]

The political differences between the two Meaghers were exposed in a dramatic and public fashion in February and March, 1848. There was a by-election in Waterford City consequent on the resignation of Daniel O'Connell Jr, and Thomas Francis Meagher resolved to be a candidate. The previous month there had been a split in the Irish Confederation, as John Mitchel and others seceded over the issue of policy and tactics. Thomas Francis, who had opposed the seceders, was now driven back on his own resources and was searching earnestly for some opportunity of public service; hence his decision to be a candidate.[166] There was already considerable bitterness in Waterford between supporters of the Repeal Association and the supporters of the Young Ireland and the Irish Confederation,[167] with the election serving to exacerbate it even more. An event of critical significance for the political relationship between the older and younger Meagher occurred at a public meeting held in connection with the election, on Wednesday 16 February. Though he was absent due to illness, some of the supporters of Thomas Francis declared his intention of contesting the seat. A Fr Cuddihy, an ardent supporter of the Repeal Association, read a letter to the meeting from Thomas Meagher, also absent due to his attending to parliamentary duties in London. Dated Monday 14 February, he stated that he had moved the election writ at Westminster and appealed for unity among the city's repealers. He then named Patrick Costello as the person most likely to prove a faithful representative of the Repeal Association.

A short time later, Thomas Francis communicated by letter to the meeting. The contents of his father's missive had been conveyed to him and he recognized the damage it could cause his candidature. He was angry because he felt that his father's letter had been used against him; he asserted that his father could not have been aware of his intentions to stand as a candidate when he wrote the letter, as he had not made up his mind to do so until Monday evening. Notwithstanding his father's sentiments, he declared that he was still putting his name forward in the election.[168]

In another letter, dated 18 February and written by Thomas Meagher, which was published in the local press, he confirmed that he was unaware of his son's plans when he had written the letter read by Cuddihy. He had not heard from his son but he intended writing to him to inform him that he was adverse to his contesting the election and that he felt bound to support Costello, whose views were shared, Meagher believed, by the majority of the city's electors.[169] Not surprisingly, his father's opposition was used as a powerful weapon against him by the opponents of Thomas Francis. The *Chronicle* was very hostile and was ready to exploit the rift between father and son. It denounced the latter for not heeding his parent's advice. Describing him as 'a rebellious son', he was attacked for standing in the election 'in opposition to the will of him, whom under God, he was most bound to respect'.[170] Cuddihy also criticized what he characterized as filial disobedience.[171]

Thomas Francis Meagher was defeated, coming in last of the three candidates. Costello was also unsuccessful, the divisions in the ranks of repealers allowing a Whig candidate to be elected.[172] To what extent may his defeat be attributed to his father's decision to withhold his support? This support was a necessary but still not a sufficient precondition for success. Meagher's defeat was due to his failure to attract, in necessary numbers, the votes of traditional repeal supporters. Many of these were already hostile to him and were loath to vote for him, the more extreme among them believing that he had contributed to the Liberator's death. His father had not created this hostility. Certainly, he did nothing to mitigate it; but, at most, he only confirmed it. Therefore, while his intervention made his son's electoral situation more difficult, this difficulty essentially pre-dated the March election, having its roots in the bitter split in the Repeal Association in July 1846. Thomas Francis also failed to attract the support of the conservative, non-repeal electors. Some of these might have been inclined to vote for him as a means of damaging the traditional repeal movement. Over these Meagher's father exercised no influence. Their votes were lost due to the intimidatory and often violent conduct of some of his son's supporters, many of them unfranchised members of the working class.[173] Thomas Francis Meagher's defeat, therefore, was due to hostility towards him among a majority of repeal voters pre-dating the election and the alienation of conservative voters because of the untoward actions of some of his supporters, rather than his father's attitude and actions.

Thomas Meagher's behaviour during the election is understandable. As a loyal supporter of the Repeal Association, he could not have supported his son. To do so would have meant discarding his political beliefs. This was something a man of his principles would never have done, not least at a time when the association was experiencing grave difficulties. It was impossible for him to support a person who had disassociated himself from the repeal movement and rejected Daniel O'Connell's leadership, even if that person was his own flesh and blood. Indeed, he was only doing what his son had advocated in June 1846, when still a member of the Repeal Association. Then Thomas Francis had argued that no man should receive electoral support who was not an enrolled member of the Association. Ironically, he had continued:

> I tell you candidly, if my father was in Parliament and had up to this period refused to join the association, were he at the next election to present himself to his constituency to ask their vote again, I would be the first to vote against him.[174]

The political relationship between Meagher and his son was sundered completely by the latter's participation in the 1848 rising. Thomas Francis wrote that his father had not 'the slightest faith' in the Irish Confederation.

> More than once, particularly when I met him in London, on my way... to present the congratulatory address to the provisional government of the French Republic, in the month of April, he warned me against being led away by the success of the continental revolutionists, to trust the fortunes of our cause to the desperate success of insurrection.[175]

On 20 July he left his father's house to participate in the rising. He described his feelings and those of his father thus:

> I gave myself up to the gay illusion of a gallant fight, a triumphal entry, at the head of thousands, into Dublin, before long. I was full of liveliness and hope at that moment, and welcomed the struggle with a laughing heart. But I recollect it well, my father was far otherwise. He seemed to me mournfully serious, and impressed with the saddest anticipation.[176]

It was little wonder that Thomas Meagher felt as he did. He was, after all, a veritable pillar of the establishment, whose entire political career had been founded on constitutional and pacific methods. He viewed his son's illegal actions not only as a rejection of all that he valued and represented but as profoundly dangerous, incurring as they did the penalty of death.

Meagher was never reconciled to his son's politics. In 1851 the *Waterford Chronicle* published, over two editions, Thomas Francis Meagher's memoirs of 1848.[177] The same journal also carried a report that it was authorized to state that Thomas Meagher had not been a party to the publication and knew nothing about it until he read the articles in the newspaper. Moreover, according to the *Chronicle*, 'the publication gave him considerable pain'.[178]

Even though he rejected his son's politics, Thomas Meagher stood by him after the 1848 rising and relations between them appear cordial. The *Waterford Chronicle* carried a report in November 1848 which observed: 'Mr. Meagher's affection for his son is extreme; and his affliction at the fate to which patriotic enthusiasm hurried him is deep and poignant.'[179] He paid the debts incurred by him during his incarceration and trial.[180] It was even rumoured that while he 'greatly deplored Tom's rebellious politics', he had 'employed four brigantines to cruise off the southern and western coasts to facilitate his escape'.[181] While certainly inconsistent with Meagher as the model of probity, it may not be with the man heartbroken at the plight of his son. He financed him while he was in Van Diemen's Land.[182] The *Waterford News* reported in May 1850 that Meagher had received a letter from his son describing his treatment in his penal home.[183] When his son escaped and arrived in America in 1852, Meagher extended hospitality to Catherine Bennett, the wife of Thomas Francis, when she stayed in Waterford, while en route to be united with her husband in New York.[184] Meagher accompanied her on her journey in the spring of 1853[185] but the re-union between husband and wife was to prove unsuccessful. During his time in New York, Thomas Meagher's health was poor. The rigours of the transatlantic journey combined with the heat of the city took its toll.[186] He was honoured by a delegation of Irish exiles from Cincinnati, who presented him with a cane cut from a tree growing above the grave of George Washington. In the accompanying address Meagher was lauded for his 'character' as a representative in the House of Commons, where 'in the midst of treachery and corruption', he was 'always found the earnest friend of the people'.[187] Now pregnant, Catherine Bennett returned to Waterford a few months later with her father-in-law and resided with him. She gave birth to a son at the beginning of April 1854, but died of typhus on 9 May. Meagher helped care for his grandson, christened Thomas Bennett Meagher.[188] Father and son continued to correspond. On the eve of his departure for Montana as territorial secretary in August 1865, Thomas Francis wrote to his father:

> I leave this evening for the far west, one of our richer new territories... I entertain the liveliest hopes that this enterprise will prove a profitable one to me and that it will enable me to pay you a visit in France next summer.[189]

Thomas Meagher was certainly generous towards his son. This generosity, in Keneally's words, 'was often exercised across a gulf of incomprehension'.[190] Not only did this gulf encompass politics, it also included personality. Thomas Francis Meagher was a handsome, flamboyant and debonair young man, who cut a dash in his splendid coats and elegantly cut trousers.[191] Such a personality and manner contrasted with the austere character of his father.[192] Though his son's political conduct, in particular, was deplorable in his father's eyes, Thomas Meagher's essential decency and integrity ensured that he acted in a fashion which some might consider beyond the bounds of paternal obligation towards a child who must have been, on occasions, the source of the deepest pain.

Other factors besides the conduct of his rebel son contributed to make the personal life of Thomas Meagher a less than happy one. He was widowed after only seven years of marriage. His wife, Alicia, died on 28 February 1827, nearly four weeks after giving birth to twin daughters. One of the girls, Christianna, died soon after being born; the other, Alicia Catherine, lived a short life of only seven years. Nor were these the only deaths of children suffered by Meagher and his wife – a son, Thomas, died soon after birth in 1821 and a daughter, Josephine Mary, died in infancy. Though premature deaths of children and wives after childbirth were not unusual in the nineteenth century, they were, nevertheless, occasions of great personal grief. The transportation of Thomas Francis effectively removed him forever from his father's life. Of his two remaining children, Christina Mary (born 1822) became a nun, and a son, Henry (born 1825) joined the military.[193] It was this son who became his only heir with the death of Thomas Francis on 1 July 1867, at Fort Benton, Montana. Henry accompanied his father when he retired to Bray and it was here that Thomas Meagher died on 27 February 1874. He was buried in Glasnevin Cemetery, Dublin.

Thomas Meagher lived during a time of great social, economic and political change in Ireland. He sought to influence that change by active political involvement, especially as Mayor of Waterford and MP for the city. A distinguished civic figure, he gave his fellow citizens leadership during the momentous events of the repeal campaign. His years of public service were characterized by integrity, honesty and loyalty. Such attributes were of special importance while a member of the Independent Irish Party, as central to the concept of independent opposition was adherence to pledges by elected representatives. Meagher was faithful to his word; had others acted likewise the party might have enjoyed a greater measure of success. Throughout much of his political life Thomas Meagher was a nationalist in the mould of Daniel O'Connell – a constitutionalist and loyal to the Crown. Equality for Catholics was a paramount objective of the Liberator's politics, to which cause Meagher subscribed with enthusiasm. His Catholicism was an integral part of his life. He served his faith publicly by striving for civil and religious liberty for his co-religionists; and in private he engaged in many acts of religiously inspired philanthropy. The generosity which was a feature of so much of his life was no less evident in the treatment of his rebel son, Thomas Francis, by whom he stood even though he had rejected, in a definite and dramatic manner, his father's deeply held political convictions. Thomas Meagher's ultimate fate was to be overshadowed by his son, who acquired heroic status in Irish nationalism at home and in America. The father of a patriot, his son's memory obscures the fact that Thomas Meagher was also a patriot. Speaking in 1847, he declared in words unusually passionate for him: 'I love Ireland. My heart beats with ardour for her welfare – it bleeds for her sufferings. And Oh! would it were in my power, by pouring out the last drop of that heart's blood to rescue the country from her misery and degradation.'[194] These are the words of a man who loved and served his country, and who deserves remembrance for more than just being the father of Thomas Francis Meagher.

NOTES

1. Matthew Butler, 'Some Waterford Notabilities', *Waterford News*, 8 Nov. 1929.
2. P.M. Egan, *History, Guide and Directory of County and City of Waterford* (Kilkenny: P.M. Egan, 1893), p.323.
3. The date of Meagher's birth is uncertain. The details on his early life in Newfoundland and Waterford are based on the research of Professor John Mannion and published in 'From Comfortable Farms to Mercantile Commerce and Cultural Politics: The Social Origins and Family Connections of Thomas Francis Meagher', *Decies* (Journal of the Waterford Archaeological and Historical Society), 59, (2003), pp.1–29.
4. *Ibid*., p.24.
5. See Fergus O'Ferrall, *Catholic Emancipation: Daniel O'Connell and the Birth of Irish Democracy 1820–30* (Dublin: Gill and MacMillan, 1985), pp.114–52.
6. *Waterford Mirror*, 27 March 1824.
7. *Ibid*., 7 April 1824.
8. James Reynolds, *The Catholic Emancipation Crisis in Ireland 1823–1829* (New Haven, CT: Greenwood Press, 1954), p.18.
9. For an account of this election, see Eugene Broderick, 'Protestants and the 1826 Waterford Election', *Decies*, 53, (1997), pp.45–66.
10. Thomas Wyse, *Historical Sketch of the Late Catholic Association of Ireland*, 2 vols, (London: H. Colburn, 1829), vol. 1, p. 267.
11. *Waterford Mail*, 23 Sept. 1826.
12. Rev. John Sheehan to Daniel O'Connell, 3 Nov. 1826, in Maurice R. O'Connell (ed.), *The Correspondence of Daniel O'Connell* (Dublin: Irish University Press, 1972), vol. iii, p.1349.
13. *Waterford Mail*, 12 Aug. 1826.
14. *Waterford Mirror*, 18 July 1827.
15. *Ibid.*
16. Quoted in Virginia Crossman, *Local Government in Nineteenth-Century Ireland* (Belfast: Institute of Irish Studies, The Queen's University, 1994), p.78.
17. *Ibid*., p.75.
18. W. Burke, 'Newport's Waterford Bank', *Journal of the Cork Historical and Archaeological Society*, IV (1898), pp.278–86.
19. Mannion, 'From Comfortable Farms', p.19.
20. Eugene Broderick, 'Waterford's Anglicans: Religion and Politics, 1819–1872', (unpublished Ph.D. Thesis, National University of Ireland, Cork, 2000), p.152.
21. For the text of the compact see James Auchmuty, *Sir Thomas Wyse 1791–1862: The Life and Career of an Educator and Diplomat* (London: P.S. King, 1939), pp.122–3.

22. *Waterford Mirror*, 9 March 1822.
23. See Eugene Broderick, 'Waterford's Minority Anglican Community during Three Crises – 1824–25; 1831–35; and 1848', *Decies*, 59 (2003), pp.166–9.
24. Broderick, 'Waterford's Anglicans', p.229.
25. *First Report of the Commissioners Appointed to Inquire into the Municipal Corporations in Ireland*, House of Commons 1835 (27), xxviii, p.39.
26. Minute Book, Waterford Corporation, 24 June 1829, Waterford City Archives, LA1/1/A/15.
27. Minute Book, Waterford Corporation, 3 Nov. 1829, Waterford City Archives, LA1/1/A/15.
28. Quoted in Crossman, *Local Government*, p.78.
29. Minute Book, Waterford Corporation, 26 Oct. 1842, Waterford City Archives, LA1/1/16.
30. *Waterford Chronicle*, 27 Oct. 1842.
31. *Ibid.*, 3 Nov. 1842.
32. *Ibid.*
33. *Ibid.*, 1 Nov. 1842.
34. *Ibid.*, 8 Nov. 1842.
35. Mannion, 'From Comfortable Farms', p.24.
36. For an account of the years of this alliance and its implications for Ireland see Gearoid O Tuathaigh, *Ireland before the Famine 1798–1848* (Dublin: Gill and Macmillan, 1972), pp.170–84.
37. R.F. Foster, *Modern Ireland 1600–1972* (London: Allen Lane, 1988), p.308.
38. Oliver MacDonagh, *States of Mind: A Study of Anglo-Irish Conflict 1780–1980* (London: George Allen & Unwin, 1983), pp.56–9; S.J. Connolly (ed.), *The Oxford Companion to Irish History* (Oxford: Oxford University Press, 1998), p.481.
39. Minute Book, Waterford Corporation, 1 Nov. 1842, Waterford City Archives, LA1/1/A/16.
40. *Waterford Chronicle*, 12 Nov. 1842.
41. *Ibid.*
42. *Ibid.*
43. *Ibid.*, 7 Feb. 1843.
44. *Ibid.*, 25 March 1843.
45. Minute Book, Waterford Corporation, 25 April 1843, Waterford City Archives, LA1/1/A/16.
46. Donal McCartney, *The Dawning of Democracy: Ireland 1800–1870* (Dublin: Helicon, 1987), pp.152–3.
47. *Waterford Chronicle*, 11 July 1843.
48. *Ibid.*, 19 Oct. 1843.
49. Minute Book, Waterford Corporation, 20 Oct. 1843, Waterford City Archives, LA1/1/A/16.
50. Minute Book, Waterford Corporation, 22 Nov. 1843, Waterford City Archives, LA1/1/A/16. For an overview of other aspects of his mayoralty see Eugene Broderick, 'A Decade of Agitation and Strife – Thomas Meagher, Mayor, 1843, 1844', in Eamonn McEneaney (ed.), *A History of Waterford and its Mayors from the 12th to the 20th Century* (Waterford: Waterford Corporation, 1995), pp.187–8.
51. Minute Book, Waterford Corporation, 25 March 1844, Waterford City Archives, LA1/1/A/16.
52. *Waterford Chronicle*, 10 April 1844.
53. Minute Book, Waterford Corporation, 31 May 1844, Waterford City Archives, LA1/1/A/16.
54. Minute Book, Waterford Corporation, 4 June 1844, Waterford City Archives, LA1/1/A/16.
55. Minute Book, Waterford Corporation, 11 Sept. 1844, Waterford City Archives, LA1/1/A/16.
56. *Waterford Chronicle*, 7 Feb. 1843.
57. *Ibid.*, 8 June 1844.
58. *Ibid.*, 3 March 1843.
59. Minute Book, Waterford Corporation, 2 May 1843, Waterford City Archives, LA1/1/A/16.
60. Paul A. Townend, *Father Mathew, Temperance and Irish Identity* (Dublin: Irish Academic Press, 2002), p.209.
61. McCartney, *Dawning of Democracy*, p.153.
62. Townend, *Father Mathew*, p.226.
63. *Waterford Chronicle*, 19 Oct. 1843.
64. Townend, *Father Mathew*, p.1.

65. *Waterford Chronicle*, 19 March 1840.
66. Townend, *Father Mathew*, p.1.
67. *Ibid.*, p.53.
68. *Ibid.*, p.5.
69. *Ibid.*, p.11.
70. *Ibid.*, p.78.
71. *Waterford Chronicle*, 3 Nov. 1842.
72. John M. Hearne, 'The Cost of Living and Standard of Living of Urban Workers in Waterford, 1834–56', *Saothar* (Journal of the Irish Labour History Society), 26, (2000), p.39.
73. Des Cowman, 'Trade and Society in Waterford city, 1800–1840', in William Nolan and Thomas Power (eds), *Waterford: History and Society* (Dublin: Geography Publications, 1992), p.444.
74. *Ibid.*
75. Hearne, 'Cost of Living', p.39.
76. Townend, *Father Mathew*, p.4.
77. *Ibid.*, p.42.
78. *Waterford Chronicle*, 7 Jan. 1843.
79. *Ibid.*, 6 May 1843.
80. *Ibid.*, 14 Sept. 1843. Meagher was on a pilgrimage to Rome in 1839 and 1840.
81. *Ibid.*, 6 May 1843.
82. Townend, *Father Mathew*, pp.56–9.
83. *Ibid.*, p.59.
84. *Ibid.*, pp.59-67.
85. Colm Kerrigan, *Father Mathew and the Irish Temperance Movement 1838–1849* (Cork: Cork University Press, 1992), pp.65–6.
86. Townend, *Father Mathew*, pp.235–60.
87. *Ibid.*, p.246.
88. *Waterford Chronicle*, 14 Sept. 1843.
89. *Chronicle*, 14 July 1847.
90. Mannion, 'From Comfortable Farms', p.25.
91. *Ibid.*, pp.25–6.
92. Anonymous, *Report of the Fanning Institute, Waterford, for the First Ten Years with the History of its Origins* (Waterford: Thomas Harvey, 1853), p.47.
93. Minute Book, Waterford Corporation, 12 Sept. 1843, Waterford City Archives, LA1/1/A/16.
94. *Waterford Chronicle*, 3 Nov. 1842.
95. This account is based on J.S. Donnelly, 'A Famine in Irish Politics', in W.E. Vaughan (ed.) *A New History of Ireland,* V: *Ireland under the Union,* I, *1801–70* (Oxford: Oxford University Press, 1989), pp.357–71; and O Tuathaigh, *Ireland before the Famine*, pp.190–202.
96. Donnelly, 'Famine in Irish Politics', p.364.
97. John. M. Hearne, 'The Sword Speech in Context', *Decies*, 59, (2003), pp.53–8.
98. *Chronicle*, 9 June 1847.
99. *Ibid.*, 23 June 1847.
100. *Ibid.*, 10 July 1847.
101. *Ibid.*, 7 Aug. 1847.
102. Mannion, 'From Comfortable Farms', p.26.
103. Sr Assumpta O'Neill, *Waterford's Presentation Community: A Bicentenary Record* (Waterford, 1998), pp.22–3.
104. Frances Finnegan, *Do Penance or Perish: A Study of Magdalen Asylums in Ireland* (Kilkenny: Congrave Press, 2001), pp.82–5.
105. S.A., *Mary Aikenhead: Her Life, Her Work and Her Friends* (Dublin: M.H. Gill and Son, 1879), pp.287, 291–3. My thanks to Mr David Smith for bringing this information to my attention.
106. Eugene Broderick , 'Thomas Meagher', in Eamonn McEneaney (ed.) with Rosemary Ryan, *Waterford Treasures* (Waterford: Granary Museum, 2004), pp.198–9.
107. David Smith, 'Obituary of Brother Edmund Ignatius Rice', *Decies*, 58, (2002), pp.47–8.

108. Catholic University of Ireland, *Report of the Committee and List of Subscriptions* (Dublin: J.M. O'Toole, 1852), p.43. My thanks to Dr John M. Hearne and Mr Ailbhe O'Donoghue for bringing this information to my attention.
109. B.M. Walker (ed.), *Parliamentary Election Results in Ireland, 1801–1922* (Dublin: Royal Irish Academy, 1978), p.79. The total electorate was 1,696.
110. *Waterford Chronicle*, 4 Aug. 1847.
111. R.V. Comerford, 'Churchmen, Tenants and Independent Opposition', in W.E. Vaughan (ed.) *A New History of Ireland,* V: *Ireland under the Union,* I, *1801–70* (Oxford: Oxford University Press, 1989), p.399.
112. J.H. Whyte, *The Independent Irish Party 1850–9* (Oxford: Oxford University Press, 1958), pp.6, 8.
113. *Ibid.*, pp.14–38.
114. *Ibid.*, Appendix A, pp.178–9.
115. *Ibid.*, p.27.
116. *Waterford Chronicle*, 8 March 1851.
117. Whyte, *Independent Irish Party*, pp.28–30.
118. *Waterford News*, 13 July 1852.
119. Whyte, *Independent Irish Party*, pp.86–90.
120. *Ibid.*, pp.92–157.
121. *Ibid.*, Appendix B, pp.180–1. In this Appendix Whyte included details of forty-eight members. In addition to the forty-two MPs who pledged themselves at the conference, six others are included on the basis of pledging support for tenant right or repeal of the Titles Act in addresses or at adoption meetings. Of these forty-eight, thirteen had died or resigned before the 1857 election.
122. *Ibid.*, p.102.
123. *Waterford Chronicle*, 14 July 1847.
124. *Waterford News*, 16 April 1852.
125. *Waterford Chronicle*, 30 Nov. 1850. The criticisms contained in the *Chronicle*'s editorials are considered later.
126. *Parliamentary Debates*, Third Series, cii, 6 Feb. 1849, 332.
127. See Donald H. Akenson, *The Church of Ireland: Ecclesiastical Reform and Revolution, 1800–1885* (New Haven, CT: Yale University Press, 1971), pp.199–201.
128. *Parliamentary Debates*, Third Series, cxl, 19 Feb. 1856, 1004.
129. *Ibid.*, cxli, 16 April 1856, 1115.
130. *Ibid.*, 15 April 1856, 1081.
131. *Ibid.*, cii, 7 Feb. 1849, 374.
132. *Ibid.*, cxli, 30 April 1856, 1796.
133. *Ibid.*, cxxxviii, 19 June 1855, 2251–2.
134. *Report of the Select Committee Appointed to Inquire into the Postal Arrangements in the City and County of Waterford*, 31 July 1855, Waterford Municipal Library.
135. *Waterford Chronicle*, 14 Dec. 1850.
136. *Ibid.*, 9 June 1847.
137. *Ibid.*, 7 Aug. 1847.
138. *Ibid.*, 14 Dec. 1850.
139. *Waterford Mail*, 17 April 1852.
140. *Waterford News*, 16 April, 7 May 1852.
141. *Waterford Chronicle*, 17 July 1852.
142. *Ibid.*, 14 Dec. 1850.
143. *Waterford Mail*, 30 June 1852.
144. *Waterford Chronicle*, 14 Dec. 1850.
145. *Ibid.*
146. *Waterford Mail*, 14 April 1852.
147. *Waterford News*, 26 March 1852.
148. Ibid., 13 July 1852.
149. Whyte, *Independent Irish Party*, p.16.

150. *Waterford News*, 13 July 1852.
151. *Waterford Chronicle*, 7 Aug. 1847.
152. *Waterford News*, 13 July 1852.
153. Comerford, 'Churchmen, Tenants and Independent Opposition', p.410.
154. Liz Curtis, *The Cause of Ireland: From the United Irishmen to Partition* (Belfast: Beyond the Pale Publications, 1994), p.61. The Ecclesiastical Titles Act, in the opinion of Professor R.V. Comerford, 'combined minimal effectiveness with a massive amount of offence to Catholics'. See 'Churchmen, Tenants and Independent Opposition', p.401.
155. R.V. Comerford, 'Ireland 1850–70: Post-Famine and Mid-Victorian', in W.E. Vaughan (ed.) *A New History of Ireland,* V: *Ireland under the Union,* I, *1801–70* (Oxford: Oxford University Press, 1989), p.373.
156. Tony Pierce, 'The "Clongowes" of Thomas Francis Meagher', *Decies*, 59, (2003), p.31.
157. Thomas Keneally, *The Great Shame: A Story of the Irish in the Old and New World* (London: Vintage, 1999), p.61.
158. For an account of his experiences see David Knight, 'Thomas Francis Meagher: His Stonyhurst Years', *Decies*, 59, (2003), pp.40–52.
159. Keneally, *Great Shame*, pp.80–1.
160. Thomas Francis Meagher, 'Recollections of Waterford', in T.N. Fewer (ed.), *I Was a Day in Waterford: An Anthology of Writing about Waterford from the 18th to the 20th Century* (Waterford: Ballylough Books, 2001), pp.133–4.
161. Hearne, 'Sword Speech', p.55.
162. *Waterford Chronicle*, 16 Sept. 1843.
163. *Ibid.*, 6 May 1843.
164. *Ibid.*, 11 July 1843.
165. *Ibid.*, 7 Aug. 1847.
166. Denis Gwynn, *Thomas Francis Meagher* (Cork: National University of Ireland, 1966), p.20.
167. See, for example, *Chronicle*, 16 Feb. 1848.
168. *Ibid.*, 19 Feb. 1848.
169. *Waterford Mail*, 23 Feb. 1848.
170. *Chronicle*, 23 Feb. 1848.
171. *Ibid.*, 1 March 1848.
172. The results of the election were as follows: Meagher, 154 votes; Costello, 301; and the Whig, Henry Barron, 318.
173. For an account of this election see John M. Hearne, 'Waterford: Economy, Society, and Politics, 1780–1852', (unpublished Ph.D. thesis, National University of Ireland Cork, 2001), pp.260–3.
174. Gwynn,*Thomas Francis Meagher*, p.10.
175. *Waterford Chronicle*, 15 Feb. 1851. The quotation is taken from an article by Thomas Francis Meagher, entitled 'Meagher's Memoir of Forty-Eight'.
176. *Ibid.*
177. *Ibid.*, and 12 Feb. 1851.
178. *Ibid.*, 26 April 1851.
179. *Waterford Chronicle*, 1 Nov. 1848.
180. Mannion, 'From Comfortable Farms', p.28.
181. S.A., *Mary Aikenhead*, p.335, footnote 1.
182. For an account of his life in Van Diemen's Land, see *Waterford Chronicle*, 3 Aug. 1850. This contains a re-print of a letter written by Meagher to Charles Gavan Duffy, dated Van Diemen's Land, 16 Feb. 1850.
183. *Waterford News*, 3 May 1850.
184. *Ibid.*, 8 July 1853.
185. *Ibid.*,12 Aug., 19 Aug. 1853.
186. *Ibid.*, 19 Aug. 1853.
187. *Ibid.*, 9 Sept. 1853. See also Broderick, 'Thomas Meagher', in McEneaney (ed.), *Waterford Treasures*, pp.198–9.
188. Mannion, 'From Comfortable Farms', p.29.

189. Quoted in James L. Thane, Jnr, 'Thomas Francis Meagher: – "the Acting One"' (unpublished MA thesis, University of Montana, 1967), p.7.
190. Keneally, *Great Shame*, p.61.
191. *Ibid.*, p.91.
192. It is difficult to write about the personal relationship between Thomas Meagher and his son because of the absence of sources. Professor John Mannion has noted that details on personal family background rarely entered Thomas Francis Meagher's public discourses and he made 'little mention in his speeches, reminiscences, or other writings of his ancestry or extended family'. Mannion, 'From Comfortable Farms', p.28.
193. My thanks to Mr David Smith for information on the family of Thomas Meagher.
194. *Waterford Chronicle*, 14 July 1847.

4

Thomas Francis Meagher: Reluctant Revolutionary

John M. Hearne

When Thomas Francis Meagher delivered what became known as the 'Sword Speech' in Conciliation Hall on 28 July 1846, it was a defining moment in nineteenth-century Irish politics. It brought to a head and into the open the simmering ideological and generational differences between Daniel O'Connell's repeal movement and the younger more belligerent faction within that movement, the Young Irelanders. While the speech itself was ambivalent, being prefaced by an adherence to the peaceful policy of the Repeal Association and having advance knowledge that it would knowingly occasion schism, it was not a composite entity. It was the second part of a trilogy of unfinished orations that began on 13 July 1846 and eventually finished on 2 December of the same year. These speeches were a riposte to Daniel O'Connell's attempt to impose an abstract concept known as the 'peace resolutions' on the Repeal Association, and in particular on the Young Ireland faction of that body. The essence of these resolutions required that all members of the Association adopt a pledge repudiating physical force in any and all circumstances in the pursuit of repeal. The ulterior motive, according to the Young Irelanders, was to prevent endangering an anticipated O'Connell–Whig alliance and the inevitable patronage that would ensue. Meagher's 'Sword Speech' thus enunciated a refusal to adhere to these 'peace resolutions' and in so doing was an implicit repudiation of this alliance. However, the 'peace resolutions' concept was not a product of 1846, its genesis can be found in the bitter confrontation between the Young Irelanders and O'Connell over the Colleges Bill a year earlier. Nonetheless, Meagher's exposition exposed repeal as a mere paradigm of ambiguity in constitutional nationalism[1] and hastened its decline as a credible political conviction. With the death of O'Connell in May 1847, the Young Irelanders, and Meagher in particular, were denounced for having embittered and frustrated the last years of the Liberator's public life.[2] The only agency that could make effective demands on the government for famine relief was now politically impotent and the Young Irelanders, the umbilical cord now severed, drifted towards their own place in history.

REPEAL

Almost immediately after the granting of emancipation in 1829, Daniel O'Connell initiated a new campaign aimed at achieving his chief political goal

– repeal of the Act of Union. But for much of the 1830s the principle of repeal was compromised as he sought to elicit practical socio-economic reforms from various British governments, with repeal used as the bargaining tool. Indeed, O'Connell used repeal as both an offensive weapon and as a defensive position: repeal was used as a threat through which other concessions might be levered from successive Whig governments, but it was always valuable as a popular fall-back if all else failed.[3] This resulted in the Lichfield House Compact of 1835. Here, O'Connell concluded an informal alliance with Melbourne's Whig government whereby repeal agitation would be put in abeyance in return for parliamentary, municipal and tithe reforms. Of more immediate advantage was the opening of large areas of official employment and patronage to those wealthy Catholics who saw such advancement as the real achievement of emancipation. Indeed many, seeing no immediate prospect of repeal, were prepared to accept office and make their way in the world while retaining, if quietly, nationalist political views.[4] And O'Connell was not slow in exploiting such patronage for his friends and family.[5] By 1838 O'Connell, aware that his co-operation with the Whigs had brought reforms, albeit minor in nature and grudgingly granted, now believed that this alliance was alienating him from the Irish people. These anxieties were manifested in his founding of three successive societies directed towards repeal: the Precursor Society, the National Repeal Association and, in 1840, with the threat of a Tory election victory looming (the Tories under Peel were returned in 1841), he reverted to a simple and more direct anti-Union strategy by forming the National Association for Full and Prompt Justice or Repeal.[6] It was only now that O'Connell's commitment to repeal of the Act of Union emerged untrammelled by the compromises of the Whig alliance.[7] As a lawyer, he had gained an unrivalled insight into the operation of Protestant control in Ireland and into the futility of using violence and outrage against oppression.[8] Such agitation that was employed was therefore subject to careful choreography, strictly disciplined and within the confines of the law. But in reality this amounted to no more than platform sedition.

YOUNG IRELAND

In November 1841, O'Connell was elected Lord Mayor of Dublin. During his tenure the Repeal Association was allowed to mark time as the old organization, used so potently and successfully in the emancipation struggle, was honed into effective action for the campaign ahead. O'Connell announced that 1843 would be 'repeal year'. His conduct as mayor had increased his popularity and ensured that he commenced his campaign with a solid backing of public opinion.[9] In 1842 Thomas Davis, Charles Gavan Duffy and John Blake Dillon launched a new nationalist newspaper. On Saturday 15 October 1842 the first edition of the *Nation* appeared and sold out before midday. In its prospectus, written almost entirely by Davis, its central theme was renewal: emancipation from old, tired themes and the direction of the popular mind and the sympathies of educated men to nationality and the blessings of domestic legislation. Moreover, the new journal would work to bring all Irishmen of whatever historical origin to a love of their common country, and to convince them to act patriotically in its behalf.[10] Although utopian, such idealism evoked an earlier Protestant republican tradition, subliminally bestowing the imprimatur of Tone and Emmet and indirectly rebutting repeal's Catholic confessional hue, and O'Connell's own ambiguous attitude towards the Protestant minority. The *Nation* quickly became the nexus for the younger intellectuals within the Repeal Association, many of whom were Protestants, graduates of Trinity College and who had already shown that they were not prepared to accept O'Connell's dicta as their law.[11] Though initially supportive of O'Connell and his policies, this faction began to be seen as a separate movement with an ideology of its own; an identity that became more apparent as repeal agitation intensified during 1843 and thereafter.

On the Tuesday of Easter week 1843, just as O'Connell's monster meetings were gathering momentum, Thomas Francis Meagher returned home to Waterford having completed his education at the Jesuit College of Stonyhurst, near Preston in England. Although absent from Ireland for almost five years, he was, nonetheless, attuned to its changing political landscape. Indeed, it was at Stonyhurst that his latent nationalism had been awakened and displayed when, in 1840, as first clarinettist in the college orchestra he refused to play at the annual commemoration of the Battle of Waterloo. Returning to Waterford he became involved in the Repeal Association where his father, then Mayor of Waterford, was a leading figure and loyal supporter of the Liberator. Indeed, both father and son were present at the Waterford monster meeting in July 1843 where O'Connell addressed a crowd of some 300,000 people. Here, sarcastically thanking *The Times* for providing the adjective 'monster' for such meetings, O'Connell's tone was more mocking than militant.[12] It was certainly less militaristic than the Mallow Defiance of a month earlier where he declared that Irishmen would soon have the alternative of living as slaves or dying like freemen and that he was prepared to resist if the government made war on the Irish people. During the same month at Drogheda, he vowed that his movement was, to a man, prepared to perish in pursuit of repeal.[13] This orchestration of rising expectations was, however, interrupted by the British Prime Minister, Sir Robert Peel who, mindful of O'Connell's respect for the law, was confident that he would back down once the threat of open confrontation with the government became a reality. Indeed, the government's growing concern regarding public order had led earlier in May to the suspension by the lord lieutenant, Clarendon, of many government officials supportive of repeal and to Peel introducing a bill regulating the use of arms in Ireland. Peel now forced the issue to a conclusion in October by proclaiming the Clontarf monster meeting.[14] O'Connell, as predicted, cancelled the meeting and a week later he, his son, John, Charles Gavan Duffy and six others were charged with conspiracy and with trying to change the constitution by illegal means. The *Nation* and Young Irelanders at that time concurred with O'Connell's policy of keeping the Repeal Association within the law.[15] Thus, by threatening force, the government had discredited O'Connell's formula of militant constitutionalism and assisted in the re-emergence of unconstitutional politics.[16]

The events of May 1843 had two important results. Firstly, O'Connell was forced into making more extreme statements than hitherto. This led the Young Ireland faction to expect more from him than he was prepared to deliver. It also helped disguise the fundamental differences between the two groups and led to a deceptive harmony of aims and methods as to how repeal might be secured. Secondly, the *Nation* leader writers, in particular, were forced to reconsider their theories as to what methods of obtaining repeal were justifiable. Davis' *The Morality of War* appeared in the paper in early June and concluded that the use of force was justifiable when all other methods had failed.[17] Thereafter, the tone of the *Nation* became more militaristic and the young men associated with it discovered that they had a common stock of ideas and aims. This initiated weekly meetings between them and thus began the Young Irelanders as a separate, albeit unofficial, group within the Repeal Association.[18]

Patrick Maume has recently questioned whether O'Connell actually expected to obtain repeal or whether he merely wished to use the agitation to safeguard the gains of the 1830s and perhaps gain further concessions in the future.[19] When launching his repeal campaign in 1843, O'Connell had addressed this question when he stated that 'a Parliament inferior to the English Parliament I would accept as an instalment... if it were offered me by a competent authority... if others offer me a subordinate parliament, I will close with any such authorized offer and accept that offer'.[20] Indeed, nine years earlier in a speech to the House of Commons, he stated that he was not willing to 'fling [the] British connection to the winds' and that 'I am sure that separation will not happen in my time; but I am equally sure that the connection cannot continue if you maintain the Union on its present basis'. And while he wanted to maintain friendly relations between the two islands, he only desired legislative independence in a way that 'both countries would afford mutual advantage to the other'.[21] Thus, repeal was only *apparently* a demand, it did not countenance formal separation of any kind, it merely represented the sloganizing of pressure designed to force a counter-offer from the government.[22] And concessions, if not an offer, did materialize a little more than a year later.

MEAGHER'S ARRIVAL

It was during O'Connell's trial, in January 1844, that Thomas Francis Meagher arrived in Dublin, from Waterford, to study law at Queen's Inns. He, however, quickly immersed himself in nationalist politics, regularly attending Repeal Association meetings and by the end of the year he had terminated his studies.

It was only then that he became more involved and more vocal in the Association; 1844 was also the year that witnessed the ideological disjunction between the Young Irelanders and O'Connell become more acute. Education was the contentious issue that precipitated this fissure. Peel, in a follow-up to the smothering of repeal, set about introducing a package of reforms to soften O'Connell's political humiliation (he was incarcerated for most of 1844, only being released in September of that year). He also hoped to divert the middle class and moderate ecclesiastics towards the quieter paths of accommodation and quiescence and dilute their repeal aspirations.[23] In 1844 a Charitable Bequests Act was passed which sought to safeguard Catholic charities by giving Catholics a greater say in the operation of bequests and donations. Peel also increased the grant to Maynooth seminary, which was warmly received by the bishops. However, it was the enactment of the Education Act in May 1845 that was to cause controversy. In establishing universities in Cork, Galway and Belfast, the government did not envisage the public endowment of religious instruction, but private funding of such teaching by representatives of each denomination would be facilitated.[24] This was to cause an open rift between O'Connell, the Catholic Church and the government, as the colleges would be essentially non-denominational. This was far short of the bishops' demands for a fully Catholic University. O'Connell opined that the bill was 'fraught with a host of evils' and 'gross violation of Catholic principle'. He denounced the colleges as 'Godless' and suggested that Cork and Galway should be Catholic while Belfast should be Presbyterian. But the Young Irelanders, and Thomas Davis in particular, openly opposed this view in the *Nation*, stating that 'we are in favour of mixed education above all, because it is consistent with piety, and favourable to the union of all Irishmen of different sects'.[25] Davis was supported by Thomas Wyse and by William Smith O'Brien (a Limerick landlord and MP for that city who was destined to play a pivotal role in the eventual split in the Repeal Association). With both sides now polarized and an open rift a distinct possibility, a conciliation of sorts was hastily brokered in order to ensure at least the fascade of unity.

In a show of unity and as an attempt to stave off public division, O'Connell agreed to address a full meeting of the Association. Prior to this meeting he was handed a document to be read by him in addressing the assembly. This was however to prove portentous. Shocked to find it contained a 'battle song, a war like song, an incitation to fight' and bearing a motto or war cry of the O'Briens, '*The strong arm prevails*', he stated that the author misapprehended the principles of the Association. 'We are not a fighting body', he continued, 'we are a peaceable body, and the author would be better out of the Association'.[26] Thus was witnessed the advent of the 'peace resolutions', a potent abstraction that was destined to inflict terminal damage on the Association. While subsequent debates in the Association on this issue were bitter and left deep scars, a gaze over the abyss of religious schism also had a chastening effect. It was the sudden death of Davis in September 1845 that led eventually to a temporary cessation in hostilities. The Colleges Bill had activated the first open confrontation between O'Connell and the Young Irelanders. But it left behind the poisonous seeds of distrust and an undercurrent of seething antipathy that would eventually explode over an issue that inadvertently surfaced during these acrimonious debates. However, the death of Davis had two important results. Firstly, it took from the political stage a voice of moderation respected on both sides of the political divide; secondly, it allowed the more strident nationalists, John Mitchel, Meagher and Michael Doheny to assume centre stage within the Young Ireland faction. After September, although an uneasy peace was maintained, the abrasive and incendiary invective of the new editor of the *Nation*, the Ulster Presbyterian, John Mitchel, ensured that tensions between the two camps were accentuated. The Famine had also begun.

The first real threat to the unity of the repeal movement arose in December 1845. With famine in the country since early autumn, Peel had decided to repeal the Corn Laws. Unable to convince all of his cabinet, his Tory government fell in early December; but Lord John Russell was also unable to construct a Whig administration, thus allowing Peel to return. The prospect of another O'Connell–Whig alliance now took root and would become an eventuality in June 1846. The *Nation* denounced any prospect of a return to a Lichfield House-type alliance. It proclaimed that the only pretext for such an accommodation with the Whigs was a promise of immediate repeal of the Act of Union. In one of his first recorded speeches on the issue, in February 1846, Thomas Francis Meagher appealed for both sides to adopt a tolerant attitude and a unified approach in pursuing repeal.[27] The tone was conciliatory and it was obvious that he had clearly not yet thrown in his lot with Young Ireland.

TOWARDS YOUNG IRELAND

It was around this time, at an '82 Club social function, that Meagher first met John Mitchel. Introduced by Thomas McNevin, Mitchel's first impression of Meagher was of 'a rather foppish young gentleman with an accent decidedly English'. No common ground was discernible among the two until both found that they shared a mutual admiration for the recently deceased Thomas Davis. Thereafter, the two men formed an unlikely yet close friendship that lasted until Meagher's death in 1867, surviving three continents and withstanding a civil war and fundamental ideological differences. Thus, from the early spring of 1846, Meagher became more involved in the *Nation* and more committed to the philosophy of Young Ireland.[28] By June, the division in the Tory Party over the Corn Laws ensured that the days of the Peel administration were numbered. It was also evident that O'Connell was set on another alliance with the Whigs, thus provoking a hostile reaction from the *Nation*, with Meagher leading the onslaught. On 15 June, Meagher made a fiery denouncement of the proposed alliance and a stinging attack on O'Connell. 'We have learned to regard the

Whig government in Ireland as little more than a State Relief Committee for the beggarly politicians that beset the country, and there is suspicion', he said, 'that the national cause will be sacrificed to the Whigs, and that the people, who are now striding for freedom, will be purchased back into factious vassalage.' But it was his reference to 'our illustrious friend Thomas Davis, our prophet and our guide'[29] that was later considered by O'Connell as 'a base attack on me'. It led to the Liberator referring to Meagher's oration as 'clap traps from juvenile orators' and accusing the Young Irelanders of ruining the repeal cause and warning that it was becoming 'impossible to work the Repeal Association with them'.[30] Meagher's reply to O'Connell a week later increased the tension and pre-empted the split, now just a month hence. Pledging loyalty to O'Connell and the right of free speech, he nonetheless refused to apologise for his remarks and stated 'the attack has begun – we have been struck... but we will not flinch... we shall leave this Hall... our honour unimpaired... asserting the right of free opinion and our determination to defend it'.[31]

An impending by-election in Kilkenny witnessed O'Connell's antipathy towards the Young Irelanders being manifested publicly. Aware that Meagher was expected to contest the vacant seat, he urged that a repealer must be returned in Kilkenny as 'I cannot possibly permit it to return either a Tory or Whig or an animal more mischievous than either of the others called a Young Irelander.'[32] While this outburst could be seen as an implicit attack on Meagher, it also demonstrated O'Connell's intent on coercing the Young Irelander's into secession. By the end of June the Tory administration had at last fallen, defeated on the Irish coercion bill by a combination of protectionist Tories, Whigs and O'Connell. The attempt to force the Young Irelanders into submission or secession now entered its final phase in Dungarvan, County Waterford.

THE SWORD SPEECH

In the summer of 1846 Richard Shiel, the sitting MP for Dungarvan, was appointed Master of the Mint by the new Whig government. Since 1842 it had been Repeal Association policy that whenever a sitting MP was granted a government position that the subsequent by-election would be contested; even if that MP was a repeal supporter.[33] Therefore, as Shiel intended standing for re-election O'Connell's action with regard to this seat was watched closely, as it would give an indication of his future policy. But O'Connell, his eye firmly on an accommodation with the Whigs, postponed naming a candidate until it was too late, thereby allowing Shiel to retain the seat uncontested. O'Connell's remark to a Whig friend that '... I have stifled all opposition to Shiel at Dungarvan... the election will not cost him a shilling', was seen by the Young Irelanders as a sell-out and a sop to Russell's new administration. To them the proposed alliance was anathema and they saw this trucking with the Whigs as sycophantic, believing that repeal was a great crusade and, as such, was not negotiable. The *Nation* accused O'Connell of cowardice[34] while O'Connell believed its constant criticism of the Repeal Association and of his own servility to the Crown would endanger the Association's influence in obtaining local famine relief, and would also inhibit political patronage. But when Lord John Russell made it clear that the Whigs regarded the Young Irelanders as republican, separatist and revolutionary in inclination, O'Connell saw the Young Irelanders as a hindrance to the alliance. He was determined to force the issue by requiring all members of the Association to adopt a direct pledge repudiating physical force in any and all circumstances. The 'peace resolutions', as they were called, seen in embryonic form a year earlier during the Colleges Bill controversy, were now publicly broached by O'Connell at a committee meeting on 9 July 1846 and carried, with only Meagher and Mitchel voting against. Four days later, 13 July, they were debated at a full Association meeting with Meagher the only dissenting voice. It was here that O'Connell insisted 'that the abstract principle of disclaiming physical force in any event must be held by every member of the Association'.[35] The intention, according to P.J. Smyth, was to 'draw a marked line between Old and Young Ireland'.[36] O'Connell was aware that the Young Irelanders would react negatively to these 'peace resolutions' and might indeed provide ample pretexts for their expulsion from the Association. Meagher retorted bitterly, castigating O'Connell for his inaction at Dungarvan, stating that it had 'cast a stain on the... Association', but, nonetheless, agreed that repeal should only be achieved by moral and peaceful means. However, if it was not possible to achieve it in that way then,

> I am prepared to adopt another policy – a policy no less honourable though it may be more perilous – a policy which I cannot disclaim as inefficient or immoral, for great names have adopted its adoption, and noble events have attested its efficiency.[37]

This was his most belligerent avowal of militarism to date and implicitly evoked the Tone and Emmet republican tradition. It also challenged the Liberator's authority. This oration was the first instalment of what became known as the 'Sword Speech'; it was continually interrupted by O'Connell and his supporters, and would not be completed for another few months. In the two weeks before the 'peace resolutions' eventually came up for determination, both camps had become more polarized. Duffy accused O'Connell of seeking a Whig alliance for no other reason than procuring patronage for himself and his friends and, in so doing, was prepared to silence and exclude opponents of this accommodation. The defining moment came, however, on 15 July in Kilrush, County Clare. Here, William Smith O'Brien, not yet a member of the Young Ireland faction, publicly supported the thrust of Meagher's speech of two days earlier, and thus reluctantly came off the fence and sided with Young Ireland in direct contradiction of O'Connell. These resolutions came up for determination in Conciliation Hall on 27 July 1846. Daniel O'Connell was not present at this meeting. He sent his son, John, to represent him and to ensure their implementation. The scene was now set for the historic encounter whereby, in his absence, the movement that O'Connell created would be all but destroyed.[38]

At this meeting John O'Connell insisted that his father's 'peace resolutions' had to be accepted if the Young Irelanders were to remain within the Association. There seems little doubt that he had been instructed by his father to make no concessions whatsoever and thus, during the second day of the meeting, pushed the dispute to extremity by attacking the militaristic tone of the *Nation* and its adherents. In asserting the right to free speech and defending attacks on the *Nation* from John O'Connell and his supporters Meagher, in a carefully crafted speech, began by berating the proposed O'Connell–Whig alliance. He condemned it as a sell-out, commenting that while a Whig ministry might improve the province, it would not restore the nation; and while the errors of the past might also be repaired, the hopes of the future would not be fulfilled. Meagher then turned on John O'Connell, accusing him of orchestrating a debate so as to force the Young Irelanders to secede from the Repeal Association.[39] But in essence, the speech was primarily concerned with upholding the right of free speech and of the free expression of opinion within the Association, as Meagher explained,

> In the exercise of that right I have differed, sometimes, from the leader of this Association, and would do so again. That right I will not abandon; I will maintain it to the last. In doing so, let me not be told that I seek to undermine the influence of the leader of this Association, and am insensible to his services... I will uphold his just influence, and I am grateful for his services... No... I am not ungrateful to the man [O'Connell] who struck the fetters from my arms, whilst I was yet a child; and by whose influence my father – the first Catholic who did so for two hundred years – sat, for the last two years, in the civic chair of an ancient city. But... the same God who gave to that great man the power to strike down an odious ascendancy in this country, and enabled him to institute, in this land, the glorious law of religious equality – the same God gave to me a mind that is my own – a mind that has not been mortgaged to the opinions of any man or any set of men. In the exercise of that right... a right which this Association should preserve inviolate, if it desires not to become a despotism – in the exercise of that right I have differed from Mr. O'Connell on previous occasions, and differ from him now.[40]

This then brought Meagher to what he called the 'question of the day', the 'peace resolutions'. Meagher gave his reasons for opposing the resolutions and why he had voted against them in committee the previous week. Firstly, he believed that they were unnecessary, 'senseless' and 'wicked' given the present state of the country; and that 'any talk of repealing the Act of Union by force of arms would be to rhapsodise... and would be a decided failure'. Continuing, he mentioned that the second reason for his dissenting was that to give his assent to the resolutions would mean pledging himself to the unqualified repudiation of physical force in all countries at all times and in every circumstance;

> This I could not do; for… I do not abhor the use of arms in the vindication of national rights. There are times when arms alone will suffice, and when political amelioration's [*sic*] call for a drop of blood, and many thousands drops of blood. Opinion, I admit, will operate against opinion… force must be used against force. The soldier is proof against an argument, but he is not proof against a bullet. The man that will listen to reason let him be reasoned with; but it is the weaponed arm of the patriot that can alone prevail against battalioned despotism. Then… I do not disclaim the use of arms as immoral, nor do I believe it the truth to say that the God of heaven withholds his sanction from the use of arms. From that night in which, in the valley of Bethulia, He nerved the arm of the Jewish girl to smite the drunken tyrant in his tent, down to the hour in which He blessed the insurgent chivalry of the Belgian priests, His Almighty hand hath ever been stretched forth from His throne of light, to consecrate the flag of freedom – to bless the patriot sword. Be it for the defence, or be it for the assertion of a nation's liberty, I look upon the sword as a sacred weapon. And if… it has sometimes reddened the shroud of the oppressor – like the anointed rod of the high priest, it has, as often, blossomed into flowers to deck the freeman's brow. Abhor the sword? Stigmatise the sword? No… for at its blow it cut to pieces the banner of the Bavarian, and through those cragged passes of the Tyrol cut a path to fame for the peasant insurrectionist of Innsbruck. Abhor the sword? Stigmatise the sword? No… for at its blow, and in the quivering of its crimson light a giant nation sprang up from the waters of the Atlantic, and by its redeeming magic the fettered colony became a daring free Republic. Abhor the sword? Stigmatises the sword? No… for it swept the Dutch marauders out of the fine old towns of Belgium – swept them back to their phlegmatic swamps, and knocked their flag and sceptre, their laws and bayonets into the sluggish waters of the Scheldt… I learned that it was the right of a nation to govern itself – not in this Hall – but upon the ramparts of Antwerp. This is the first article of a nation's creed, I learned upon those ramparts, where freedom was justly estimated, and where the possession of the precious gift was purchased by the effusion of generous blood. I honour the Belgians, I admire the Belgians, I love the Belgians for their enthusiasm, their courage, their success, and I, for one, will not stigmatise, for I do not abhor, the means by which they obtained a citizen King, a Chamber of Deputies.[41]

At this juncture John O'Connell intervened to prevent Meagher continuing, insisting that Meagher was expressing views entirely in opposition to the principles of the Association; Meagher must cease to be a member of the Association or the Association must cease to exist. He would himself withdraw, if the meeting approved such sentiments, but he was there as the official representative of the Liberator. Most of Daniel O'Connell's senior acolytes concurred with his son's ultimatum. But when William Smith O'Brien defended Meagher (as he had previously done at committee meetings on 9 and 13 July) 'not for his sentiments but for having made an honest avowal of his opinions after he had been invited to express them', the die was cast. When Meagher's attempts to resume his interrupted speech were persistently stifled by John O'Connell the Young Irelanders, led by O'Brien, Meagher, Mitchel and Duffy walked out of Conciliation Hall for ever. The irony of this turn of events was that the 'Sword Speech' was itself merely a continuation of the speech Meagher had made in the same venue two weeks previously, and that had also been stymied by O'Connell's supporters. It was here that the Rubicon had been crossed. The 'Sword Speech' can therefore be seen as no more than an encore to the events of 13 July. When Meagher eventually concluded his oration, on 2 December 1846 at the Rotunda, he rounded on the O'Connells accusing them of conjuring up a deliberate and premeditated plan on 13 July to facilitate the expulsion of the Young Ireland faction. 'Had we assented to the peace resolutions', he explained, 'others would have been introduced to which we could not with common sense have subscribed.'[42] Although attempts at reconciliation had up to now been unsuccessful, the success of the Rotunda meeting forced Daniel O'Connell to make another attempt to heal the breach. But when he again insisted on adherence to the 'peace resolutions', he was accused by Duffy of entering the discussions in bad faith. O'Connell then personally wrote to Meagher inviting him back into the Association, but to no avail.[43] Duffy and Meagher had at this time proposed developing the '82 Club as a Young Ireland forum but O'Brien advised against, lest it be seen as a rival association. He did not want to close the door on eventual reconciliation. Encouraged by the support they received at the December meeting the Young Irelanders arranged another one for January 1847. It was here that the Irish Confederation was set up. Young Ireland now looked to William Smith O'Brien for leadership, but such strength was not forthcoming. Thus, Young Ireland was about to launch a leaderless party in the naïve hope that such an organization could avoid division and give a clear direction to Irish nationalism.[44]

THE IRISH CONFEDERATION

On 13 January 1847 the seceders met at the Rotunda, Dublin, and formally set up the Irish Confederation. Resolutions were drawn up and a governing council elected, which subsequently acquired offices in D'Olier Street, Dublin. But in essence the Confederation was little more than the Repeal Association minus the peace resolutions. The Confederation's first action was to contest the

Galway by-election in February, occasioned by the death of the sitting repealer, Sir Valentine Blake. Meagher delivered a robust speech in rallying support for a cause he said was 'unstained by the glittering poison of the English Treasury' and for a victory that would 'lay the foundations of a future nation'.[45] The candidate supported by the Confederation, Anthony O'Flaherty stood little chance in reality. His opponent, James Monahan, the official repeal candidate, was also solicitor general, had the Liberator's imprimatur and the support of the clergy.[46] At the next meeting of the Confederation on 7 April, two items took precedence; reconciliation and the Famine. On the former, the meeting was kept apace of recent attempts to broker an acceptable peace, but in a follow-up meeting with John O'Connell in early May, no progress was made. The famine issue dominated the meeting with many calling for a scheme of public works to alleviate distress. Meagher, showing an acute awareness of the impending disaster, made an impassioned plea for government intervention concluding, 'the people will not consent to live another year in a wilderness and graveyard... Ireland will be burnt into one black, unpeopled field of ashes rather than this should last'.[47] But any chance that the Confederation harboured of emerging as a serious political force was dealt a terminal blow by the death of Daniel O'Connell in May 1847, in Genoa, Italy. As a mark of respect, the *Nation* was black-bordered and Smith O'Brien moved a resolution of sympathy in the Confederation. Nonetheless, the *Pilot*, mouthpiece of the Association, accused Young Ireland, and Meagher in particular, of sending him to an early grave. But one member of the Confederation was unsympathetic. Fr John Keynon, one of the few priests who was a member of the Confederation, ended any chance of a reunion with a vitriolic attack on O'Connell and, what he described as, 'his huckstering politics'.[48] An inference from the O'Connell family that members of the Confederation should not attend the obsequies and a decision to delay the funeral until August, just before the general election, copper-fastened the schism. More than any other event the 1847 general election highlighted the disorganization within the Confederation. With no electoral strategy or countrywide network, few Confederation members even contested the election and even fewer were elected. Paradoxically, it was in the midst of this election that an embryonic structure crystallized: the confederate clubs.

Meagher and Duffy envisaged the clubs as the basis of a mass political party. O'Brien endorsed this opinion and proposed the establishment of confederate clubs 'in every town and parish in Ireland'. This was adopted by the Confederation on 26 August. Peopled mainly by unfranchised artisans, the clubs, their names evoking earlier nationalist republican traditions, quickly sprang up throughout urban Ireland. Dublin had the Swift, Davis and Grattan Clubs, Limerick, the Sarsfield, Cork, the Desmond and Waterford had the Wolf Tone Club. Clubs were also formed in many of the larger British cities such as Manchester, Glasgow and Liverpool,[49] thus giving the impression of an ideological unison within the British Isles. However, just when it seemed that the Irish Confederation was about to become a potent political force, the seeds of division were already germinating.

By December 1847, the Irish Confederation still had not developed a coherent policy on how repeal was to be achieved. But the introduction of the Crimé Prevention Bill in the same month accentuated the quest. It was the question of force that disrupted the progress of the Confederation, as the coercion bill now allowed the differences that had developed during the previous year to come into the open. Mitchel, in particular, argued that the disarming clauses of the bill were 'a direct invasion of the common rights and prerogatives of manhood' and proclaimed that 'every man has the right to bear arms'.[50] He now advocated the formation of a militia for mutual defence. Duffy and O'Brien, alarmed at this turn to naked militarism, realized that the Confederation faced its first major obstacle. In January 1848 Duffy, proprietor of the *Nation*, argued that Mitchel's articles propagating an abandonment of constitutional agitation were diametrically opposed to his own and, as a result, Mitchel, along with Devin Reilly, left the *Nation*. Within a month they had started a new newspaper, the *United Irishman*. Earlier in the same month Meagher, in a letter to O'Brien on the subject, lamented,

> My heart sinks under a weight of bitter thoughts, and I am almost driven to the conclusion that it would be better to risk all – to make one desperate effort – and fix at once the fate of Ireland... has any country ever suffered so much, ever had such terrible provocation, and been so jealous of the law, so anxious to keep it sacred. Oh! That poor Davis could come to life, even for one short day, and beckon us, like a pillar of flame to some pathway in this wilderness – some sure track – so that we might be redeemed out of this uncertainty, this bewilderment, this despair, in which we now so feebly wander.

Still, Meagher could not accept that the Mitchel policy would be successful at this time and stated that 'an unconstitutional mode of action would not in the present circumstances, succeed. I am convinced that the only mode we can adopt... successfully is the constitutional policy.'[51] A special meeting of the Confederation was arranged for 2 February at which Smith O'Brien put forward proposals in support of achieving repeal by constitutional means. The meeting overwhelmingly rejected Mitchel's militaristic policy. Meagher had missed the first two days of the meeting, being in Manchester addressing a Chartist rally. On his return he adopted the same stance as that outlined in his letter to O'Brien, adding that the question to decide upon was between following a constitutional policy and insurrection. He knew of 'no nation that has won its independence by an accident' and while he agreed in principle with Mitchel, he did not think insurrection was a practical alternative. 'I support the constitutional policy not from choice', he said 'but from necessity.' Then, in concluding, Meagher made a curious remark in outlining the obstacles that insurrection would face:

> So much for the war of the classes. No, I am not for a democratic, but I am for a national movement – not a movement like that of Paris in 1793, but for a movement like that of Brussels of 1830... If you think differently say so. If you are weary of this constitutional movement...let this night terminate the... Irish Confederation.[52]

This throwaway remark sheds a lot of light on the type of insurrection that Meagher was prepared to countenance; it certainly was not one that envisioned a radical social tumult. Indeed, when one takes a look at the personnel constituting the council or governing body of the Confederation, the majority were from the middle classes; eleven of the forty were barristers, four were doctors and four were justices of the peace. There was a solitary architect along with a few merchants and landlords.[53] This was hardly a body that had any incentive to disturb the prevailing social order. Mitchel and his supporters were clearly in a minority and the result, which was overwhelmingly in favour of O'Brien's proposals, was not unexpected. This led to Mitchel, Reilly and Martin retiring from the council. They did not leave the Confederation, and this would later cause its own problems for that organization. All concerned could not have but been cognisant of the irony involved. Men who only eighteen months earlier had themselves been forced out of the Repeal Association by O'Connell's 'peace resolutions', were now supporting O'Brien's 'peace resolutions', with a similar result: schism. Thus did the protagonists rehearse the conflict between the constitutional and revolutionary brands of nationalism that would persist into the next century.[54] However, the victors were given little time to consolidate their success. A confluence of endogenous and exogenous events quickly conspired to redefine the political topography and offer the prospect of independence. It would, however, turn out to be no more than an illusion.

In the general election of 1847 Thomas Meagher Jr, father of Thomas Francis and, Daniel O'Connell's son, Daniel, were elected as MPs for Waterford City. By the following January, Daniel O'Connell Jr had resigned his seat having accepted the position of British consul in Boulogne, France. In the subsequent by-election Thomas Francis Meagher stood representing the Confederation, confident that he would be chosen as the sole repeal candidate in the city. But the recriminations evident following the Liberator's death the previous May again surfaced with his candidature. Divisions became apparent within the repeal movement in the city. His fate was sealed when at the selection committee meeting a letter was read which seemed to suggest that Meagher's father was supporting a rival candidate, Patrick Costello. Meagher was not endorsed and was forced to appeal to the Tories in the city for support. As Costello did not have the unanimous support of the Repeal Party this seemed like good political strategy. Initially promised the *bloc* Tory vote, his prospects were encouraging especially as the Tory *Waterford Mail* was unambiguous in its support for him. However, the repeal newspaper, the *Waterford Chronicle*, launched a vitriolic attack on Meagher just one week before the election. It branded him a traitor and pronounced that in Waterford 'the public mind is too well trained to receive the base impressions of the Young Ireland spawn. Away then with the political impostor.'[55] This sealed Meagher's electoral fate. Though he was badly defeated the official repeal candidate, Costello, was also unsuccessful. Victory went to the Whig, Henry Winston Barron. From early in the polling it was evident that Meagher was not going to be victorious. Thus, with defeat a certainty, Meagher and his supporters cast their votes for Barron, ensuring his victory. But in many respects Meagher was the author of his own defeat. He and his supporters had been accused of intimidation prior to the election and of attacking the repeal newsroom in the city. This soured many neutral repealers and, importantly, lost him many Tory votes.[56] However, he had little time to feel sorry for himself. Just as the election result was being conveyed, news filtered through of a successful revolution in Paris and the proclamation there of the Second French Republic. Intoxicated on wild expectations and naïve assumptions drawn from this bloodless revolt, the temper of the *Nation* and of the Young Irelanders changed dramatically. The ideological differences that only a few weeks earlier had split the Confederation were now temporarily blurred. An example of the type of revolution Young Ireland wished for was at hand and the aspirations, once theoretical, now took practical form and propelled them headlong towards their destiny.

TOWARDS REVOLUTION

If the growth of liberalism was the greatest political challenge to the established order in Europe between 1815 and 1848, the growth of nationalism was a close second. And in the decades after 1848 nationalism would prove to have an even stronger appeal. Indeed, nationalism as a modern political force was born with the French Revolution. The nation, wrote Sieyes 'is prior to everything. It is the source of everything. Its will is always legal. The manner in which a nation exercises its will does not matter; the point is that it does exercise it.'[57] This philosophy seemed to permeate the Confederation meeting of 2 March, where Duffy announced that the long talked of opportunity had come and that Ireland would be free before summer sunk into winter. He also suggested that 'a deputation be sent to France to tell its people and government how entirely the Irish people sympathized in their success'.[59] What is interesting about this congratulatory address is that at a time when even the most conservative of Young Irelanders, including O'Brien, were making militaristic noises, Duffy, Dillon and Meagher were cautious. Indeed, while all three had, like O'Brien, contributed to the increasing tension and were prepared to countenance a bloodless coup, they were still worried lest any revolution be democratic. This, they believed, would lead to 'death and exile to the middle and upper classes' and would end, they believed, with them being exterminated on 'a Jacobin scaffold'.[59] This merely echoes Meagher's earlier reservations regarding the democratization of any revolutionary intent. One sentence included in the address declared that 'in imitation of your example we propose to exhaust all resources of constitutional action, before we resort to other efforts for redress'. Following the adoption of the address Meagher gave perhaps the clearest impression of the type of independence he envisaged. A deputation should, he said,

> proceed to London and in the name of the Irish people demand an interview with the Queen. Should the demand be refused, let the Irish deputies pack up their court dresses – as Benjamin Franklin did, when repulsed from the court of George III – and let them ... make solemn oath, that when next they demand admission to the throne room of St James's, it shall be through the accredited ambassador of the Irish Republic. Should the demand be conceded, let the deputies approach the throne, and, in firm and respectful terms, call upon the Queen to exercise the royal prerogative, and summon her Irish Parliament to sit and advise her in the city of Dublin.

In such circumstances, he continued 'may we bless the constitution we have been taught to curse and Irish loyalty ... become a sincere devotion to the just ruler of an independent state'. While portents of the future Home Rule movement are evident here, Meagher continued by propounding that if such claim be rejected 'if the throne stand as a barrier between the people and their supreme right – then loyalty will be a crime and obedience to the executive, will be treason to the country ... it will then be our duty to fight ... if the constitution opens to us no path to freedom ... then up with the barricades and invoke the God of Battles'.[60] For these sentiments Meagher, along with O'Brien and Mitchel (for printing them in the *United Irishman*) was arrested for sedition. This only accentuated Meagher's recklessness and on leaving Dublin, whilst still on bail, as part of the delegation to meet the French government, he stated that 'the language of sedition is the language of freedom'.[61] The representatives met with Alphonse de Lamartine, Foreign Minister of the French Provisional Government, at the *Hotel de Ville* on Monday 3 April. However, they failed to elicit support (other than moral) for their proposed revolution. In fact the game was over even before O'Brien, Meagher and the delegation had arrived to play. Prior to the Irish leaving for France the British had been successfully working hard behind the scenes to dissuade Lamartine from offering support. Lamartine did not want to antagonize the British and so jeopardize France's new-found independence; moreover the Irish had the misfortune to meet the most conservative of French ministers and the only one that liked England.[62] Disappointed, the delegation arrived home and was fêted at a reception in Dublin on 13 April. It was at this meeting that Meagher presented to the chairman, Andrew Stricht, a tricolour flag of orange, white and green which he said 'I present ... to my native land and I trust that the old country will not refuse this symbol of a new life from one of her youngest children'. Mitchel replied that he hoped one day to see the flag waving as the national banner.[63]

In the immediate aftermath of the visit to France the revolutionary fervour intensified throughout the country. This passion was accentuated by Mitchel's invective in the *United Irishman*. Whereas most of the confederate leaders still hoped for an accommodation with John O'Connell's Repeal Association and hoped eventually for a domestic legislature within the Empire, Mitchel's call for an independent republic highlighted the ideological aperture now evident within the Confederation. His denouncing of Daniel O'Connell as an aider and abettor of English plunderers and calling him an enemy of the Irish working man, prejudiced any alliance and resulted in a physical assault on O'Brien whilst in Limerick recruiting for a proposed National Guard. With the confederate leaders clearly on divergent ideological paths and becoming increasingly impatient with Mitchel's radicalism, Duffy's pronouncement in the *Nation* that he would prefer a republic to be won by negotiation rather than by revolution led to Mitchel's resignation from the Confederation. But of more immediate concern were the upcoming trials of O'Brien, Meagher and Mitchel. O'Brien and Meagher were both accused of sedition, but their juries failed to convict. Mitchel was not so fortunate. In April 1848 the government passed the Treason Felony Act. This proved to be an ingenious measure which enabled the authorities to strike at the instigators of disaffection, especially the press, without having to invoke the charge of treason which carried a mandatory death sentence, or sedition which carried only minor penalties.[64] John Mitchel was the first major victim of this act when convicted on 26 May and sentenced to fourteen years transportation. There had been expectations within the Confederation that an attempt would be made to rescue Mitchel but Meagher, in an emotional speech, advised against such a futile venture, reminding his audience of the implications of such an act of unconstitutionalism.

Mitchel's conviction had chastened the Confederation leaders. Aware that they could be subjected to a similar fate for past offences, they were forced to abandon overt displays of militarism. A half-baked plan to effect a revolution after the harvest had not been afforded serious military consideration. Thus, convinced of the government's resolve to prevent any attempt at insurrection, the leaders hastened to develop a coherent plan of action. This was realized when Fr Kenyon proposed the creation of a smaller council to effect the blueprint for revolt. A council of twenty-one was subsequently elected from the original council, not from the Confederation in general. Meagher and Kenyon topped the pole with thirty-one votes each. In the absence of O'Brien, Meagher assumed leadership of this inner council and then proceeded to deliver a speech proclaiming 'We shall be martyrs or the rulers of a revolution', which seemed to put the Confederation on a war footing.[65] A formal conspiracy was now commenced with plans drawn up to procure arms from America, France and England.[66] As O'Brien had not been at these meetings, when he became aware of their import he intensified efforts to reach an accommodation with John O'Connell. In early May a confluence of sorts did eventuate when the Irish Confederation and the Repeal Association both dissolved, leading to the creation of the Irish League.[67]

In the immediate aftermath of the trials there was a noticeable proliferation of confederate clubs throughout the country. O'Brien had, however, ensured that the clubs had not been affiliated to the Irish League, thus alleviating the League from any legal responsibility resulting from the clubs' actions. Nonetheless, in a public letter welcoming the new body, O'Brien's intemperate language stating that 'Our controversy will soon narrow itself into the single question . . . *when shall the Irish nation strike?* Upon this question we ought to invite the deliberation of men who are cautious as well as resolute',[68] seemed to John O'Connell and the Catholic Church to imply a willingness to adopt physical force in pursuit of repeal. This provoked O'Connell, at a conference on 20 June, to yet again attempt to impose the 'peace resolutions' on the new body.[69] This was met with derision from O'Brien. O'Connell reacted by announcing, in late June, that he was to retire from politics. He later clarified his position by stating that he had not in fact retired from politics, but that he had refused to join the Irish League.[70] Mindful of the church's opposition to unification, and of his own perceived subservient position within the new organization, his decision ensured that the Irish League would be stillborn. He thereafter closed Conciliation Hall and embarked on a tour of the Continent.[71] But the Church and O'Connell had good reason to be worried; events in Paris in late June would have their own eventful consequences.

The expansion of confederate clubs around the country worried the lord lieutenant, Clarendon. Although aware of the division between the more conservative bishops and a clergy seemingly more supportive of the philosophy of Young Ireland and who in many cases assumed leadership roles in the clubs, he still worried that the Catholic Church would support insurrection. But any chance a Young Ireland rebellion had of being supported by the Catholic Church suffered a terminal blow when, on 23 June, the workers of Paris rose up in a revolt that became known as the 'June Days'. As Europe witnessed a lesson in the horrors of popular insurrection, well over 1,000 people died. Among those killed was the Archbishop of Paris, Denys-Auguste Affre. More than any other event this brought home to the clergy the reality, and consequences, of revolution; it also helped tilt the balance of opinion against Young Ireland. Clarendon, now confident that the bishops would refrain from supporting insurrection, began preparing the ground to prevent the seeds of sedition taking root. Thus, a month before Ballingarry, the French, the original creators of all the excitement, had struck the first blow in the defeat of Ireland's revolution.[72]

Indeed, two months earlier the Catholic hierarchy had already begun to organize resistance to any revolutionary intent. On Friday 21 April a meeting of the Catholic clergy of the diocese of Waterford and Lismore convened in the city's cathedral. Resulting from this assembly an address was prepared and delivered to Queen Victoria. While outlining to the sovereign the inevitability of violence unless the privations endured by the ordinary people as a result of famine abated, nonetheless, the clergy pledged unequivocal loyalty to their queen.[73] This was an important development. In erecting a moral bulwark between constitutionalists and revolutionaries, the Catholic Church had managed to sunder from the political purveyors of revolution any pretensions of moral righteousness that might be used to justify their actions. Thereafter, the Church's support for insurrection was unreservedly withdrawn. The government's actions of April (Treason Felony Act), combined with the position now being adopted by the Catholic Church, along with the horrors emanating from Paris, ensured that any attempt at insurrection would be unsuccessful.

JULY 1848

By early July the country was gripped in an atmosphere of fear and anticipation, especially with the harvest just a month away. A rebellion, if it transpired, was not expected until after the harvest. Indeed, this was the information the government spy, John Donellan Balf, a member of the Confederation, had been giving Clarendon since early in the year. But June witnessed a dramatic increase in the proliferation of the confederate clubs and in the reckless militaristic vituperation from even moderate Young Irelanders. Balf was now urging the lord lieutenant to apprehend the Confederation leaders immediately, as he believed insurrection would eventuate earlier. On 8–9 July, Clarendon reacted by using the prevailing sedition legislation to arrest the more prominent leaders, Duffy, O'Doherty and Doheny. Meagher was apprehended a few days later on Tuesday 11 July at his father's house in Waterford. Although his supporters erected barricades on the bridge over the Suir to prevent his conveyance to Dublin, Meagher interceded with the crowd to refrain from any action that might be deemed unconstitutional and to allow the warrant be executed.[74] Commenting on Meagher's arrest, an editorial in the *Waterford Chronicle* the following day urged that caution be adopted and that nationalists should 'wait until England is involved in a major European war' then 'the *Chronicle* will equip 20,000 men to fight against England'.[75] Subsequently released on bail, Meagher appeared on Sunday 16 July at the 'monster meeting' at the summit of Slievenamon, where he delivered his most bellicose oration in calling the country to arms. The same evening he arrived triumphant into Waterford City at the head of a 20,000 strong procession. The *Waterford Mail*, alarmed at what it perceived as a rapid descent into anarchy, called for the confederate clubs to be closed down. With rumours circulating in Waterford of a possible revolution on 8 August, the newspaper lamented that,

> this overthrow of the constitution is to be attempted at harvest time when in return to the all merciful giver of all good . . . this country is to be deluged in blood, and given over to the demons of anarchy, republicanism and demonism to work their will.[76]

Revolution now seemed inevitable. A diary kept by Mary Smith, housekeeper at Lord Waterford's residence at Curraghmore, Portlaw, outlines in graphic detail the fears and apprehensions of the Protestant community, in particular.

> My Lord [Waterford] says he will barricade the house and get some men in...I only wish all the stablemen were protestants, we should have a better chance, but...fear there are not many...that have not joined the Clubs, and what chance would we have if they all turned out.[77]

A later entry mentions that 'I wish we could hear of Smith O'Brien's head being taken off, he would himself decapitate millions if he could, not forgetting the queen'.[78] Events moved quickly during the next two weeks. On 18 July the cities of Dublin, Cork, Waterford and Drogheda were proclaimed and, four days later, Habeas Corpus was suspended. This seemed to catch the Young Irelanders by surprise. They had only the day before, 21 July, instituted a 'war directory' of five that would have responsibility to decide whether or not a rebellion would take place. But as Meagher said on hearing of the government's decision, 'death itself could not have struck me more suddenly than this news. I had fully calculated...that nothing would occur for three or four weeks at least, to precipitate a rising.'[79] But, as Meagher indicated, the suspension of Habeas Corpus which found the would-be rebels unprepared and in disarray, induced rather than caused the subsequent insurrection. As most of the Young Irelanders had already left Dublin to organize the confederate clubs prior to the government's announcement, Meagher stayed overnight with his friend, P.J. Smyth. Aware that they had been outmanoeuvred, Meagher exclaimed 'We are driven to it...there is nothing for us now but to go out; we have not gone far enough to succeed, and yet too far to retreat'.[80] There was no turning back. Meagher would later, in a letter to Duffy, explain his reason for embarking on this unconstitutional course of action outside of Dublin:

> had we taken a different course, a desperate fight would have taken place in the streets of Dublin [that] would have been stifled in a pool of blood. This...our...followers might not have deplored. But it is one thing to offer to the cause of liberty the tribute of your own life, and another to exact the lives of others. To justify the exaction there must be...belief that the outlay will be repaid by an equivalent result.[81]

And what, according to Meagher, was the equivalent of a nation's blood? Was it the gratification of a just revenge; the vindication of the public spirit, or even the attainment of heroic fame? His conclusion has a chilling resonance for what was to transpire some seventy years later. Answering his rhetorical inquisition, Meagher concluded that none of these aspirations could vindicate the loss of life. However,

> for the liberty of the island...for the power which would enable her to shape her own course through the world, and build up an honourable renown and fortune out of her own soil and genius – for this alone – would we be justified in requiring so great a treasure.[82]

The ideological link with '98 had now been created, and before the week had ended, a bridge for future revolutionaries would be erected on the embers of Ballingarry.

The week leading up to Balingarry was one of frenetic activity as the Young Irelanders attempted to raise an effective fighting force. However, any hope the militants might have had of posing a threat to the government vanished in the face of their own inefficiency, and of a population too confused by faction and demoralized by hunger and disease to have any will to fight. Meagher, in particular, realized this fact when journeying through Wexford, admitting that 'we were aiming far beyond our strength and launching our young resources upon a sea of troubles, among which the Divine Hand alone could guide and save us'. At that moment, he recounted,

> I entertained no hope of success. I knew well the people were unprepared for a struggle; but at the same time, I felt convinced that the leading men of the confederation were bound to go out, and offer to the country the sword and banner of revolt, whatever the consequences might result to themselves from doing so.[83]

Spurred into unprepared action by government coercion, the Young Irelanders crossed through south-east Tipperary, Meagher's ancestral homeland, and south Kilkenny, and found a stratum of dispossessed, broken smallholders and rural proletarians on the edge of economic ruin. While curious regarding this band of middle-class militants, most were dissuaded from joining them by the strenuous admonitions of their priests (themselves under instruction from their bishops), many of whom were themselves leading members of confederate clubs.[84] On 29 July 1848, belligerent Young Irelanders, led by Smith O'Brien managed to besiege a heavily armed group of Tipperary constabulary at the widow McCormack's house at Farrenrory near Ballingarry. But when faced with a constabulary refusing to surrender, O'Brien, paralysed by his own aversion to bloodshed and to the destruction to property, failed to take the initiative. His motley band of would-be rebels was quickly scattered by hostile gunfire. Though Smith O'Brien was quickly captured, hostilities moved southwards to Carrick-on-Suir. This ill-conceived objective lacked organization and a coherent military strategy. An attempt to destroy Grannagh Bridge just outside Waterford City also failed, as did half-hearted assaults on police barracks in Portlaw, Glenbower, and in Kilmacow, County Kilkenny. These, along with other similar failures, convinced the rebels to abandon the attack on Carrick. Thus, after less than a week of ineffectual campaigning the rising was at an end. By the autumn of 1848 most of the leaders were either in prison or on their way to exile. The remaining rebels, including Meagher, Terence Bellew MacManus and O'Doherty, were transported to Van Diemen's Land in June and July of 1849. A last attempt to effect a revolution was made in September 1849, when Joseph Brenan and a band of Young Irelanders attempted to take the constabulary barracks in Cappoquin, West Waterford. However, the attack was repulsed and the leaders fled. Thus ended the revolution.

The 'Sword Speech' propelled Thomas Francis Meagher into the forefront of nationalist politics and along a career path which even he could hardly have envisaged. A revolution of sorts did occur in 1848 and for his part Meagher was transported to Van Diemen's Land from where, in 1851, he escaped to America. Although the Young Ireland Movement achieved little in practical terms, it did, nonetheless, graft itself glue-like upon the increasingly complicated and many-branched tree of Irish nationalism. And while the 1848 rebellion did not bring any degree of finality to the work of 1798, it was in later years seen to have done just that. Thereafter, Irish nationalism would oscillate between the shifting attractions of two traditions – the O'Connellite and that produced by the uneasy amalgam of Young Ireland's romanticism and Wolf Tone's republicanism – each full of contradictions and by their interaction bequeathing a legacy capable of further ambiguities.[85] Nonetheless, the importance that Arthur Griffith attached to the Young Ireland pedigree is illustrated in the manner in which, as the debate on the Third Home Rule Bill progressed and the prospect of Sinn Fein becoming the official opposition in a Home Rule Parliament presented itself, he published editions of writings of Mitchel, Doheny and Davis and of Meagher, implying thereby that Sinn Fein was their direct heir.[86] It would not take much mental dexterity to extend that lineage to Tone and Emmet.

CONCLUSION

The 'Sword Speech', it would be fair to conclude, moved the country a step closer to revolution. But revolution was not inevitable; nor was that its intention. While the 'speech' enunciated a moral justification for the use of physical force in pursuit of political independence, that was a last resort. Meagher's introduction to the 'speech' cautioned against such militarism, deeming it to be impractical given the prevailing circumstances. Nor did he envisage a social revolution; rather, the preservation of social order was his priority. A social order where the Irish middle classes, Catholic and Protestant, governed by a benign constitution, would be enabled to avail of, and access freely, the benefits thereof. Neither were his intentions separatist. His Ireland would be an independent nation within the British Empire, shrouded in a republicanism that was more atuned to and embedded in Jacksonian idealism than the more radical French model. Indeed, the move towards revolutionism had to a large degree been initiated by O'Connell and his glorification of 'historic' violence, a characteristic that adorned the monster meetings. Moreover, it was the apparent subservience and appeasement that characterized the Clontarf climbdown that created the Repeal Association's soft underbelly and made it an easy target for criticism. But O'Connell's action was in keeping with his overall repeal strategy. On this particular occasion the modus operandi adopted was defensive, which in time did elicit practical results.

While the Young Irelanders, in general, failed to comprehend the complexity of O'Connell's overall repeal strategy, O'Connell was also apprehensive with regard to the Protestant hue he perceived was adulterating the Young Ireland Movement. And with Protestant influence waning in the wake of the Municipal Corporations Act of 1840, he (O'Connell) had no intention of allowing that influence to recast nationalism so as to accommodate a Protestant ethos. But it was the worsening famine, and the inimical response by Lord John Russell's Whig government, that was to completely erode O'Connell's credibility and initiate the Repeal Association's terminal decline; and ironically, his death facilitated this process.

Thomas Francis Meagher was a constitutional nationalist. Although not of the same political stature as Daniel O'Connell, one could argue that he was the closest, ideologically, to the Liberator. At best, Meagher was a reluctant revolutionary. Ballingarry was, in many respects, for him an uncharacteristic, albeit necessary, act of unconstitutionalism and of self-sacrifice. As a middle-class Catholic, Meagher was fully aware of the privileges and obligations his status bestowed on him. Thus, having orchestrated secession and preached rebellion, when push came to shove, it was the obligations of leadership and honour and, a keen eye on posterity, that reluctantly propelled him into insurrection.

NOTES

1. O. MacDonagh, *States of Mind. Two Centuries of Anglo Irish Conflict, 1780–1980* (London: Pimlico, 1992), pp.58–9
2. D. Gwynn, *Thomas Francis Meagher* (Cork: National University of Ireland, 1966), p.17.
3. A. Jackson, *Home Rule. An Irish History 1800–2000* (London: Weidenfield & Nicholson, 2003), p.14.
4. K.T. Hoppen, *Ireland Since 1800: Conflict & Conformity* (New York and London: Longman, 1989), p.23. See also, H.F. Mulvey, *Thomas Davis & Ireland. A Biographical Study* (Washington, D.C.: Catholic University of America Press, 2003), p.98.
5. Michael O'Loghlen became Solicitor General and Attorney General in 1835; another friend, David Pigot became Baron of the Exchequer, James Monahan, also became Solicitor General and O'Connell's son, Daniel, was appointed consul in Boulogne, France, in 1847, resulting in a by-election in Waterford City where Thomas Francis Meagher unsuccessfully contested the vacant seat.
6. Mulvey, *Thomas Davis & Ireland*, p.98.
7. Jackson, *Home Rule*, p.15.
8. F. O'Ferrall, *Daniel O'Connell* (Dublin: Gill & Macmillan, 1981) pp.17–18.
9. R. Clarke, 'The Relations between O'Connell and the Young Irelanders', *Irish Historical Studies*, 111, 9, (1942–43), p.18.
10. Mulvey, *Thomas Davis & Ireland*, p.61.
11. T. Garvin, *The Evolution of Irish Nationalist Politics* (Dublin: Gill and Macmillan, 1981), p.51 and Hoppen, *Ireland Since 1800*, p.28.
12. The *Nation*, 15 July 1843.
13. O'Ferrall, *Daniel O'Connell*, pp.117–18.
14. R.F. Foster, *Modern Ireland 1600–1972* (London: Penguin, 1988), p.313.
15. *Nation*, 21 Oct. 1843. See also C.G. Duffy, *Young Ireland: A Fragment of Irish History, 1840–1850* (London: M.H. Gill, 1880), p.386.

16. Garvin, *Evolution of Irish Nationalist Politics*, p.51.
17. *Nation*, 10 June 1843.
18. Clarke, 'The Relations between O'Connell and the Young Irelanders', p.20.
19. P. Maume, 'Young Ireland, Arthur Griffith, and Republican Ideology: The Question of Continuity', *Eire–Ireland*, 34, 2, (1999), p.159.
20. Quoted in MacDonagh, *States of Mind*, p.58.
21. M.F. Cusack (ed.), *The Speeches and Public Letters of the Liberator* (Dublin: McGlashan and Gill, 1875), pp.433–4.
22. MacDonagh, *States of Mind*, p.58.
23. Hoppen, *Ireland Since 1800*, p.27.
24. R. Sloan, *William Smith O'Brien and the Young Ireland Rebellion of 1848* (Dublin: Four Courts Press, 2000), p.128.
25. *Ibid.* See also *Freeman's Journal*, 13 May 1845 and *Nation*, 17 May 1845.
26. *Freeman's Journal*, 20 May 1845. The author was J.C. O'Callaghan, a well-known contributor to the *Nation*.
27. Arthur Griffith (ed.), *Meagher of the Sword. Speeches of Thomas Francis Meagher in Ireland 1846–1848* (Dublin: M.H. Gill & Son, 1915), pp.1–4. This speech took place in Conciliation Hall, Dublin on 16 Feb. 1846.
28. *Irish Citizen*, 4 Nov. 1867. This is contained in Mitchel's warm and obsequious eulogy to Meagher following his death a few months earlier.
29. *Nation*, 20, 27 June. Daniel O'Connell was not present at this meeting. He expressed his criticism by letter.
30. Quoted in Sloan, *William Smith O'Brien*, p.158.
31. Griffith, *Meagher of the Sword*, pp.16–20. Meagher delivered this speech in Conciliation Hall on 22 June 1846.
32. Sloan, *William Smith O'Brien*, p.158. O'Connell's son, John, by standing for election in two constituencies, Limerick and Kilkenny, had caused the by-election. Successful in both, he chose Limerick thus necessitating a by-election in Kilkenny where the repeal candidate, Michael Sullivan, won.
33. Clarke, 'The Relations between O'Connell and the Young Irelanders', p.29.
34. *Nation*, 18 July 1846. See also Clarke, 'The Relations between O'Connell and the Young Irelanders', p.29.
35. *Nation*, 18 July 1846.
36. P.J. Smyth, *The Life and Times of Thomas Francis Meaghar* (Dublin: The Irishman, 1867).
37. *Nation*, 18 July 1846.
38. Sloan, *William Smith O'Brien*, p.161.
39. Griffith, *Meagher of the Sword*, pp.27–9.
40. *Ibid.*, pp.32-3.
41. *Ibid.*, pp.35-7.
42. *Ibid.*, p.46.
43. M. Cavanagh, *Memoirs of General Thomas Francis Meagher, Comprising The Leading Events of His career* (Worcester, MA: The Messenger Press, 1892) p.75. O'Connell would have known Meagher since he was a child. He was also a close family friend and felt that he could draw on this friendship to prise him away from the Young Ireland faction.
44. Sloan, *William Smith O'Brien*, p.176.
45. Griffith, *Meagher of the Sword*, p.72.
46. B.M. Walker, *Parliamentary Elections in Ireland, 1801–1922* (Dublin: Royal Irish Academy, 1978), p.282. O'Flaherty was, however, successful in the 1852 general election.
47. Griffith, *Meagher of the Sword*, p.91.
48. *The Pilot*, 28, 31 May 1847; *Nation*, 29 May, 10 June 1847.
49. Sloan, *William Smith O'Brien*, p.193; also see Cavanagh, *Memoirs*, pp.76–89. This gives a good insight into the differing ideologies driving the various arguments within the Confederation between December 1847 and the eventual split in January 1848.
50. Sloan, *William Smith O'Brien*, pp.199–201.
51. Cavanagh, *Memoirs*, p.82.

52. *Ibid.*, p.88.
53. *Ibid.*, p.77. The full list of the Council of the Confederation is outlined here along with their occupations/professions.
54. Sloan, *William Smith O'Brien*, p.207.
55. *Waterford Mail*, 26 Feb. 1848 and *Waterford Chronicle*, 18 Feb. 1848.
56. *Waterford Chronicle*, 23 Feb. 1848.
57. A. Cobban, *Aspects of the French Revolution* (London: Paladin, 1968) pp.23–4.
58. Cavanagh, *Memoirs*, p.100.
59. Sloan, *William Smith O'Brien*, p.212.
60. *Ibid.*, p.106.
61. *Ibid.*, p.119. The members of the official delegation to meet the French were, O'Brien, Meagher, Edward Hollywood, Richard O'Gorman, Martin McDermott and Eugene O'Reilly.
62. Sloan, *William Smith O'Brien*, p.218.
63. Cavanagh, *Memoirs*, pp.164–5.
64. R.V. Comerford, *The Fenians in Context: Irish Politics and Society 1848–82* (Dublin: Wolfhound Press, 1998) pp.15–16.
65. Cavanagh, *Memoirs*, pp.206–7. O'Brien was not present at these meetings and on hearing the outcome, was annoyed. Cavanagh mentions that he believed Meagher was unconvinced regarding the course of action being advocated but that 'he was impelled to by others – against his own feelings and convictions', p.207.
66. Charles Gavan Duffy, *Four Years of Irish History 1845–1849* (New York: Cassel, Pelter, Galfin and Co., 1882), p.608. One of these agents was John Mitchel's brother, Michael.
67. *United Irishman*, 22 April 1848. See also Sloan, *William Smith O'Brien*, pp.225–7.
68. Letter from O'Brien dated 1 June 1848 and read to a meeting of the council of the Confederation and the committee of the Repeal Association. Quoted in Cavanagh, *Memoirs*, p.213.
69. *Nation*, 17 June 1848.
70. Sloan, *William Smith O'Brien*, p.236. Also see *Nation*, 1 July 1848.
71. Cavanagh, *Memoirs*, p.214.
72. Sloan, *William Smith O'Brien*, p.273. Though not the only incident to inhibit support for rebellion, it was nonetheless important in highlighting the consequences of a 'bloody' confrontation.
73. G. Flynn, 'The Young Ireland Movement in Waterford', Part 1, *Decies, Journal of the Waterford Historical Society*, 18 (1981), pp.4–7.
74. *Waterford Chronicle*, 12, 17 July 1848.
75. *Ibid.*, 12 July 1848.
76. *Waterford Mail*, 22 July 1848.
77. Augustus C. Hare, *The Story of Two Noble Lives: Being Memorials of Charlotte, Countess Canning and Louisa, Marchioness of Waterford* (London: George Allen, 1893), p.307.
78. *Ibid.*
79. D. Gwynn, *Young Ireland and 1848* (Cork: National University of Ireland, 1949), p.176.
80. Duffy, *Four Years*, p.184.
81. Waterford City Archives, Ms. P11/03, *Letter from Thomas Francis Meagher to Charles Gavan Duffy*, 16 Feb. 1850.
82. *Ibid.*
83. *Ibid.*
84. Comerford, *Fenians in Context*, pp.16–17.
85. Hoppen, *Ireland since 1800*, p.30.
86. Maume, 'Young Ireland, Arthur Griffith, and Republican Ideology', p.169. For a comprehensive analysis of this theme see Patrick Maume, *The Long Gestation. Irish Nationalist Life 1891–1918* (Dublin: Gill & Macmillan, 1999).

5

The Final Days of Meagher's Irish Uprising

William Nolan

Following the suspension of Habeas Corpus on 22 July 1848, the Young Irelanders had left Dublin for the country in an attempt to raise support for rebellion.[1] Having by various ways, mainly accidental, reached County Tipperary their chief, William Smith O'Brien, and the Irish Confederation leaders came together for the last time in an upstairs room in Sullivan's public-house in the coal-mining village of Blackcommon. Here they joined the colliery engineers and workers for a drink and a discussion on Ireland's future.[2] They then adjourned for a private session to consider their rather uncertain situation. From the beginning the plan was to organize the country by sending the various emissaries, such as Meagher, Doheny and the others, to the regions in which it was presumed they could rouse the people. It was clear from the events of the past days that neither Doheny nor Meagher, nor indeed any of the Irish Confederation principals, had the degree of local support necessary to defy the Catholic clergy. Meagher had been singularly unsuccessful in his quest to raise 1,000 men in Waterford and was unable to muster a single combatant; indeed it is not certain if he ever reached the city. Yet, the evidence from the state trials shows that he had attained a degree of fame among the public, with many of the witnesses testifying that their primary purpose in attending the impromptu meetings was to both see and hear Meagher.

FINAL PLANS

The meeting on Friday 28 July and the subsequent events of Saturday 29 July sealed the fate of the would-be revolutionaries. Though defiantly insisting that he himself would remain with the colliers, O'Brien advised (ordered) the others to disperse to their own districts and prepare the people for the revolution when the harvest would be in. It was, in effect, the return to the original plan of regional organization that had been pre-empted by the suspension of Habeas Corpus and the subsequent flight of the leaders from Dublin to the south-east. Meagher was partly responsible for this decision, drawn as he was to home territory and the central places of Cashel and Kilkenny, which appealed to the Young Ireland sense of history. Indeed, he had visions of the tricolour flying over the Rock of Cashel where once O'Brien's ancestors ruled, and he was equally aware that the last 'native' parliament had met under the aegis of the Catholic Confederation in Kilkenny during the seventeenth century.

All of the retrospective narratives agree that Meagher was posted to the Comeragh Mountains from where he would organize Waterford City and its hinterland, including Carrick-On-Suir. Doheny was to take command of the district north of Slievenamon. In his narrative, John O'Mahony makes it clear that the Carrick-men preferred to have Meagher rather than their own countyman, Doheny. Meagher's family connections with the district and the economic linkages of Waterford with the tidal Suirside town of Carrick, would have made Meagher better known. The confederates dispersed from Blackcommon with the jarveys ferrying them to safe houses. Meagher left in the company of Maurice Leyne and Patrick O'Donohoe. On his way towards Slievenamon, Meagher gave a red flag – a kind of handkerchief, as one witness was to describe it – to a party on its way to join O'Brien. There is no reference in any of the manuscript or secondary sources of a green, white and orange flag being displayed during the week of revolution in Tipperary.

There has been much subsequent discussion on the decision to disperse rather than remain with O'Brien. James Stephens was to glorify his refusal to leave, and others like Doheny and O'Mahony agonized over what might have happened if they (the only ones to know the Tipperary countryside) had remained. Terence Bellew McManus, who had come from Liverpool via Dublin to join his revolutionary companions in Tipperary, also stayed with O'Brien. It was he, rather than O'Brien, who provided some semblance of leadership the following day. Meagher and his fellow travellers were placed by O'Mahony in a secluded farmhouse on the southern slopes of Slievenamon. The house, which belonged to the Hanrahan family, is now in ruins and almost engulfed by a sitka-spruce plantation. The visitors were hospitably treated and the neighbours came to see Meagher whose speeches they had read in the *Nation*. Some of them may also have participated in the mass meeting on Slievenamon in early July, which was addressed by Meagher and Doheny.

It was a farm servant of the Hanrahans delivering milk to the town of Callan who brought the news of the debacle at the Widow McCormack's house on Saturday 29 July. Callan was also the town from where Sub-Inspector Trant and his men had marched on that fateful morning to effect Smith O'Brien's arrest. The news was confirmed with the arrival of McManus, who had participated in the siege of the house in which the police-party, fearing an attack from the protectors of the confederates, had taken refuge. McManus, as did O'Brien and Stephens, escaped the police and military cordon in place around the collieries. Like all his fellow-confederates, strangers for the most part in Tipperary, McManus turned to John O'Mahony in his hour of need in Tipperary. None of them, apart from Michael Doheny, would have known O'Mahony previously; and it was ironic that it was he who took command of the floundering confederates and was to rally them for a second rising in the autumn.

ON THE RUN

Patrick O'Donohoe in his narrative, recorded how two Dublin confederates, 'P.J. Barry, secretary of the Grattan Club and Grey, secretary of the Swift Club arrived' after tracking the fugitives to Hanrahan's house. In their agitated state they suspected the visitors to be government spies and directed them to return to Dublin. They again tried to meet up with Doheny, crossing and criss-crossing Slievenamon to no effect. Having failed they decided, with O'Mahony's advice, to make for Keeper Mountain which stood out as a blue block some twenty miles north-west of Slievenamon. Meagher, O'Donohoe and Leyne were taken through the old medieval town of Fethard on to Holycross, where they would have glimpsed the ruins of the Cistercian Abbey, and then entering the hill country which stretched west to the county boundary with Limerick. Their guide was local confederate, James Cantwell.[3] It is of interest that the confederates, like the rapparees and tories of the seventeenth century, and Michael O'Dywer and his Wicklow-men in the eighteenth century, perceived the hills as safe refuges. But unlike the hardy mountaineers of earlier days the confederate trio were not suited to rough marching.

John O'Mahony seems to have organized a safe house with a kinsman who had been a Repeal Warden in the parish of Clonoulty. Here they 'slept that night on wet straw in a hay loft and at 5 next morning . . . climbed a range of hills at the base of Keeper Hill'. Dublin Castle was already aware of the felon's track. James Johnston, a surveyor employed in the great mapping programme of Ireland under the direction of the Ordnance Survey, wrote telling of their presence in the vicinity of Clonoulty on 2 August. On the same day, the Tipperary town magistrate reported that 'O'Brien, Meagher, Doheny and Dillon slept in an outhouse of a man named Mahony near Clonoulty on the night of August the first'. It appears that they were still intent on some type of confrontation with the military or police, as the magistrate also noted that 'at the Iron Mile Bridge at the entrance on the New Anglesey line Meagher addressed the people that they were going to Keeper Hill to raise the people'.[4]

As the fugitives were dining in the hill village of Kilcommon, O'Donohoe recalled how the local parish priest, Fr Moloney 'called on us' and 'having admonished the people they deserted us'. It was now that the party split up with McManus remaining in the precincts of Keeper Hill and Meagher, O'Donohoe and Leyne retracing their steps towards Clonoulty. 'We now', O'Donohoe wrote,[5] 'abandoned all hope'. They wandered around aimlessly for the next few wet days – all accounts constantly refer to the wet July and August of 1848. They 'slept in a bog'; 'got lodgings in a farmer's house'; 'the following night and day we were walking through the fields, the people being all afraid to shelter us'. Then a message was sent by Fr Mackey, parish priest of Clonoulty, 'requesting us to surrender and that he would proceed to Dublin Castle to intercede for mercy'. O'Donohoe's narrative has no reference to the following days before their eventual arrest on 12 August, but there are plenty of other accounts from both the police and the priests of Clonoulty parish.

It is misleading to infer that the confederates were totally purposeless in their Tipperary travels. Their long-standing logistical plan was to affect a strategic link between the Suir and Shannon. Meagher was to organize Waterford and its hinterland; Doheny was to do likewise in South Tipperary; Cane was to bring in Kilkenny City; Fr Kenyon, who had promised so much from his base in North Tipperary, was to be the final link in the chain joining the south-east to Limerick City and county to where Richard O'Gorman had been sent in late July. Kenyon backed down under the threat of losing his parish and had dismissed as total folly the Tipperary escapade when Meagher had visited him in late July. None of the others managed to enrol a single fighting man. Yet the evidence from McManus's narrative suggests that the original plan had not been abandoned. McManus wrote two accounts, one for Charles Gavan Duffy, who was even then collecting material for his two-volume history of Young Ireland, and the other for John Dillon, who had managed to evade arrest (with help from the priests) and flee the country. McManus in his narrative for Dillon agrees substantially with O'Donohoe, but he makes it clear that their travelling to the Limerick side of Keeper Hill was to effect a junction with O'Gorman and the Limerick men. But then he added 'if we failed that I was to escape the others to surrender'.

McManus could be implicated in all the major events of the week, particularly the attack on the Widow McCormack's house, whereas none of the others were in Farrenrory that day. 'We had just reached the foot of the mountain [Kilcommon]' he wrote, 'when an evil spirit in the form of a Father Moloney crossed our path and just when we had sat down in a public house to eat some sort of refreshment the Holy Spirit came in and threw down Redington's latest proclamation on the table and by the threats of advancing troops and friendly hints induced them to turn back.' Fr Moloney's intervention forced the confederates to split up, as O'Donohoe recalled, and McManus was to go back up Keeper Hill the next day to light a signal fire which, if answered by other fires, he was instructed to come down and again join his revolutionary companions and their 1,000 men. But there was nobody to meet him when he returned next day, and he turned again towards Slievenamon country, a subsequent adventurous journey to Cork, embarkation on the *N.D. Chase*, bound for the United States and chance arrest on board as Constable Crowley, searching for another suspect passenger, identified him.

SUPPORT OF CLERGY

On 8 August, the *Tipperary Vindicator* reported that Fr Moloney had advised his parishioners that any attempt at insurrection would only end like Ballingarry.[6] Moloney gave his own version of the confederate/Young Ireland incursion to his hill parish in a letter published on 12 August. He wrote:

> persons seemingly connected with the late unfortunate insurrection appeared in this parish. They were persons of the mildest, most gentlemanly, and unobtrusive demeanour, and seemed to take refuge in these mountains to evade the vengeance of the law and not for any other purpose – and repeatedly and fervently did I pray with many others that God may deliver these martyrs of designing and despotic government from the hands of their enemies and the enemies of their country.[7]

This account contrasts with the vehemence of McManus's denunciation, but Moloney went on to refer to another person (McManus), separated from the first group 'disposed to say and do very foolish things but the people took my advice, left him immediately though many told me they "may as well die in war, as die from starvation in the course of the coming winter"'. Moloney was pleased that his decisive actions had 'saved my poor people from bloodshed and further notoriety'.

Fr Tom O'Carroll, in his account,[8] noted how

> the parish priest and curate (O'Carroll) arranged a meeting and were introduced to them in an open field at Parke on 4th of August at around 7pm. The fugitives were forlorn figures; They were somewhat dishevelled from constant walking, the shoes of one or two of the party were quite broken, soiled by many days wear. Their coats and trousers were clotted with mud and heavy with damp.[9]

The account published in the *Freeman's Journal* on 14 November entitled 'Thomas Francis Meagher – his last days in the Tipperary mountains' appears from internal evidence in the text to have been written either by Fr Mackey or his curate, Fr O'Carroll, or both. It has more to say concerning the negotiations with Dublin Castle than Fr Carroll's retrospective and, though at times it reads suspiciously like a composition made with the benefit of hindsight and for the purpose of sanctifying Meagher's honourable course of action, it does articulate the moral burden faced by the Young Irelanders as to the probity of their future actions. Indeed, those like Doheny, who managed to evade arrest, spent much time afterwards justifying the flight and emphasizing that it was not desertion. One imagines that in retrospect the government was quite pleased that it managed to snare such a small catch. Handling four high-profile political prisoners – O'Brien and Meagher were the only national figures of these – was much easier than managing the trials of fourteen. Meagher's rationale in not accepting the means (which were available to him) to escape was grounded on two premises. Firstly, such a course would save him from the suspicion of 'treachery, of desertion, of fear; thus may I still serve the country, by proving that the leaders were faithful to it, even to its fall [and then in pure Meagherism] – that when the ship struck, and the sea was rushing in, they stood to it, and preferred to sink with it, rather than abandon it'.[10]

Such fidelity would do much to counter the government's propaganda machine, which maligned the courage of the Young Irelanders and highlighted their incompetence. But for the confederates, with a keen sense of their future destiny and status in the annals of Irish history yet to be written, there was a second premise. Meagher told the priest that the people would be pleased initially that the leaders had escaped retribution but

> it would be for a time only. I see this as clearly as I see that stream there, that were I to escape, men bidding for popularity against our memory would hereafter say – those leaders incited the people to a certain point – disaster met them there – many of the poorer classes became involved – they were arrested, imprisoned, tried and punished, whilst the leaders, availing themselves of their superior facilities, made off and left these poor fellows – their honest and devoted followers to bear the whole brunt.[11]

Although Fr Mackey stated that his intervention and subsequent negotiations with Dublin Castle were exercises in damage limitation

> fearing that any attempt to arrest them might lead to a collision similar to that which took place at Ballingarry and as the country had declined to act under their guidance a surrender to the government was their most judicious and honourable course.[12]

Yet when the parish priest and his curate first met the fugitives they endeavoured to dissuade them from persevering any longer in the hopeless struggle and recommended them to fly from the country altogether. Meagher declared that although 'many facilities were already afforded him for that purpose' he scorned to 'preserve his life at the expense of his honour'. Certainly Meagher had the network of influential friends and the monetary resources of his wealthy family who were anxious to get him out of the country but the others, particularly O'Donohoe, had no such avenues open to them. 'I had been led to believe', Meagher told the priests, 'that the nation was prepared for totally disassociating itself from England – I and my friends have made the experiment: we have found that the people are not up to the mark, and from this day forward we consider that the death of one man in our defence would be wilful murder, and for that very reason we carry no arms about us'. Although many would have professed a contrary opinion concerning the leaders, it was now clear that Meagher's party had no earthly idea of what to do.

Initially the fugitives refused to entertain Fr Mackey's proposal to act as an intermediary with the government. But their circumstances were so hopeless that they finally consented, and Fr Mackey set off for Dublin on the morning of 7 August with the following proposition to place before the government: 'Mr Meagher and his friends will surrender themselves to the government on condition that they and all others concerned in the late outbreak be permitted to leave the country altogether.' The Clonoulty priests were in a rather delicate situation. They were clearly harbouring those proclaimed by the government for treasonable practices, a crime punishable by death. But perceiving themselves as a parallel jurisdiction to the civil law, they were now about to negotiate with the state for an amnesty not only for Meagher's party, but for all others implicated in the rebellion. It was the total disregard of the local functionaries, the resident magistrates and the police authorities, and their championing of those who had been their bitterest political opponents, which makes the drama enfolding at Clonoulty so compelling a vignette of the complexity of Ireland in the mid-nineteenth century.

Buoyed by the decision, the priests now had no qualms of admitting the confederates to the comforts of Carrigeen for the night of 6 August; and the prospect of clean comfortable beds must have appealed to men on the run for some two weeks. The servants were deployed as sentinels parodying in a curious way O'Brien's armed guards of the previous week. Fr Carroll did not get to bed until 3.30 a.m., 'having visited the outposts'. Fr Mackey was up early next day and left to catch the recently established train connection for Dublin, to place his propositions before the government in the person of Under Secretary Thomas Redington. The visitors breakfasted at 11 a.m., entertained themselves in the garden until dinner time, and it was then agreed that they should remain another night at Carrigeen. It was an amiable social evening. Mr Leyne sang 'The memory of the dead' in a rich fine voice and they retired to bed at 11 p.m. It may have been on this evening that Fr Carroll recorded the account of the previous week's activities, which was to surface and be published by Fr Fitzgerald in 1868. The curate obviously enjoying the military logistics went to bed at 2.30 a.m. after again visiting the watches. Next day, Fr Carroll casually enquired of some parishioners if they knew the whereabouts of the 'outlaws' and he was pleased to discover that they were convinced that they had proceeded in the direction of Tipperary town. Dinner was at five that evening but it was then decided that Meagher's party would be safer elsewhere, and they were lodged by the curate in a farmer's house. The following day Fr Carroll attempted to get more secluded lodgings from a parishioner in a 'very retired and solitary spot' but he was rebuffed.

Mackey wrote informing them that the under secretary, Redington, had made great promises (including a meeting with Lord Lieutenant Clarendon) at his first meeting, but retracted them on the following day. The fugitives were still at Carrigeen on 10 August when they had to flee through the parlour window on hearing of the approach of the dragoons. On 11 August the curate found to his dismay that the *Evening Mail* had distorted the object of Fr Mackey's mission, representing him as an emissary of the insurgents sent to bargain and beg for their lives from the government. The *Mail* charged Meagher with offering to surrender, on condition that his life would be spared. Carroll wrote to Fr Mackey emphasizing the necessity of 'contradicting so base a falsehood' and probably on the prompting of the 'outlaws' then decided to travel to Dublin to ensure that the *Mail*'s damaging report was challenged. Caught up in the drama, Carroll left

Thurles on the 5.30 p.m. train, met Fr Mackey in Dublin who had the story contradicted in the papers of 12 August:

> Sir,
> I am grieved to be under the necessity of addressing you on this occasion but a regard for truth, and a respect for the character of gentlemen who cannot now defend themselves, render my silence any longer possible. The grossest misrepresentations have appeared in some of the newspapers in reference to a communication I have made to the government on behalf of Mr Meagher and some of his friends. I have abstained until now from publishing anything on the subject, lest I might cause embarrassment in any quarter. And besides, I felt confident that the character of the gentlemen in question for honour and disinterestedness were too well established to suffer any detriment from these calumnies. I now give the simple facts of the case, and the public will be able to judge whether or not I have formed a just opinion on the subject. About a week ago, when I heard that those gentlemen had arrived on the borders of my parish, fearing that any attempt to arrest them might lead to a collision similar to that which took place in Ballingarry, I sought and procured an interview with them. I then said that though there were no other reasons, as the country had declined to act under their guidance, a surrender to the government was their most judicious and honourable course. The great obstacle in the way to their following my advice was the fear they entertained, that by so doing, they might appear to abandon those to whom they were committed, or be attempting to secure any special advantage to themselves. They ultimately consented to my making the communication to government, into the details of which it is now unnecessary to enter. It is enough to say it was not of the nature described. *It was not a bargaining for mere life*, as has been asserted. It did not propose any advantage special to themselves. It was conceived in the spirit of brotherly affection and devotion. It contemplated the peace of the country and the speedy restoration of order, and in proof of the perfect disinterestedness that governed this proceeding, I beg to add that one of these gentlemen, Mr Meagher, refused to comply with the more urgent entreaties to escape from the country when the means of escape were offered to him, and this because he had determined to share in whatever penalty awaited his friends.[13]

Meagher likewise, wrote probably from Carrigeen, to the editor of the *Evening Packet*:

> My Dear Mr Mansfield
> A statement has appeared in the *Mail* and *Freeman* of Wednesday, in which I and other parties are charged with making stipulations for our lives with the government.

I need not assure you that this statement has bitterly, most bitterly, indeed cut me to the heart's core. A letter will be sent to you denying this statement and giving the true facts.

You have been so kind and honourable in your conduct towards me always that I rely fully on your kindness in inserting this; and I leave the vindication of my motives in your hands.

My character is now more dear to me than my life, and it is not I am sure too much to expect from a generous opponent like you, a refutation, full and complete of a slander – and which (if unanswered) will deprive me of all that now remains to me – my reputation, my honour and my fame.[14]

ARREST

Carroll returned on 12 August on the 11 a.m. train, reached Thurles at 3 p.m. and met the confederates at Clonoulty at 8 p.m. He impressed on them the necessity of adopting some decided course but found them still as undetermined as ever – they would neither surrender nor try to escape. As the priest arrived he found three policemen outside the chapel gate in charge of a proclamation offering £300 for the arrest of Richard O'Gorman. James Cantwell, who had local connections, had left them the previous day and successfully evaded the authorities. On 13 August, having celebrated the last Mass in Clonoulty, Fr Carroll learned that Leyne, Meagher and O'Donohoe had been arrested close to the police barracks at Rathcannon: 'it appears', he wrote, 'that they left at about eleven last night, with the intention of going to Cashel, and not knowing the country went in the direction of Holycross'.

It seems that the decision of Meagher's party to leave Clonoulty was precipitated by the failure of Fr Mackey's mission to the government. The police account of their arrest differs from that given by Fr Carroll and it details Meagher's views on the Mackey mission and the government response. Gore Jones, the resident magistrate at Thurles, related every aspect in minute detail. In a covering note to his despatch, he told how he had taken a written statement from Meagher who, when writing it,

> was highly excited in consequence of some severe strictures and animadversions which had been made by the *Mail* and by other papers and which had come to his observation when a fugitive, his object in writing this was that his true feeling might be known.[15]

Gore Jones immediately read Meagher's statement to Lord Hardinge and General MacDonald, and they both considered it should be sent to the lord lieutenant. Unfortunately, Meagher's letter is not in the police files but the account of the arrest and detention carries the substance of his chagrin.

The report records that Meagher, Leyne and O'Donohoe were proceeding on foot from the village of Clonoulty towards Holycross when, near the police barracks of Rathcannon (to which the police had returned within the last two days), they encountered a 'Sergeant Madden and a body of police who were patrolling the roads. Sergeant Madden accosted the gentlemen saying "fine night gentlemen", "Good night Boys", rejoined Mr Meagher. A few more ordinary words passed between them and both parties moved off.' Then, obviously suspicious of the strangers a party of six police, armed with carbines, overtook the fugitives and arrested them. Meagher demanded the reason of this, upon which Sergeant Madden replied 'that he had strict orders to act as he was doing'.

O'Donohoe, remembering his legal training, asked the arresting sergeant if they had any warrant and the sergeant replied that he had not. Madden then demanded their names and both O'Donohue and Leyne gave theirs immediately. Sergeant Madden drew Meagher aside and asked him in a whisper 'what was his name'. Mr Meagher said: 'Anything you have to say to me I beg may be said publicly before all, I will not hold any private conversation with you', then (said Sergeant Madden) 'I ask your name publicly, what is it?'. 'My name is Francis Meagher', was the reply.[16]

In the dark early August morning the police fell in two by two on either side of the confederates and marched them back to the barracks about a mile down the road. The prisoners were shown into the kitchen while the police entered into a council of war in an adjoining room and made arrangements to proceed to Thurles. Gore Jones, the resident magistrate, arrived and asked Meagher, 'did he come to surrender'. Meagher replied that he had not the least intention of surrendering. We now have a verbatim account of Meagher's position concerning Mackey's negotiations and we can presume it is substantially the same as he wrote in the statement forwarded to the castle authorities:

> Mr Meagher added that he was most anxious to state this for he had been grossly misrepresented and freely calumniated in some of the papers within the last two or three days. He had been *charged with striking a bargain for his life* – he had done no such thing. The Revd Mr Mackey of Clonoulty had begged of him to surrender and come to terms with the government but that he (Mr Meagher) had refused to make any terms for himself, but pressed by the Rev. Mr Mackey, had authorised him to state that he (Mr Meagher) would surrender on condition *that all parties* involved in the late proceedings should have permission to leave the country. The government had not entertained this proposition, but had offered to spare his (Mr Meagher's) life if he would surrender and plead guilty to the charge of high treason.
>
> That being the condition offered by the government, he had determined not to surrender, he scorned any such condition. He had not begged for his life, he never would, but now awaited his fate whatever that might be, with pride. He rejected the terms of the government that morning in a letter read

> to Revd Mr Mackey and he had done so in the strongest most indignant manner.[17]

The 14 November account in the *Freeman* indicates that there was a further condition laid down by the government – that the arms of the insurgents in the south and the arms in all the disturbed districts, should be delivered up without delay. *The Times* of London carried the following details. 'Meagher was dressed in a blue surtout and battered up trousers of grey tweed. He wore a wide-awake hat (straw) disposed rather theatrically on his head.' O'Donohoe's features were described

> as enormously large and coarse wears no whiskers and the sallow complexion of his face is rendered more repulsive by the puckered seams and harsh lines. He wore on his head an immense fur-cap from beneath which extended the stiff ends of his back hair. Clothes were a cut-away black coat, seedy from wear, dirty light waistcoat and a pair of trousers with a light blue stripe down the side.[18]

Having ensured that O'Donohoe's features consigned him to the criminal class *The Times* dismissed Leyne as a lightweight juvenile with 'an impression of silly enthusiasm' in his face. Sergeant Madden received the considerable sum of £100 as a reward for arresting the fugitives and his companions got £50 each.

CARROLL'S PERSONAL ASSESSMENT

Fr Carroll learned from his visitors that the organization for rebellion had been more extensive than had been imagined, but the suspension of Habeas Corpus precipitated the crisis, with the confederate clubs taken by surprise. These same clubs, he alleged, showed the white feather when asked to match their words with actions, an outcome that did not surprise him. He had obviously listened to much criticism of O'Brien during his contact with Meagher's party and he penned a pithy but reasoned analysis of the movement's leadership:

> Nor is my opinion of the principal leaders much higher. With a few exceptions, they are men totally incapable of conducting a movement to a successful issue, though they had at their command all the elements of success. I never heard of so many instances of incapacity in any one pretending to be a leader as Smith O'Brien. If a country were to be revolutionized solely from the rostrum or editor's desk they would have been powerful agents, but they were entirely unfitted for the drudgery of a camp or the toil or fatigue of a campaign.[19]

Carroll did not sever connections with the imprisoned Young Irelanders and was adopted as a kind of spiritual director by some of them. Leyne wrote to him for some religious books as he was anxious to perform a retreat during his imprisonment and, after a holiday in the Isle of Man, he visited Leyne and O'Donohoe at Kilmainham. Because of the train connection it was as easy for Carroll to travel to Dublin as to Clonmel where the prisoners were moved to await their trials at the State Commission in October. On 12 September, Carroll left Carrigeen at 9 a.m. and did not reach Clonmel until 3.30 p.m. He met Meagher on that evening and on the next day spent an hour or two with the prisoners with the permission of the High Sheriff. This was when Carroll met McManus for the first time; his trial had just terminated and he had been sentenced that morning. Carroll, as did the other priests who encountered McManus, spoke highly of him:

> He is a fine handsome young fellow, full of soul and longing to have another opportunity of doing some service for his country. Had the other leaders possessed the same energy of mind and acted on his suggestions, the movement would have been more general and formidable, and would not have terminated so contemptibly.[20]

In a fashion of the time, McManus presented Fr Carroll with a small dressing case and the priest was pleased that 'His fellow-prisoner must have been speaking of me to him, otherwise I could not expect to have so much of his confidence and regard.' He also encountered McManus's relative, the Rev. Mr Tierney, parish priest of Clontibret, who had been one of the state prisoners in 1844.

O'Donohoe was not as upbeat as the others – referred to by Carroll as 'poor O'Donohue', he asked the priest to stop in town and hear his confession 'as' said he, 'I am a great sinner this time past'. It was the second time O'Donohoe had sought confession in Tipperary and both times he was unsuccessful. Previously, Fr Corcoran of Mullinahone had refused him because of his principled objection to his request and Carroll did likewise 'being of another diocese [Cashel and Emly] and not having faculties in the diocese of Waterford [in which Clonmel was located]'. Meagher was 'the general favourite' among the prisoners and was advised by Carroll 'to prepare himself as a Christian for his impending fate'. He remarked on O'Donohoe's despondency and his tendency to 'drink grog to keep up his spirits' and the others were of the opinion 'that you [Carroll] are the only person most likely to bring him to a sense of his situation and the grave duties it enjoins'. Even failure had bestowed on the prisoners heroic status and they 'are occupied the greater part of the day in giving autographs to ladies etc.'. Meagher, ever the gallant young gentleman, sent a letter by Fr Carroll to Anne Mackey, Fr Mackey's sister and housekeeper, with a gift of a book thanking her for looking after them:

> Clonmel Jail, October 18th, 1848
> My Dear Miss Mackey
> I should have to accuse myself of great unkindliness and ingratitude, did I

not avail myself of Fr O'Carroll's visit to convey to you my warm and sincere thanks, for the anxious care you bestowed on me when I was an outcast in the land of my birth, my love and my ambition.

Indeed I ought to have done so long since, but perhaps these thanks are the kinder for having been deferred till now, and may prove to you that I have retained from the first to the last day of my imprisonment, a lively recollection of your sympathy and attention.

In these sentiments my friends, Mr. Leyne and Mr. O'Donoghoe, most warmly concur, and as a slight testimony of their truth, we beg your acceptance of the accompanying book, the only one we can procure in time for Father O'Carrolls' departure.

I know you will not judge of our feelings from the poverty of the present, many a plain coarse stone in our old green church-yards commemorates more virtue than the gilded costly effigies that crowd the Cathedral aisles of rich and noble cities; and there is more heart, God knows, in these poor church-yards, on funeral days, than ever throbbed in the glittering wake of kings and princes.

With sincere esteem and gratitude,
Believe me, my dear Miss Mackey,
Your, most faithfully,
Thomas Francis Meagher.[21]

On Saturday, 22 October Meagher was found guilty of high treason. His death sentence was later commuted to transportation for life to Van Diemen's Land, to where he was transported, along with his accomplices in 1849. He was destined never to return to Ireland.

NOTES

1. Most had left Dublin prior to the announcement.
2. For the best analysis of the background of the 'Rising' see Richard Davis, *The Young Ireland Movement* (Dublin: Gill and Macmillan, 1987); for a recent account of the week of revolution see R. Sloan, *William Smith O'Brien and the Young Ireland Rebellion of 1848* (Dublin: Four Courts Press, 2000); Brendan O'Cathaoir's *John Blake Dillon, Young Irelander* (Dublin: Irish Academic Press, 1990) has detailed information on Meagher's departure from Dublin in the company of John Dillon. It was their journey to Wexford to inform O'Brien of the suspension of Habeas Corpus that precipitated all the subsequent events in Tipperary. Because Meagher, McManus and O'Donohoe were arrested and tried for their alleged activities in Tipperary, there is much reportage of the various trials in the daily reports in the *Freeman's Journal* and other newspapers. Maurice Leyne, who was arrested with Meagher and O'Donohoe was not regarded as having played as significant a role and he was released from prison when the initial excitement had waned. O'Donohoe's narrative with notes by G. Owen, was published in M. Bourke (ed.) *Tipperary Historical Society Journal*, (Thurles: Tipperary Historical Group, 1998).
3. For a biography of James Cantwell see W. Hayes (ed.), *Moyne – Templetouhy a life of its own. The Story of a Tipperary Parish* (Roscrea Moyne: Templetouhy Historical Group, 2002), vol.

2, pp.168–9. Cantwell escaped to America but in later life returned to Dublin where he owned a hotel.
4. National Archives of Ireland. Outrage Reports 27/1734, 2 Aug. 1848.
5. We are fortunate that almost all of the confederates left accounts of their experiences in Tipperary. For the purposes of this essay the most pertinent are: Patrick O'Donohoe's narrative account, NLI, Ms. 770; Terence Bellew McManus's two accounts which are contained in NLI, Ms. 5886 and the retrospective narrative of Richard O'Gorman Jr, which is also in NLI, Ms. 5886. O'Gorman's account was written in 1881 when in New York. Meagher's own account of events was published in D. Gwynn's, *Young Ireland and 1848* (Cork: National University of Ireland Press, 1949), pp.275–97, but it only deals with the early part of the week in Tipperary and has no reference to his travails in the Clonoulty district.
6. *Tipperary Vindicator*, 8 Aug. 1848.
7. *Tipperary Vindicator*, 12 Aug. 1848.
8. The most comprehensive and interesting account of the revolutionaries in the Clonoulty district is in Rev. Dr Phillip Fitzgerald, *A Narrative of the Proceedings of the Confederates of '48 from the Suspension of the Habeas Corpus Act to their Final Dispersion at Ballingarry* (Dublin: James Duffy, 1868). Fitzgerald's primary purpose in writing a second account of the events of 1848 was to highlight his own role. Fortunately he also included a detailed account of the events which occurred both during and after the 'Rising' itself. He received this material from Fr James Carroll, who was a brother of Fr Thomas Carroll who hosted the 'outlaws' at the parochial house at Carageen, Clonoulty. I have failed to locate the original manuscript or indeed any of Dr Fitzgerald's other papers, but it would appear that Fitzgerald's account of their provenance is accurate. Both Carrolls were inveterate diarists and typescript copies of material relating to ecclesiastical matters, and written recently by the Carrolls, were issued recently by Monsignor Feehan, Boherlahan, Tipperary. For biographical details of the priests referred to here, see W.G. Skehan, *Cashel and Emly Heritage* (Holycross: Abbey, 1993).
9. *Freeman's Journa*l, 14 Nov. 1848.
10. *Ibid.*
11. *Ibid.*
12. *Ibid.*
13. *Ibid.*, 14 Aug. 1848.
14. *Evening Packet*, 12 Aug. 1848.
15. NAI, Outrage Reports, 27/1791, 14 Aug. 1848.
16. *Ibid.*
17. *Ibid.*
18. The *Freeman's Journal*, 14 Nov. 1848.
19. Fitzgerald, *A Narrative*, pp.110–11.
20. *Ibid.*
21. *Ibid.*

* I wish to acknowledge the assistance of Michael Hall and Denis Gahan in locating the Hanrahan house.

6

O'Meagher in Australia

Elaine Sullivan

From late October 1849 to early April 1850, seven members of the Young Ireland Movement were transported to Van Diemen's Land as state prisoners. The majority were intellectuals and well educated, men of influence who had been actively involved in the failed uprising at Ballingarry in 1848. Found guilty of high treason at Clonmel in October 1848, four of these men, O'Brien, Meagher, McManus and O'Donohoe were sentenced to death. These sentences were later commuted to life sentences and transportation. Consequently, in July 1849, the four were transported aboard the *Swift* from Kingstown. William Smith O'Brien, a Protestant landlord and lawyer, had been a Member of Parliament for Ennis, 1828–31 and for Limerick, 1835–1849. Educated at Harrow and Trinity College, Cambridge, O'Brien was a direct descendant of the ancient high king of Ireland, Brian Boru. Thomas Francis Meagher was the son of a wealthy Catholic merchant who had been Mayor of Waterford and who was then the sitting Member of Parliament for the City of Waterford. Terence Bellew McManus was also from a middle-class background in Tempo, County Fermanagh. The fourth, Patrick O'Donohoe, from Clonegal, County Carlow, was a law clerk and journalist in Dublin. Though less prosperous, he was no less committed a nationalist than the others.

Two other Young Irelanders, John Martin and Kevin Izod O'Doherty, were both sentenced to ten years transportation. Martin, a Presbyterian and proprietor of an estate in County Down was a graduate of Trinity College, Dublin, and was also the publisher of the *Irish Felon*. O'Doherty was a Dublin-born medical student and co-publisher of the *Irish Tribune* and, prior to his transportation, was engaged to Eva Kelly, a poet of the *Nation*. Initially they were taken on the *Trident* from Dublin to Cork, then aboard the convict ship *Mount Stewart Elphinstone* they went to New South Wales, Australia. On board the *Emma*, in which these two state prisoners had specially fitted cabins, they then sailed for Hobart.

Among the Young Ireland rebels John Mitchel had been the first to be convicted and in May 1848 was sentenced to fourteen years transportation. Son of a Unitarian clergyman, he was born in 1815 near Dungiven, County Derry. Educated at Trinity College, Dublin, he practised law in County Down but later joined the *Nation* as editor following the death of Thomas Davis. The founder of the later *United Irishman*, Mitchel was a fiery and strongly principled republican and his voyage to Van Diemen's Land, via Bermuda and Capetown, took almost two years. Unlike the other prisoners who had experienced intense personal hardships upon this voyage, Mitchel was alone in not being granted a conditional pardon upon his arrival in Australia.[1] Undoubtedly amongst this group of exiles Thomas Francis Meagher was the most charismatic; a powerful and persuasive writer/orator Meagher romantically believed that 'An eloquent speech is enough, of itself, to disorganize the police force of Ireland.'[2]

ARRIVAL IN VAN DIEMEN'S LAND

Van Diemen's Land, their destination, was an island marginally smaller than Ireland and had been a penal colony since 1803. Situated at the extreme south-east of Australia, it had been discovered in 1642 by Abel Tasman who had been sent by the Governor of the East Indies, Anthonie Van Diemen, to explore the southern and eastern waters of the Pacific Ocean in an attempt to counter the Spanish who, from their colony in the Philippines, tended to dominate the trade of the area. Initially thought to be part of the mainland of *Terra Australis*, it was Matthew Flinders and George Bass' circumnavigation of the island in 1798 that proved that it was separated from mainland Australia by a large strait later named Bass Strait. In 1803, Lieutenant-Colonel David Collins was sent to establish a penal settlement at Hobart and the first shipment of 200 convicts arrived in 1812 on the *Indefatigable*. By a royal proclamation in 1825 Van Diemen's Land was declared a separate colony and Colonel George Arthur was appointed governor.

With the arrival of both free settlers and cheap convict labour the population grew and agriculture flourished on the island. During the 1840s, as many as 5,000 convicts arrived annually and by 1846 the free settlers began lobbying for an end to the convict transportations. In response the authorities suspended transportation for two years and the last shipload of convicts arrived in May 1853. When the discovery of gold in Victoria in 1851 increased crime and encouraged the arrival of freed convicts from Van Diemen's Land, similar objections were echoed from the mainland.The Victoria gold strike resulted in the cost of convict administration to escalating greatly and consequently, to the relief of the free settlers on the island, the transportations ended. To mark the occasion, and to celebrate the end of the felon stigma, the island was renamed Tasmania after its initial discoverer.[3]

The transportation of Meagher and his three Young Ireland colleagues in 1848 aboard the *Swift* was largely uneventful until the ship made its way into the Indian Ocean where gales and heavy rains drove the '...sprightly, handsome, little brig... southwards towards the icebergs of the Antarctic'.[4] The accommodation for the four felons consisted of a large saloon and a bunkroom with four small bunks and was better than they had expected. Captain Aldham treated the four Irish rebels with courtesy and respect while at the same time maintaining his authority. Their days were spent reading their small supply of books, writing letters, verse and journals, and playing backgammon. They dined on simple fare and bottled porter (O'Brien abstained) and spent time on the deck. Spriggs, a marine, was assigned to them as a servant and the four were allowed a large degree of liberty until the curfew at 9 p.m. when their saloon was locked and the key delivered to the captain. Their only conversation, however, was largely restricted to Spriggs, the captain, the ship's surgeon and amongst themselves. During the trip Meagher and O'Brien drew closer in friendship but O'Donohoe, according to O'Brien, was '... an impecunious tippler', a man with few social pretences who tended to be aggressive by nature.[5] McManus, it seems, spent much time fishing on deck and it was during the voyage that Meagher announced that while in exile he would be known as O'Meagher.

After more than 100 days upon the voyage the *Swift* finally made her way up the Derwent River to Hobart. O'Meagher was immediately struck by the natural beauty of the region for, he noted, 'Nothing I have ever seen in other countries – not even my own – equals the beauty, the glory, of the scenery.'[6] Moored at the wharf in Hobart for two nights, the Irish rebels amused themselves by training their telescopes upon the local sights of the port. On their third day at anchor the assistant comptroller and his clerk arrived to inform the prisoners that the governor, Sir William Denison, had received instructions that they were to be granted tickets-of-leave, a form of parole for a six-month period. Although this privilege had been granted in light of their previous good conduct aboard the *Swift*, O'Brien, unlike his three companions, declined the offer for to accept required a promise not to try and escape.[7] Life for O'Meagher, O'Donohoe and McManus, however, would initially be relatively unrestricted as the terms of their tickets-of-leave were generous; while they were not to leave their allotted district, they could live where they pleased, had to report once a month to the police magistrate in their district and promise to observe a 10 p.m. curfew. The three Irishmen also had to give their assurance that they would not frequent places of entertainment such as the theatre or billiard room.[8]

Sir William Denison's instructions had come from Earl Grey, Secretary of State for the Colonies, but Denison himself was appalled by their leniency; he also felt that the lenient conditions were an affront to other prisoners who had exhibited good behaviour during their years of hard labour prior to receiving their own tickets-of-leave. Grey, on the other hand, felt that the gentleman status of the new political prisoners precluded them from hard labour. Transportation itself was, he felt, penalty enough and an actual prison sentence was reserved for second offenders. However, the three ticket-of-leave men were to be settled in districts far from each other and refusal to agree to the terms would result in a prison sentence, a fate which awaited O'Brien.[9]

Actual transportation brought with it varying degrees of punishment and in a seven-year sentence the felon would be initially sent to a convict station for two years; for a fourteen-year sentence the felon would be sent to a convict station for three years. Following this time, and if the convict had remained on good behaviour, the prisoner became a pass holder. With this pass a convict could obtain paid employment, own property and generally enjoy certain liberties. Again, if there were no complaints, the convict could receive a ticket-of-leave. When the prisoner's sentence had elapsed he was free to leave the colony.[10] The districts of settlement a felon could be placed in were somewhat arbitrarily drawn and difficult to check, for usually only natural geographic features marked their boundaries. Nonetheless, the Young Irelanders could not meet outside their designated district. As the *Swift* four had been transported for life, escape would be the only way they would ever see their families or friends again, but escape would, however, preclude them ever returning to Ireland. Their only hope of redemption was continued agitation by their friends for their release and pardon by Queen Victoria.

Before their disembarkation from the *Swift* the four prisoners were visited by the young Irish parish priest of St John the Evangelist church at Richmond, Fr William Dunne, and by the assistant registrar whose task it was to take an inventory of their heights, facial features, colouring of hair and eyes. Following this the prisoners were informed of their various destinations; O'Meagher was sent to Campbell Town, McManus to New Norfolk, O'Donohoe to Hobart and O'Brien was sent to the prison at Maria Island. They also learnt that John Martin and Kevin O'Doherty had also arrived aboard the *Emma* although they were not allowed to communicate with them. During his eighty-two mile carriage trip to Campbell Town O'Meagher continued to marvel at the beauty of the countryside but, as he noted, he was overcome by remorse for although 'I was in raptures with my drive' he remembered that he was being taken 'still further from my own poor country'.[11] Arriving in mid-afternoon with a hat-case and portmanteau his short, quick inspection indicated that he had been sent to a mean, vulgar town whose inhabitants, who were mainly Anglo-Irish, were too intrusive for his taste. Consequently, O'Meagher applied for and was granted permission to move to Ross, seven miles to the south.

O'MEAGHER IN ROSS

Three days later O'Meagher was in Ross and found it much to his taste; it was quiet, unpretentious and offered him the ability to live more privately. He rented two rooms in a small cottage from a Methodist couple, the Andersons, who also offered to cook his meals for him.[12] A solitary life became his lot with visits to Hope's Hotel, a little out of town, where he began a written correspondence with the other six Young Irelanders. Informed that O'Doherty's district was not too far away from his own, O'Meagher arranged to meet with him where their two districts met at Tunbridge, seven miles south of Ross, at the Blackman River. O'Meagher and O'Doherty met on a number of Mondays each technically staying in his own respective district by meeting on the bridge over the river. Here they enjoyed numerous meals together provided by a local inn.[13] A restless man, O'Meagher explored the bush and soon became familiar with his small district and when he found out that Martin's district actually met both his and O'Doherty's in the mountainous area called The Tier, a meeting was arranged between the three at Lake Sorell just north of Crescent Lake. Here every Monday at 11 a.m. the three continued to meet and take long rambles along the lake shore 'talking of old times, singing the old songs, weaving fresh hopes among the old ones that had ceased to bloom'.[14] These were happy days for O'Meagher, '... summer days, all of them; all through the sunshine have floated the many coloured memories, the red griefs, the golden hopes of our sad, beautiful old country'.[15] In time, many of their widening circle of friends also joined them at the lake; Father Bond, Dr McNamara (a Clare man, from Ross), John Connell, the Rev. Thomas Butler and a Mr Clarke. The entertainments were simple and included reading letters from home, reciting poems and plays and singing the well-loved ballads. Nonetheless, O'Meagher was feeling the severity of his exile but felt, at this stage, he and his colleagues had been fairly treated.[16] They had played for high stakes, he wrote to Gavan Duffy, the editor of the *Nation*, 'the highest that could be played for; we lost the game by a wretched throw...we ought, like honourable men, to pay the forfeit, and say no more about it'.[17]

In his own exile, however, O'Donohoe continued to play a risky game. Frustrated at being unable to find permitted employment in Hobart he refused offers of help and accommodation from Bishop Willson, and began a weekly newspaper called the *Irish Exile*, later renamed the *Freedom's Advocate*. Both O'Meagher and Martin had attempted to dissuade him from this venture fearing that O'Donohoe's continued political activity would bring them all into disrepute with the authorities. Although O'Donohoe agreed with these sentiments, he, unlike the others, had no private resources and needed to work to survive. Satisfied of his sincerity and desperation, O'Meagher indicated that he would endeavour to get subscribers for him. While O'Meagher himself took no active part in politics while in exile he did support anti-transportation candidates such as a Mr Kermode. While staying at the Avoca Hotel John Mitchel noticed a number of political tracts left on a table by the candidate and in reading them recognized immediately O'Meagher's style; '...the sharp pen of the hermit of the lake' was pointed in every sentence and in every line Mitchel recognized the 'fine touch of his claw'.[18] O'Meagher's concerns regarding the conditions of O'Brien's confinement, however, did lead him to direct action.

A man more respected for his unbending integrity than his leadership, O' Brien had initially been put under the supervision of a Mr Lapham, a transplanted Kildare man. Under his regime O'Brien had been allowed certain liberties such as exercise, a limited interaction with others and access to written communications. O'Brien's continued resistance to give his parole not to escape, however, continued to embarrass the authorities and finally Dr Hampton, the comptroller of convicts, removed many of the original concessions extended to O'Brien in an attempt to force him to accept a ticket-of-leave. When he received a letter from Maria Island detailing O'Brien's new condition a distressed O'Meagher wrote to Sir William Denison on 17 January 1851 detailing his concerns. Refusing to remain silent upon the matter, O'Meagher demanded an inquiry 'into the treatment pursued towards Mr Smith O'Brien and the state to which, in consequence of his treatment, his health has been reduced'.[19] Although his letter received only a four line acknowledgement from the governor, O'Meagher's intervention had been noted and questions were raised in London regarding O'Brien, leading to the conditions of his captivity noticeably improving.[20]

Largely left to his own devices, O'Meagher leased land on the edge of Lake Sorell and built himself a cottage, an activity that both temporarily absorbed some of his energy and gave him some purpose. While he loved the Australian bush, O'Meagher never came to accept his exile nor embrace the felonious society he despised. While he had made friends such as Fr Dunne and Dr McNamara, he continued to feel a general sense of isolation from the general population of whom almost half were either convicts or ticket-of-leave holders. He acquired a six-oared boat and had it hauled up from Hobart by a wagon and twelve bullocks converting it into a yacht, named *Speranza*', the pen name of Jane Elgee the Young Ireland poet and later mother of Oscar Wilde, which he launched on St Patrick's Day, 1850.[21] On an island in the middle of the lake O'Meagher also leased some sixty acres of land and put his convict farm servant, Tom Egan, to work growing oats and turnips. The lake was well stocked with fish, silver eels and all kinds of wild duck to supplement O'Meagher's diet.[21]

In early April 1850, John Mitchel finally arrived in Van Diemen's Land after his two year voyage on the *Neptune*. He was ill and frail for, as O'Meagher noted, 'the old demon asthma' had taken its toll. Fortunate to have survived, Mitchel's poor health persuaded him to take a ticket-of-leave and he was assigned to Bothwell whose moderate climate aided his recovery. His improving health soon led him to undertake the twenty-four mile ride to The Tier with Martin where he happily reunited with both O'Meagher and O'Doherty. As unbending as ever, O' Brien attempted an escape from Maria Island in August 1851 at the behest of the Irish Directory, a secret society of Young Irelanders in New York City.

The Irish Directory in New York was interested in organizing the possible escapes of all the Young Irelanders in Australia and had indicated its willingness to financially support such bids, in particular for O'Brien.[22] A Hobart physician, Dr McCarthy, along with O'Meagher and O'Donohue, was involved in organizing and setting up the attempt. O'Brien insisted that he would recompense the parties concerned for the expenses incurred. A Captain Ellis, himself a pass holder who regularly plied the waters around Maria Island in his ship *Victoria*, was approached by O'Donohoe to make the attempt. This attempt failed however, due to the duplicity of Ellis who, as O'Brien rushed into the water, made no attempt to pull him in. As a result, Ellis and his first mate, Hunt, were arrested, the *Victoria* was confiscated and they were each fined £60. Being unable to pay, their fines were paid by Dr McCarthy who, unaware of their deceit, was nonetheless worried lest O'Meagher and O'Donohoe be embroiled in the intrigue, thus threatening their ticket-of-leave status, and leave O'Brien more vulnerable. Ellis, however, made good his own escape to America with his ship. The expense for this failed attempt fell heavily on O'Meagher and his father, Thomas Meagher Jr eventually paid all the costs, a rather substantial sum of £550, while rebuking his son that he found the whole episode both improvident and fruitless.[23] O'Brien, who was later to reimburse O'Meagher's father, thought the whole escapade had cost closer to £800 and he wrote in his *Journal*, '... £800 a large sum sacrificed to disappointment and treachery'.[24]

This fiasco was to have important repercussions. Concerned about his future the citizens of Hobart petitioned O'Brien to accept a ticket-of-leave and pressured by both friends and the authorities to do so, O' Brien finally agreed and relocated to the Elwin Hotel in New Norfolk. When O'Meagher, McManus, O'Donohoe and O'Doherty visited him there they officially broke their parole by leaving their districts and while the latter three were arrested O'Meagher, due to the speed of his horse, escaped capture. Although the magistrate dismissed the detainees with a verbal reprimand, Sir William Denison was outraged and he overruled the magistrate, sentencing the three delinquents to three months' hard labour in three different penal stations while revoking their tickets-of-leave. The press was sympathetic to the Irishmen and the *Hobart Town Courier* attacked Denison for attaching '... an infamous penalty to a mere infraction of a petty regulation' and for throwing the three companions amongst 'thieves and murderers' without a hearing.[25] Bishop Willson, the Catholic bishop of Hobart, urged Denison to reconsider and as a result O'Doherty's sentence was reduced but McManus had to serve the full three months although this sentence was later overturned by a higher court. O'Donohoe completed his sentence and was later transferred by Denison to Oatlands but McManus' troubles had not ended for Denison again intervened to quash his dismissal. Having already lost his ticket-of-leave, McManus finally went into hiding prompting the Hobart weekly *Irish Exile* to exclaim 'This last atrocious act of our Domitian has filled the measure of his crimes against the Colony, and the name of Denison the tyrant, is now in every mouth, coupled with the most opprobrious epithets.'[26]

MARRIAGE AND ESCAPE

During the latter part of 1850 O'Meagher met Catherine Bennett. While walking one day he came across Dr Hall, the medical superintendent of Ross, who was in some difficulty as his carriage had become wedged in a rut on the road. Dr Hall's six children were with him, as was their governess, Miss Catherine Bennett, the beautiful nineteen-year-old daughter of Bryan Bennett from Cavan. Bryan Bennett had been convicted of robbing the mail at Trim, County Meath, and having served his time was granted 100 acres of land at New Norfolk. Having assisted the travellers in their plight, O'Meagher accompanied them on their journey and he became a regular visitor at the Hall residence. By Christmas 1850, O'Meagher secured a promise from Catherine that she would be his bride and the wedding date was eventually set for Saturday, 22 February 1851. O'Meagher's proposed wedding was controversial news amongst his friends. The general reaction was that it was folly and inappropriate for him to marry a girl from an inferior social standing. Martin could hardly 'imagine a pleasant or instructive word to say on the subject. God help the poor fellow! – I fear – I fear – one of the very finest fellows that ever lived is in great danger of rushing head foremost and with his eyes open to the very pit of destruction: – and all for want of something to do.' He was also scathing of O'Meagher's application to Denison for permission to marry; 'That he should condescend to make an English jailer the confidant and arbiter of his "great love and affection"', wrote Martin 'and beg the English jailer's permission to marry a wife'![27] O'Doherty, on the other hand, congratulated O'Meagher and in return received a letter from him expressing his thanks; '... I have to thank you, and I do so with the deepest and most grateful affection, for your warm and noble-hearted congratulations'.[28] O'Brien recorded his impression of Catherine in his *Journal* on 24 February 1851. 'She was', he wrote, 'in person and manner very pleasing but in a worldly point of view the connexion cannot be considered advantageous for him.'[29]

The wedding took place at the home of Dr Hall and was conducted by Bishop Willson and later the couple settled into his cottage at Lake Sorell. He seemed much happier and in a letter to O'Doherty exclaimed, 'Glory! Glory! be to Heaven, I am myself again – and for this sole reason, that I have faced the World in this quarter of the earth, have laughed the tinselled and grinning Devil in the face, and gone my own way, calmly, proudly, and defiantly.'[30] O'Meagher's happiness made Martin change his assessment of the marriage and in a letter to O'Doherty he wrote that O'Meagher '... was in great spirits skipping about like a four year old and entertaining Mrs O'M. and the Hall girls who are staying there'.[31] McManus bravely left his hiding place in Hobart to attend the wedding after which he went to the house of a Dean Butler in Launceston to plan his own escape. While a fellow Irishman, John Galvin, pretended to be an 'ill' McManus and kept Dr Dawson, the chief medical officer, busy, McManus boarded the *Elizabeth Thompson* and was on his way to San Francisco. When Galvin confessed his charade Lady Denison ruefully remarked 'what a mistake it was to treat these men so differently from ordinary convicts'.[32]

The Young Ireland exiles had arranged their domestic situations very differently, for while O'Brien never considered bringing his family to Van Diemen's Land, Mitchel had made arrangements for his wife Jenny and their five children to make the journey. They arrived in June 1851 and within a few weeks they had moved to Nant Cottage, three miles from the town of Bothwell where many English and Scottish settler families had made their home. Martin joined them at Nant and he and Mitchel planned eventually to farm the 200 acres surrounding the cottage. A life of domesticity in the Australian bush only temporarily satisfied O'Meagher and the rustic, damp conditions caused him concern regarding his soon pregnant wife. Bennie, as he called her, was never robust and although O'Meagher seemed attentive to her condition and needs, Martin detected a growing irregularity in their relationship. In a letter to O'Doherty he indicated that there had been a serious quarrel between O'Meagher and Dr Hall over his treatment of Bennie and that 'injurious representations' regarding his behaviour towards his wife had been made. Martin added '... I am vexed beyond expression at the vile entanglements he gets himself into – he has hardly any common sense in some respects'.[33] While the Young Irelanders were, in general, romantics who valued the emotions and feelings of other people, perhaps O'Meagher had treated his wife as a social inferior and had been inconsiderate. Maybe O'Meagher did see Bennie as socially inferior and therefore not worthy of consideration. On the other hand, O'Meagher could have just been concerned with the medical advice of Dr Hall for he later wrote to O'Doherty, 'Bennie is much better – indeed, quite convalescent. But those doctors have had some misunderstanding, which makes me exceedingly unhappy. Of that I shall tell you by and bye.'[34] Although evidence clearly indicates that O'Meagher cared for his wife during her pregnancy, it is also evident that McManus' successful escape played on his mind and O'Meagher began to plan his own escape.[35]

O'Meagher made elaborate plans and took his friend John Connell of Glen Connell into his confidence. He would play a crucial role in O'Meagher's escape for it was arranged that at strategic places along O'Meagher's route of escape his friends would give aid and shelter to him. It was also arranged for an appropriate ship to pick him up and that if he was successful in escaping that Bennie and her yet unborn child would follow him to freedom. On Saturday 3 January 1852, O'Meagher sent a letter to the local magistrate informing him that he was resigning his ticket-of-leave and therefore withdrawing his parole. He went on to say:

> I write this letter, therefore, respectfully to apprise you, that after 12 o'clock to-morrow noon, I shall no longer consider myself bound by the obligation which that parole imposes. In the meantime, however, should you conceive it your duty to take me into custody, I shall, as a matter of course, regard myself as wholly absolved from the restraint which my word of honor to your Government at present inflicts.[36]

The letter was signed and delivered to the magistrate by 11 a.m. and O'Meagher remained at the cottage until 7 p.m. when four friends arrived on horseback to warn him that the police were on their way to arrest him. All five then rode into the bush about 300 yards from the cottage and waited, sending a servant back to the cottage to inform the police of their position. At first reluctant to follow O'Meagher and his party, the police eventually approached the group and O'Meagher, standing up in his stirrups, informed them that he was the prisoner they had come to arrest. His friends cheered and with that he spurred his horse and rode into the bush, his friends in pursuit. Following a route determined by the tracks of Bushmen, O'Meagher proceeded towards Westbury via the Western Tier Mountains, rested, took some refreshments at the hut of Job Sims, and shaved off his moustache.[37] From Westbury he rode to the north-east coast where the two fishermen Barrett brothers rowed him to Waterhouse Island, four miles from the coast. The expected ship was late and for the first three days the Barrett brothers waited with O'Meagher, after which he waited alone on the desolate island for seven days, surviving on shellfish and seabird's eggs. Eventually, on his eighth day alone he heard a gunshot, saw the *Elizabeth Thompson* and was taken on board. The trip took him via Cape Horn to Pernumbuco (Brazil) where he transferred to the *Acorn* which took him to New York City and freedom. Following his arrival,[38] 27 May 1852, O'Meagher learned that Bennie had given birth to a son in February, Henry Emmet Fitzgerald O'Meagher. In a lengthy letter to O'Doherty, Martin was highly critical of how O'Meagher had actually broken his parole, making his escape on the same day the authorities received his letter. Mitchel and O'Brien were less critical and the latter indicated that O'Meagher had acted like a gentleman and had given the authorities ample time to arrest him after which he was within his rights 'to use any stratagem for escaping from their hands'.[39]

THE LATER ESCAPES

Transportation, the lack of meaningful employment and the separation from both country and friends undoubtedly increased the exiles' feelings of powerlessness in Van Diemen's Land. This sense of loss, of alienation and of injustice was actually enhanced in their exile by the realization that their trials had been far from fair, a realization brought home when they encountered both John Donnellan Balfe and John Whitty, two previous acquaintances from Ireland. Whitty had been the foreman of the packed jury at the Green Street court-house when Mitchel was convicted of treason and, presumably as a reward, he had been appointed a magistrate on the bench in Australia, a position which carried with it a salary of £800 per annum.[40] Balfe, on the other hand, had a more intimate relationship with the Young Irelanders for he had attended, like O'Meagher, Clongowes Wood College and had also been a member of both O'Connell's Repeal Association and the Irish Confederation. Balfe had also, however, been a government informer and he had fed to Lord Clarendon, the lord lieutenant of Ireland during the 1848 rising, information regarding the rebels' plans. Paradoxically perhaps, as a reward he had also found himself in Van Diemen's Land as the deputy assistant controller of convicts and the recipient of a land grant. Accused of treachery by Duffy in the *Nation*, in August

1852, Balfe responded that O'Meagher had acted dishonourably himself by breaking his parole, an accusation which attracted a stinging reply from O'Donohoe in the *Launceston Examiner*.[41] Sir William Denison again made an example of O'Donohoe by withdrawing his ticket-of-leave and imprisoning him in the Cascades probation station for three months. Bishop Willson's intervention would again help get O'Donohoe freed, but he had decided during his incarceration to follow McManus' and O'Meagher's example and escape.

After one failed attempt O'Donohoe managed to get passage to Melbourne on the *Yarra Yarra* from where he hoped to sail to the United States. Betrayed by a ship's captain who took his money and left him stranded, O'Donohoe, now ill and almost destitute had little option but to take a ship to Sydney in the hope of finding a sympathetic captain who would take him to America. In February 1853, he finally managed to board the *Oberon* for Tahiti and, from there, the *Otranto* bound for San Francisco. He then made his way to New York City where he waited to meet his wife and daughter who were sailing from Ireland to be with him.[42] If O'Donohoe had also broken his parole, he was also a broken man, for the harsh treatment inflicted by Governor Denison had destroyed his health. Denison, perhaps because of O'Donohoe's lower social status, had often used him as a scapegoat and singled him out for punishment. Consequently, O'Donohoe did not long enjoy his freedom for he died hours before his wife was able to land in New York City.

On 8 June 1852, young Henry Emmet Fitzgerald O'Meagher died of influenza just as Catherine was planning to rejoin her husband in New York. His burial, arranged by Fr Dunne at St John's Church, was just three months after his baptism. Near the front door of the church is a tiny grave with the following inscription:

In
Historic Memory Of
Henry Emmet Fitzgerald
Infant son of
Thomas Francis Irish Exile To V.D.L.
And Catherine O'Meagher
Died June 8th 1852
Aged 4 Months
Suffer Little Children To Come
Unto Me For Such Is The
Kingdom Of Heaven Matt. XIX 14

Shortly afterwards Catherine received a letter from her father-in-law, Thomas Jr and Henry, O'Meagher's younger brother. This was the first communication she had had from her husband's family and a bond of friendship was created between them. O'Meagher himself was to receive the news of the death of his son while on a lecture tour in New York.[43] O'Brien was particularly attentive to

Catherine and called to see her often; he had been a regular visitor to the Bennett family before, as had McManus. He sent the following to Catherine:

When snatched from ills that years await
A sinless infant dies
Sweet Babe! How happy is thy fate
The pious pastor cries

Though if thy first born here bereft
Fond Mother, weep no more!
Grateful that he this world has left
To seek a happier shore[44]

In January1853, a compatriot and childhood friend of Meagher slipped quietly into Hobart. Patrick J. Smyth, a Young Ireland exile in New York, had been sent to Van Diemen's Land by the New York Directory to organize the escapes for the remaining four captives. O'Brien, their first choice, had, following his earlier failed attempt, no longer any heart for escaping and feared the financial burden another such failed attempt would place on both him and others. However, John Mitchel was keen to escape but his own bid for freedom would be complicated by the necessity of disposing of his farm and the need to also smuggle Jenny and the children out of Van Diemen's Land.

Following news from Smyth in Melbourne that arrangements had been made for his family's escape Mitchel wrote to Governor Denison on 8 June 1853 that he was resigning his ticket-of-leave and advising him that he personally would present a copy of the note to the magistrate in Bothwell. With Smyth, Mitchel rode to the magistrate's office and handed him the note informing him of his actions and invited Mr Davis, the magistrate, to take him into custody. When Davis did nothing, possibly due to the many Mitchel supporters and friends standing outside his office, Mitchel repeated his offer then bade Davis a 'good morning' and walked outside. His bravado was probably enhanced by having '... a ponderous riding whip in my hand, besides pistols in my breast-pocket'.[45] They galloped off towards Oatlands, and having exchanged horses, turned north towards the mountains guided by a friend who knew the terrain, John Howells, and made for Westbury, a town of Irish settlers. Mitchel stopped at Job Sim's hut, had breakfast and, like O'Meagher, removed his moustache.[46] Mitchel was given refuge by various settlers. He stayed at Dan Burke's for a week while Smyth, in Launceston, was making further plans. With the Westbury police constantly patrolling, Mitchel remained hiding in Burke's attic. When Smyth sent a message of the arrival of a ship, the *Don Juan*, five days hence at Point Sorell, Mitchel, with the Burkes and other settlers, headed off again with eighty miles of rough terrain to cover. By this time Smyth had gone to Hobart intending to cross to Melbourne on the mainland to organize further shipping.

Stormy weather had brought flooding which delayed their journey and prevented Mitchel's planned escape. After further unsuccessful attempts, Mitchel was forced to go to Launceston where the prospects of transport were more encouraging. But severe storms forced Mitchel to take refuge with Fr Butler of St Joseph's, Launceston. Plans were then made for him to go by coach to Hobart in clerical attire as the Rev. Mr Blake. Once in Hobart Mitchel met with O'Doherty and Smyth who did not recognize him in his clerical disguise. It had been five weeks since his departure from Bothwell. It would be another week before he boarded the *Emma*, heading for Sydney. Now as a Mr Wright, Mitchel boarded the ship and was taken to his cabin where Smyth was already waiting. Mitchel had seen his wife and children on the poop deck and, while they had seen him, no word was spoken.[47]

On 29 November 1853, after an escape lasting almost six months, Mitchel arrived in New York City. Another epic journey was over and he had survived the tempestuous rain, floods and storms and sleeping out-of-doors in the unforgiving Australian bush. It was an incredible feat given that he was a chronic asthmatic and had been constantly in wet clothing. But all this was to become a distant memory for, waiting on the pier to welcome him and his family, were his brother Michael and his friend, Thomas Francis Meagher (O'Meagher reverted to Meagher once in America).

EPILOGUE

In February 1853, Catherine Bennett Meagher left Hobart on the *Wellington* to travel to Ireland. Another passenger was Bishop Willson who was able to see to her care. Meeting her father-in-law in Dublin they travelled to Waterford where a crowd, estimated at 20,000, extended an affectionate welcome to her. Shortly afterwards, Thomas Jr and Catherine sailed for New York where Catherine lived with Meagher for a short time. Again Catherine became ill and she returned to Waterford with her father-in-law while her husband went to California for a lecture tour. It was arranged that Catherine would return in the summer, but Catherine was again pregnant and another son, Thomas Bennett Meagher was born in April 1854 and baptized at the Holy Trinity Cathedral, Waterford. Unfortunately, Catherine died a little more than a week after the birth of her son.[48]

For Governor Denison, Mitchel's escape had drawn unwelcome attention to the conditions in Van Diemen's Land and as a result he felt unable to penalize his last three Young Irelander prisoners, O'Brien, Martin and O'Doherty, who were now in the spotlight of world media attention. They, however, were living a quiet life; O'Brien, writing his journal, letters and historical dissertations; Martin, tutoring children; O'Doherty worked as a surgeon at Port Cygnet, south of Hobart. In May 1854, the three were granted conditional pardons. These were achieved by pressure from many of their supporters in America and

Ireland, including O'Brien's brother, Sir Lucius O'Brien.[49] Ironically, P.J. Smyth had been sent back to Van Diemen's Land by the New York Directory in 1854 to arrange their escapes but his arrival coincided with their conditional pardons. Smyth, who had successfully masterminded Mitchel's escape the previous year, had, during that time, met and married Jeanie Regan, daughter of the prominent Hobart merchant, John Regan. On 8 February 1855, Bishop Willson married Smyth and Jeanie Regan in St Joseph's church, Richmond.[50]

The release of O'Brien, Martin and O'Doherty and their departure from Australia was fêted in Hobart, Launceston and Melbourne, where O'Brien was presented with a gold cup. Nineteen inches high and made of 125 ounces of Victorian gold, it was crafted by William Hackett, a young Irish goldsmith in Melbourne. The value of the cup at the time was between £840 and £860.[51] Martin and O'Doherty each received 200 sovereigns. The cup was exhibited at the Paris Exhibition in 1855 and is currently displayed at the National Museum of Ireland, Collins Barracks, Dublin; Mitchel's pistol, given to Dan Burke in Westbury, is also there.

On receiving a full pardon in 1856 O'Brien, who had gone to Brussels to meet his family, returned to Ireland but kept a low profile for the remainder of his life. He subsequently travelled to America, Canada and Europe and died in 1864 while on a visit to Wales. After a large funeral in Dublin he was laid to rest in the family vault at Rathronan in County Limerick. Martin lived in Paris for a time and then returned to Ireland where his brother and sister-in-law had died, leaving their seven children in Martin's care. Remaining in Ireland he raised and educated the children and later married John Mitchel's sister, Henrietta. He died in 1875, aged 63 years, ten days after, and in the same house as, his close friend John Mitchel.

O'Doherty, after secretly returning to Ireland, married Eva in London then returned to Dublin to live quietly until 1856 when the full pardon was received. Arranging to complete his medical studies he graduated in June 1857, with a Fellowship of the Royal College of Surgeons in Dublin. Shortly afterwards he received the Licentiate of the Kings and Queens College of Physicians. He was also awarded a Diploma in Obstetrics from the Coombes Maternity Hospital.[52] Dejected by family concerns and by the apathy of the Irish to solve their own problems, O'Doherty and family emigrated to Queensland, Australia where he became a distinguished surgeon, politician and leader of the Catholic laity. After briefly returning to Ireland (long enough to receive the Freedom of the City of Dublin and become MP for Dublin at Westminster), they again returned to Queensland, but he was unable to resume his practice as successfully as before. With his circumstances in decline he died in July 1905, aged 81 years. Eva died in May 1910 in virtual poverty, and was survived by one daughter. Her other seven children had pre-deceased her.[53]

McManus did not have great success in America. There, his business pursuits were unprofitable. Possibly debilitated by his many punishments and unfamiliar with the cut and thrust of the American business scene, he died in January 1861, aged 37 years. Following a Requiem Mass at St Patrick's Cathedral, New York, Archbishop Hughes in his sermon proclaimed the '... right of an oppressed people to struggle for their liberation'. The remains of McManus were then taken to Ireland; but there, Archbishop Cullen would not permit a Requiem Mass as it would honour a revolutionary. But regardless of the bishop's strong feeling, the Irish people decided to turn out for McManus's funeral. The crowd of mourners stretched for miles behind the casket on the route to McManus's final resting-place at Glasnevin Cemetery.[54]

John Mitchel settled in New York and published the *Citizen*. He was soon at loggerheads with the Catholic clergy as well as those opposed to Catholicism. He later published his *Jail Journal*, and moved his family to Tennessee to farm, supplementing his income with lecture tours and writing. The family stayed in Paris on numerous occasions, eventually returning to America where Mitchel was a staunch supporter of the South in the American Civil War. After the war he was editor of New York City's *Daily News* but his pro-southern opinions again made him unpopular and he was briefly imprisoned. Released on 30 October 1866 (after pressure from Fenian supporters) he resumed newspaper work in New York City where he was persuaded, against his better judgement, to join the Fenian movement. He later became its financial agent in Paris. On returning to America he was twice asked to accept the presidency of the Fenian Brotherhood, but declined; he felt the movement 'no longer offered a chance of success' and that the activities they were proposing were 'inconsistent with their duties as American citizens'. With his health deteriorating a testimonial was launched raising $10,000 for him. But after a serious illness he returned to Ireland.[55] In 1875, Mitchel accepted nomination as the Independent Nationalist parliamentary candidate, and was subsequently elected MP for Tipperary. Declared void by British Prime Minister, Benjamin Disraeli, another poll was organized and Mitchel was again elected, but on petition, Mitchel was again declared ineligible and his seat was assigned to the Conservative, Stephen Moore, in May 1875.[56] However, by that time, Mitchel was already dead. On becoming ill, he returned to Newry and the family home at Dromalane, where he died on 20 March 1875, aged 59 years.

The Vandemonian experiences of the seven state prisoners, their harsh treatment, the feelings of loss and loneliness associated with exile, and the constant boredom and inactivity, took their toll. Thus, the illnesses and premature deaths that ensued were not surprising. Although there were compensations such as a supportive clergy and a sympathetic settler population, Ireland was always in their thoughts. For those who escaped, America proved a fertile ground for Irish pursuits. The life of Meagher, spent on three continents, was colourful and adventurous. Throughout that life he often expressed the hope that he would be remembered for his devotion to Ireland. He was mindful of the quality of those who were of like mind, working alongside him, and whom he described as '... the very pick and pride of the population... I shall never cease to pray that Ireland may be made worthy of them'.[57]

So should I triumph o'er my fate,
And teach this poor desponding State,
In signs of tenderness, not hate,
Still to think of her old story,
Still to hope for future glory.[58]

Thomas Francis Meagher

NOTES

1. S. MacCall, *Irish Mitchel: A Biography* (London: Thomas Nelson & Sons, 1938), p.256.
2. A. Griffith, *Meagher of the Sword* (Dublin: M. H. Gill & Son, 1915), p.202.
3. L. Robson, *A Short History of Tasmania* (Melbourne: Oxford University Press, 1997), p.25.
4. Griffith, *Meagher of the Sword*, p.237.
5. R. Davis, *Revolutionary Imperialist: William Smith O'Brien 1803–1864* (Dublin and Darlinghurst: Crossing Press, 1998), p.295.
6. Griffith, *Meagher of the Sword*, p.239.
7. P. Adam-Smith, *Heart of Exile* (Melbourne: Thomas Nelson, 1996), pp.200–1.
8. R. and H. Patrick, *Exiles Undaunted: The Irish Rebels Kevin and Eva O'Doherty* (Melbourne: University of Queensland Press, 1989), p.64.
9. *Ibid.*, p.60.
10. B.M. Touhill, *William Smith O'Brien and his Revolutionary Companions in Penal Exile* (Columbia, MO, and London: University of Missouri Press, 1981), p.30
11. Griffith, *Meagher of the Sword*, p.248.
12. *Ibid.*, p.252.
13. *Ibid.*, p.257.
14. *Ibid.*, p.255.
15. *Ibid.*
16. *Ibid.*
17. Griffith, *Meagher of the Sword*, p.253.
18. J. Mitchel, *Jail Journal* (Dublin: M. H. Gill & Son, 1913), pp.259–60.
19. Griffith, *Meagher of the Sword*, p.263.
20. *Ibid.*, p.264.
21. T. Kiernan, *The Irish Exiles in Australia* (Dublin: Clonmore & Reynolds, 1954), p.79.
22. T. Keneally, *The Great Shame. A Story of the Irish in the Old World and the New* (London: Vintage, 1998) p.225.
23. Kiernan, *Irish Exiles*, pp.99–100.
24. R. Davis (ed.), *To Solitude Consigned* (Sydney: Crossing Press, 1995), p.341.
25. R. and H. Patrick, *Exiles Undaunted*, p.76.
26. Kiernan, *Irish Exiles*, p.110.
27. *Ibid.*, p.95.
28. Kiernan, *Irish Exiles*, p.97.
29. Davis (ed.), *To Solitude Consigned*, p.212.
30. Kiernan, *Irish Exiles*, p.97.
31. *Ibid.*, p.98.
32. Keneally, *Great Shame*, pp.236–7.
33. Adam-Smith, *Heart of Exile*, p.232.
34. Kiernan, *Irish Exiles in Australia*, p.101.
35. M. Cavanagh, *Memoirs of Gen. Thomas Francis Meagher, Comprising the Leading Events of His Career* (Worcester, MA: The Messenger Press, 1892), p.306.
36. *Ibid.*, p.307.
37. Mitchel, *Jail Journal*, p.295.

38. Cavanagh, *Memoirs*, pp.308–9.
39. Kiernan, *Irish Exiles*, p.102.
40. Mitchel, *Jail Journal*, p.434.
41. Keneally, *Great Shame*, pp.258–9.
42. *Ibid.*, p.276.
43. *Ibid.*, p.256.
44. Davis (ed.) *To Solitude Confined*, p.340.
45. Mitchel, *Jail Journal*, p.291
46. *Ibid.*, p.295.
47. *Ibid.*, p.391.
48. *Waterford Mail*, 2 July 1853 and *Waterford News*, 8 July 1853.
49. R and H. Patrick, *Exiles Undaunted*, p.85.
50. B. Kiely, *The Waterford Rebels of 1849. The Last Young Irelanders and their Lives in America, Bermuda and Van Diemen's Land* (Dublin: Geography Publications,1999), pp.57–8.
51. K. Fahy, 'The William Smith O'Brien Gold Cup', *Australian Antique Collector*, Jan.–June 1981, pp.115–17.
52. R and H. Patrick, *Exiles Undaunted*, pp.110–11.
53. *Ibid.*, pp.263–4.
54. Touhill, *O'Brien and his Revolutionary Companions*, pp.211–12.
55. MacCall, *Irish Mitchel*, pp.358–60.
56. B.M. Walker (ed.), *Parliamentary Elections in Ireland 1801–1922* (Dublin: Royal Irish Academy, 1978), p.314.
57. Griffith, *Meagher of the Sword*, p.186.
58. *Ibid.*, p.331.

7

'Saving the South With All My Might': John Mitchel, Champion of Southern Nationalism

Michael Toomey

In the long history of transatlantic politics the Irish have played an important role. This was especially true in the period of the American Revolution as it would be in the later era of the American Civil War. Irish radical exiles, such as the United Irishmen, often helped shape the tenets of American republicanism itself and those Irish immigrants who arrived after the 1820s, especially the Famine Irish, had to adapt to an American republic that was increasingly suffering the tumults of hardening sectionalist attitudes. While only approximately 84,000 of the 1.2 million Irish immigrants in the United States by 1860 had settled in the eleven states which would later make up the Confederacy, they constituted in ten of those states the largest foreign-born element. As the South, perhaps more so than the North, was becoming more of a distinct and self-conscious region, these southern Irish had to become not only American, but southern as well. Nonetheless, the process of assimilation was common to all and many of the generalizations about the Irish in the North are equally applicable to those who settled in the South.[1]

In the tragedy that became the American Civil War the careers of no two Irish exiles came to personify greater the division that split Irish opinion than did those of Thomas Francis Meagher and his friend, John Mitchel. Thomas Francis Meagher has occasionally been accredited with accelerating the process of Irish assimilation into American society but often overlooked, however, is the role John Mitchel played in the creation of southern nationalism and the similar process of the assimilation of the Irish emigrants into southern society. Patrick Pearse once called Mitchel the supreme evangelist of nationalism, but Mitchel's nationalism was intimately bound up with his notorious rejection of nineteenth-century progress and the liberalism it brought in its wake. For Mitchel, the benefits of modernity were a fraud, a swindle created by a decadent commercial elite and their allies; philanthropists and professors who spouted little more than the laws of the shop till. Mitchel's arrival in the United States in 1853 coincided with the rise of a vocal southern nationalism increasingly identified with the institution of slavery and, in the antebellum years preceding the Civil War, Mitchel came to reflect the opinions of its leading spokesmen. Indeed, parallels can be seen between the development of Mitchel's ideas and those of another disciple of Thomas Carlyle, the controversialist, George Fitzhugh of Virginia.[2] While Meagher and many of his colleagues in the North did not hesitate to offer their services to the Union, Mitchel offered his pen to the Confederacy and, as the war dragged on, Mitchel perhaps came to personify better than Meagher developing Irish public opinion towards the war.

Although Mitchel's passion for southern nationalism was never a forgone conclusion, it was a brand of nationalism that he was nonetheless ideologically more attuned to. Thus, to Irish southerners Mitchel's republicanism could easily be reconciled with the opinions of their region. Indeed, his opposition to the union between Ireland and Britain appeared to mirror the growing conflict during the late 1850s between North and South in the United States. Many northern opponents of slavery had strong connections with anti-Catholic American nativists as well as close ties with anti-slavery British evangelicals, among them Charles Trevelyan who had stated that the Irish Famine was 'the direct stroke of an all-wise Providence'. Irish southerners could draw easy parallels between resistance to the evangelical influence in Britain on the one hand, and the South's zeal to prevent a similar influence permeating the federal government in Washington on the other.[3]

The opening shots of the American Civil War were two years in the future when John Mitchel sat down at his new home in Washington, D.C., to write a letter to his sister. Mitchel was a celebrated Irish patriot and a recent convert to the cause of southern nationalism. Aware that the issues separating the northern and southern states were escalating rapidly he sought neither reconciliation nor believed it was possible. Like the most rabid of southern 'fire-eaters' with whom he had aligned himself, Mitchel had come to believe that the southern states were already in effect a separate nation and, therefore, entitled to a separate government. Should the northern states refuse to recognize this fact Mitchel was prepared to support armed rebellion. In fact, Mitchel had relocated to Washington, D.C., in the hope that he might be able to influence events to bring on an independent South. As he explained to his sister, 'I am saving the South with all my might – indeed so violently that a great part of the South (besides the whole North) think me mad.'[4]

Mitchel was, perhaps above all, a revolutionary. Although he played no part in the Young Ireland rebellion of 1848, his arrest for treason, subsequent conviction, exile and escape, had played well in the American press and made him, like Meagher and other Irish rebels, a celebrity. However, his early years in America had been marked by controversy that left him frustrated, so much so that he abandoned activism in favour of a self-imposed exile in the foothills of Appalachia. There he seemed content to live the modest, reclusive life of an independent farmer. It would prove to be a short-lived contentment and, in hindsight, it is difficult to imagine that John Mitchel, given his own character, would have willingly remained detached from the events that swept the United States toward civil war. Mitchel would also remain a discontented exile for he longed to return to Ireland and when many of his fellow exiles rushed to serve their adopted country, he interpreted the crisis of the Union in a distinctly personal context. Basically he thought, the 'South and the North are two nations' and every year 'widens the breach and reveals the incompatibility of the two systems'.

Frankly admitting 'I prefer the South in every sense', Mitchel saw the quest for southern independence as the product of a unique heritage which set the South apart from the rest of the Union.[5] His support for the movement was a logical extension of his life-long commitment to national self-determination and it was for his commitment to Irish nationalism that Mitchel had been arrested and sentenced to exile, first to Bermuda and then, because of his ill health, to Van Diemen's Land, now Tasmania, in 1851. With the assistance of friends he, like Meagher before him, escaped and finally arrived in New York City in 1853.

CONTROVERSIAL JOURNALIST

In the cosmopolitan atmosphere of New York City Mitchel should have thrived, and for a while he did. His arrival generated the same interest as Meagher's had before him and he was the guest of honour at banquets and receptions. Mitchel was understandably gratified but at the same time he was eager to resume his former life as a revolutionary and journalist. In partnership with fellow Young Ireland exiles Meagher, John McClenahan and John Savage, Mitchel began the publication, in January 1854, of the *Citizen* which quickly reached an impressive circulation of 50,000 copies an issue. While Meagher's own celebrity status left little time for an active role in the paper, Mitchel set much of the tone and provided most of the energy in its publication. The *Citizen* should have provided Mitchel with a secure and effective pulpit from which to renew his struggle for Irish nationalism. Instead, Mitchel seemed from the outset to be bent on antagonizing the very people and groups whose opposition might prove most damaging to its success, including the Mayor of New York City, Jacob Westervelt.[6]

Controversy was Mitchel's preferred intellectual approach to his editorials and an excellent opportunity appeared almost immediately when he and the other Young Ireland exiles were asked to state their position on the slavery issue. There was no issue in America that was more important or more explosive and while a few, including Meagher, prudently refused to offer an opinion Mitchel was straightforward in his endorsement of slavery. Attacked for an endorsement which many thought made him a willing participant in its evil, Mitchel's response to his critics was unequivocal: 'As for being a participant in the wrongs', he wrote, 'we, for our part, wish we had a good plantation, well-stocked with healthy Negroes, in Alabama.'[7] Among those who took immediate offence at Mitchel's 'Alabama plantation' remarks was Henry Ward Beecher, one of the more charismatic leaders of the abolitionist movement. His letters in response were eloquent and forceful in his condemnation of Mitchel, but Mitchel found the whole exchange amusing. To Beecher's claim that historical slavery was illegal, Mitchel claimed that abolitionism itself was 'not only nonsense, but treason'.[8]

The abolitionists were a large and dynamic reform group with an active press in New York City and Mitchel had badly underestimated their following. Even so, he almost immediately moved on to another target, the American nativist movement, the Know-Nothings, which Mitchel viewed as the natural ally of the abolitionists. Anti-Catholic and anti-immigrant, the Know-Nothings attempted to exclude all but native-born Protestants from the political process. A significant political force in the North in the 1850s, Mitchel, himself the son of a Presbyterian minister, found the movement ridiculous. He had never experienced, he wrote, 'so foolish, so filthy, so imbecile a movement as this of the Know-Nothings'.[9] Again, Mitchel failed to grasp the extent of his opponents' support, yet these clashes were minimal in comparison with his clash with the powerful Archbishop of New York City, John Hughes.

Within the pages of the *Citizen* Mitchel exchanged views with Archbishop Hughes on the continuing temporal power of the Pope. Hughes had advised the members of his flock to remain aloof from the slavery issue, suggesting that domestic American institutions were not of their immediate concern. When he attacked Mitchel on his Alabama plantation remarks, Mitchel, in August 1854, responded that it was only natural for Hughes to scorn a profitable plantation in the South as he had a much more profitable undertaking in charging five dollars for each internment in his church cemetery. In fact, Mitchel wrote, he was 'almost tempted, instead of a well-stocked plantation in Alabama, to wish for a well-peopled grave-yard on Long Island'.[10] Mitchel later realized that such an exchange, while clever, was perhaps ill advised. More important, given the constituency of his readers, it was a conflict he was bound to lose. It was, he wrote, 'an unfortunate controversy' which was not only damaging to his own reputation, it was also detrimental to 'the purposes and objectives of the *Citizen*, in as much as most of the readers of that paper, those indeed, to whom it was mainly addressed, were just the flock of this very prelate, and of the rest of the Catholic clergy'.[11] Thus, within seven months of the appearance of the first issue of the *Citizen*, John Mitchel had created enemies among the most visible social reform movement of his day, one of the most energetic new political parties in the North and the most powerful Roman Catholic clergyman in the United States. In the spring of 1854, however, Mitchel had had an epiphany; invited by the Mayor of Richmond to give a talk, Mitchel visited Virginia.

Leaving the *Citizen* to the supervision of his partners, Mitchel was unprepared for the enthusiasm and excitement with which he was received. In Richmond he perhaps realized for the first time the true extent of the division that existed between North and South. As he later explained, he began to understand what he had long suspected, that 'on this land of the United States there are two nations, not only one, and that the two are divided not more sharply by a geographic line than by their institutions, habits, industrial requirements and political principles'. If these two nations did not separate peacefully it would, he predicted, come to war and in such an eventuality 'I think all my sympathies would be with the South'.[12]

While in Richmond Mitchel accepted an invitation to return in June to deliver the commencement address at the University of Virginia in Charlottesville. His address was entitled 'Progress in the Nineteenth Century' in which he complemented the South on her institutions and her ability to resist what mistakenly was viewed as progress. It was progress, he argued, that had caused most of the contemporary problems in the civilized world. It was progress that had brought the British to Ireland and it was progress that had built factories and created a system of class exploitation. The South, however, had resisted such change and its agricultural economy was more stable than that to be found in the North. If her economy was based upon slavery this was less evil than the circumstances which maintained the poverty of the Irish peasant or even perpetuated wage slavery in northern and British factories. The new capitalists, he believed, treated their workers as slaves and if anything, these wage slaves of New England were more in need of emancipation than slaves of the South. Meagher had also been impressed with the South and although he was usually unwilling to involve himself in the slavery issue, he had admitted in a candid moment that in the South he had found none of the social corruptions that are said by northerners to disfigure southern society. Finding the people intelligent, high-minded and patriotic he concluded that he had noticed the absence of the 'squalid misery of the labouring classes of the North'.[13]

Mitchel's rousing reception in Virginia, together with his growing disdain for 'progress' and its accompanying problems, made it increasingly difficult for him to feel at ease among the reformers, nativists and bureaucratic clergymen of New York. Moreover, he was certain now that his continued involvement with the *Citizen* would certainly be counterproductive. He therefore announced in the paper that 'various personal considerations (including a rapid deterioration of eyesight)' had compelled his resignation from the *Citizen*. With no immediate prospects, and disgusted with the hostile reaction to his articles and opinions, Mitchel considered his alternatives. It was readily apparent that his personal philosophy and politics suited him better to the South. Looking through the available literature, he came upon *The Annals of Tennessee*, a recent publication by Dr James G.M. Ramsey. Mitchel was apparently impressed by the sweeping narrative account of Tennessee's early exploration and settlement, and by Ramsey's account of the heroic settlers who waged a successful struggle for independence against the British and their Native American allies. Ramsey's story of the people and events was no less impressive than his description of the rolling hills and well-watered valleys of East Tennessee, and it was there that Mitchel determined to go.

MITCHEL IN TENNESSEE

After divesting himself of his partnership in the *Citizen*, Mitchel began preparations for moving his family and their belongings to Knoxville, the major urban centre of East Tennessee. Knoxville was more than 600 miles from New York City and the absence of a rail line made such a journey difficult in the spring of 1855. Mitchel seemed little concerned with the distance or the difficulty of the upcoming trip, despite the fact that he himself had never been to East Tennessee or spoken to anyone who had been there. He did, however, feel compelled to defend his decision to friends and colleagues, and perhaps to himself, writing that he desired 'to fly from the turmoil of New York, and to try whether life may be possible for us in the woods. Other folks had found it so: so why not us?'[14] Travelling by coastal steamer to Charleston, South Carolina, Mitchel met a number of the leading southern nationalists who were then advocating the reopening of the African slave trade, a cause Mitchel himself became associated with.

In June 1853, Leonidas Spratt, a non-slaveholding South Carolinian, had suggested in the *Charleston Southern Standard* that the slave trade, abolished in 1808 by congressional action, be reopened. This proposal was seen as shocking by many, yet it quickly became a cause supported by the more vocal southern nationalists. A number of political and economic factors recommended such a move. Firstly, in the economic downturn of the 1850s the southern economy had weathered the storm better than the North, convincing many that the southern system was superior. This was the logic of George Fitzhugh's first book published in 1854, *Sociology for the South, or the Failure of Free Society*. The price of slaves had, however, soared and if ownership was to be extended the trade needed to be re-established. Increasing the number of slaves would allow poor whites to become owners, thus allying this class with the planting elite and unifying the South in defence of its institution. Reopening of the slave trade would increase the labour force, help create increased southern self-suffiency and protect southern institutions from northern economic imperialism. Furthermore, and the logic would not be lost on Mitchel, if the institution of slavery was a positive good for the Negro, the reopening of the slave trade would benefit the Africans themselves. While not all slave trade advocates were southern nationalists, most southern nationalists, hoping to unite the South in such a campaign, supported the repeal of the ban on reopening the trade.[15]

Mitchel's arrival at Knoxville did not go unnoticed and he was greeted by the town's mayor, William G. Swan, and a delegation of other dignitaries. Mitchel was pleased to learn that his political ideology was similar to Swan's and the two men immediately became friends. Swan was well read, subscribed to several European newspapers and, more important, his commitment to southern independence was intense; he would later serve as a member of the Confederate Congress. William McAdoo, the attorney general for the state of Tennessee's second district, was also to become a close friend of Mitchel's while he resided in Knoxville.[16] Both men spent the next several days helping Mitchel get acquainted with Knoxville. It was certainly a dramatic change from the frantic pace of life in New York City as the town had only 'two or three decent streets' and these were unpaved and dark after sunset as there were no gas lines in Knoxville. Nor was there any direct railway service into the town but Mitchel believed that the town 'has a great future, and occupies itself much in contemplation of that good time'.[17]

Over the next few days, Mitchel learned that others had noticed his arrival. Most disturbing were the local members of the Know-Nothings who mistakenly, because he was Irish, thought his arrival was linked to the recent construction of Knoxville's first Roman Catholic church; the arrival of so prominent an Irish revolutionary, they believed, could hardly be a coincidence. Mitchel's arrival was also noticed by the town's resident celebrity, William Gannaway Brownlow, better known as the 'Parson'. As Mitchel explained to a friend, Brownlow was 'systematically, frantically chronic in his personal abuse on all and sundry and is generally understood to be perfectly ready to gouge any fellow creature at a moment's notice'. A former circuit-riding Methodist minister, Brownlow was then the editor of the *Knoxville Whig*. As a minister, it was said he had preached his sermons with two loaded pistols beside his Bible on the pulpit in front of him and his vitriolic editorials had earned him many enemies. Brownlow represented the yeoman class in the region for he hated the abolitionists and the planter class with equal ferocity; while not an opponent of slavery, he was a staunch unionist. Nor did he take to Mitchel, yet noted that at least Mitchel was 'genteelly dressed' and appeared to have been well raised. Brownlow reserved judgement on Mitchel for he treated a stranger 'as a gentleman until he proved himself none'.[18]

If Brownlow and the local Know-Nothings offered scant hospitality to Mitchel, Swan and McAdoo, along with other leading citizens, were genuinely excited to have such a well known personality among them. Yet despite their best efforts to persuade him otherwise, Mitchel made it clear that he had no desire to live in Knoxville. Instead, he intended to purchase property in the surrounding countryside and become a farmer. When entering Tuckalechee Cove at the very foot of the Smoky Mountains, Mitchel was immediately enthralled by the wild beauty of the region. The cove was divided by the Little River, a clear mountain stream that Mitchel was forced to cross five times as he made his way up the valley. When he arrived at the last house at the upper end of the cove, he discovered to his delight that the owner was very willing to sell his property. A deal was soon struck whereby John Mitchel became the owner of 137 acres of land and a two-room log cabin with a loft. While his friends attempted to warn Mitchel of the difficulties of such an isolated, rural life and, that the mountain people tended to be barbarians, Mitchel merely replied that he 'intended to become a barbarian myself, and bring up my family in that line of life'.[19]

In May 1854, Mitchel moved wife Jenny and their four children into the property and they immediately learned that the roof leaked badly and that the cabin was cramped and 'excessively desolate'. Mitchel and his family also found that the management of even a small farm was hard work, work he was not terribly efficient at. Though disappointed with the results of his first harvest and aware that farming 'is not very likely to make me rich' he enjoyed the life, especially the independence, claiming 'I am a poor devil enough, but I am done with paying rent. I am free.' To his friends who wondered at his inexplicable decision to take his wife and children to live in what he himself called 'our remote and solitary wigwam at the back of the Alleghenies', there was a simple explanation: 'To some such place I was obliged to bring them, or else submit to a species of life in New York which... is to me the most wasting drudgery.'[20] As Mitchel became used to his new surroundings he concluded 'I rather like all this' and he wrote to a friend in Dublin waxing lyrical regarding the mountains, the forests, the natural beauty of the area as well as the interesting flowers and fauna.[21] Regarding his neighbours, however, he reserved his final judgement. While he found them to be largely 'excessively ignorant and cunning' he liked their sense of independence; if any of them worked for him, he noted, 'I am not only expected to pay them but feel obliged'. He was particularly grateful, he claimed, to have settled in a place 'where I was not known' and he proclaimed that he was done with public life, with activism, factions and raising money.[22] The reality was somewhat different; Mitchel never became a successful farmer and his family increasingly continued to feel cramped in their small cabin and out of place in their remote valley.

By 1856, Mitchel was concerned over his increasing inability to support his family by farming alone and he saw little option but to return to the lecture circuit as 'one evening's average lecturing is a more profitable harvest to me than all the cereal grains and livestock I raise in a year'. He not only scheduled a series of lectures through the north-eastern states during the winter of 1855, he also decided to move his family back to the relative comfort of Knoxville. In his lectures he again spoke of his 'determined abhorrence of the British government' and consoled himself with the hope that he was 'doing some good, and at any rate doing no harm'. Although he was clearly unenthusiastic about lecturing, Mitchel did appreciate the opportunity to travel through the country, and was especially grateful for the opportunity to visit family and friends when his travels took him to New York. Still, as he prepared for a second lecture tour to take place the next year, he was at a loss as to 'what I shall vociferate on... but vociferate I must'. In September 1856, his family left Tuckalechee Cove; looking back one last time Mitchel lamented 'I knew that I should never again call my own so lovely a spot of earth'. From William Swan, Mitchel purchased three adjacent lots just outside of Knoxville for $3,000 and began the construction of a new home. The house was to be built 'among tall oak trees, close to a small stream, with a hill and a wood between us and the "city"... our immediate environs will be sylvan enough'. A fifteen-minute walk took him to the heart of the town where he had access to the excellent libraries of William Swan, William McAdoo and other friends.[23]

In the United States Mitchel proved to be as restless as Thomas Francis Meagher. He clearly missed Ireland and he named his new house 'Nowhere Else'. No sooner had he begun constructing his new house than he abruptly decided to sell it and return to New York City and resume his law career, a decision that disappointed his new southern friends. William McAdoo attempted to change Mitchel's mind by offering him a partnership in his law firm, but Mitchel was not interested. Once the house was sold he was determined to move as his fascination with East Tennessee had been partially based on an idealistic rural life that had not in fact materialized. As mercurial as ever, and although he liked Knoxville, Mitchel wrote that 'no bribe would induce me to live in it a day longer than I must'.[24] As the United States was again experiencing an economic downturn in the summer of 1857, Mitchel had trouble selling his house and the force of circumstance would keep him in the South. Learning that two associates, William B. Reese, president of East Tennessee College in Knoxville (later the University of Tennessee), and Albert Miller Lea, a professor of mathematics at the same institution, had been invited to a conference at Lookout Mountain near Chattanooga, Tennessee, Mitchel decided to join them as an unofficial delegate. His attendance would change his life.

THE SOUTHERN CONVENTIONS

The conference had been called by bishops and laymen of the southern Episcopal Church to create a new university, one that was to be free of northern influence. The three arrived in Chattanooga in early July and Mitchel found himself surrounded by delegates and dignitaries who were for the most part strong southern nationalists; many would later serve prominently in the Confederate army or government. It was a conference designed to perpetuate the best ideals of southern society within the confines of a college campus, and John Mitchel responded with enthusiasm. Together with a crowd of 400 or 500 other spectators, he walked to the top of Lookout Mountain to witness the opening ceremonies. He later described the convention as an effort 'to organize a great southern university... independent of your Harvards and Yales'. Not only was the proposed university intended to benefit the youth of the South, he said, it was intended to 'offer to northern youths the sort of education that will do them good, amend their morals, enlighten their intellect, and purify their hearts'. The trip had exposed him to some of the most ardent of southern nationalists of the day and he was 'exhilarated by the events'.[25] When he returned to Knoxville the town was preparing for another event which would also greatly influence the course of Mitchel's career; in 1857 Knoxville had been selected as the site of the annual southern commercial convention.

The southern commercial conventions had gradually evolved from a conference of Georgia and South Carolina delegates who had met in Augusta, Georgia, in October 1837, to discuss how to improve southern economic development. In April 1838, another convention attended by delegates of seven states met in Augusta to discuss the creation of a southern banking system. This was followed by other conferences in Charleston, Memphis and New Orleans. By 1851, the conferences gradually became dominated by southern nationalists who rejected increased commercialism and, instead, began to champion the southern system. The conference that met at Charleston in 1854 became a political forum dominated by politicos and agitators. During the Savannah conference of 1856, the year Fitzhugh's *Cannibals All! Or Slaves Without Masters* was published, a resolution to reopen the African slave trade gained a great deal of support. At the Knoxville convention, which met in the First Presbyterian Church, just three blocks from Mitchel's house, the delegates elected the southern nationalist, James D. DeBow, editor of *DeBow's Review*, to preside over the proceedings.[26] The reopening of the African slave trade again dominated the convention and although not an official delegate, Mitchel attended the conference and played a prominent role. Appreciative of his activities, the pro-slave trade delegates appointed Mitchel as paid secretary for next year's conference.[27]

At the end of the convention, Mitchel and Swan agreed to jointly publish a newspaper to protect southern rights and agitate for the reopening of the slave trade. Mitchel forgot his plans to return to New York and happily returned to political activism to awaken the South to the abolitionist danger developing in the North in his weekly newspaper, the *Southern Citizen*. First published in October 1857, the paper stated its clear objective; it was to be a journal which addressed itself to first

> rousing the somewhat indignant and too good-natured southerner to their danger; *second* of discussing in all points of view the whole matter of negro slavery, both in Africa and here, so as to make the hesitating and frightened better satisfied with the institutions which their fathers handed down to them, and third (as means to both ends) to advocate earnestly the reopening of the African slave trade in the interest both of blacks and of whites.[28]

Such a position was bound to create a sensation in East Tennessee where sentiment was evenly divided between those who supported the movement for southern rights and those who saw themselves as only marginally involved in the dominant plantation economy. Unionism would prove strong in the region during the Civil War and this was undoubtedly due to the fact that in East Tennessee, unlike Middle and West Tennessee, conditions were not conducive to slavery. In East Tennessee the slave population averaged around 7 per cent, and in some mountainous counties slavery accounted for less than 2 per cent of the population. For many poor whites the option to actually purchase a slave was unrealistic, for the cost of an unskilled field hand could range anywhere from $750 to more than $1,200.[29]

CONTROVERSIAL DEFENDER OF SLAVERY

Mitchel could have hardly selected a less likely region of the South for a paper that advocated the return of the African slave trade, and it is hardly surprising that there was little enthusiasm among most East Tennesseans for his cause. At best, they saw it as a scheme that would serve the interests of the planter class and at worst they found it morally repugnant. Among those whose reaction fell into the latter category was John H. Fleming, editor of the *Knoxville Register*. The *Register* tended to support the American Party, an outgrowth of the Know-Nothing movement, and following the publication of the first issue of the *Southern Citizen*, Fleming published a column which not only ridiculed the notion of reopening the slave trade, it also contained a thinly veiled criticism of Mitchel. During an unexpected meeting between the two a couple of days later outside the Lamar House, Knoxville's most fashionable saloon and hotel, a few heated words led Mitchel to assault Fleming with his walking cane. So forceful were Mitchel's blows that the wooden cane splintered into several pieces and Fleming responded by drawing a loaded pistol. Although the police broke up the altercation the affair was not over. Later the same day Mitchel and Fleming, both armed and accompanied by friends, again met outside the Lamar House in what was clearly a prearranged meeting. Harsh words were again exchanged and a more serious exchange was only prevented by the intervention of their friends. Their ill feeling toward each other, however, continued to simmer for the next several weeks in the pages of the *Southern Citizen* and the *Register*, as well as other papers throughout the region.[30]

Mitchel described the *Southern Citizen* as a 'handsome paper' and his writing continued to prove sharp and effective. He took particular pleasure in attacking any issue that he found absurd, such as the growing fad of vegetarianism, or, as Mitchel called it, the 'potato gospel'. In a review of the book *Christianity in the Kitchen*, wherein the author sought to blend the virtues of religion with those of vegetarianism, Mitchel wrote that the book offered 'a new light on the correspondence between charity and cuisine', . . . the innate antagonism between conscience and conserves . . . [and the] 'universal affinity between turkey and turpitude'. He was likewise amused to learn that a forthcoming edition of *Webster's Dictionary* was to include the word 'telegram'. It was, he claimed, a 'newly-coined word without sense or reason' but one that would be accepted as it had been adopted by both *The Times* of London and the 'Longmires of Paternoster Row'. To balance this silliness, Mitchel suggested that the dictionary insert another word that was likewise gaining usage and popularity: 'bogus'.[31]

Old enemies were attacked and old friends, such as Meagher himself, were defended in the *Southern Citizen*, but Mitchel never forgot that the paper was intended to propagate the concept of restoring the African slave trade and many of the columns in the paper eventually found their way back to that subject. Reporting on an article he had seen in the *Londonderry Journal*, for example, Mitchel wrote that 'the present condition of the peasantry of the wilds of Donegal can, we believe, find no parallel . . . throughout Ireland'. While this was a consequence of the British system, on the other hand, he pointed out, the 'poor negro slave is provided by his master with food sufficient to preserve health and strength'. In a lengthy column entitled 'Africa and Africans', Mitchel described a continent of petty kings, depravity, squalor and cannibalism. No one could argue, he maintained, that any individual living in such circumstances would not be better off as slaves in the American South.[32] With the *Southern Citizen* as a platform, Mitchel returned to the lecture circuit, taking with him a degree of enthusiasm that had been absent in his two previous tours.

His schedule for the winter of 1857 included the major towns of the South rather than the more lucrative cities of the north-east, for his message was intended to rouse the apathetic southerner to impending danger. The solution to this threat was invariably the same: the renewal of the African slave trade. But his reception, even in the Deep South, was not always cordial. The *Mobile Advertiser* described Mitchel as a 'foreign born Don Quixote' and reviewed his presentation in that city under the headline 'An Impertinent Foreign Meddler Rebuked'. The editor claimed that Mitchel's 'ability and boldness seems to surpass his discretion and modesty and he now vapours and struts as if the whole South belonged to him'.[33]

In 1858, Mitchel attended the annual southern commercial conference in Montgomery, Alabama, which was again dominated by the advocates of the African slave trade. As the upper southern states were becoming concerned over the lower South's increasing radicalism they refused to send delegates to Montgomery, and only ninety-five delegates attended the conference.[34] Even without the opposition of the upper South delegates, the proposal to reopen the slave trade was again defeated and Mitchel had to report in the *Southern Citizen* that there was little support for reopening the African slave trade. He noted that 'some of the Southern Journals, to say nothing of the northern, affect, I observe, to make light of this convention and its whole procedures'.[35] For both Mitchel and William Swan this attitude was inexplicable and unacceptable. They eventually determined that their message should be placed in the hands of a more influential audience and thus it was decided that the *Southern Citizen* should be moved to Washington, D.C., and its publication in Knoxville was thus stopped in December 1858. While Swan remained in Knoxville and continued as a partner, Mitchel went with the paper to Washington, D.C.

In Washington the Mitchel family found a comfortable family house on Capitol Hill where he entertained William Smith O'Brien, who returned to America for a visit in February 1858. He introduced O'Brien to many of his political contacts and no doubt renewed his friendship with Meagher who was in the capital to help defend Dan Sickles in April 1859. Mitchel rekindled his interest in Irish affairs by publishing a series of letters in the *Southern Citizen* to Alexander Stephens of Georgia, the future vice president of the Confederate States, on the history of the Young Ireland movement which Mitchel later published as *The Last Conquest of Ireland*. In the summer of 1859, Mitchel made another of his lightning decisions and closed his paper to visit Paris in August 1859. Believing that Britain and France were close to war, Mitchel hoped such an eventuality would be Ireland's opportunity and he wanted to be on hand. Leaving his family in Washington, Mitchel hoped to support himself as a correspondent to American newspapers including the *Irish American*. With the outbreak of the Civil War in April 1861, Mitchel, whose two eldest sons were serving with the Confederate army, decided to return to America. Arriving in New York City in September 1862, Mitchel, with some difficulty, made his way through federal lines and successfully made it to Richmond, Virginia, the Confederate capital.

MITCHEL AND THE CONFEDERACY

At the time of his return Meagher had already become the commander of the Irish Brigade and, like many other Irish in the South, Mitchel volunteered for service in the Confederate army. His poor sight, however, prevented this and, aware of his journalistic abilities, President Jefferson Davis of the Confederacy appointed Mitchel editor of Richmond's pro-administration paper, *The Enquirer*. Joined by Jenny, who became a nurse in Richmond, Mitchel used his ability with a pen to defend the Davis administration, attack the North for prolonging the war for private profit, accuse Lincoln of wishing to foster a race war and castigate Britain for not recognizing the Confederacy.[36] True to character, however, Mitchel became disillusioned with the Davis administration's handling of the war, especially in Tennessee where he thought Davis' pet general, Braxton Bragg, was losing the war, and in the autumn of 1863 he abandoned Davis and joined the opposition paper of John M. Daniel, the *Daily Examiner*. Mitchel was precise in defining his role; 'I point out diligently and conscientiously what is the condition of a nation which suffers itself to be conquered... such as we have experienced in Ireland, and endeavour to keep our good Confederate people up to the fighting point.'[37] Although he refrained from attacking his old friend Meagher when he wrote about the butchering Union generals, Mitchel did attempt to prevent the Irish from being recruited into the Irish Brigade. All Irishmen, he argued, did not support the North. Proportionally in regard to the respective populations, he suggested in January 1863, there were more Irish fighting for the South than there were in Lincoln's army. Unlike the northern Irish, however, they did not flaunt green flags nor '*sunbursts*, nor shout *Fontenoy!* Nor *Limerick!* They are content to fight simply as Virginians, or as Georgians.'[38]

Alexander Stephens thought that Mitchel 'did a great deal in bringing on the war' and Mitchel would suffer personally because of it. His youngest son, William, was killed carrying the colours of the 1st Virginia during Pickett's Charge at Gettysburg. Another son, Captain John Mitchel, was killed commanding Fort Sumter outside of Charleston. Captain James Mitchel lost an arm in 1862 and was later wounded at Chancellorsville. His son, Mitchel's grandson, John Purroy Mitchel, was later elected Mayor of New York City paradoxically, given Meagher's own career in that city, as an anti-Tammany candidate.[39] The end of the war did not bring an end to Mitchel's own suffering for, in June 1865, he was arrested by the military authorities and confined with Jefferson Davis at Fortress Monroe. Receiving very harsh treatment, he was finally released in ill health on 30 October 1865, eight years to the month since he had first started publishing the *Southern Citizen*. In the years that remained to him, Mitchel dedicated himself to Irish affairs and journalism, publishing his *History of Ireland* in 1867. Unlike his friend and former colleague, Thomas Francis Meagher, Mitchel was allowed to return to Ireland in 1874, after twenty-six years of exile.

CONCLUSION

In the United States Mitchel had become a fervent southern nationalist and by far a more controversial figure than Meagher. If Meagher's decision to support the Union was seen as a betrayal of his previous support of nationalist revolutions, Mitchel's support for the institution of slavery has been equally viewed as contradictory to his revolutionary principles. His continued devotion to nationalism, however, made it easy for him to connect the events of his life into a single purpose. 'All the time', he explained, 'I was thinking of Ireland, and contending for the South as the Ireland of this continent'.[40] No less significant than Mitchel's commitment to nationalism was his disgust with 'progress' and the ensuing problems it created. It was this somewhat retrogressive viewpoint that would allow him to entertain a rather idealized image of the South. The past as we all learn, is not as simple as we would like to believe yet at a crucial time in his life Mitchel chose the course of southern nationalism. For him, unlike perhaps a number of Irishmen in the United States, his course of action was not a matter of geography but one guided by what he perceived as revolutionary principles. Mitchel died at Dromlane, Newry, on 20 March 1875.

NOTES

1. David Gleeson, 'Parallel Struggles: Irish Republicanism in the American South, 1798–1876', *Eire–Ireland*, 34, (1999), p.98 and his, *The Irish in the South, 1815–1877* (Chapel Hill, NC: University of North Carolina Press, 2001), p.98. Also, see David A. Wilson, *United Irishmen, United States. Immigrant Radicals in the Early American Republic* (Ithaca, NY and London: Cornell University Press, 1988), pp.1–11.
2. P. Maume, 'Young Ireland, Arthur Griffith and Republican Ideology: The Question of Continuity', *Eire–Ireland*, 34 (1999), p.161. For an introduction to the ideas of Fitzhugh see George Fitzhugh, *Cannibals All! Or Slaves Without Masters*, C. Van Woodward (ed.), (Cambridge, MA: Harvard University Press, 1988), pp.vii–xxxix.
3. Gleeson, 'Parallel Struggles', pp.99–100.
4. John Mitchel to Matilda Dixon, 10 April 1859, Pinkerton Papers, Mitchel Correspondence Public Records Office Northern Ireland hereafter, PRONI.
5. William Dillon, *Life of John Mitchel* (London: K. Paul Trench & Co., 1888), p.107.

6. *Ibid.*, p.38.
7. *Citizen*, 14 Jan. 1854. Also see Rebecca O'Connor, *Jenny Mitchel, Young Irelander* (Tuscon, AZ: The O'Connor Trust, 1988), p.194; Dillon, *Life of John Mitchel*, pp.43–9 and John Hughes to *The Daily Times* (New York) 11 Aug. 1854, quoted in *Citizen*, 19 Aug. 1854; also cited in R. Knowlton, 'The Politics of John Mitchel: A Reappraisal', *Eire–Ireland*, 22, 2, (1987), p.42.
8. Mitchel to Henry Ward Beecher quoted in *Citizen*, 11 Feb. 1854; also cited in Knowlton, 'Politics of Mitchel', p.42.
9. Dillon, *Life of John Mitchel*, pp.52–3.
10. *Citizen*, 19 August 1854
11. Dillon, *Life of John Mitchel*, p.50.
12. *Ibid.*, p.54–5.
13. Brendan O'Cathaoir, *John Mitchel* (Dublin: Clodhanna Teoranta, 1978), p.7. On Meagher, see Denis Gwynn, *Thomas Francis Meagher* (Cork: National University of Ireland Press, 1966), p.44. For Mitchel's view of the concept of 'progress' and his belief in the South, see James Quinn, 'John Mitchel and the rejection of the nineteenth-century', in *Eire–Ireland*, 38, 1 & 2 (2003), and Bryan McGovern, 'John Mitchel: Ecumenical Nationalist in the Old South', *New Hibernia Review*, 5, 2 (2001), pp.99–100.
14. Dillon, *Life of John Mitchel*, p.64.
15. Vicky V. Johnson, *The Men and Vision of the Southern Commercial Conventions, 1845–1871* (Columbia, MI: University of Missouri Press, 1992), pp.134–5. Also see, Ronald T. Takaki, *The Pro-Slavery Crusade: The Agitation to Repeal the African Slave Trade* (New York: Free Press, 1971), pp. 23–85; John McCardell, *The Idea of a Southern Nation. Southern Nationalists and Southern Nationalism, 1830–1860* (New York: Norton & Co., 1979), pp.49–90.
16. Brief biographies of Swan and McAdoo are in Mary U. Rothrock (ed.), *The French Broad-Holston Country: A History of Knox County, Tennessee* (Knoxville: The East Tennessee Historical Society, 1946), pp.443–4, 493–4.
17. Dillon, *Life of John Mitchel*, pp.65, 71.
18. *Ibid.*, pp.69–71. The standard biography of Brownlow remains E.M. Coulter, *William G. Brownlow: Fighting Parson of the Southern Highlands* (Chapel Hill, NC: North Carolina University Press, 1937).
19. Dillon, *Life of John Mitchel*, p.72.
20. Mitchel to Matilda Dixon, 6 Aug. 1855, Pinkerton Papers, Mitchel Correspondence, PRONI.
21. Dillon, *Life of John Mitchel*, p.74.
22. *Ibid.*, pp.73–8. Mitchel to Mrs. Williams, 24 July 1855, in *Collections Relating to Australia*, PRONI. Dillon, *Life of John Mitchel*, pp.73, 78.
23. *Ibid.*, pp.84, 87–8, 90, 97–8.
24. *Ibid.*, p.98.
25. O'Connor, *Jenny Mitchel*, p.228; Dillon, *Life of John Mitchel*, p.97. The university founded would become the University of the South located at Sewanee, Tennessee. See Arthur Ben Chitty, *Reconstruction at Sewanee; the Founding of the University of the South and its First Administration* (Sewanee, TN: University of the South Press, 1954).
26. Johnson, *The Men and Vision of the Southern Commercial Conventions*, pp.95–6, 134–5 145–6; McCardell, *The Idea of a Southern Nation*, pp.91–140.
27. O'Connor, *Jenny Mitchel*, p.226.
28. Dillon, *Life of John Mitchel*, pp.99-100.
29. Chase C. Mooney, *Slavery in Tennessee* (Bloomington, IN: University of Indiana Press, 1957), pp.37, 100. See also Stanley Engerman, *Time on the Cross: Evidence and Methods: a Supplement* (Boston, MA: Little, Brown & Co., 1974), p.73; Wilma A. Dunway, *Slavery in the American Mountain South* (Cambridge, CT: Cambridge University Press, 2003).
30. *Knoxville Register*, 24 Sept., 1 Oct. and 15 Oct. See also O'Connor, *Jenny Mitchel*, pp.229–30. Unfortunately, Mitchel's version of this affair as recorded in the *Southern Citizen* is no longer available.
31. *Southern Citizen*, 21 Jan., 18 March 1858.

32. *Ibid.*, 21 Jan. 1858, 18 March 1858.
33. The *Mobile Advertiser* comments were republished in Brownlow's *Knoxville Whig*, 24 July 1858.
34. Johnson, *The Men and Vision of the Southern Commercial Conventions*, p.27; McCardell, *The Idea of a Southern Nation*, pp. 131–5.
35. *Southern Citizen*, 3 June 1858.
36. Kelly O' Grady, *Clear the Confederate Way! The Irish in the Army of Northern Virginia* (Mason City, IA: Savas Publishing, 2000), pp.40–5.
37. *Ibid.*, p.45.
38. Cited in Thomas Kenneally, *The Great Shame and the Triumph of the Irish in the English-Speaking World* (New York: Knopf, 1998) p.376.
39. O'Grady, *Clear the Confederate Way!*, pp.207–8; Kenneally, *Great Shame*, pp.385, 391–9. See also Ernest B. Ferguson, *Ashes of Glory. Richmond at War* (New York: Knopf, 1996) pp.278–9.
40. Dillon, *Life of John Mitchel*, p.101.

8

An Irish Republican Abroad: Thomas Francis Meagher in the United States, 1852–65

Rory T. Cornish

On 27 May 1852, a rather handsome, short man with a strange English upper-class lisping accent presented himself at the law office of Dillion and O'Gorman, William Street, New York City. By 9 p.m. that evening 7,000 fellow Irish exiles milled around the neighbourhood to catch a glimpse of one of Ireland's greatest national orators, and companies of the largely Irish 69th New York State Militia paraded in his honour.[1] American politicians such as Senator Henry Foote of Mississippi, Daniel Webster, the Secretary of State, and even the President himself, Millard Fillmore, had interested themselves in securing this young Irish republican's release from political exile in Van Diemen's Land. However, Thomas Francis Meagher had engineered his own dramatic escape and arrived in the American Republic.

Having broken his parole to escape, Meagher would be exempted from the conditional pardons later issued for the Young Ireland rebels of 1848 by Lord Palmerston in 1854. Consequently, Meagher's dramatic arrival in the United States would compel him to remain in exile. Becoming perhaps the most assimilated of all Irish exiled leaders in the antebellum United States, Meagher became an American citizen in May 1857, and during the American Civil War, 1861–65, he gained fame as a Union soldier. Meagher would become the founder and first commanding general of the Irish Brigade, the most famous ethnic unit to fight for the preservation of the Union in the Army of the Potomac.

Meagher was not the first of his family to face political exile from Ireland. In the seventeenth century, many O'Meaghers had supported the unfortunate James II and had left Ireland as Wild Geese to find their fortune in the service of the Catholic armies of France and Spain. Following his own transportation to Van Diemen's Land in 1849, he had dramatically changed his name to O'Meagher and would later extol the bravery of exiled Irish soldiers, including a number of O'Meaghers, who had taken part in the French defeat of the English at Fontenoy in May 1745. A number of his own collateral ancestors had served in the French Irish Brigade including Major O'Meagher of Dillion's Regiment, Major Patrick O'Meagher of Bulkeley's Regiment and Captain Philip O'Meagher of O'Brien Regiment.[2] The most famous of the Meagher Wild Geese was undoubtedly Thaddeus Meagher (1690–1765), who was later known as Chevalier de Maar. Following service in the French army he was commissioned in the Saxon lifeguards of Frederick Augustus II, King of Poland

and elector of Saxony, later rising to the rank of lieutenant general in the Polish army, 1752.[3]

His own immediate family had also left Ireland to seek their fortune. His grandfather had left Tipperary for Newfoundland to build up a successful transatlantic provision trade, which served the many Waterford immigrants who had emigrated to the province. His father, Thomas Meagher Jr (1789–1874), had been born in Newfoundland but returned to Ireland to manage the family's growing mercantile concerns in Waterford. Elected Mayor of Waterford in 1843, he later represented the city in the British House of Commons, 1847–57, as a political ally of Daniel O'Connell. Thomas Francis Meagher was thus the scion of a prosperous, urban mercantile family of some standing but his adoption of a more radical republican outlook would change his life forever.

While the British authorities remained largely silent regarding Meagher's escape to the United States, the Irish nationalist newspaper the *Nation* was ecstatic; 'Meagher in America', it boomed, 'what a triumph . . . we conceive a great career for him under the flag of Washington'. To the republic, which had previously welcomed many other Irish republican exiles, especially the rebels of 1798, the *Nation* called upon American citizens to honour Meagher for he would undoubtedly 'fulfil a great destiny there' and open a new chapter in the history of Ireland.[4] Many of Meagher's contemporaries in the United States would later emphasize the importance of Meagher's career there. Eager to promote the symbolic importance of Meagher's commitment to both the cause of Irish independence and the preservation of the Union, his supporters often overstated their case. For example, Michael Cavanagh claimed that 'save for Lafayette alone, no foreign visitor to this Republic was accorded such a generous, hearty and spontaneous welcome as that given to Thomas Francis Meagher on his arrival in New York'.[5] Similarly, upon reflecting on Meagher's military career his orderly, William McCarter, a Derry-born private of the 116th Pennsylvania Infantry, thought Meagher's military skill and courage made him a general 'second to none in the Army of the Potomac'.[6] Regarding Meagher's short career in the United States a number of points need to be made.

Firstly, Meagher was not the only 1848 European republican rebel ecstatically welcomed by the citizens of the United States who, proud of their republican principles, flocked to listen to the oratory of their European republican allies. In the year of Meagher's own arrival Louis Kossuth, the 1848 Hungarian rebel recently released from a Turkish jail, was being equally feted and was playing an important role in the Whig presidential campaign of 1852.[7] Meagher's Young Ireland colleague, John Mitchel, would be similarly welcomed in New York City upon his own escape to the United States in 1853; in Mitchel's case the furore lasted for days.[8] Secondly, Meagher would not be the only Irishman to don the uniform of a Union general during the American Civil War, and while he may have been the most colourful figure to do so, he was clearly not the most successful of the twelve Irish-born Union generals. At the beginning of the war James Shields of County Tyrone was equally as famous as Meagher, and Thomas William Sweeny of County Cork was undoubtedly more successful as a general than Meagher would ever be.[9]

These Irish generals would be joined by twelve German-born generals a number of whom had also been 1848 rebels, and who were also political exiles in the United States. The most colourful of these was perhaps August Von Willich, a Prussian officer turned 1848 rebel who later became a Marxist. At the outbreak of the American Civil War, Von Willich personally recruited 1,500 fellow Germans for the Union cause within a matter of days.[10] Lastly, it should also be noted that the welcome extended to such foreign republican exiles was not without qualification. Not only did their views attract the hostility of the nativist Know-Nothing Party, but the anti-clerical views of Kossuth, Meagher and Mitchel also attracted the hostility of the Catholic pulpit and, in both Meagher's and Mitchel's case, criticism in the Irish-American press.[11] As Meagher admitted to Smith O'Brien in 1856, 'I spoke favouringly of Kossuth, and the European movements for liberty, and that was the whole of it. For this I was denounced from the pulpits and through the bigoted Catholic press, and in the highways and byways.'[12] From the early clash with the Church and conservative Irish-American opinion Meagher, unlike Mitchel, learnt the language of caution and moderation and he frequently kept his more radical opinions to himself. This, after all, would be the language of assimilation.

ASSIMILATION

Upon his arrival in New York City, the American republic's largest and most cosmopolitan city, Meagher found an instant constituency in the city's Irish-born population which constituted one-quarter of its entire population. Since 1850, some 60 per cent of Irish-born exiles were residing in the four states of New York, Massachusetts, Pennsylvania and Illinois. There was also a sizeable Irish-born population in the Midwest and the cities of Chicago, St Louis, Cincinnati and Detroit each had an Irish-born population ranging between 12 to 15 per cent. The South, especially the cities of Charleston and New Orleans, also had a large Irish-born population and even San Francisco had an Irish-born population of well over 25,000 residents.[13] As the Irish were the most nationalistic ethnic community within the Republic, as well as the most politically active, the Democrat Party machine had long manipulated the Irish ethnic block vote and, eager to consolidate its recent victory over the Whigs in the 1852 presidential election, the Democrats were quick to entertain such a prominent Irish hero. The President-Elect, Franklin Pierce, invited Meagher both to his New Hampshire home and to his inauguration, March 1853, where Meagher, accompanied by James Shields, the Irish hero of the Mexican War and a Democrat Senator for Illinois, met many prominent national leaders. Pierce endorsed Meagher's first lecture tour of New England and in April 1853,

Meagher followed this by a lecture tour of the South where he received an especially warm welcome in both Charleston and New Orleans.[14]

This first public speaking tour, which would end in Boston in August 1853, was crucial to Meagher's early American career. Not only did it physically introduce him to the larger Irish-American community as well as other interested American citizens, it also provided Meagher with an early grasp of the sheer size of the United States and its enormous potential. To facilitate the success of this first speaking tour Meagher, an ambitious man conscious of his public image, edited thirty of his speeches which were published in early 1853 by Redfield, as the *Speeches on the Legislative Independence of Ireland with Introductory Notes by Thomas Francis Meagher*. Prefaced with an attractive portrait of the author, the collection, of course, contained his famous July 1846 speech 'Freedom of Opinion – Morality of War', which is better known as the 'Sword Speech', numerous other speeches against the English power, but also his 1846 speech on the Polish Insurrection, reflections on Greek independence, his 1848 speeches in favour of the French Revolution as well as four letters to the *Nation* on the Belgian Revolution.[15] The book and the speaking tour helped establish Meagher's credentials in the United States as not only an Irish ethnic spokesman, but also an international republican of some note.

In concluding the tour in Boston, Meagher took as his topic American republicanism. While Meagher had been impressed with his tour of the South, he rejected the notion that grave sectional differences seriously threatened the Union. Both North and South, he announced, were the same fraternal nation joined together under the Stars and Stripes, that 'unviolated and unviolable flag', the symbol of republican unity. The states themselves were moulded by the Constitution, a crucial political document which supported important freedoms, 'freedom of thought, freedom of speech [and] freedom of discussion'.[16] It is clear that Meagher, quite early on, came to admire the United States, and this feeling of affinity for the young, vibrant republic almost immediately began to colour his old relationships.

In August 1853, his wife, Catherine Bennett Meagher arrived in New York City with his father, Thomas Meagher Jr. Meagher and Catherine had married in Van Diemen's Land in 1851, and although there appears to have been no bad blood between father and son, his feelings towards his wife had cooled. When Meagher eagerly accepted an offer from the California Steamship Company for a free visit to San Francisco he used this as an excuse to cut short his wife's and father's trip. Catherine would return to Waterford pregnant and following the birth of their second, and only surviving son, Thomas Bennett Meagher, she would die in Waterford in May 1854. Similarly, Meagher also welcomed his colleague John Mitchel to New York City in November 1853, and while he was happy to give an oration welcoming him to America and help him establish the *Citizen*, Meagher soon began to distance himself from Mitchel's controversial editorials and was unwilling to commit any large amount of money to the journal. As a newly minted American citizen in 1857, Meagher also kept

1 Home of Thomas Francis Meagher Jr and his wife Alicia, O'Connell Street, Waterford, 1820–1823 (Courtesy of John Mannion)

2 Thomas Francis Meagher (1846) (Courtesy of the National Library of Ireland, R13165)

3 Portrait of Thomas Francis Meagher by Rev. John Rooney (c. 1847) (Courtesy of the National Library of Ireland)

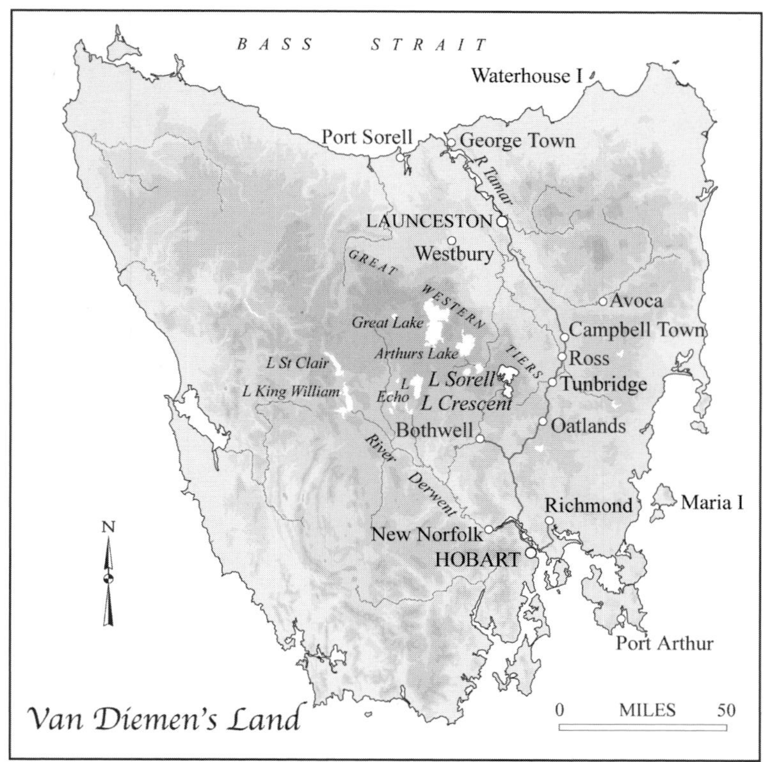

4 Map of Van Diemen's Land, now called Tasmania
(Courtesy of PIWE, Tasmania)

CON 37/5

Meagher Thomas Francis

Transported for

Tried Clonmel ... October 1848 Life

Embarked

Arrived ... 1849

Trade	Height	Age	Complexion	Head	Hair	Whiskers	Visage	Forehead	Eyebrows	Eyes	Nose	Mouth	Chin	Nat. Place
Law Student	5 9	26			brown				brown			do	do	Waterford City

Marks

Period of Labour

Station of Gang

Class

Offences and Sentences		Remarks
	6 November 1849	3/1/52 Abs^d Gaz 13/1/52.

5 O'Meagher's convict record (CON 37/5 Archives, Tasmania)

6 Sketch by John Mitchel of the house built at Lake Sorell by O'Meagher (NS 23/3/29 Archives, Tasmania)

7 Grave of O'Meagher's first born son, Henry Emmet Fitzgerald O'Meagher, at St John's Church, Richmond, Tasmania (Courtesy of Elaine Sullivan)

8 John Mitchel (1846) (Courtesy of the National Library of Ireland, R16415)

9 Thomas Francis Meagher
(By kind permission of
Montana Historical Society.
Photography by A.C. Carter)

10 The hanging of James Daniels,
1 March 1866, for the murder of
A. J. Gartley, Helena, Montana (Photographer
unknown. By kind permission of Montana
Historical Society)

11 Bryan Bennett, father of O'Meagher's first wife, Catherine (Bennie) (Courtesy of Reg A. Watson)

12 Wilbur Fisk Sanders, Lewis photographer, New York City (By kind permission of Montana Historical Society)

13 Thomas Francis Meagher statue in front of Montana Capitol Building, Helena, Montana (By kind permission of Montana Historical Society, photograph by Terry Murphy)

(a) and (b). Medals: Fort Sumter Medal and Kearney Cross were presented to Meagher in 1863.

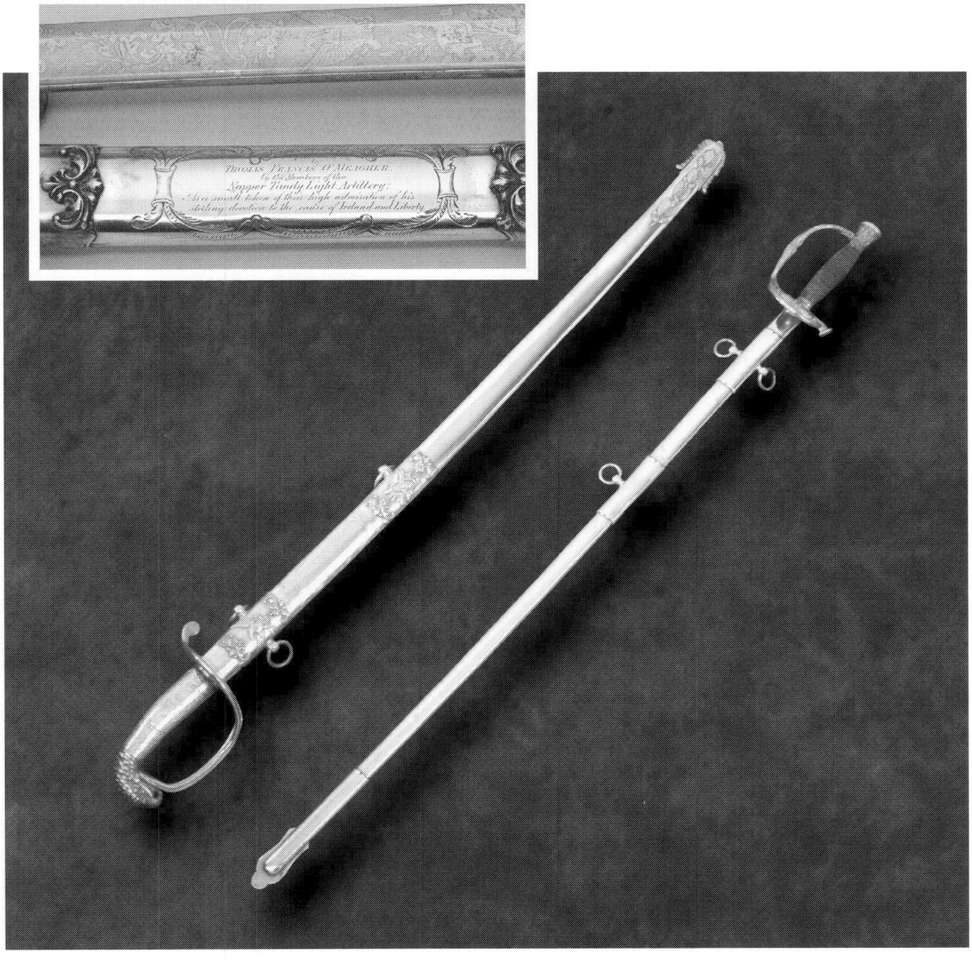

(c) Sword: A specially commissioned staff officer's sword presented to Thomas Francis Meagher in 1863 by the Napper Tandy Light Artillery, Brooklyn. This was gifted to Waterford Corporation in 1886 by Meagher's widow, Elizabeth.

14 Images from the Waterford Museum of Treasures

(d)

(e)

(f)

(d) 'Sprig of Green' similar to that worn in caps of soldiers of the Irish Brigade and used to identify the brigade's dead after the battle of Fredericksburg, 1862. A Union Army general's buff coloured silk sash, which belonged to Meagher. Both these items were gifted by Meagher's widow to Waterford Corporation in 1886.

(e) Painting: A portrait of Meagher (c. 1865) by the Waterford-born artist, T.F. Gallagher. Gifted to Waterford Corporation by Meagher's widow, Elizabeth, it was presented personally by Gallagher to the Mayor of Waterford, Richard Power in 1886.

(f) Coatee and Clarinet: Meagher's original coatee specially designed by him for the '82 club. This was donated to Waterford Corporation in 1886 by a Mr Donegan of Cork. This is Meagher's clarinet, used by him as first clarinettist in the Stonyhurst College orchestra, but which he refused to play during a concert celebrating the anniversary of the Battle of Waterloo. He subsequently brought it with him into exile to Van Diemen's Land.

14 Images from the Waterford Museum of Treasures (continued)

somewhat aloof from the Fenian movement. While he was willing to entertain the Fenian, James Stephens, when he arrived on a fund raising trip in 1858, and was willing to take him to Washington, D.C. to make contacts, Meagher was, by January 1859, eager to distance himself from the movement.[17]

Many of Meagher's contemporary biographers tended to idealize Meagher as a disinterested republican nationalist; as Michael Cavanagh noted, Meagher was never interested in the spoils of office, he was an individual never 'fitted to deal with tricksy politicians – these were a class he always despised and detested'.[18] Undoubtedly, Meagher remained true to the cause of eventual Irish independence and to the ideals of international republican government yet Meagher, the permanent exile, had also to look to his own self-interest. Simply put, he had to make a living and although the San Francisco *Daily Herald* announced in January 1854 that he had 'for his own support' decided upon the role 'lecturer as his avocation', this is far from the truth.[19] If Meagher's lecture tours proved lucrative and his noted oratory kept him in the public eye, such a career was both transitory in nature and not one fitting a gentleman of Meagher's background and education. The careers of his contemporary exiles Patrick O'Donohoe, Terence McManus, William Smith O'Brien and even John Mitchel himself, well illustrated the transitory nature of a professional Irish nationalist in the United States.[20] Consequently, Meagher would become a familiar figure in the antebellum republic; a professional ethnic spokesman who hoped to eventually broker with the establishment a more lasting, permanent and suitable station in mainstream American society. In short, Meagher hoped his leadership of the Irish-American community would finally lead to a government appointment and possibly elected public office.[21]

The death of Catherine Meagher in 1854 tended to focus Meagher's attention on such a new, respectable career, for he began to court Elizabeth Townsend, the daughter of the prosperous Peter Townsend, owner of the New York Sterling Ironworks. Elizabeth Townsend's social credentials were impressive and their marriage in November 1855 helped make Meagher a peripheral member of upper-class New York society. Elizabeth's father was not particularly happy that his daughter had married an Irish political exile or that she had become a Roman Catholic and, as Meagher gazed out of the windows of his father-in-law's house on Fifth Avenue, he must have been increasingly aware of his failure to transform his public standing into a more lasting social position. This frustration may help explain Meagher's violent outbursts of temper during these years and a developing drinking problem commented upon by both contemporaries and historians alike.[22]

Encouraged by Judge Charles Patrick Daly, a Townsend family friend and Tammany Hall politician, Meagher resumed his study of the law. Tutored by Judge Robert Emmet, the son of Thomas Addis Emmet, who had become the Attorney General of New York, Meagher was called to the New York bar by special license on 4 September 1855.[23] To become a lawyer is one thing, to build a successful practice is another and Meagher found his days in his law office at

20 Anne Street, near New York City Hall, tedious. Occasionally, to supplement his income, he returned to the lecture circuit.

As a prominent Democrat Party ethnic leader Meagher decided, in April 1856, to create his own newspaper, the *Irish News*, which quickly established a circulation of 50,000. While Meagher announced that he had created the newspaper to give the poor and ignored New York City Irish a political voice, the timing of its creation coincided with the upcoming presidential election of 1856. The *Irish News* increased Meagher's political profile and strongly supported the Democratic Party. Noticeably pro-southern and somewhat neutral on the slavery issue, the *Irish News* characteristically reflected the language of the New York City Democrats: that sectional differences were not worth destroying the Union for and that the South's peculiar institution be tolerated. The Democrat Party's candidate in 1856, James Buchanan, won the election but lost New York State. He did, however, carry New York City and Meagher, who became an American citizen in May 1857, began to bombard the new president for preferment, preferably a diplomatic appointment in Central or South America. Eager to prove himself useful to the Democrat Party he travelled to Central America to promote a railway link from the eastern seaboard to the Pacific, defended American filibusters prosecuted under the Neutrality Act of 1818, and in April 1859, travelled to Washington, D.C. to defend one of President Buchanan's favourite political friends, the Tammany Hall insider and congressman, Daniel Sickles of New York. A man noted for his own numerous amorous adventures, Sickles shot his wife's lover dead in broad daylight on a Washington street. As part of Sickles' eight-man legal team, Meagher helped gain Sickles' acquittal on the grounds of temporary insanity, the first time such a legal device was successfully used in the United States.[24] Disappointed that the national interest in the Sickles' trial failed to generate more clients for his neglected law practice, Meagher again went on his travels. Following another lecture tour of the South he and Elizabeth embarked upon a trip to Costa Rica to explore financial business opportunities as well as promote the construction of a railway across the isthmus.[25] During his absence Abraham Lincoln was elected president in the impassioned election of 1860, and upon his return to New York City in January 1861, Meagher encountered a nation in the grip of a national crisis, a crisis which threatened civil war.

As the presidential candidate of the Republican Party, Lincoln had stood upon a political platform which wanted to prevent the further expansion of slavery into the western territories. His election prompted the secession of South Carolina in December 1860, and early in the new year it was followed out of the Union by six other southern states that formed the Confederate States of America. Meagher, who had voted for his Democrat Party friend, Senator Stephen A. Douglas, was surprised by Lincoln's election and, between January and April 1861, he attempted to remain neutral regarding the slavery issue and, like many in New York City, was anti-Lincoln and pro-southern. However, the crisis over the continued Federal possession of Fort Sumter in Charleston harbour finally led to Confederate forces under General Pierre Beauregard firing upon the fort and its garrison under Major Robert Anderson on 12 April 1861. This act sparked the American Civil War as President Lincoln called for 75,000 volunteers to suppress the rebellion in the South, an act which prompted the secession of four other southern states who joined the Confederacy.

SUPPORTING THE UNION

The effect upon the New York City Irish was profound and from 15 April to 23 April 1861, over 500 Irishmen flocked to the colours of the 69th New York Militia under the well known Fenian, Colonel Michael Corcoran. While some were Fenians themselves, the majority, who were older, married men and who had become American citizens, were not.[26] Irish-Americans joined northern or southern armies for a number of reasons and for some it may have just been a matter of geography. As the *Tipperary Advocate* noted on 10 August 1861, 'In our opinion adhesion on the part of the Irish-American to North or South is a mere question of locality.'[27] In the North, however, it is clear that many volunteers, like Peter Walsh of the 28th Massachusetts Infantry, later part of the Irish Brigade, did so to preserve the Union.[28] The early patriotism many Irish-Americans in the North felt towards the Republic should not be underestimated. On 20 April 1861, Major Anderson, the late commander of Fort Sumter, arrived in New York City with the Sumter flag. Following a monster meeting in Union Square the influential weekly newspaper the *Irish American* proclaimed,

> Irish Americans, we call on you by the sacred memories of the past, by your remembrance of the succour extended to you suffering brethren, by the future hope of your native land here taking root and springing towards a vigorous maturity to be true to the land of your adoption in the crisis of her fate.[29]

On 22 April 1861, Meagher made the important decision to volunteer for Union service. Commissioned captain of Company K, the 69th New York Militia, the Irish Zouaves, Thomas Francis Meagher was about to go to war.[30]

As the American Civil War became the first modern war of attrition, Meagher would be later criticized by both the Irish-American community and critics in Ireland herself for his decision to support the Union.[31] More recently, Kelly J. O'Grady in his book *Clear the Confederate Way! The Irish in the Army of Northern Virginia* has, while celebrating the military reputation of the Irish in the South who fought for the Confederacy, attacked the military reputation of Meagher. The hero of O'Grady's book is clearly John Mitchel and Meagher's support of the North was, O'Grady believes, a betrayal of his own 1848 revolutionary roots and his break with Mitchel, who supported the Confederacy, 'one of the sorrowful mysteries of Irish history'. Similarly, Robert G. Athearn has also been critical of Meagher's seeming political inconsistency.[32] If O'Grady's own grasp of Irish history is shaky, on one specific point regarding Meagher he is totally incorrect. Meagher's decision in April 1861 to fight for the Union was not an 'abrupt turn of events', a seeming betrayal of a lifetime of resistance against central authority.[33] Meagher had never opposed central governmental authority; he had, however, opposed arbitrary authority, the establishment of a government which ignored the freedom and rights of the governed. Although Meagher was willing to rebel to win Irish independence, it is doubtful, unlike his colleague John Mitchel, that he had ever been a social reformer. His preface to his edition of *Letters of a Protestant on Repeal*, which defends the social division of society, certainly suggests he was something of a conservative regarding Irish society.[34]

In his speech 'The Irish Soldier. His History and Present Duty to the American Republic', which he delivered at the Boston Music Hall on 23 September 1861, Meagher reviewed his political past.[35] Freely admitting his continuing allegiance to the Democrat Party, his previous sympathy for the South and the fact he had not voted for Lincoln in 1860, Meagher reminded his audience that Lincoln, whatever his political platform, had been legitimately elected President. Once Lincoln had taken the oath of office from Chief Justice Taney to support the Constitution, all political platforms, he believed, were subordinated to the maintenance of that Constitution. Consequently, all reasons for opposing the government, the commonwealth, were inexcusable. Believing he could not find 'one substantial reason or pretext for the revolution' and the following unnatural brothers' war, Meagher securely placed the outbreak of the American Civil War on self-interested, hot-headed southerners, especially those in South Carolina. To his own critics who noted that 'Oh, you were once a revolutionist, and why should you not be a revolutionist now' Meagher put his own decision to support the Union in context. Political consistency in all questions was not necessarily a political strength and the conditions in Ireland were not the same as those in the American Republic. Consequently, it could not be expected of any gentleman that 'he is never to change', that 'under all circumstances, in every climate, and on every stage [he] is to be the same'. While he had been, he added, a 'revolutionist in Ireland, I am a conservative in America' because the circumstances were different. Meagher had also long been an admirer of the American Republic.[36]

Interested in the United States since his Stonyhurst schooldays, many of his Irish and American speeches before the outbreak of the American Civil War indicate he was a champion of American constitutional freedoms. In his famous 'Sword Speech' of July 1846, he had praised the Republic as he had complimented American generosity during the Famine. The United States was Ireland's true sister, a nation by whose example other poorer and oppressed nations could learn how to become great. His arrival in the United States in 1852 had created in Meagher an increased appreciation for both American constitutional freedoms and the progress it promoted. Unlike his friend, John

Mitchel, Meagher was no enemy to progress and he considered the Republic a 'symbol' of hope and salvation to the oppressed peoples of Europe.[37] His fellow Irish and European revolutionaries of 1848 had hoped to achieve and establish the freedoms and progress the United States actually enjoyed. Indeed, if Ireland herself had enjoyed the same privileges that the South enjoyed under the American Constitution, Meagher argued, he would not have found himself in exile for,

> had Ireland been under the enjoyment of such privileges and such rights, and such a guaranteed independence as South Carolina enjoyed, I would not have been here tonight, the scaffold would not have been stained with one drop of martyrs' blood, and Ireland would have been spared many a generation of martyrs and exiles.[38]

The experience of war only hardened Meagher's initial belief that the cause of southern independence could not be compared to European nationalistic revolutions. As he wrote to James Roche in September 1863, 'One must be able to discriminate between the unjustified and treacherous revolt of the South and the revolutions which occurred in Europe' for the latter did not aim to destroy a sacred compact, but destroy unnatural 'mastership and domination'.[39] In another of his important pre-war speeches, that welcoming Mitchel to New York City in January 1854, Meagher had given full vent to his belief that the United States outshone the old monarchies of Europe. 'Look to America – look to Austria' he thundered, 'look to Italy and even Russia and who will have the temerity to say they stand the competition with America.' Praising the United States for its freedoms Meagher reached his oratorical crescendo:

> When a nation is free, the nation is active, adventurous, occupied with great projects, competent to achieve greater ends. When a nation is enslaved, she is spiritless, inert and sluggish; is stirred by proud conception; her strength enervated, she is unequal to an industrious career. The most prosperous days, which nations have enjoyed, have been those in which their freedom was most conspicuous.[40]

Believing that the preservation of the Union was crucial to preserving the American republican experiment, Captain Thomas Francis Meagher joined his regiment in Virginia, May 1861. Meagher was not the only one of his name to fight for the Union for over 300 O'Meaghers, Meaghers, Marrs and Mahers also fought for the North.[41]

At the Battle of Bull Run, the first major engagement of the war, July 1861, the 69th New York Militia fought as well as any other northern unit that day. When the Union retreat turned into a rout however, the regiment broke up and joined the flight from the battlefield. While attempting to rally his men Colonel Corcoran was captured as he defended the regimental colours. Meagher had his horse shot from under him and rising to his feet he waved his sword over his head exclaiming 'Boys! Look at the flag and remember Ireland and Fontenoy.' Concussed, Meagher joined the general retreat and although his actions in this first battle have been the subject of some debate, the *Waterford News* noted that every citizen of 'Waterford feels a just pride in the glory Thomas Francis Meagher has won for himself'.[42]

Commissioned a captain in the regular United States Army, Meagher furthered both his military reputation and his standing in the northern Irish-American community by the publication of his *The Last Days of the 69th in Virginia*. The disaster at Bull Run had shocked the North and Meagher defended his comrades from nativist attacks claiming that 'no soldiers could have rushed to battle with a heartier elasticity and daring than did the soldiers of the 69th'. While, Meagher suggested, native-born soldiers had begun the Union rout, the 69th initially refused to 'abandon the Stars and Stripes' until the situation became hopeless. Their valour was even more praiseworthy, he concluded, given pre-war nativist attacks on their religion and the treatment their brigade commander, Colonel William T. Sherman, inflicted upon them in the days preceding the battle. Sherman was, Meagher thought, a 'crude and envenomed martinet', an officer who exhibited 'the sourest malignity towards the 69th'.[43] When 500 of the old 69th New York Militia re-enlisted for three years service as the new 69th New York Infantry, Meagher was promoted to colonel. Offered the command of the regiment Meagher never really assumed the position for he was already planning the creation of an Irish Brigade, a brigade which, he hoped, would rival the fame of Wild Geese brigades that had fought in the service of both France and Spain.

THE IRISH BRIGADE

During August 1861, Meagher's role was clearly that of recruiting officer for the projected brigade, a brigade to be commanded by James Shields who had been commissioned a brigadier general that month. The brigade, Meagher hoped, would consist of two New York regiments, the 69th under Nugent and the 88th New York commanded by Meagher, and two other Irish regiments raised in Boston and Philadelphia. However, this was not to be and initially the brigade was an all New York unit which also consisted of the 63rd New York Infantry and the 2nd New York Artillery Battalion. Meagher created the brigade structure and proved to be a successful recruiting agent for Irish regiments in New York, Boston and Philadelphia.

In August 1861, he delivered a speech at the Jones Wood pleasure grounds on the Upper East Side before an estimated 100,000 people. In September he delivered his 'Irish Soldier' speech in Boston. Appearing as a citizen in arms for the national government, Meagher proclaimed in Boston, a city known for its nativism, that 'Know-Nothingism is dead' and the present war would prove worth the sacrifice when the Irish soldier could 'take his stand proudly by the side of the native-born, and will not fear to look him straight and sternly in the face, and tell him that he has been equal to him in his allegiance to the Constitution'. Admitting that he could not find it in his heart 'to disparage my countrymen down South', Meagher forcefully rejected the 'foolish cant about Irishman fighting Irishman' in this war for any student of Irish history knew, he remarked, that this had often happened in the past. In a speech which celebrated the bravery of the Irish soldiers on previous American battlefields he regretted that all too often Irish valour had been wasted in establishing the ascendancy of the British Empire. Reminding his Irish audience of the haven the United States had become to them and the freedoms they enjoyed under both its flag and Constitution, he called upon his fellow countrymen to 'take sword in hand' and follow General Shields down to the Potomac.[44]

General Shields, however, would not be the first commander of the Irish Brigade for he had requested, as an experienced former general officer of the Mexican War, the command of a division, a request Lincoln granted. With Michael Corcoran remaining a Confederate prisoner until August 1862, Meagher seemed to many, including Shields and Colonel Nugent, to be the logical choice to command the brigade he had done so much to create. Meagher obviously welcomed the appointment and in October 1861, he was appointed acting brigadier commanding the Irish Brigade. Congress confirmed his commission on 3 February 1862, and together with Shields, Meagher rode down to Virginia from the capital to take command of the brigade on 11 February 1862.[45]

Formally designated the second brigade of the First Division, II Corps, Army of the Potomac, Meagher took command in a formal ceremony in which he reminded his officers that while they may later take up the cause of an independent Ireland, in the present crisis they were Union officers and all personal considerations should be subordinated to restoring the authority of the American Republic. This sacred duty must be undertaken, he ordered, while ignoring newspaper opinion, political speeches and the possible death rate of those involved 'until the Stars and Stripes float over every inch of their legal domain'. They were to plunge themselves 'into the thickest of the most desperate fight' and Meagher promised his officers that he personally would always lead them into battle and, if killed in action, he would be happy that he had served the Irish exiles' 'happiest, proudest, and most prosperous home', the United States of America.[46] There can be no doubt, however, that Meagher conceived the Irish Brigade not just as another unit of the United States Army but as a symbol of continuing Irish glory. For Meagher, the brigade would become the living embodiment of the Wild Geese who had fought for England's European enemies.[47]

Meagher's command of the Irish Brigade, February 1862 to May 1863, clearly constituted the most important phase of his career in the United States. It was not, however, without controversy as both contemporaries and historians alike have commented upon his drinking problem, and the mounting casualty rates of his brigade led some of his contemporary critics to accuse Meagher of sacrificing his men unnecessarily to gain personal glory and advancement. As Irish opinion became disillusioned with war, Meagher was even accused of complicity with various unnamed Yankee Know-Nothings in promoting Catholic genocide.[48] While there can be no doubt that Meagher hoped that his military service would help promote a post-war political career, this was a hope shared by many of his fellow officers. What was different about his service, however, were the constant nativist attacks upon him which reflected the prevalent anti-Catholic, anti-Irish prejudices of his day; prejudices which, Joseph G. Bilby has noticed, many modern historians are themselves, whether subliminal or otherwise, not immune to.[49]

As the first commander of the brigade Meagher played a dominant role in establishing its reputation for ferocity in battle. The brigade did sustain a heavy casualty rate but this was largely due to the fact that it was viewed as a fine combat unit that could always be relied upon to do its duty and, consequently, was often thrown into the vortex of battle at critical times. Meagher alone cannot be blamed for this as he was, of course, required to follow the orders of his superior officers.[50] It should be noted that following Meagher's resignation, the brigade under its later commanders continued to sustain unusually high casualty rates, especially at Spotsylvania in May 1864 and at Cold Harbor, in June 1864. It should also be noted that, unlike the later brigade commanders who served under General U.S. Grant, Meagher served under Generals McClellan, Burnside and Hooker, officers unequal to the tactical abilities of the celebrated Confederate general, Robert E. Lee, a commander who was also more than willing to sacrifice his own men in fruitless charges to establish his elusive quest for southern independence.[51]

As a political general, Meagher had no formal military training but there can be no doubt he was a courageous officer whose sense of duty and honour compelled him to lead from the front. Many of his officers and enlisted men were veterans of previous European wars, yet they never seem to have questioned his personal bravery and seemed genuinely saddened by his resignation. Meagher, like many European officers in the war, had a tendency to wear ornate uniforms and be followed by a glittering staff. Consequently, Meagher presented himself as a conspicuous target on many a battlefield. It was a miracle, Robert Athearn has noted, that Meagher was never wounded.[52] There can equally be no doubt that the horrors of war and the slaughter on the battlefield had a deep and personal effect on Meagher. The critical historian would do well to take note of D.P. Conyngham's reflections on the nature of war in his post-war, *Sherman's March*. To those unacquainted with the horrors of war, the battlefield may well seem a field of honour and glory but if this sounded well in historic fiction it was not reality;

> Could these fireside heroes but witness a battlefield, with its dead, its dying and wounded, writhing in agonizing tortures, or witness the poor

> victims under the scalpel knife, with the field hospital clodded with human gore, and full of maimed bodies and dissected limbs of their fellow creatures, war would lose its false charm for them.[53]

The brigade had its baptism of fire at the Battle of Fair Oaks, 1 June 1862, during General McClellan's Peninsular Campaign, which was designed to capture the Confederate capital, Richmond, Virginia. Within sixty miles of the city, the Union army was attacked by General Joseph E. Johnson and, in the battle, both the 69th and 88th New York distinguished themselves. Meagher personally brought the 88th up to the firing line and was indefatigable in riding along the line cheering his men on. Both McClellan and Meagher's corps commander, General Edwin V. Sumner, praised the brigade for its gallantry; if his Irishmen ever ran from the field, Sumner noted, he would also have to run.[54] McClellan continued his cautious advance towards Richmond but his campaign was brought to a vicious conclusion by a series of battles called the Seven Days which were launched by the new Confederate commander, Robert E. Lee, to destroy the Army of the Potomac.

Reinforced by the 29th Massachusetts Infantry, a non-Irish Yankee unit, which Meagher came to regard as Irishmen in disguise because of their bravery, the brigade distinguished itself at Gaines Mill, 27 June 1862, where the brigade covered the army's retreat across the Chickahominy River. In this action Meagher and his staff were the last to cross the river. At the battle of White Oak Swamp, 30 June 1862, the brigade spent most of its time supporting Union batteries. Under the hottest fire, Captain Horgan of the 88th New York saw Meagher riding up and down the line oblivious to danger. When implored to dismount, he refused stating, 'No I will not dismount. If I am killed I would rather be riding this horse than lying down.'[55] Again at Malvern Hill, the final battle of the Seven Days, 1 July 1862, the brigade distinguished itself under fire and later engaged in vicious hand-to-hand fighting with Irish Confederate troops from Louisiana.[56] McClellan's failure in the Seven Days led to his recall to Washington and many of his troops were placed under the command of General John Pope. The luckless Pope was defeated by Lee at the second battle of Bull Run in August 1862, a Confederate victory which prompted Lee's first invasion of the North. In the four months that followed, September 1862 to December 1862, Meagher's Irish Brigade secured its reputation as one of the finest combat units in the Army of the Potomac.

At the battle of Antietam, 17 September 1862, General McClellan, who had returned to command, would misuse his superior numbers in attempting to dislodge Lee's army from a strong position. In the bloodiest single day of the war, Meagher would personally lead the brigade upon an attack on Confederate forces secure in a sunken road later known as the 'Bloody Angle'. Charging over a hundred yards under a murderous fire which, Meagher reported, 'literally cut lanes throughout the approaching line', the brigade advanced under Meagher's personal command to within thirty paces of the enemy.[57] Conspicuously mounted and in a gorgeous uniform, Meagher's horse was shot from under him while he attempted to persuade his men to mount a bayonet charge. Carried from the field unconscious, Meagher's fall stimulated a rumour, first noted by Colonel David Strother, a staff officer over a mile from the front, that Meagher had been drunk during the battle. Whether true or not, Meagher did little to enhance his reputation in Washington, D.C. after the battle. When McClellan allowed Lee's shaken army to escape back to Virginia he was again removed from command and in protest Meagher had his colour bearers throw down their regimental colours before McClellan's feet upon his departure from the army. The 'gentlemen in the White House' Meagher imprudently wrote to a friend, had committed a crime 'which the Army of the Union will never forgive'.[58]

FREDERICKSBURG AND MEAGHER'S RESIGNATION

The decimation of the Irish Brigade began during the Seven Days and was continued at Antietam and later at Fredericksburg, where General Burnside, McClellan's successor, ignored all of his senior commanders and threw his army against Lee's entrenched position on Marye's Heights. Before the battle, the 29th Massachusetts had been reassigned and replaced by the 28th Massachusetts, an Irish regiment recruited by Meagher in Boston in 1861. The brigade's strength was further augmented by the addition of the 116th Pennsylvania Infantry, an inexperienced and under-strength regiment. Meagher's effect on this new regiment was, however, almost immediate as Lieutenant Colonel St Clair A. Mulholland noted: the regiment did not 'know him as well as the other regiments as it had not served so long' but it had 'learned to admire him' and gladly followed him into two hard battles.[59]

The charge of the Irish Brigade on 13 December 1862 was one of the most dramatic events of the battle of Fredericksburg. Before the advance Meagher, mounted and surrounded by his staff, addressed each regiment in 'burning, eloquent words, beseeching the men to uphold in the coming struggle the military prestige and glory of their native land'. As the famous green battle flags had been sent back to New York City for refurbishment, Meagher instructed each soldier to place a sprig of green boxwood in their caps.[60] Dismounting, Meagher initially led his regiments out of Fredericksburg towards Marye's Heights where the command had a clear view of the destruction being inflicted upon the commands of Generals French and Zook which had preceded them. As all senior officers had been ordered to enter battle on foot, Meagher, who had been suffering from an ulcerated knee, made the brigades' dispositions and returned to Fredericksburg to retrieve his horse. He watched as his brigade surged forward with shouts of an old Irish cheer *Faugh-a-Bellagh* (Clear the Way) and charged amidst the dead and human wreckage of the previous assaults. As the Confederate artillery tore gaps in their formation, the brigade continued forward until it finally was halted by repeated Confederate volleys, the survivors being pinned down for the rest of the day.

The charge at Fredericksburg has been romanticized as a glorious example of Irish bravery. *The Times* of London correspondent reported that never, not even at Fontenoy or Waterloo, had the undaunted courage of the son of Erin been better displayed. The 69th New York, in this 'heroic' charge, lost all of its sixteen commissioned officers present, and only sixty-one enlisted men returned from the action. Of the 1,300 men of the brigade who went up Marye's Heights, 545 were either killed, wounded or missing; as one Mississippi soldier reported 'We almost annihilated general Megearks Ireish (*sic*) Brigade.'[61] After Fredericksburg, both Irish-American support for the war, and Meagher himself, would never be the same. As Thomas Keneally has suggested, before Fredericksburg Meagher had spoken of the debt the Irish owed to the American Republic, after Fredericksburg he began to think darkly of the need for the Union to express its debt to the Irish Brigade.[62]

Two days after Fredericksburg Meagher obtained a twenty-day medical furlough due to his injured knee. Once in New York City he initiated a press campaign, supported by the *Irish American*, to bring the brigade out of the line, an initiative which gave offence to the War Department. Following a Requiem Mass in January, at St Patrick's Cathedral, in which his wife thought Meagher looked shaken, Meagher toasted the bravery of both armies during a wake at Delmonico's. Meagher seemed very reluctant to return to duty and, when he finally returned to the army on 14 February 1863, he had to explain his period of absence without leave to a military commission under General Oliver O. Howard. In Washington, D.C. he had ignored official channels and personally appealed to President Lincoln to grant a furlough to his brigade, a request he repeated in a strongly worded letter to Edwin Stanton, the Secretary of War, on 19 February.[63] In March, he made another successful request for medical leave and returned to his brigade just in time to take part in the battle of Chancellorsville in May 1863.

The new commander of the Army of the Potomac, General Thomas Hooker, began this campaign well on 27 April by outflanking Lee's Army of Northern Virginia. Lee, however, divided his army in the face of the enemy and sent General Thomas Jackson on a counter outflanking movement. When Jackson's troops hit the unsuspecting Federal XI Corps on the morning of 2 May, the Irish brigade was in reserve guarding the corps' ammunition train. Hearing the firing, Meagher put the brigade in line and tried to check the disorderly flood of retreating Union soldiers who had been routed by Jackson's surprise attack. Early the next morning the brigade was ordered into line at Chancellor House and stubbornly held its position while Meagher 'in full uniform, walked up and down the brigade line' encouraging his men. When Hooker decided to retreat on 4 May, Meagher was put in charge of the rear guard to cover the retreat, the 88th New York being one of the last Union regiments to leave the field.[64]

Following Chancellorsville, Hooker refused Meagher's request to grant the brigade a furlough. Already frustrated at official refusals to allow his depleted regiments home to rest and recruit, Meagher resigned from command on 8 May 1863. To put his dramatic decision in context it should be noted that during the war 110 of the 583 Union generals resigned from the service.[65] In a frank letter to the assistant adjutant general, Meagher complained that the Irish Brigade no longer existed, that its heroic attack at Marye's Heights at Fredericksburg had reduced its numbers to that of a regiment. Reminding Major Hancock of his previous requests that the brigade be allowed a furlough to recruit, he noted the bravery of his brigade at Chancellorsville, a 'mere handful, my command did its duty' and with a 'fidelity and resolution, which won for it the admiration of the army'.[66] It was a forceful letter, but Meagher's resignation has never been adequately explained; was it caused by fatigue, weariness, frustration at the continued official refusal to allow the brigade a leave of absence, his wish to seek another command or, the vain hope that his resignation, as a fine gesture, would prompt the government to grant the brigade a much earned furlough? Whatever Meagher's hopes were, his eloquence was ignored and a week later his resignation was accepted. Following a touching ceremony on 19 May in which Meagher personally shook the hand of every surviving soldier of the brigade, he returned to a hero's welcome in New York City. If Meagher expected to be reassigned he was to be sorely disappointed, for he spent a frustrating seven months on the shelf.

Meagher's resignation from the Irish Brigade did not, however, lead to its disbandment. Its regiments were initially consolidated into one battalion under the command of Colonel Patrick Kelly of the 88th New York. The Galway-born Kelly commanded the brigade (in name only) at Gettysburg, where in the Wheatfield on the second day of the battle, the brigade once again distinguished itself. In repulsing the Confederates, the brigade at last made a bayonet charge and engaged in the close-quarter fighting Meagher had long hoped for.[67] In the winter of 1863–64, the brigade was reinforced and placed under the command of Fermoy-born Colonel Thomas A. Smyth. In May 1864, the brigade's command was turned over to Colonel Richard Byrnes of the 28th Massachusetts. The Cavan-born Byrnes led the brigade through Grant's Wilderness Campaign in the spring of 1864 where it distinguished itself at Spotsylvania in May 1864, and at Cold Harbor in June 1864.[68] Following Byrnes' death at Cold Harbor, the brigade was finally placed under the command of Colonel Robert Nugent of the 69th New York.

Although once again vastly reduced in numbers and consolidated with other New York regiments into the Consolidated Brigade, II Corps, the Irish Brigade survived as a command unit and Nugent led the brigade from Petersburg to Lee's surrender at Appomattox, April 1865. Meagher continued to visit his old command during these years and perhaps his biggest regret regarding his wartime service, apart from never becoming a major general, was that he was not permitted to lead his old Irish brigade down Pennsylvania Avenue during the Army of the Potomac's victorious grand review in Washington on 22 May 1865.

In June 1863, General Lee began his second invasion of the North, which culminated in his defeat at the battle of Gettysburg. Frustrated by inactivity, Meagher proposed the raising of another Irish brigade of 3,000 men. Another such command, the Irish Legion, had been raised by Michael Corcoran upon his exchange in August 1862, and Lincoln proved lukewarm in raising a further Irish command. The possibility of such a command disappeared following the New York draft riots of July 1863 in which the Irish-American community played a prominent role. When Meagher attacked Peace Democrats and Copperheads for fanning the flames of sedition he was, in turn, attacked by the *Irish American* as a Lincoln man.[69] Irish opinion had never been unified behind Meagher's crusade to preserve the American Republic by force and, in September and October 1863, he began to answer his critics by writing directly to the Irish newspapers in Cork and Dublin defending his actions and opinions. Believing the Irish people to be ungrateful, especially as American aid was then relieving the suffering of another potential famine in Ireland, he recorded his 'scornful disappointment' with the growing partisanship between the Irish public and the 'aristocrats of Carolina and Virginia'. Increasing hostile Irish opinion had been noted in the North, Meagher warned P.J. Smyth, and the 'unnatural partisanship' of the Irish for the slaveholding South 'has done more harm to Ireland than, in the present circumstances, it could possibly do to the United States'. Meagher's letters to the Irish press were later reprinted in the *Loyalty Tract No. 38* and circulated in the North.[70]

MEAGHER REINSTATED

Meagher's continuing loyalty, however, was noted by the administration and on 23 December 1863, he was recalled to active duty though he was not actually given a command. His re-appointment was undoubtedly motivated by the death of Michael Corcoran in a riding accident the previous day. As James Shields had resigned from the army and relocated to San Francisco in March 1862, Meagher remained the most prominent symbol of continued Irish support for the Union in the East. Meagher, a lacklustre Fenian at best, was never a serious contender to succeed Corcoran as commander of the Irish Legion, for it was strongly Fenian in membership and his appointment to command, even after his oration praising Corcoran in New York on 23 January 1864, would not have been welcomed. The two rising dominant stars in the Northern armies, U.S. Grant and William T. Sherman, were reluctant to appoint Meagher to an active command as they both held him in low esteem.[71] In an increasingly modern, professional war of attrition, amateur political generals, especially those such as Meagher who were becoming marginalized by their own constituency, were considered military dinosaurs by their professionally trained colleagues. General Sherman, however, was reluctantly pressurized into finding Meagher a command and he was ordered to Nashville, Tennessee, where he was finally appointed to command two convalescent brigades rather grandly named the Provisional Division of the Army of Tennessee.

Reporting to General James Steedman, another War Democrat civilian general who commanded the Etowah military district south of Chattanooga, Meagher's initial role was to help defend vital railways in the area. When Steedman was ordered to Nashville to help defend the city against General Hood's invading Army of Tennessee, Meagher temporarily commanded the district and efficiently performed his duties defending the area from Confederate guerrillas.[72] Following General Hood's decisive defeat at Nashville on 23 December 1864, Meagher was ordered to transport his command to North Carolina to link up with General Sherman's main army then beginning its destructive march through the Carolinas. This proved to be a difficult mid-winter manoeuvre and Meagher so mismanaged the transport that when he finally got the division to New Bern via Annapolis, Maryland, General Innis Palmer, the local commander, reported that Meagher's division was little more than a mob in uniform. Meagher's rumoured reputation for intoxication had also preceded him and General Grant used Meagher's poor handling of the transport to relieve him in February 1865. Meagher was sent back to New York City to await orders which would never come; it was an inglorious conclusion to a military career which had begun with the fighting 69th New York at Bull Run in July 1861.[73]

Meagher's American career, however, was far from over as he still had important political connections and, following President Lincoln's assassination on 11 April 1865, he was invited to Washington, D.C. to form part of the general officer Honour Guard which accompanied the dead president's lying in state. In accordance with General Order No. 79, Meagher, like all temporary volunteer generals commissioned for the duration of the war, submitted his resignation, which was accepted on 15 May 1865. Whether this resignation was cancelled and Meagher actually made a brevet major-general is questionable, but his friend Major James O'Beirne, President Andrew Johnson's military aide, was certainly working behind the scenes to advance Meagher's career.[74] Johnson himself had reason to be grateful to Meagher . While in Tennessee, Meagher had made a number of speeches supporting the re-election of Lincoln and of his new vice presidential candidate Andrew Johnson, another War Democrat.

Meagher, like James Shields before him, had long had an interest in the West. Both viewed the region as a place the Irish could escape the tenements of the eastern cities and regenerate themselves into an agricultural people. Denied the governorship of Idaho, Meagher headed west to deliver speeches on his new project when news reached him that Johnson, as a political favour, had offered him the vacant position of Secretary of Montana Territory. Happily accepting the appointment, Meagher set off from Minneapolis to Montana on 16 August 1865. Aware that Governor Sidney Edgerton was eager to resign his post and return east, Meagher, no doubt, projected a great future for himself as he travelled west; from secretary to acting governor, to governor and, eventually, to even the United States' Congress. However, this last great adventure on the western frontier would not bring Meagher the post-war fame he craved but only further political controversy and an untimely, mysterious death in July 1867.

CONCLUSION

There can be no doubt that in his short, fifteen-year career in the United States Thomas Francis Meagher was both an important and controversial political figure. There can also be no doubt that he was a vain, mercurial and ambitious individual who clearly often drank to excess on a number of occasions. It is also true, however, that Meagher's commitment to the preservation of the American Union was deeply felt and that he was a brave and courageous, if untrained, officer whose military services to his adopted country proved to be an important watershed in Irish-American history. Meagher's biographer, Robert G. Athearn, however, proved to be strangely hostile to his subject. In his conclusion Athearn noted that few foreigners had arrived in the United States with so many apparent qualifications for success as had Meagher, yet Meagher had proved to be a failure in America. He never gained more than guest status in the United States and, Athearn added, had lived there almost completely upon his name, a name whose reputation was based upon a youthful indiscretion. In short, Meagher's life in the United States had proved to be an anticlimax and his greatness illusionary.[75] It is certainly true that Meagher's career in the United States was marked by frustration and failure and, it is also certain, that if he had not become involved in radical Irish politics his career in his native land could have become conventionally successful. He may well have followed his father into the British House of Commons or like his brother Henry, who became an officer in the Waterford Artillery and High Sheriff of Waterford, become a local Waterford dignitary. To term Meagher's involvement in the Repeal Association, Young Ireland and the rebellion of 1848 a youthful indiscretion, however, is to miss the point about Meagher's own personal commitment to national self-determination and republican principles, two dominant nineteenth-century ideals shared by many of his Young Ireland colleagues.

Whether Meagher proclaimed his beliefs in the upper-class English lisping accent affected in Dublin or the Irish brogue he cultivated in the United States, the message was the same. In the Belfast Music Hall he told his audience on 20 September 1847 that in the 'history of all nations, you will find that, with the decline of freedom, the decay of virtue has been contemporaneous'. Restrict the freedom of a nation and you check all those passions which make it noble and progressive. The nation that does not possess the power to shape its own destiny 'will have no heart, no courage, no ambition'. Seven years later in the San Francisco Music Hall, Meagher would proclaim to his American audience that his career had been dedicated to the imperishable word 'FREEDOM' and because of this he had been 'cast from a wreck upon these shores'. In America, however, he had found the fruits of liberty in full bloom; it was a society in which 'Labour is Nobility' and 'Democracy is sovereignty'. In inhaling the free air which lifts the folds of 'your inviolable flag', he announced, he was conscious of the freedom which penetrates the soul of 'all those who settle here, and to citizenship aspire'.[76]

It was to save this promise of freedom defended by the American constitutional union that Meagher took up the sword in 1861, and in doing so he became a symbolic figure in the story of the assimilation of the Irish into mainstream American life. If the veterans of the Irish Brigade and later historians have romanticized Meagher's career to further this process of assimilation, as Kelly O'Grady has forcefully argued, it should be noted that this was exactly what Meagher had hoped to achieve by the valour and heroism of the Irish Brigade. If Meagher's career in the United States was marked by failure, it was also characterized by achievement and national attention. It was a career that helped persuade the Irish in America that the United States was not just a temporary refuge but a permanent home, a society in which their assimilation was a desirable social and political goal. Meagher's own career in the United States, far from being a failure, exemplified this transition.

NOTES

1. Both John Blake Dillion and Richard O'Gorman had been active in the Young Ireland movement and had also participated in the 1848 rebellion. For Meagher's reception in New York City see Robert G. Athearn, *Thomas Francis Meagher: An Irish Revolutionary in America* (Boulder, CO: University of Colorado Press, 1949) pp.28–9 and Thomas Keneally, *The Great Shame and the Triumph of the Irish in the English Speaking World* (New York: Doubleday, 1999), pp.241–53.
2. For these O'Meagher's see Joseph Casimer O'Meagher, *Some Historical Notices of O'Meaghers of Ikerrin* (New York: privately published, 1890), pp.21, 40–4 and 136–7.
3. On de Maar, see my entry on Thomas Francis Meagher in H.G. Matthews and Brian Harrison (eds) *The Oxford Dictionary of National Biography*, 60 vols (Oxford: Oxford University Press, 2004).
4. Cited in Michael Cavanagh, *Memoirs of General Thomas Francis Meagher, Comprising the Leading Events of His Career* (Worcester, MA: Messenger Press, 1892) pp.311–13. Regarding the later American careers of the 1798 exiles see David A. Wilson, *United Irishmen, United States Immigrant Radicals in the Early Republic* (Ithaca, New York and London: Cornell University Press, 1998).
5. Cavanagh, *Memoirs*, p.309.
6. Kevin E. O'Brien (ed.), *My Life in the Irish Brigade: The Civil War Memoirs of Private William McCarter, 116th Pennsylvania Infantry* (Campbell, CA: Savas Publishing, 1996), p.16.
7. Michael F. Holt, *The Rise and Fall of the American Whig Party, Jacksonian Politics and the Onset of the Civil War* (New York: Oxford University Press, 1999), pp.692–7.
8. Keneally, *Great Shame*, pp.268–70.
9. For the brief biographies of all these mentioned Union generals, as well as other foreign-born Union generals, see Ezra J. Warner, *Generals in Blue. Lives of the Union Commanders* (Baton Rouge: Louisiana State University Press, 1964). Warner's account of the career of Meagher is not very flattering, pp.317–18. For a brief corrective to this account see my entry on Meagher,

together with an entry on the Irish brigade as well as that on the career of Thomas Sweeny, in David S. Heidler and Jeanne T. Heidler (eds), *Encyclopedia of the America Civil War. A Political, Social and Military History* (New York: Norton, 2000) pp.1038–40, 1297–8 and 1912–13.

10. Warner, *Generals in Blue*, pp.565–6.
11. Athearn, *Thomas Francis Meagher*, pp.34–6 and Keneally, *Great Shame*, pp.270–2.
12. Cited in Denis Gwynn, *Thomas Francis Meagher* (Cork: National University of Ireland Press, 1966), pp.40–1.
13. Kevin Kenny, *The American Irish. A History* (New York: Longman, 2000), pp.105–6.
14. Athearn, *Thomas Francis Meagher*, pp.36–41 and Keneally, *The Great Shame*, pp.258–60.
15. Thomas F. Meagher (ed.), *Speeches on the Legislative Independence of Ireland with Introductory Notes by Thomas Francis Meagher* (New York: Redfield, 1853) pp.18–33, 85–90, 183, 234–54, 255–61, 281–7, 288–93, 294–9 and 300–6. Meagher dated his preface, Irving Place, New York, November 10, 1852.
16. Keneally, *Great Shame*, p.259.
17. William L. Burton, *Melting Pot Soldiers. The Union's Ethnic Regiments* (New York: Fordham University Press, 1998), pp.9–12; Keneally, *Great Shame*, pp.270–1 and Pat McCarthy 'Reluctant Fenian: Thomas Francis Meagher and Militant Irish-American Nationalism', *Decies (Journal of the Waterford Archaeological and Historical Society)*, 59 (2003), pp.101–11.
18. Cavanagh, *Memoirs*, pp.43, 493.
19. Cited in Athearn, *Thomas Francis Meagher*, p.43.
20. On their brief careers in the United States see Keneally, *Great Shame*, pp.236–8, 256–60, 268–73 and 307–11.
21. Burton, *Melting Pot Soldiers*, pp.9, 209–10.
22. For Meagher's outbursts of temper and his attack on James McMaster, editor of the *Freedom Journal*, and his battle with Henry Raymond, editor of the *New York Times*, see Athearn, *Thomas Francis Meagher*, pp.57–8 and Keneally, *Great Shame*, pp.255, 299. Meagher proved very touchy about the question of breaking his parole before his escape and how this reflected upon his position as a gentleman.
23. Athearn, *Thomas Francis Meagher*, pp.49–51. Judge Robert Emmet was the nephew of the Irish nationalist hero, Robert Emmet.
24. For Meagher's role in the Sickles case see Thomas Keneally, *American Scoundrel. The Life of the Notorious Civil War General Dan Sickles* (New York: Anchor Books, 2002), pp.152–4, 192–7.
25. For Meagher's interest in developing the economic potential of Costa Rica see his 'Holidays in Costa Rica', *Harpers New Monthly Magazine*, 20 Dec. 1859, Jan. 1860, Feb. 1860.
26. Kerby A. Miller, *Emigrants and Exiles: Ireland and the Irish Exodus to North America* (New York: Oxford University Press, 1985), p.359.
27. Cited in Joseph M. Hernon, *Celts, Catholics and Copperheads. Ireland Views the American Civil War* (Columbus, OH: Ohio State University Press, 1968), p.12. For Irish-American motives for joining the armies see Burton, *Melting Pot Soldiers*, pp.52–3, 112–54: Dean B. Martin, *The Blessed Place of Freedom. Europeans in Civil War America* (Dulles, VA: Brassey's, 2002), pp.21–8: Florence E. Gibson, *The Attitudes of the New York Irish Toward State and National Affairs, 1848–1892* (New York: Columbia University Press, 1951), pp.121–7, 133–6: Ella Lonn, *Foreigners in the Union Army and Navy* (Baton Rouge: Louisiana State University Press, 1946), pp.68–79, and Jason H. Silverman, 'Stars, Bars and Foreigners: The Immigrant and the Making of the Confederacy', *Journal of Confederate History*, 1, 2, (1988), pp.265–85.
28. Lawrence F. Kohl and Margaret C. Richards (eds), *Irish Green and Union Blue. The Civil War Letters of Peter Walsh* (New York: Fordham University Press, 1986), pp.1–11.
29. Cited in Paul Jones, *The Irish Brigade* (London: New English Library, 1969) p.38.
30. Cavanagh, *Memoirs*, pp.367–74 and Athearn, *Thomas Francis Meagher*, p.38.
31. For an excellent analysis of Irish opinion regarding the use of force to preserve the Union see, Hernon, *Celts, Catholics and Copperheads*, pp.81–113.
32. Kelly J. O'Grady, *Clear the Confederate Way! The Irish in the Army of Northern Virginia*

(Mason City, IA: Savas Publishing, 2000), p.43.
33. Athearn, *Thomas Francis Meagher*, pp.169–70.
34. Thomas F. Meagher, *Letters of a Protestant on Repeal: By the Late Thomas Davis* (Dublin: William Holden, 1847), pp.IV–VI.
35. The full text of this speech is printed in W.F. Lyons, *Brigadier-General Thomas Francis Meagher: His Political and Military Career* (New York: D.J. Sadlier, 1870), pp.91–121. Lyons, however, misdates the speech as being given on 23 June 1863, although he refers to Meagher as a colonel. A fellow Irish Brigade officer D.P. Conynham also misdates the speech as being delivered on 6 October 1861; Lawrence F. Kohl (ed.), D.P. Conyngham, *The Irish Brigade and its Campaigns* (New York: Fordham University Press, 1994), p.48. Athearn correctly notes the date by reference to the report of it in the *Boston Morning Journal*, 24 Sept. 1861. See, Athearn, *Thomas Francis Meagher*, p.105. Athearn briefly reviews the speech but does not do it or Meagher justice, pp.103–4.
36. Meagher, 'The Irish Soldier', in Lyons, *Brigadier-General Thomas Francis Meagher*, p.103; pp.92–3, 95–7.
37. Thomas F. Meagher's 'Freedom of Opinion – Morality of War', Dublin, 28 July 1846; 'American benevolence-Irish Gratitude', Dublin 4 May 1847 and 'Reply to the Common Council of the City of New York', 10 June 1852 in, Thomas Francis Meagher (ed.), *Speeches*, pp.89–90, 142–3 and 316–17.
38. Meagher, 'The Irish Soldier', in Lyons, *Brigadier-General Thomas Francis Meagher*, p.105.
39. Cited in Hernon, *Celts, Catholics and Copperheads*, pp.94–5. This letter was part of a debate between pro-Union and pro-Confederate Irish leaders and Meagher's letter was published in the *Cork Examiner* on 20 Oct. 1863.
40. This, one of Meagher's most interesting American speeches, is published in full in Lyons, *Brigadier-General Thomas Francis Meagher*, pp.230–41; 239. This notion that liberty motivated economic and social progress was a common theme in Meagher's speeches. See, for example, 'Spirit of the North-European Examples', Belfast, 19 Nov. 1847, in Meagher (ed.), *Speeches*, pp.183–4.
41. O'Meagher, *Some Historical Notices*, pp.157–67. In his 'American Notes', O'Meagher also noted the southern Meaghers, descendants of James Meagher of Rathcash, Kilkenny, who migrated to Newfoundland. His sons relocated to Mobile, Alabama, and seem to have been involved in the illegal African slave trade, pp.175–8. William O'Meagher of New Orleans and Thomas W. Meagher of Kentucky both served as surgeons in the Confederate army, p.182.
42. Cited in Hernon, *Celts, Catholics and Copperheads*, p.17. For accounts of the 69th and Meagher at Bull Run see Conyngham, *The Irish Brigade*, pp.30–46; Cavanagh, *Memoirs*, pp.388–405; Jones, *The Irish Brigade*, pp.55–67 and Christopher M. Garcia, 'The Fighting 69th New York State Militia at Bull Run', in Pia Seija Seagrove (ed.), *The History of the Irish Brigade. A Collection of Historical Essays* (Fredericksburg, VA: Sergeant Kirkland's Museum and Historical Society, 1997), pp.35–56.
43. Thomas Francis Meagher, *The Last Days of the 69th in Virginia. A Narrative in Three Parts* (New York: Lynch and Cole, 1861) p.11; pp.5–6. Lynch and Cole were the publishers of the *Irish American* which had a weekly circulation of 30,000, and Meagher's narrative was initially serialized in this newspaper.
44. Meagher, 'The Irish Soldier', in Lyons, *Brigadier-General Thomas Francis Meagher*, p.118; 107–10, 117–19.
45. On Meagher's appointment see Athearn, *Thomas Francis Meagher*, pp.105–11; Burton, *Melting Pot Soldiers*, pp.119–20; Cavanagh, *Memoirs*, pp.425–31 and Conyngham, *The Irish Brigade*, pp.67–70.
46. The whole text of Meagher's address to his officers is printed in Cavanagh, *Memoirs*, pp.433–9; p.439.
47. Conynham, *The Irish Brigade*, pp.336, xi–xii; Joseph G. Bilby, *The Irish Brigade in the Civil War* (Conshohoken, PA: Combined Publishing, 1998) p.137; Philip T. Tucker, 'Celtic Warriors in Blue', in Pia Seija Seagrove (ed.), *History of the Irish Brigade*, pp.1–4 and O'Brien (ed.) *My Life in the Irish Brigade*, pp.i–ii.
48. Bilby, *The Irish Brigade*, p.136; Burton, *Melting Pot Soldiers*, p.126.

49. Bilby, *The Irish Brigade*, p.137.
50. *Ibid.*, p.137; Lawrence F. Kohl (ed.), *The Irish Brigade and its Campaigns*, p.xii; William Corby, *Memoirs of Chaplin Life. Three Years With the Irish Brigade in the Army of the Potomac* (Chicago, IL: LaMonte, O'Donnell and Co., 1992), pp.131–2.
51. On Lee see Alan T. Noolan, *Lee Considered. General Robert E. Lee and Civil War History* (Chapel Hill, NC: University of North Carolina Press, 1991), pp.91–106.
52. Athearn, *Thomas Francis Meagher*, p.113. Although Kelly O'Grady questions Meagher's personal bravery, *Clear the Confederate Way!*, pp.127–9, this is not the general view of other historians or his own troops. See, for example, Farewell Address of the Officers of the 69th, 63rd and 88th Regiments, N.Y.S.V., Irish Brigade, 20 May 1863, Non-Commissioned Officers of the 88th regiment to General Meagher, 21 May 1863, and Resolutions of the Officers of the 116th Regiment Pennsylvania Volunteers, Irish Brigade, 13 May, 1863, published in Cavanagh, *Memoirs*, Appendix, pp.28–32.
53. Cited in Conyngham, *The Irish Brigade*, p.xxii.
54. For Meagher's report on his first battle with the Irish Brigade see, United States War Department, *The War of the Rebellion: A Compilation of the Official Records of the Union and Confederate Armies*, 128 vols. (Washington, DC: Government Printing Office, 1880–1901), vol.11, part 1, pp.775–9. Also see, Cavanagh, *Memoirs*, pp.432–47 and Conyngham *The Irish Brigade*, pp.141–62. For an account of the entire campaign see Stephen W. Sears, *To the Gates of Richmond. The Peninsula Campaign* (New York: Ticknor and Fields, 1992).
55. Athearn, *Thomas Francis Meagher*, pp.112–13.
56. Terry L. Jones has suggested that Meagher's troops fought with either the 1st or 10th Louisiana and not the Louisiana Tigers as usually noted in previous works, *Lee's Tigers. The Louisiana Infantry in the Army of Northern Virginia* (Baton Rouge: Louisiana State University Press, 1987), p.110.
57. For Meagher's Report of 30 September 1862, see *War of the Rebellion*, vol. 19, part 1, pp.293–5. For an account of the Irish Brigade at Antietam see, Bilby, *The Irish Brigade*, pp.51–61; Conyngham, *The Irish Brigade*, pp.296–308, 309–22; Kevin E. O'Brien 'Sprig of Green: The Irish Brigade', in Pia Seija Seagrove (ed.), *History of the Irish Brigade*, pp.59–94, and Stephen W. Sears, *Landscape Turned Red. The Battle of Antietam* (New York: Ticknor and Fields, 1983), pp.242–4.
58. Cited in Sears, *Landscape Turned Red*, pp.342–3.
59. St Clair A. Mulholland, *The Story of the 116th Regiment Pennsylvania Volunteers in the War of Rebellion*, (New York: Fordham University Press, 1996), Lawrence F. Kohl (ed.), p.111.
60. *Ibid.*, pp.43–4, 24–62. For other accounts of the brigade at Fredericksburg see, Bilby, *The Irish Brigade*, pp.64–72; O'Brien (ed.), *My Life in the Irish Brigade*, pp.154–86; Conyngham, *The Irish Brigade*, pp.341–53.
61. Cited in Daniel E. Sutherland, *Fredericksburg and Chancellorsville* (Lincoln, NE: University of Nebraska Press, 1998), p.55. For Meagher's battle reports of 20 December 1862 see *The War of the Rebellion*, vol. 20, pp.240–6.
62. Keneally, *Great Shame*, p.375.
63. *Ibid.*, pp.375–6, 378–80. Meagher's letter to Edwin Stanton is reprinted in Cavanagh, *Memoirs*, pp.23–6.
64. Conyngham, *The Irish Brigade*, pp.388–403; Mulholland, *The Story of the 116th Regiment*, pp.94–102. For Meagher's report of 18 April 1863 see, *The War of the Rebellion*, vol. 25, part 1, pp.326–7.
65. Warner, *Generals in Blue*, p.xxi.
66. Meagher's resignation, 8 May 1863, in Cavanagh, *Memoirs*, Appendix, pp.26–7; Conyngham, *Irish Brigade*, pp.405–14.
67. Conyngham, *Irish Brigade*, pp.415–23; Myles Dungan, *Distant Drums. Irish Soldiers in Foreign Armies* (Belfast: Appletree Press, 1993), pp.33–4 and Kevin E. O'Brien, 'The Irish Brigade in the Wheatfield', in Pia Seija Seagrove (ed.), *History of the Irish Brigade*, pp.95–114.
68. Barry Lee Spink, 'Colonel Richard Byrnes: Irish Brigade Leader', in Pia Seija Seagrove (ed.), *History of the Irish Brigade*, pp.119–76; Bilby, *The Irish Brigade*, pp.449–54, 455–9. Thomas

A. Smyth was promoted to brigadier general on 1 October 1864 and was mortally wounded at Farmville, Virginia, 7 April 1865. He has the unfortunate distinction of being the last Union general to be killed in the war.

69. Keneally, *Great Shame*, pp.393–6; James M. McPherson, *Battle Cry of Freedom* (Oxford: Oxford University Press, 1998), pp.595–611 and generally, Ernest A. McKay, *The Civil War and New York City* (New York: Syracuse University Press, 1990). In his recent study Iver Bernstein has portrayed the riots in a wider context indicating that they were more than just an Irish-American anti-establishment outburst of violence: *The New York City Draft Riots; Their Significance for American Society and Politics in the Age of the American Civil War* (Oxford: Oxford University Press, 1990).
70. Meagher's letters to the Dublin Irishmen and to the Dublin Citizen in September 1863 can be found in the *Loyalty Tract No. 38*, pp.1–15. The whole debate is covered well in Hernon, *Celts, Catholics and Copperheads*, pp 93–108.
71. Keneally, *Great Shame*, p.389. Meagher's oration on Corcoran is published in Cavanagh, *Memoirs*. Cavanagh covers this period of Meagher's life but rather overestimates his commitment to the Fenians, pp.489–92.
72. Lyons, *Brigadier-General Thomas Francis Meagher*, p.39; Cavanagh, *Memoirs*, pp.492–3; and Keneally, *Great Shame*, pp.393–4. Robert G. Athearn, *Thomas Francis Meagher*, pp.143–9.
73. Keneally, *Great Shame*, pp.394–5; Bilby, *The Irish Brigade*, p.140.
74. The issue as to whether Meagher was also promoted to brevet major general when he was appointed to his new office in Montana is discussed in Keneally, *Great Shame*, pp.398–9 and 649. This idea is dismissed by Robert G. Athearn, *Thomas Francis Meagher*, p.145. It seems that Meagher may have promoted himself.
75. Athearn, *Thomas Francis Meagher*, pp.170–1.
76. Meagher, 'The Spirit of the North', in *Speeches*, p.183. His speech in San Francisco is reprinted in Lyons, *Brigadier-General Thomas Francis Meagher*, pp.242–52. Lyons, however, misdates the speech as 24 January 1864. This is clearly incorrect for Meagher was in New York City in January 1864. The speech was clearly part of his western lecture tour in January 1854.

9

The Lost Leader? Thomas Francis Meagher and the Fenian Brotherhood

Pat McCarthy

In July 1865, Thomas Francis Meagher made a call on the New York offices of the Fenian Brotherhood.[1] He arrived to say goodbye to many of his friends since he was about to depart for the West and in the offices he met an old friend, Captain John Hearne.[2] A native of Dungarvan, County Waterford, Hearne had been been active in the Young Ireland Movement and was arrested in 1849; he spent ten months in prison before being released. Later emigrating to the United States, he fought in the Irish Brigade and had been a staff officer to Meagher himself. Hearne had also called into the Fenian offices to say farewell as he was returning to Ireland to take part in a planned Fenian rising. No record was kept of their conversation but their parting was symbolic; as one old comrade returned home to renew the fight for Irish freedom, the other, Meagher, was turning westwards to renew the lustre of his somewhat fallen reputation. For Meagher, it could be seen as the final break with militant Irish nationalism after a period of years when he had flirted with the Fenian movement.

Fenianism was the logical and lineal descendant of Young Ireland. It also created a transatlantic nexus between militant Irish nationalism in the United States and in Ireland, a link that has persisted to the present time. In both countries Irishmen dedicated to revolutionary action emerged to lead new organizations. Known initially as the Irish Republican Brotherhood (IRB) in Ireland, and as the Fenian Brotherhood in the United States, the term Fenian soon came to be applied indiscriminately to members of both organizations and indeed to successor bodies such as Clan na Gael. The founders of both bodies were men who had been 'out' in Ireland during the 1848 Rising – James Stephens, Thomas Clerk Luby and Philip Gray, Michael Doheny and John O'Mahony, both of whom lived in the United States. Not all the former leaders of Young Ireland embraced the new movement however, and in the United States two names were conspicuous by their absence – John Mitchel and Thomas Francis Meagher. For Mitchel, his refusal to be associated with the new movement was the culmination of a growing disillusionment with Irish politics and his commitment to the Confederacy. Thomas Francis Meagher's relationship with fenianism was more complex and it is this relationship that is explored in this essay.

THE EMMET MONUMENT ASSOCIATION

On 27 May 1852, the 28 year-old Thomas Francis Meagher stepped ashore in New York after his dramatic escape from Van Diemen's Land and other escapees such as Patrick O'Donohoe and Terence Bellew McManus would soon join him and the other Young Ireland exiles in New York City. All would face the new challenge of earning a living in their new homeland and, at the same time, they formed a secret directory which maintained contact with some of their erstwhile colleagues in Ireland such as John O'Leary, Thomas Clark Luby, Philip Grey and Joseph Brenan. They also had control over a substantial sum of money originally collected among the emigrant Irish in 1848.[3] It was this directory that had financed Meagher on his arrival in New York City. While he became a member of the organization his series of lecture tours took him away from New York City and, consequently, he was not a very active member of the 'directory'. In 1854, Great Britain and her allies France, Turkey and Sardinia declared war on Russia and invaded the Crimea. The campaign soon became bogged down in a protracted siege of Sevastopol. To some it seemed that 'England's difficulty was Ireland's opportunity'. Doheny, O'Mahony and Michael Corcoran formed the Emmet Monument Association, a title redolent of Robert Emmet's stirring speech from the dock. Its aim was to organize an armed expedition of not less than 5,000 trained volunteers to Ireland while the greater part of the British army was in the Crimea. Doheny and O'Mahony entered into negotiations with the Russian ambassador to the United States and convinced him of their ability to raise and lead such a force. In return, the ambassador was authorized by his government to pledge both arms and money. The movement spread rapidly and, according to Michael Cavanagh,

> It numbered within its ranks the greater portion of the organised Irish nationalists throughout the chief cities of the Union, while in New York it numbered more armed and disciplined men, pledged to the cause of Ireland's freedom than there have been at any period since.[4]

Meagher, however, did not join even though he must have been aware of the existence of this secret oath-bound society but his lectures at least helped to inspire others in the cause. Before anything could come of the drilling and plotting the Crimean War ended in March 1856. The association was dissolved and the members released from their pledges. The leadership, however, formed a committee of thirteen to await that elusive opportunity to strike for Irish freedom. They did not have to wait long.

MEAGHER AND FENIANISM: THE FIRST ENCOUNTER

In 1857 the British Empire was shaken to the core by the Indian Mutiny. The repercussions extended beyond the sub-continent and, when added to the growing

French threat to British naval supremacy, it seemed to the directory that the elusive opportunity had arrived. This time, Irish American efforts would be supplemented by a parallel movement in Ireland. On St Patrick's Day, 17 March 1858, James Stephens, Thomas Clarke Luby and Peter Langan established the Irish Republican Brotherhood in Dublin as a secret oath-bound revolutionary society.[5] A short time later O'Mahony and Doheny established the Fenian Brotherhood in America. Both societies expanded steadily after initial difficulties. In Ireland, Stephens undertook an extensive organizing tour and by the autumn he felt confident enough to visit America to ensure a steady flow of money to finance the operations in Ireland. In particular, he had his eye on the money controlled by the directory. At this point the money lying dormant in the account amounted to a very substantial $30,000 (about £6,000 at the prevailing rate of exchange).[6] To obtain access to this Stephens knew that he would have to gain the support of Meagher and Mitchel, still the most visible and influential of the Irish-American leadership. Access to the fund would not only provide an immediate financial boost, but the endorsement of the directory would be the best way to ensure a continuous flow of funds across the Atlantic.

On Wednesday, 13 October 1858 Stephens landed in New York City, alone and unexpected.[7] He immediately sought out Michael Doheny, but their meeting was marred by a personality clash as Stephens sought to impose his personal control on all aspects of the movement on both sides of the Atlantic. In addition, Doheny resented the emphasis that Stephens was putting on Meagher and Mitchel, both of whom were standing aloof from the new movement. Doheny could not have been aware of Stephens' real opinion of Mitchel and Meagher. In his diary Stephens wrote:

> These were my opinions before I left Ireland. I was certain of the cooperation of both Mitchel and Meagher. Not that I had high opinion of – or even believed – in their patriotism. But I believed that they would not dare hold out against the facts I had to state . . . they dare not because by so doing, it would be evident to all that they were shams, had been shams probably at all times and had abandoned their country.[8]

Despite his deepest feelings, Stephens persisted and finally Doheny agreed to contact Mitchel. While he waited for a reply Stephens focussed on recruiting Meagher. On 19 October both he and Doheny met Meagher at the Fifth Avenue residence of Meagher's in-laws, the Townsends, where he then lived. Stephens remembered that,

> As Meagher had met me but once in Ireland, I was not surprised at his not being able to recognize me. On being presented he gave me a patronizing hand, inviting us up to his study. I had been told of his obesity; but, in spite of this, he appeared by no means imposing on this occasion. The intellectual and moral portion of his head is small, and his measured way of speaking would scarcely reconcile one to the genius of Shakespeare.

> Briefly stated our position at home. He seemed greatly struck; pronounced me the Tone of our generation, expressed not only sympathy but a desire to forward my views as far as he could. On hearing of the letter to Mitchel, and the telegram sent to him, was pleased, seeing the importance of his cooperation. He would present me to the directory (for he also deemed it better to see Mitchel before applying for the money in the hands of the directory) on my return, and, as a member propose that it should be given to me. All this, though pleasant, had one drawback; he said nothing about going heartily to work with us. He said however that he would give the matter his most earnest consideration. On leaving, he asked me to meet him next day at the office of the Irish News.[9]

When they met the next day, Meagher said he had considered Stephens' proposals and was ready to throw himself 'heart and soul' into the new movement.

Buoyed up with Meagher's assurances, Stephens decided to travel to Tennessee to meet Mitchel. As he had business in Washington, D.C., Meagher, along with another former Young Irelander, Thomas D'Arcy Magee, travelled with Stephens as far as the capital. On their parting Meagher gave Stephens a letter of introduction to Mitchel stating that 'This will be handed to you by our gallant friend, Stephens – one of the truest of the true – and, I verily believe, the Wolfe Tone, of our generation.'[10] The initial meeting between Stephens and Mitchel was very successful. Mitchel was won over by Stephens' enthusiasm and tales of the organization being built up in Ireland. Stephens was invited to stay at the Mitchel home, and for two days they conversed eagerly together, remembering their Young Ireland days and planning the forthcoming struggle. Mitchel later recalled:

> For two days he remained with us, telling me romantic tales of his armed, sworn, organised forces in Ireland, all he wanted was that I should publicly call on my fellow countrymen in America for money, and more money, and no end of money to be remitted to him for revolutionary purposes.[11]

For the moment at least, all that Stephens wanted of Mitchel was his support in accessing the funds controlled by the directory and this Mitchel promised to do, saying that he would write to each of its five members. Buoyed up by this Stephens returned to New York. He was not long there when he had a further meeting with Mitchel who told him that he had changed his mind, even though he had already dispatched the letters as he had promised. Although he personally supported Stephens' efforts, he would not do so publicly, nor would he further petition the directory. Disappointed, but not downhearted, Stephens waited in New York City for the return of Meagher, consoling himself with the thought that 'there are two gentlemen, however, members of this present directory that are good and true, Robert Emmet and T. F. Meagher'.[12]

This belief in Meagher's commitment did not last long. On 25 January 1859,

O'Mahoney mentioned that Meagher was back in New York but had made no mention of Stephens or his support for fenianism. With a sense of foreboding Stephens decided to seek out Meagher. A few days later he called to him at his office. After a perfunctory greeting, Meagher said to him, 'I left in a letter for you in case you did not call.' Stephens opened the letter, as he said himself, 'with a misgiving'. It was brief and to the point:

> New York,
> 26 January 1859
> My Dear Stephens,
> I have come to the conclusion, after some days of conscientious reflections, that, if it be not criminal, it is unworthy of me, in any way, however trivial or indirectly, to urge or authorize a revolutionary movement, in the hazards of which, from a conviction of their utter uselessness, I feel at present no disposition whatever to participate. You will, therefore, be so good as to erase my name from the paper you did me the honour to submit to me for my signature a few weeks ago, since by this letter it is virtually withdrawn. And with sincere regards – and friendship,
> Believe me,
> Very faithfully yours, Thomas F. Meagher.[13]

Without comment Stephens concluded his American journal with that cold and dismissive letter. With these words it must have seemed that 'Meagher of the Sword' had turned his back forever on fenianism. Stephens, with all hope of immediate American funding shattered, returned to Ireland to continue his indefatigable work in building up the IRB. For the time being at least, Mitchel chose to have nothing to do with Irish nationalism but focussed his formidable talents as a newspaper editor on defending the South and the institution of slavery. For Meagher, however, there remained a certain ambivalence in his attitude to fenianism. Stephens must have felt that there was still some hope that Meagher would play some part, for he confided to his diary:

> As to the Man of the Sword he has performed such patriotic feats within the last lustrum as most assuredly make the angels weep. Still I must do Meagher the justice to say that I believe his heart (filled) infinitely more with everything generous, and even noble, than Mitchel's is and but for his proverbial weakness, he would, as in his best moments do good service to Ireland.[14]

ON THE FRINGES OF FENIANISM

Over the course of the next two years the Fenian Brotherhood developed slowly but steadily. Several Phoenix regiments of armed Irishmen were formed and began drilling with arms, while others joined the 69th New York Militia, 'The Fighting Irish', to gain military experience. Several times in that period it seemed that Meagher was about to join as he was, according to Cavanagh, inspired by the sight of the ranks of uniformed and armed men marching in parade. On the morning of 17 March 1861 Meagher went to the Fenian office to meet Doheny but as Doheny was absent he conversed with Cavanagh.[15] Meagher expressed 'admiration of the disciplined column of armed Irishmen that had paraded that morning' and of his determination to join them. Typically Meagher would only deal with Doheny and he left promising to return. However, later events would overtake Meagher as the crisis of the Union developed. Following the attack on Fort Sumter, 12 April 1861, Meagher decided to take up arms in defence of the Union, a decision which led to the eventual creation of the Irish Brigade and his commission as a brigadier general. To recruit and motivate his men Meagher often invoked the spirit of Irish liberation; that the experiences gained in the American Civil War would be useful in the fight for Ireland's freedom. As his brigade advanced from Yorktown in May 1862, it became scattered in a violent rainstorm. An officer of the brigade recalled the general's reaction:

> General Meagher could have been found pacing back and forth in an abandoned shanty, worrying about his command. 'Great God' he said to one of his officers, 'the Irish Brigade will be brought into action at daybreak and the work of a brigade will be expected from them, while I have scarcely two hundred men. Are these the men that I expected at some future time to free Ireland with'![16]

Despite these sentiments Meagher did not join the brotherhood although many of his officers and men were Fenians.[17] One of the leading Fenian organizers in the Irish Brigade was Dr Lawrence Reynolds, a native of Waterford and, also like Meagher, another Young Ireland exile. Fenian meetings within the Irish Brigade were held openly every month, but despite his known sentiments Meagher continued to remain aloof from the organization.[18] While the image of a victorious general leading a uniformed disciplined mass of Irishmen into the field may have appealed to his vanity Meagher seemed unwilling to take on the task of creating a secret revolutionary society. Nonetheless, as his standing remained high amongst the Irish-American community of the North, the Fenian leadership was not slow in using Meagher's name for their own purposes.

On 15 January 1861, Meagher's fellow Young Irelander and escapee from Van Diemen's Land, Terence Bellew McManus, died in San Francisco.[19] The following day he was buried in Calvary Cemetery; but in death he was destined to perform one last service for the cause of Irish nationalism. The local Fenian circle in San Francisco conceived the idea of exhuming the remains and carrying them in state to Ireland for reburial. It was believed that such an action would provide an ideal opportunity for a popular demonstration of militant nationalism. The idea was taken up enthusiastically by the Fenian leadership in America, but Stephens and Luby in Ireland took some convincing. Eventually, Stephens saw the potential advantages and took control of the organizing committee in Ireland.[20] In America, Doheny and O' Mahoney were the principal organizers of the project. All local committees were filled by sworn members of the brotherhood and all reported to the Obsequies Committee of Doheny and O'Mahoney. Though not a Fenian, Meagher was immediately co-opted to the Obsequies Committee. Apart from his Young Ireland connection, his social standing in New York City and his friendship with Archbishop Hughes were obvious advantages to the Fenians who, as a secret society, were disliked by the Church on both sides of the Atlantic.

On 21 August 1861 the corpse was put on a train travelling from San Francisco to New York City and as it crossed the continent the funeral cortege was met by large demonstrations of Irish men and women. It arrived in New York City on 15 September and Meagher was prominent in the official welcoming party. The next day Meagher had a meeting with Archbishop Hughes and persuaded him to officiate at the Requiem Mass for McManus in St Patrick's Cathedral. In the meantime, the coffin rested at the Steven's Hotel where uniformed Fenians mounted a guard of honour. It was there that Meagher paid his formal respects and wept at the sight of the coffin and the memory of the days that he and McManus had spent together trying to raise the people in 1848. At a Mass held on 18 September, Archbishop Hughes gave a stirring sermon. The corpse lay in New York until 4 October when it was put on board ship. When it reached Ireland it had the same rousing, emotional effect on the people even though both the Bishop of Cork and Cardinal Cullen, Archbishop of Dublin, refused permission for a lying in state in any church in their dioceses. Meanwhile Meagher, his temporary service to the Fenian Brotherhood over, returned to his army duties.

MEAGHER TAKES THE OATH

Meagher's Irish Brigade suffered appalling losses at the Battle of Antietam and Fredericksburg in 1862. Further losses at Chancellorsville in 1863 reduced his brigade to only about 10 per cent of its original strength. Repeated applications to the War Department for a period of rest and recruitment for his small band of survivors had met with refusal. A despondent Meagher decided to resign his commission. On 8 May 1863 he wrote to the Secretary of War that,

> I beg most respectfully to tender you my resignation as Brigadier General, commanding what was once known as the Irish Brigade. In tendering my resignation, however, as the Brigadier General in command of this poor vestige and relic of the Irish Brigade, I beg sincerely to assure you that my

> services in any capacity that can prove useful, are freely at the summons and disposition of the Government of the United States.[21]

On 14 May the resignation was accepted and Meagher returned to New York City. That summer as the American Civil War moved to an important climax at Vicksburg and Gettysburg, Meagher watched as an impotent witness, a general without a command. It must have been galling for 'Meagher of the Sword' to be a 'mere' civilian at this particular moment, especially when he read in the newspapers of the heroic fight of his brigade at Gettysburg. Restless for some form of action or involvement he approached Doheny and a week later, 11 July 1863, Thomas Francis Meagher was sworn into the Fenian Brotherhood.[22] Throughout that summer he was a frequent visitor to the Fenian headquarters in New York and it seemed that he was ready to play a major role again in militant Irish nationalism.

When news reached him that Meagher had taken the oath James Stephens was naturally elated. He at once saw an opportunity to help IRB recruitment in Ireland and specifically in Waterford. In a letter to Doheny, dated 14 October 1863 he wrote:

> Waterford City is the most backward spot in Munster... As General Meagher is so desirous of forwarding the work, it struck me that a spirited address to the manhood of his native city would have a good effect, and so being last week there I asked my friends if such were the case. They were quite of my way of thinking. That address, then, I am desirous of having at the General's convenience. It would be best in form of a private letter, addressed to a third party, in which the General might express his wonder and regret at hearing how dull his townsfolk are, at the very time there is such reason for faith and activity. The reasons for this faith and activity he could give with effect by stating the numbers willing and bound to come over here at the close of the year. There should be nothing about a war with England: the people should be taught to look to our own race and efforts solely. Of course, you will show this to the General. Mind, it would not do to publish an address from the General to his townsmen; that, while stirring up a fire would certainly neutralise the efforts of many more. Should the General make me the recipient of his address I shall look on it as a favour.[23]

In the same letter he appealed to Doheny to ask Meagher to use his influence to raise £500 to cover the costs of launching the Fenian newspaper, the *Irish People*. There is no reply from Meagher to Stephens' suggestion extant, nor was one likely since it seems that the general's new-found enthusiasm was already beginning to wane. Nor does he seem to have raised any funds for the newspaper venture. Less than a month after the launch of the paper, on the 28 November 1863, it was in dire financial straits and O'Donovan Rossa, the editor, was forced to draw on his own meagre resources to pay the wages of the printers.[24]

That autumn the Fenian Brotherhood decided to capitalize on their growing strength and to hold a national convention in Chicago.[25] The purpose of the convention was to adopt a new constitution, elect an officer-board and to publicize their activities. It was also an attempt by the American organization to assert equality with, if not primacy over, the IRB in Ireland where Stephens tended to view America simply as a source of funds. Fenian circles in twelve states and in the Union armies of the Cumberland, the Tennessee and the Potomac selected delegates to meet in Chicago on 3 November 1863. One of the most powerful and influential circles was that of the Army of the Potomac, home of the Irish Brigade. General Michael Corcoran's Irish Legion, a garrison unit and numerous other units with a large Fenian membership were also prominent in the East. Meagher was nominated to represent the Army of the Potomac and, as the eighty-two delegates gathered, it must have seemed that this would be an ideal stage for Meagher to play a leading role. He had made arrangements with John O'Mahony to be present for the opening of the convention but instead he headed for Washington on, what he claimed was, army business. On his return to New York he sent a telegram to the convention:

> New York, Nov. 4, 1863.
> John O'Mahony,
> Fenian Hall,
> Chicago.
> Had to go to Washington on call of War Department. The call imperative. Have to go again on Saturday. Will proceed to the Army next week. I heartily concur in plan and regulations of reorganization as proposed by you, with such modifications as the Convention adopts.
> Fraternity and happiness and honor to all.
> Thos. Francis Meagher.[26]

Although the convention continued for four days, Meagher made no effort to join it. One of the immediate outcomes of the convention was a successful recruiting drive that winter, but Meagher seems to have taken no part in it. Instead, he went south again to visit his old comrades in the army and spent November there being royally entertained. Just before Christmas, Meagher decided to return to New York City. General Michael Corcoran accompanied him to Fairfax station to say goodbye but while riding back to camp was thrown from his horse and killed. Corcoran had been the leading Fenian in the United States Army and his death was a major blow to the movement.

The movement held a memorial service for Corcoran at the Cooper Institute in New York City, on 22 January 1864, and Meagher was the main speaker to a huge audience. Mindful that the occasion was sponsored by the Fenian Brotherhood, he paid stirring tribute to the dead general and concluded his speech with a detailed review of Corcoran's commitment to the cause of Ireland's freedom;

> Thus with him did the glorious project of having Ireland established as a nation become the ultimate aim of his military life. Hence it was that, convinced they were upon the true road, he joined the Fenian Brotherhood under the auspices of which these words commemorative of their brother are this night spoken, and finding in that brotherhood men of his own high aim, he remained faithful and serviceable to it to the last... Brothers see to it that his wish, his prayer, his hope shall be fulfilled.[27]

Despite these stirring words Meagher does not seem to have played any further role in fenianism. Although he eulogised Corcoran, his friend and one-time commanding officer, and repeated those sentiments at a series of lectures that spring, he carefully avoided making any public commitment to the movement himself but concentrated his efforts on reviving his military career.[28] Corcoran's death prompted the War Department to place Meagher once more on active service, 23 December 1863, yet he remained without a command. Significantly, he was not offered the vacancy created by Corcoran's death and how Meagher might have been influenced by the strongly Fenian regiments of the Irish Legion we can only speculate. Sent to Tennessee, the final phase of Meagher's military career was hardly glorious and on 12 May 1865 Meagher, for the second time, submitted his resignation.

As Meagher drifted away from fenianism his position as a leader of the Irish-American community began to fade. Throughout the summer of 1864, as the presidential election loomed, he became more and more vocal in his support of Lincoln and the Republican administration – both anathema to the traditionally Democrat supporting Irish. This move was noted with sorrow and anger by the *Irish American*, voice of the Irish community. On 15 October 1864, it intoned, 'Between him and the people who loved and trusted him once, he has opened a gulf he can never bridge over.' A few weeks later Meagher called on the Irish to vote for Lincoln. The *Irish American* newspaper saw this as the final betrayal and responded on 12 November:

> In General Meagher's fall from the high position he once held in the esteem and affection of his countrymen, we see only a subject of regret. Our indignation at his unprovoked attack upon our people has long since subsided into contempt, and we have no desire to add a deeper tint to an act that has gone so far to darken the whole record of a life, of which the promise was once so fair.[29]

Despite the condemnation of the *Irish American*, Meagher retained the friendship and affection of his former comrades and he continued to be a frequent visitor to the offices of the Fenian Brotherhood. Still probably a nominal member, they seemed to have accepted his token assistance and harboured no grudge.

EPILOGUE

In August 1865 Meagher was appointed secretary and later acting governor of Montana Territory. Whilst there, the Irish-American community was agog with preparation for a Fenian rising, with many former soldiers making their way to Ireland. Others prepared to strike at a more convenient target, Canada. The papers were filled with stories of Fenian military preparations for the invasion of Canada and inevitably Meagher's name was linked to the movement. The rumours crossed the Atlantic and gained wide circulation. On 21 January 1866, the *Waterford News* carried an item, *General Meagher's Plans*, which stated that

> ... my informant has reliably learned that the latest move of the Fenian body is to appoint Thomas Francis Meagher as Dictator. His plans are said to divide the Fenian Army into two immense bodies and with one to invade Canada and with the other to join the Emperor Napoleon in sustaining the throne of Maximilian in Mexico. By this stroke of policy it is stated that Meagher hopes to secure the eternal goodwill of the Emperor and to gain his support to the scheme of establishing an Irish Republic.[30]

Appalled at the thought that his government contacts might think of him as an active Fenian, Meagher wrote to Secretary of State Seward, begging him to regard any such reports as 'absurd'.[31]

Truly the wheel had turned full circle; the young Irish rebel had become a middle-aged American conservative. To the Fenian movement in the United States he was a lost leader, one whose ability, prestige, charisma and national record could have unified that fractious movement and fulfilled its potential. We can possibly get an intimation of Meagher's true thoughts on fenianisn from his private correspondence. In a letter from Virginia City, Montana, to a friend in San Francisco dated 27 October 1866, he expressed himself on Fenian matters thus;

> In the hands of thoroughly capable and reliable men it (fenianism) would have been and yet may be an organisation powerful enough to command for the Irish race on this continent the recognition they are entitled to, which, with such an opening as a war between England and France, or a war between England and the United States, it would be more than adequate to the liberation of Ireland and her triumph as an independent nation permanently guaranteed. Vast resources have, however, in the mismanagement of this magnificent organisation been scandalously wasted.[32]

Is this what Meagher had subconsciously sought but had shied away from? Was he the 'thoroughly capable and reliable man' the movement needed? We shall never know. We do know, however, that he had several opportunities to put himself forward but he chose to walk away. Nominal membership of the movement and friendship with his comrades was sufficient for him but the movement needed more. It needed his undoubted charisma and leadership; unfortunately these were not forthcoming. Truly he was the lost leader.

NOTES

1. M. Cavanagh, *Memoirs of Gen. Thomas Francis Meagher, Comprising the Leading Events of His Career* (Worcester, MA: Messenger Press, 1892), p.493.
2. M.H. Kane, 'American Soldiers in Ireland, 1865-1867' *The Irish Sword*, 23, No. 91, (Summer 2002), p.123.
3. J. Belchem, 'Irish American Nationalism in 1848', *Irish Historical Studies*, 24, No. 113, (1994), p.44.
4. Cavanagh, *Memoirs*, p.344.
5. T.W. Moody (ed.), *The Fenian Movement* (Cork: Mercier Press, 1968), pp.11–19. See also, R.V. Comerford, *The Fenians in Context: Irish politics & society* (Dublin: Wolfhound Press, 1998), p.47.
6. K.J. Quigley, 'American Financing of Fenianism in Ireland, 1858–1867'. (Unpublished MA thesis, Maynooth, 1983), pp.29-30. See also Charles Gavan Duffy, *My Life in Two Hemispheres* (London: T. Fisher Unwin, 1898).
7. James Stephens kept a detailed, if self-serving, diary of his American trip. Never published, the original is held in the Public Record Office, Belfast, Northern Ireland. A copy is also held in the manuscript section of the National Library of Ireland, Ms. 6418, and is referred to as the 'Stephens' Diary, *1859*'.
8. *Ibid.*
9. *Ibid.*
10. *Ibid.*
11. W. Dillon, *Life of John Mitchel*, vol., 2, (London: Kegan Paul, Trench & Co., 1883), p.120.
12. Stephens' Diary, *1859.*
13. *Ibid.*
14. *Ibid.*
15. Cavanagh, *Memoirs*, p.362.
16. T. Keneally, *The Great Shame. A Story of the Irish in the Old World and the New* (London: Vintage, 1998), p.351.
17. W.L. Burton, *Melting Pot Soldiers. The Unions Ethnic Regiments* (New York: Fordham University Press, 1998) pp.159–61.
18. J.G. Bilby, *The Irish Brigade in the Civil War* (Conshchoken, Pennsylvania: Combined Publishing, 1995), p.74. See also P. Jones, *The Irish Brigade* (New York: Robert B. Luce), pp.121–2.
19. T.G. McAllister, *Terence Bellew McManus, 1811–1861* (Maynooth: Department of History, St Patrick's College, 1972) pp.43–7
20. D. Ryan, *The Fenian Chief. A Biography of James Stephens* (Dublin: University of Miami Press, 1967), pp.170–80.
21. Cavanagh, *Memoirs*, p.485.
22. *The United Irishman*, 14 October 1886. See also Cavanagh, *Memoirs*, p.489 and Keneally, *Great Shame*, p.400.
23. Stephens to Doheny, Fenian Papers, National Library of Ireland, p.740.
24. Quigley, 'American Financing', p.37.

25. R.G. Athearn, *Thomas Francis Meagher: An Irish Revolutionary in America* (Boulder, CO: University of Colorado Press, 1949), p.132. See also W.D'Arcy, *The Fenian Movement in the United States, 1885–1886* (Washington: Catholic University of America Press, 1947) p.20.
26. Cavanagh, *Memoirs*, p.486.
27. *Ibid.*, pp.350–6.
28. See, for example, his speech in Boston, 9 February 1864 quoted in the *Irish People*, 24 February 1864.
29. *Irish American*, 12 November 1864.
30. *Waterford News*, 21 January 1866.
31. Meagher to Seward, 20 February 1866, in *Territorial Papers of Montana*, vol. 1. Quoted in Athearn, *Thomas Francis Meagher*, p.151.
32. Letter quoted in memoir of Maj. Gen. Thomas Francis Meagher with Diary, Correspondence, Speeches, etc. – compiled by Frederick Kearney (National Library of Ireland, Ms. 9728).

10

With Courage and Undaunted Obstinacy: Meagher in Montana, 1865–67

Jon Axline

Few figures in Montana's short history have continued to generate as much controversy as Thomas Francis Meagher. Arriving in the territory with the best intentions, he clearly left it in a worse condition than he had found it. Like many Americans, Meagher viewed the West as a land of opportunity, a region that would give him a chance to revitalize his sinking post-Civil War military and political career. He found Montana a territory much to his liking; its booming economy, rudimentary government, rowdy and unsophisticated inhabitants and an Indian population which defied pacification, all appealed to him. Positive that unlimited possibilities for personal advancement lay before him, Meagher tackled his new position with the characteristic enthusiasm and bravado that had marked his Civil War career. His activities in Montana, however, would create powerful political enemies. Their deep-felt personal hostility would help discredit him in contemporary eyes as well as continuing to influence any assessment of Meagher into our present century.

At the time of his appointment to the secretarial position in the territory, conditions in Montana were extremely volatile. In August 1862, prospectors discovered gold on Grasshopper Creek in south-western Montana. The Bannack mining camp appeared almost overnight as men (and some women) stampeded to the new placer mines from the nearly depleted diggings in Idaho. In the spring of 1863, prospectors fanned out across the territory in search of richer gold deposits. In May 1863, Bill Fairweather and four other miners made a major gold strike at Alder Gulch, about seventy-five miles east of Bannack. Within a few months as many as 10,000 miners worked the gravel along the gulch in search of pay dirt. The following year, prospectors also struck gold at other gulches with evocative names such as Last Chance, Confederate and Ophir. Many Montana miners had fled the East to escape service in the Civil War, but political conditions in Montana were soon to reflect the pro-Union and pro-Confederate prejudices of the rest of the country at war. While small, vocal minorities of Democrats were southern sympathizers, Republicans vehemently portrayed all Montana Democrats as secessionists and potential traitors.[1]

TERRITORIAL POLITICS

In May 1864, President Abraham Lincoln had signed the Organic Act officially creating the Montana Territory. He later appointed a governor, territorial secretary and judges while the white male residents of the territory elected local officials. This system of Republican federal appointees and locally elected Democrat Party officials created an explosive situation in remote Montana. The Republicans comprised the minority of the territory's population, while the Democrats, many of whom were Irish or of Irish descent, were in the majority.[2] In early 1865, territorial governor Sidney Edgerton moved the capital from a log cabin in Bannack to a substantial two-story building in the more populous Virginia City. Before the relocation, however, the first territorial legislature met in Bannack in December 1864. The assembly consisted of about the same number of Republicans as Democrats. The Republicans, however, held all the federally appointed posts, while the Democrats held the elected positions, such as county commissioners, clerks and treasurers. Despite the political friction in both the US Congress and in the territory, most Montana residents were too busy trying to strike it rich to pay much attention to politics.[3]

The first territorial legislature accomplished a great deal in establishing the foundation for a territorial government. It established the basis for a tax system, delineated county boundaries, and chartered a network of toll roads. It did all this, moreover, without the benefit of federal funds. Due to the Civil War, Congress had largely forgotten remote Montana and had failed to allocate funds for it. Even if Congress had distributed funds to the territory, only the territorial secretary was empowered to distribute the money under the terms of the Organic Act. Consequently, Governor Edgerton, a Republican, paid for much of the legislature's expenses out of his own pocket. Although the Republicans were well represented in the legislature, the prospect of paying for it must have galled him since the despised Democrats were still in the majority.[4] The *Montana Post*, Virginia City's Republican newspaper, often commented on the legislators' lack of sobriety and called them 'the most ungodly pack of sinners who ever sought to do business upon the hypothesis that it was advisable to keep up a show of decency'. Edgerton's son-in-law, the lawyer Wilbur Fisk Sanders, called all Democrats 'rebels and traitors', who were 'unfit to exercise the right of self-government'. When the raucous gathering adjourned after a few weeks, it had not named the date of its next annual meeting, a requirement of the Organic Act. This failure allowed Edgerton, with Republican support, to refuse to allow the legislature to meet again, a step which threw the territory in political chaos. For the Republicans, faced with a Democrat majority, it was better to have no government than one they could not control. In September 1865, General Thomas Francis Meagher stepped into this political maelstrom.[5]

In the two years before Meagher arrived in the territory, miners, ranchers and some businessmen had banded together to form vigilance committees to impose order on the lawless mining camps. Until federal judges arrived the vigilantes, many of whom were freemasons, brutally enforced law and order in the mining camps through banishment and the noose. At the time of Meagher's arrival in

Bannack, the vigilance committees still exercised a tremendous amount of influence in the territory through intimidation and fear. Radical Republicans, who comprised most of the vigilante leadership during the 1860s, portrayed outlaws as southern sympathizers and vice versa. For much of the next decade constant and sometimes vicious battles between the Republican/vigilante minority and the Democratic majority were a feature of Montana politics.[6] While Meagher's administration of the territory would be significantly influenced by these factors, he also became increasingly aware of the continued Native American threat to the 8,000 white settlers who were mainly concentrated in the south-west, and around Fort Benton at the head of the Missouri River. Eastern and northern Montana remained the realm of the Blackfeet, Crow, Lakota, Northern Cheyenne and the Assiniboine. Of the four trails that connected the territory to the mid-western states, the Bozeman Trail cut through the heart of the last great buffalo hunting grounds and, since 1865, both the Lakota and Northern Cheyenne had been attacking the forts along the trail.[7]

MEAGHER'S APPOINTMENT

Thomas Francis Meagher had always hoped that his military service would lead him into a political career or government service in his adopted republic. Following the end of the war in April 1865, Meagher had lobbied President Andrew Johnson for a political appointment in the West. Hoping for a governorship, he was disappointed that Johnson proved lukewarm to his constant applications. Johnson, a Union Democrat, did not want to upset the delicate political balance in Congress by appointing a fellow Democrat to a territorial governorship. Instead, he appointed the former commander of the Irish Brigade to the post of Secretary of Montana Territory. Having previously resolved to seek his fortune in the West, Meagher was in Minnesota when word of his appointment reached him. Travelling to Montana via Salt Lake City Meagher had, perhaps prophetically, pleaded with a friend to visit him before he had left New York City for it 'may be the last time... you shall see me, for I go to a fierce and frightful region of gorillas!'[8]

Upon Meagher's arrival in Bannack, Governor Edgerton, who was both unhappy with Meagher's appointment and eager to return to Ohio, briefly summarized the conditions in Montana. Having introduced Meagher to several leading prominent local citizens, mainly his own Republican supporters, he quickly decamped on the return stagecoach leaving Meagher as acting territorial governor. With the territorial papers in his pocket and the territory's $500 treasury stowed securely in his saddlebags, Meagher left Bannack for Virginia City where he was warmly greeted by its mining community. He told the crowd he would 'never be yoked, coaxed or otherwise teamed to any party'. Although he would eventually become associated with the Democrat Party majority in Montana, Meagher was determined to be his own man, to do what he thought best for the territory and, of course, what would also benefit his own political future. Frequently impulsive and not always good or deeply thought out, Meaghers' decisions often caused more problems than they solved. While historians would later attribute much of this to his tremendous ego and the bad advice of the sycophants who attached themselves to him, Meagher's initial gullibility and willingness to listen to the Republican faction would also influence his judgement.[9]

As a Union Democrat, Meagher tended to initially mirror the hostility the Republican faction felt for the southern sympathizers in Montana. He believed these 'turbulent men' were 'Favourers and abettors of treason', men 'not fitted to govern'. Initially, he refused to oppose the will of the Republican federal appointees, namely judges Hezekiah Hosmer and Lyman E. Munson, and he supported the Republican minority in the territory headed by vigilante Wilbur Fisk Sanders. With Meagher on their side, the Republicans hoped to continue business as usual and manipulate Meagher to their continued advantage. Similarly, the Democrats initially assumed that Meagher would ally himself with them and Meagher's own attempts to juggle the interests of both factions, with his eye on his own political advantage, would prove a difficult, if not impossible, task at best.[10]

DETERIORATING RELATIONS

Like any good politician, one of Meagher's first acts as acting governor was to make a fact-finding tour of the territory. This happened to coincide with an outbreak of hostilities between the Blackfeet in northern Montana and the old trading post settlement of Fort Benton on the Missouri River. Unhappy about the increasing number of white settlers in the region, the Blackfeet were angry about the effects the whiskey trade had on the tribe. The deteriorating relations between the whites and the Indians would plague Meagher's short career in Montana. In early November 1865, Meagher, Judge Munson, Indian Agent Gad Upson, an interpreter, and an armed escort met with representatives of the Blackfeet near Fort Benton. Meagher had little knowledge of, or experience in dealing with Native American's but fortunately he had the good sense to leave much of the negotiations to Munson and Upson. The judge later reflected that the meeting 'was a panoramic scene of Tribal costume, interlaced with painted faces and fantastic paraphernalia of Tribal ornaments requiring the graphic touch of the painter's brush on canvas to convey a realistic impression'.[11] After several days of negotiations the Montana delegation finally concluded a treaty with the Blackfeet. In return for a $7,500 annuity they agreed to cease their attacks on the outlying settlements around Fort Benton and move to a reservation closer to the Canadian border. Meagher's first trip to Fort Benton had important ramifications on the future development of his career in Montana.

While initially impressed with the Blackfeet, Meagher continued to view the Native Americans as little more than ignorant savages, an obstacle to both civilization and progress. Native American continued opposition to pacification would, Meagher believed, offer him an opportunity to reclaim his lost military glory. A few months after the treaty was signed a Blackfeet war party killed the Chouteau County clerk and, as attacks continued, Meagher regularly petitioned General William Tecumseh Sherman, commander of the military District of Missouri, for the permanent posting of a cavalry unit to Montana. In March 1866, the Civil War hero found he was unable to raise enough support from the federal government to rescue a stranded wagon train on the Missouri River from Indian attack. As a man of action this inability to shield his adopted territory from its enemies was irksome. It resulted in increased appeals to Sherman and General Ulysses S. Grant to provide Montana with a military force adequate to defend itself.[12] His trip had also provided Meagher with first-hand experience of the territory and his experiences indicated that the Republican view of the majority of the territory's white population was inaccurate and untrue.[13] It was this growing independence from his initial advisors which led to the unfortunate Jim Daniels affair, an incident that would have important political ramifications on Meagher's career.

In Helena on 29 November 1865, a drifter named Jim Daniels mortally wounded Andrew Gartley in a dispute over a poker game in a saloon after he caught Gartley cheating at cards. When Daniels had confronted him about it, Gartley pulled a revolver and Daniels responded by stabbing him twice. Immediately after the incident, the Helena vigilantes turned Daniels over to Judge Munson for trial. A jury convicted Daniels of manslaughter and Munson sentenced him to three years hard labour at the Virginia City jail.[14] While in itself not a particularly unusual event in a frontier society, Meagher would later be convinced that Daniels had acted in self-defence and he would grant Daniels a full pardon. This political blunder would compound Meagher's worsening relations with his powerful Republican enemies. Before January 1866, Meagher had largely managed to stand aside from the differences separating the Republicans and Democrats in Montana by not taking sides on any important issues concerning the governance of the territory. As time went on, however, he chafed at Republican control believing they exercised too much influence in the territory and impeded his own personal ambitions. Increasingly, he found himself in agreement with the 'Turbulent Men' in the territory whom he at first abhorred. That many were of Irish descent undoubtedly came to influence Meagher's reappraisal of his former opponents. Gradually, Meagher came to be seen as a spokesman for the majority Democratic Party in Montana.[15]

THE TERRITORIAL LEGISLATURE

At the urging of the territory's Democratic leaders and against the advice of the Republicans, Meagher called for the convening of a territorial legislature to meet in Virginia City in March 1866. This proved to be a controversial decision as both Hosmer and Munson, the influential judges, informed Meagher that he did not have the authority to call an assembly as the first territorial legislature had failed to meet the provisions regarding reconvening under the provisions of the 1864 Organic Act. Meagher, who had thoroughly studied the Act, ignored the protests of the judges and claimed that he did indeed have the authority to call the legislature under special circumstances. The dispute caused the final break between the Meagher and the Republican Party federal appointees. In his own defence, Meagher would later claim to a Helena audience that he had previously fallen under the influence of a 'bad advisor' (Sanders) who had led him to believe that the legislature would be dominated by 'rabid secessionists', and that he had been used by 'political rascals' to 'achieve their foul ends'.[16]

The Republicans had reason to fear a Democratic Party-controlled legislature, as it would undoubtedly challenge their control of the territory. Meagher complicated the problem by also issuing a further call for a constitutional convention to meet in Helena to draw up a constitution as the first step towards statehood. Meagher fully understood the ramifications his actions would have for the Republicans for he wrote in February 1866 to Secretary of State, William Seward, that 'everything...is delightful to me with the exception of the malignity of those ill-bred bigots, who...disappointed in their factious design by the just and liberal course I have considered it my duty to pursue, vent their vexation against me in vulgar and infamous detraction'. In response, the Republicans did not participate in the legislature and threatened to take their grievances to the United States Congress.[17]

The fierce debate over the constitutional convention intensified the conflict between Meagher and the Republicans. Many Republicans, and a few Democrats, believed it too early in the territory's history to consider statehood. The potential addition of more Democrats to Congress irked fewer people than did the idea of a Democrat Party-controlled state legislature. Even after the convention convened, the Republicans questioned Meagher's authority to call the gathering. Wilbur Fisk Sanders later claimed that Meagher surrounded himself with flatterers and toadies who had urged him to call the constitutional convention with the promise of a seat in the Senate when Montana was admitted to the Union, a pledge which would have certainly appealed to Meagher's ego. In December 1865, Meagher had informed Seward that were 'Montana admitted as a state tomorrow, the Union would have to encounter in Congress equivocal friends, if not flagrant mischief makers from here'. For his perceived betrayal of the Republicans and his increasing sympathy for the Democrats, his new enemies began to refer to Meagher as 'The Acting One', a derisive sobriquet which marked his decline as a legitimate politician in Montana.[18]

THE SECOND TERRITORIAL LEGISLATURE

Meagher called the second territorial legislature to order on 5 March 1866. While the legislature considered applications for toll road licences, established county boundaries, granted divorces and chartered ditch companies, Meagher's enemies began a systematic destruction of his reputation. The accusation that Meagher was addicted to drink had constantly bedevilled his career and deputy marshal Neil Howie recorded in his diary that Meagher had been drunk when he opened the legislative session. Federal tax collector and one-time vigilante, Nathaniel Langford, called Meagher a 'disgrace to our Territory' while Meagher's most vocal critic, Wilbur Fisk Sanders, a man Meagher had referred to as a the 'most vicious of my enemies... an unrelenting and unscrupulous extremist', compared Meagher to a 'Missouri Bushwhacker' and called him a traitor who was 'dead beyond any hope of resurrection'. Sanders, however, did later admit a grudging admiration for the general. In 1902 he wrote,

> I can well appreciate the affection which General Meagher inspired among his race and countrymen. His form was manly, his manners cordial, his demeanor gracious, his conversation instructive, his wit kindly, his impulses generous and I agree with Horace Greeley, who once said to me that General Meagher was one of the finest conversationalists he had ever known.[19]

Sanders' brother-in-law, William Chumasero, a Helena attorney, believed that Meagher 'wallow(ed) his days away in his room polluting his bed and person in the most indecent and disgusting manner', making his executive office 'a place of rendezvous for the vilest prostitutes'. In early 1866, even the *Montana Post*, which had previously been supportive of Meagher, thought his vanity clouded his vision and that the general continually surrounded himself with a 'gang of bibulous politicians and flatterers'.[20]

Meagher however, proved to be a responsible administrator. He regularly vetoed bills he considered not prudent or those for which he saw no reason. During much of his administration, he tried to dodge criticism at home and defend himself to his superiors in Washington. Meagher continually sought to head off any reports they might receive from his enemies, and his letters either justified his actions or continued to plead for military assistance against the Indians. In one letter he displayed his famous tenacity and will to succeed in his adopted territory: 'I am resolved not to turn my back on the Rocky Mountains until I have the means to whip my carriage and four through the New York Central Park, and sail my own yacht, with the Green Flag at the mizzen-peak, within three miles of the Irish coast.'[21] Recently a document has surfaced that throws new light on Meagher and his controversial character.

In the 1980s, researchers in Virginia City discovered a collection of business ledgers from the 1860s, one of which included the charges made to saloons by Meagher for liquor, beer and food. The amount of spirits shown to be paid for by Meagher was prodigious and, at first glance, it seemed to support reports of Meagher's drunkenness and rowdy behaviour during the 1866 territorial legislature. Historian Elliott West, however, has proposed a different theory. Professor West claims that while much of the alcohol may have been consumed by the general, much of it also may have been used in the negotiations for legislation; in essence, to 'buy' the support of key legislators on important bills. What is also interesting about the ledger is that Meagher paid his bills in full despite his refusal to accept a salary during the first months of his tenure in Montana.[22]

THE DANIELS AFFAIR

Throughout the legislative session, Sanders and his political allies were confident that the Republican judiciary would nullify the laws passed by the 'Bogus Legislature'. While judges Hosmer and Munson had hitherto kept relatively quiet about the proceedings in Virginia City, the reappearance of the Jim Daniels affair provided the catalyst that caused the deterioration of Meagher's relations with them. In his book *Vigilante Days and Ways*, Nathaniel P. Langford later wrote that Meagher was 'under the influence of an unfortunate habit' when he granted Daniels a reprieve on 22 February 1866. Whatever the circumstances, Daniels proved to be very imprudent for, having served only three weeks of this sentence, he headed north to Helena to wreak vengeance on those who had testified against him.[23] Meagher either did not understand his legal authority or chose to ignore the law when he granted Daniels the pardon. Under the terms of the Organic Act the territorial governor had only the power to grant a stay of execution for prisoners convicted of capital crimes. The authority to grant reprieves or pardons rested solely with the President of the United States. Since Daniels had not been sentenced to death, Meagher did not have the authority to grant a reprieve or a pardon.[24]

An enraged Judge Munson wrote to Meagher on 1 March 1866, demanding that he revoke the order and return Daniels to jail. When Meagher declined, Munson ordered Deputy Marshal Neil Howie to apprehend Daniels. Unfortunately for Daniels, when he finally arrived in Helena on 2 March 1866, the vigilantes immediately surrounded him and hanged him within the hour with Meagher's pardon still in his pocket. The vigilantes attached a note to the back of Daniels' coat threatening Meagher with a similar fate if he continued to grant clemency to miscreants. The body remained suspended from the hanging tree until the next day when it was cut down and buried in the local cemetery. The lesson apparently worked, for Meagher never again granted a reprieve, pardon or directly confronted the territory's still powerful vigilance committees. But the damage had been done and Meagher had been seen to exceed his authority.[25]

When the territorial legislature met on 5 March 1866, Meagher denounced the judges, declaring that he would force them to recognize the validity of the assembly. Munson ignored the threat and became, henceforth, an implacable enemy to Meagher for the remainder of his career in Montana. When the Democrat Party-controlled legislature denied the judges permission to supplement their incomes by taking on extra work in June 1866, Munson declared all the laws of the second territorial legislature null and void. Accusations about the judges' and Meagher's own character swirled back and forth and, with neither side willing to compromise, there seemed no solution in sight. However, in July 1866, a new development helped shatter Meagher's credibility as acting governor when President Johnson appointed the Kentuckian, Green Clay Smith, a veteran of the Mexican War, a Union major general and former congressman, as the new territorial governor.[26] A member of a prominent Unionist family, Smith was politically more adept than Meagher, and his arrival in the territory promised resolution to Montana's miasmatic politics. The editor of the *Montana Post*, Henry Blake, applauded Smith's appointment and called Meagher a 'notorious individual' who was now the 'most unimportant member of the community'. Incensed, Meagher challenged Blake to a duel. Perhaps shaken by the prospect of a duel, Blake softened his stance, suggesting that Meagher would 'now have a chance to enjoy the roses of the Secretaryship [sic] and not be annoyed by the thorns of the gubernatorial chair'.[27] Before Smith arrived in the territory in October 1866, Meagher issued a proclamation calling for a third territorial legislature to assemble. Never one to pull any punches, Meagher declared that the delegates should not be 'weak in the legs [or] pliant in the backbone' in the dispute over the second session. He also accused the Republicans and their allies of being 'pimps and blackguards'.

Under Smith's administration, Montana's volatile political situation would ease but unhappy at being superseded, Meagher soon tendered his resignation as territorial secretary to Smith. Meagher may have been planning to stand for Congress himself or finally launch himself into one of the commercial schemes he had been planning, but Smith persuaded Meagher to stay in office. It is somewhat surprising, given Smith's evangelical outlook and temperance, that he and Meagher genuinely respected each other. Within a few weeks after his arrival, however, Smith applied for a leave of absence and following his departure for Washington, January 1867, Meagher once again found himself 'The Acting One' and the political situation again degenerated into political factionalism.[28]

With Smith's departure, Judges Munson and Hosmer now challenged the legality of the third territorial legislature which had convened in Virginia City, on 5 November 1866. Attacked as the 'Jeff Davis Legislature' the delegates were determined to punish the judges. The Democrat-controlled legislature established new judicial district boundaries and exiled Munson and Hosmer to the eastern part of the territory where they could only rule against Indians and buffalo. Munson, who was also on leave in Washington when the legislators made this decision, lobbied Congress to nullify the laws of both Montana legislative sessions. Momentum picked up in the campaign when Wilbur Fiske Sanders also arrived in Washington and joined Munson in his crusade against 'The Acting One'. In March 1867, the Radical Republican-controlled United States Congress voided the laws passed by the second and third Montana legislatures, authorized the creation of new legislative districts, and called for new elections. In the same month, President Johnson appointed James Tufts to replace Thomas Francis Meagher as territorial secretary and it now seemed that Meagher's stormy political career in Montana was over.[29]

INDIAN WAR

As Meagher's influence on territorial politics weakened he began to look elsewhere to recapture his fading prospects in Montana. Fortunately for him, the war between the Lakota, the Northern Cheyenne and the US army on the Bozeman Trail in south-central Montana had escalated since 1866. Two of the three forts on the trail were under constant siege by the Indians. In December 1866, they had attacked and killed eighty-six men under the command of Captain William Fetterman near Fort Phil Kearney. The Indians closed the trail to emigrants and made re-supplying of the isolated posts dangerous. The war continued into 1867, with neither side willing to make concessions to end the conflict.[30] Although the settlements in south-western Montana were not directly threatened, nervous Gallatin Valley settlers sent frequent petitions to Meagher asking for military protection. In turn, Meagher increased his pleas to General William Sherman for the stationing of cavalry units in the territory. Indeed, his appeals had become so frequent and insistent, that he became a nuisance to Sherman. In February 1866, Sherman replied to Meagher that,

> I have received your several letters . . . on the subject of troops for Montana and routes leading thereto – untill [sic] Congress fixes the establishment it is idle for us to calculate what proportion of troops can be assigned to any part. Were I to grant one tenth the part of the calls on me from Montana to Texas I would have to call for one hundred thousand men, whereas I doubt if I should expect to have ten thousand men in all.

It became increasingly clear to Meagher that Sherman would do nothing to protect Montana and he would be left to his own devices, yet it also seemed to him that the war on the Bozeman Trail was a perfect opportunity to reclaim his reputation on the battlefield.[31]

When the Lakota raided the upper Yellowstone River Valley, capturing more horses than scalps, their real objective was to evict the military from the Bozeman Trail and keep whites out of their hunting grounds rather than force the abandonment of the gold mines in south-western Montana. The Indians did not threaten the majority of the territory's population, also largely located in south-western Montana. Meagher did not really understand the reasons behind the Bozeman Trail war, but resolving the muddy political situation in the territory proved almost impossible for him to solve and he happily abandoned his political career to follow what he thought was his true destiny as a soldier. The Lakota and Northern Cheyenne, however, were not Confederate regulars, and the pool of men available for him to lead in Montana did not possess the same motivations or *esprit de corps* of his old Irish Brigade. Sherman, who had developed a low opinion of Meagher during the American Civil War, thought that Meagher was little more than a 'stampeder'. Indeed, most of the depredations in northern Montana that had generated the outrage of local citizens, were nothing more than the usual activity of the Blackfeet; horse theft, robbery or the occasional murder. The sense of urgency also faded as the Blackfeet turned away from the harassment of whites and, instead, concentrated on the summer buffalo hunt.[32]

While hostilities on the upper Missouri River eased, they intensified along the Bozeman Trail in south-central Montana. After the crushing blow suffered by the military at the Fetterman fight, the tribes increased their attacks on the military posts. Lakota war parties ranged far up the Yellowstone Valley and came into contact with the few white ranchers and prospectors living there. In March 1867, Gallatin County entrepreneur, Tom Cover, wrote a letter to General Meagher on behalf of John Bozeman, who had blazed the contested trail in 1862. Among other things, the letter claimed that an Indian attack on the valley was imminent and a 'whole area of the Territory' would be 'emptied of its population' unless Meagher did something to remedy the situation. Meagher believed the letter's implications and remonstrated with Sherman that the entire Lakota was on the move to the Gallatin Valley.[33]

The following month, Blackfeet or Lakota Indians killed Bozeman on the Yellowstone River about forty miles east of the Gallatin Valley. Both he and Tom Cover were travelling the Bozeman Trail to the besieged military posts to secure contracts for flour. Cover survived the attack and made his way back to the Gallatin Valley. Referred to as the 'Bozeman Massacre', the incident further fuelled the hysteria already pervading the valley's residents and prompted Cover to send another plea to Meagher for help. After making an inspection of the valley, Meagher declared it wide open to attack and increased the number of telegrams he sent to Sherman in St Louis. Sherman's reluctance to accede to Meagher's demands was partly based on a letter he received from a Helena miner named William Nowland. Nowland attributed Bozeman's death to carelessness on his own part, and he vehemently condemned Meagher's reasons for forming a militia believing it his own duty 'to call your attention to the efforts that are being made to distract this Territory, and plunging us into debt, by a few persons, who unfortunately hold such positions under Government as to make the public lend a willing ear to their cry of danger from Indians'. Although Sherman agreed partially with Nowland's assessment of the situation in Montana, he did authorize the shipment of 2,500 rifles to Montana via the Missouri River. Sherman also began discussions with General Ulysses Grant and Edwin Stanton, the Secretary of War, regarding the formation of territorial militias and dispatched Major William Lewis to Montana on a fact-finding mission.[34]

In early May 1867, Sherman suggested to Meagher that he 'might informally call out the citizens who could defend themselves as best they might' if the situation really warranted it and Meagher, consequently, issued a call for 800 volunteers. The few men who volunteered were mainly unreliable drifters more interested in prospecting for gold in Indian country than protecting the territory. They also became easily bored and many drifted away from the camp in the Gallatin Valley. Valley merchants knew the federal government was not financing these volunteers and refused to honour vouchers for supplies presented to them by their recruitment and supply officers. A correspondent for the *New York Herald* wrote that these volunteers were hardly needed at all as 'Meagher is as good at palaver as at a fight... He will quiet [the Indians] by talking their heads off.'[35] Sherman, meanwhile, brokered a deal with General Grant and Stanton to establish a policy for territorial militias. Only Sherman could call out the militias, which would then be properly provisioned and paid by the federal government as a paramilitary unit. While evidence suggests that Sherman established the policy specifically because of General Meagher's constant clamour for troops, it is also clear that Sherman continued to have reservations about the situation in Montana. In a letter to General Christopher Augur at Omaha, Nebraska, Sherman confided that he believed that Montana had suffered nothing more than a bad scare from the Indians. He also confided in Augur, a regular officer, that 'I have no faith in the parties who want to raise and command the volunteers'.[36]

Shortly after Sherman's envoy, Major Lewis, reached Virginia City on 19 May 1867, he received a telegram reluctantly authorizing him to muster in a battalion of 800 men for two months' service. The federal government would pay the men 40 cents a day, but the men would have to furnish their own horses and weapons. Lewis showed the telegram to merchants around Virginia City who promptly opened up their stores to the militia. Meagher, however, mistakenly believed Sherman had formally authorized him to raise volunteers at government expense. Sherman had cautioned Lewis about causing the government 'any unnecessary expense' and warned Lewis not to allow Meagher to exploit the situation, which is exactly what happened.[37]

More interested in taking the field than watching his finances, Meagher bought supplies wherever he could at whatever the cost, ignoring the fact that often these supplies never actually materialized. The militia company was also top heavy with officers who numbered between half to three-quarters of the fluctuating numbers of volunteers and never amounted to more than 200 men. Meagher told those who chose not to serve as officers that they could keep whatever property they captured from the Indians and he divided the militia into two camps, one located in the Gallatin Valley and the other on the Yellowstone River, near present day Livingston. When not involved in drills, the men frequently wandered off to pan for gold in likely-looking streams near the camps, or patronized local drinking establishments.[38] By all accounts, the militia spent most of its time on patrol to keep the lines of communication open between the territory's major settlements, although one commentator complained that they spent more time patrolling the local saloons than they did looking for Indians.

Indeed, by the time the militia disbanded in the late summer of 1867, they actually did not have any contact with the Indians. Discipline in the camps was almost non-existent: stabbings, gunfights and mutinies were common. There was also considerable friction between the officers over rank. All-in-all, it was a motley collection of businessmen, former vigilantes, lawmen, miners, bullwhackers and frontier ne'er-do-wells. The stampede Sherman feared had happened.[39]

General Meagher did not take an active role in the day-to-day operation of the militia. Although replaced as territorial secretary by James Tufts on 28 March 1867, he still maintained an office in Virginia City but it is unclear how much time he spent there. In June, Meagher began writing a series of articles about Montana under the penname of a close friend, Colonel Cornelius O'Keefe, for *Harper's New Monthly Magazine*. Called 'Rides Through Montana', the magazine published the first instalment posthumously in October 1867. Ironically, Meagher never visited the region he wrote about in the magazine article. It is likely that he gathered the information from his friend, Cornelius C. 'Baron' O'Keefe, who was a resident of the western Montana. The article, however, reflected Meagher's love of the outdoors and confirms his 1865 statement about the beauty of the territory. The *Harper's* articles and the militia offered him a way out of the territory's ugly politics and allowed him to do what he wanted to do all along, enjoy a frontier adventure and perhaps reclaim his faded glory.[40]

Like every thing Meagher was involved in, the militia drew criticism from some people. While the *Montana Post* was initially supportive of the militia, by June 1867, it had become one of its loudest critics. One man later called Meagher's Indian 'war' the 'biggest humbug of the age, got up to advance his political interests and to enable a lot of bummers who surround and hang on to him to make a big raid on the United States treasury'. The accusations of drunkenness and rowdyism on duty continued to dog Meagher. The militia never took to the field against the Indians and was more like a summer camp for the recalcitrant. Like Lieutenant Colonel George Armstrong Custer, Meagher seemed more interested in the adventure and glory than in the drudgery of commanding troops. It manifested itself in irresponsible behaviour that his detractors were quick to point out. In the end, the militia ran up bills totalling over a million dollars, and had done nothing to justify the expenditure. On 15 June 1867, Meagher closed his office in Virginia City and headed north to Fort Benton with eleven militia officers to pick up the rifles sent up the Missouri River to Fort Benton by General Sherman earlier that spring.[41]

MEAGHER'S DEATH

Late in the afternoon of 1 July, Meagher and his companions rode into Fort Benton. The trip had been a hard one for the general. The scorching early summer heat caused him to suffer a recurring bout of dysentery at Sun River

Crossing, about thirty miles west of Fort Benton. The illness caused a six-day delay in the party reaching the trading post. By the time the group reached the river port, Meagher was physically and mentally spent. He sought shelter in the backroom of I.G. Baker's log store next to the river levee. Although one report claims that Meagher busied himself reading a newspaper and writing letters, another witness told an entirely different story. According to an unknown soldier, who was also the last man to see Meagher alive, the general arrived at Fort Benton dehydrated and weakened, still suffering from dysentery. He escaped the afternoon heat in the backroom of Baker's store where he remained for several hours with his head resting on his hands, the misery heightened by frequent trips into the brush behind the store 'where the violence of the disorder assailed him'. The storekeeper offered Meagher some blackberry wine to help fortify him. While at Baker's store, Meagher learned that the expected arms shipment had not arrived in Fort Benton. Instead, low water had forced a steamer to off-load it at Camp Cooke about 120 miles downstream. The prospect of continuing on downriver could not have pleased the ailing general.[42]

Sick and disoriented with three glasses of the strong wine under his belt, Meagher left Baker's store in the early evening with Johnny Doran, the pilot of the steamer *G.A. Thompson*. Doran later described an almost surreal evening, where he and the general enjoyed a nice dinner together before they strolled through the settlement, turning down numerous invitations for drinks before arriving at the steamboat, where the men settled down to a pleasant evening of cigars, tea and conversation. Because of Meagher's weakened condition, Doran offered the general the use of his stateroom aboard the *G.A. Thompson*.[43]

Coincidentally, Meagher's political arch-enemy, Wilbur Fisk Sanders, also happened to be in town that day. He later reported that while seated in front of Baker's store, his

> attention was arrested by abnormally loud conversation, and as the party came nearer I saw that it came from General Meagher. As the party came to the place where I was, it was apparent that he was deranged. He was loudly demanding a revolver to defend himself against the citizens of Fort Benton, who, in his disturbed mental condition, he declared were hostile to him.[44]

After attempting to calm him down, Meagher's companions, including Sanders, took him to his stateroom on board the steamer. Although much of Sanders' claim can be discounted, there may be some element of truth to Meagher's fear that the people of Fort Benton wanted to kill him. When Meagher arrived in town earlier that day, he overheard a man say 'There he goes'. In his weakened state, he interpreted the comment as a threat. He later told Johnny Doran that his life had been threatened in the settlement. It was only after Doran showed Meagher two loaded revolvers that he eventually retired to the stateroom. Doran left him with a promise to return shortly. Although much of Doran's version can be also be discounted, both he and Sanders agreed that the general was not in his right mind the day he died.[45]

A few minutes after the pilot left Meagher in his stateroom a sentry patrolling the deck of the steamboat saw a figure clad in underclothes moving toward the stern. Believing it an officer who had come on deck to relieve himself, the soldier turned away to give the man some privacy. When he heard a shout and a splash the sentry immediately raised the alarm which brought most of the crew on deck. The rescuers directed the feeble light from the lanterns toward the river, threw out life buoys and launched a boat in an unsuccessful effort to rescue the general before he drowned. Some men dropped into the water while others ran downstream in a fruitless search to pull Meagher from the river. The body was never recovered.[46]

CONCLUSION

The death of General Thomas Francis Meagher is one of Montana history's most enduring mysteries. The simple truth is that Meagher likely came on deck that dark night because of another attack of dysentery. Missouri River steamboats were notoriously unsteady while anchored in a swift current. In his weakened condition on an unsteady deck he probably lost his footing or tripped on a coil of rope, hit his head and fell unconscious into the river. The handrails that normally encircled the deck had been removed as a result of a collision down-river, so there was nothing for the general to grab on to if he could. Although a barber later claimed to have witnessed him purposely jumping from the boat, suicide is unlikely considering Meagher's religious convictions.

At the time of Meagher's death there is little in the contemporary records that suggests he was murdered. Like many high profile deaths, the suggestion of a conspiracy came much later. Forty years after the event, Frank Diamond claimed to have murdered Meagher for an $8,000 bounty offered by the Montana vigilance organization. Diamond, however, later recanted his confession.[47] While Sanders' presence in Fort Benton that day is also interesting, it alone is not evidence of foul play. Likewise, some contemporary accounts state that Meagher died in a drunken accident but many eyewitnesses, including Sanders, were equally sure that Meagher was not drunk but ill and delirious. Unfortunately for Meagher's reputation, it is not unusual in many recently published Montana histories to still see the claim that Meagher's death was the result of his intoxication even though the evidence suggests otherwise. In his biography of Meagher Robert Athearn concluded that 'the extreme bitterness of his enemies had spread the legend of his insobriety so far and wide in Montana that the story of a drunken demise fell on willing ears'. Meagher had in his own lifetime, Athearn added, often been obliged to defend his honour against such rumours. Upon learning of General Meagher's death, territorial governor, Green Clay Smith offered a $1,000 reward for the body and ordered that the militia's headquarters and federal offices be draped in mourning for a period of thirty days. Judge Munson even went as far as to suspend judicial proceedings in his court for several days in honour of a man he detested.[48]

On 4 July 1905, thirty-eight years after his death, the Montana chapter of the Ancient Order of Hibernians unveiled to a 'cheering throng' a statue sculpted by Chicago artist Charles K. Mulligan of General Meagher. A powerful fraternal organization in Montana since the late nineteenth century, the Hibernians' core membership in the state rested with Irish emigrants in Butte and Anaconda. The statue portrays Meagher as the gallant Civil War hero that most Irish would prefer to remember him as; in full uniform astride a magnificent horse with sword upraised – challenging those who dared question his decisions or his courage. The statue rests on a high granite pedestal in front of the Montana State Capitol building overlooking the Helena Valley.[49] Meagher's legacy in Montana is difficult to assess. For most of his career in Montana he was on the defensive, trying to protect both his political agenda and his reputation from his opponents who successfully depicted him as a drunkard, womanizer and glory seeker, more interested in personal gain than in the good of the territory. While partially true, the historical record also indicates that Meagher was a responsible, if somewhat erratic and unskilled politician, who only signed laws he felt were in the best interests of the territory. By 1867, however, his Republican adversaries had the laws passed by two Democratic Party-controlled legislatures successfully overturned. If he was a soldier who enjoyed the company of men and strong drink, there is no reliable evidence that drunkenness affected his political or military decisions while he was in Montana.

Today, Meagher's supporters prefer to remember him as a courageous Irish patriot, idealist and renowned orator who commanded the legendary Irish Brigade during the American Civil War. Others still revile him as an unrepentant partier. After nearly 140 years there still does not appear to be any middle ground on this issue, for Thomas Francis Meagher was too complex a figure to be viewed in simple black and white terms. He clearly generated controversy whilst in Montana, as his career continues to do among historians and the public generally within the state. Indeed, at a recent meeting of the Montana Historical Society's annual conference, a presentation which portrayed Meagher as a scoundrel prompted the local Thomas Francis Meagher Chapter of the Ancient Hibernians to direct a barrage of criticism against the organization itself. If Meagher continues to be criticized, it is clear that while he remains one of Montana's most debated politicians he was also one of Montana's more colourful pioneers.

NOTES

1. Michael Malone, Richard B. Roeder and William L. Lang, *Montana: A History of Two Centuries* (Seattle, Washington: University of Washington Press, 1991), pp.65, 67, 97–8; Merrill G. Burlingame, *The Montana Frontier* (Helena, Montana: State Publishing,1942), pp.86–91.

2. Malone, *Montana*, pp.96–7.
3. James L. Thane, Jr, 'Thomas Francis Meagher: 'The Acting One', (unpublished MA thesis, University of Montana, 1967), pp.2, 17.
4. James McClellan Hamilton, *History of Montana: From Wilderness to Statehood* (Portland, OR: Binfords and Mort, 1957), pp.158–9.
5. Thane, 'Thomas Francis Meagher', pp.15, 87-8.
6. For general histories of the Montana vigilantes see Thomas Dimsdale, *The Vigilantes of Montana* (Norman, OH: University of Oklahoma Press, 1977) and Nathaniel P. Langford (ed.) *Vigilante Days and Ways* (Helena, Montana: Falcon Press, 1996). Also see, Malone, *Montana*, pp.80–1; Burlingame, *Montana Frontier*, pp.98–100; Frederick Allen,'Montana Vigilantes and the Origins of 3-7-77', *Montana The Magazine of Western History*, 51, 1, (2001), p.6; Robert G. Athearn, *Thomas Francis Meagher: An Irish Revolutionary in America* (Boulder, CO: University of Colorado Press, 1949) pp.144–5.
7. Lists for the Election of 24 October 1864 to Establish Montana as a Territory, Montana Historical Society, Helena.
8. Athearn, *Thomas Francis Meagher*, p.145; W.F. Lyons, *Brigadier-General Thomas Francis Meagher: His Political and Military Career* (New York: Sadlier, 1870), pp.192–3; Thane, 'Thomas Francis Meagher', pp.6–7; Martin Maginnis, 'Thomas Francis Meagher', in *Contributions to the Historical Society of Montana*, VI (Helena: State Historical Society, 1907), p.102; 'Arrived', *Montana Post* (Virginia City), 23 Sept. 1865.
9. Athearn, *Thomas Francis Meagher*, pp.146–7; Clark C. Spence, *Territorial Politics and Government in Montana, 1864–1889* (Chicago, IL: University of Illinois Press, 1975), p.35; James Callaghan, 'Montana's Meagher of the Sword', *Tombstone Epitaph*, May, 1978: Maginnis, 'Thomas Francis Meagher,' p.103; Thane, 'Thomas Francis Meagher', p.20; Malone, *Montana*, p.100.
10. Athearn, *Thomas Francis Meagher*, p.147; Spence, *Territorial Politics*, pp.36–7; Malone, *Montana*, p.100; Thane, 'Thomas Francis Meagher', p.23.
11. 'How General Meagher Acquired Much of Northern Montana from the Indians for a Very Modest Sum', *The Dillon Examiner*, 14 April 1919; Thomas Francis Meagher, 'A Journey to Benton', reprinted in *The Montana Magazine of History*, 1, 4, (1951), pp.46–58, p.47; Callaghan, 'Montana's Meagher'.
12. *Dillon Examiner*, 14 April 1919; Spence, *Territorial Politics*, p.51; M.A. Leeson, *History of Montana, 1739–1885* (Chicago: Warner, Beers, 1885) p.103; John Bruce (comp.), *Lectures of Gov. Thomas Francis Meagher in Montana* (Virginia City, Montana: Bruce & Wright, 1867), p.41; Meagher, 'Journey to Benton', pp.48–9; Thane, 'Thomas Francis Meagher', p.26.
13. *Dillon Examiner*; Spence, *Territorial Politics*, p.51; W.T. Henderson to Meagher, 27 Feb. 1866, Thomas Francis Meagher Papers, Short Collection 309, Montana Historical Society; Meagher to the Honorable Speaker of the House of Representatives, Montana Territory, 12 March 1866, Meagher Papers, Short Collection, 309, Montana Historical Society; Athearn, *Thomas Francis Meagher*, pp.149, 158; Leeson, *History of Montana*, p.103; Bruce, *Lectures*, p.42.
14. Jon Axline, 'Vigilante Justice', *More From the Quarries of Last Chance Gulch* I (Helena, Montana: Independent Record, 1995), p.12; Athearn, *Thomas Francis Meagher*, p.151; Langford, *Vigilante Days*, p.296; Allen, 'Montana Vigilantes', pp.8–9.
15. Spence, *Territorial Politics*, pp.36–7; Lyons, *Brigadier-General*, p.200; Malone, *Montana*, p.101.
16. Spence, *Territorial Politics*, pp.36–8; Athearn, *Thomas Francis Meagher*, pp.149–50; Harriett Fitzgerald Sanders, *History of Montana*, 3 vols (Chicago, IL: Lewis Publishing, 1913), vol.1, pp.332–3; Callaghan, 'Montana's Meagher'; Maginnis, 'Thomas Francis Meagher', p.105; Lyons, *Brigadier-General*, p.199 ; Leeson, *History of Montana*, p.249; Malone, *Montana*, p.101; Bruce, *Lectures*, pp.43–5, 61.
17. Spence, *Territorial Politics*, pp.36–8; Athearn, *Thomas Francis Meagher*, pp.149–50; Maginnis, 'Thomas Francis Meagher', p.105; Thane, 'Thomas Francis Meagher', pp.27–8, 35; Lyons, *Brigadier-General*, p.199; Leeson, *History of Montana*, p.249; Malone, *Montana*, p.101.

18. Spence, *Territorial Politics*, pp.37–8 ; Athearn, *Thomas Francis Meagher*, pp.149–50; Sanders, *History of Montana*, vol. I, pp.333, 354 ; Callaghan, 'Montana's Meagher'; Malone, *Montana*, p.102 ; Bruce, *Lectures*, pp.46–7, 61.
19. Spence, *Territorial Politics*, pp.37–9 ; Athearn, *Thomas Francis Meagher*, pp.150–3; *Montana Post*, Jan.–April 1866 incl.; Wilbur F. Sanders, 'How General Meagher Met His Death', *Butte Inter Mountain*, 15 March 1902; Callaghan, 'Montana's Meagher'; Maginnis, 'Thomas Francis Meagher', pp.103–4; Lyons, *Brigadier-General*, pp.197–202; Vivian A. Paladin, 'Proper Bostonian, Purposeful Pioneer', *Montana The Magazine of Western History*, 14, 4, (1964), pp.39–41, 38; *Council Journal of the Second Session of the Legislative Assembly of the Territory of Montana* (Helena, Montana: Wilkinson and Ronan,1870).
20. Spence, *Territorial Politics*, pp.37–9; Athearn, *Thomas Francis Meagher*, pp.150–3; *Montana Post*, Jan.–Apri1 1866 incl.
21. Thane, 'Thomas Francis Meagher', p.54; Athearn, *Thomas Francis Meagher*, p.154.
22. Elliott West, 'Thomas Francis Meagher's Bar Bill', *Montana The Magazine of Western History*, 35, 1, (1985), pp.19–21.
23. Axline, 'Vigilante Justice', pp.14–15; Athearn, *Thomas Francis Meagher*, pp.151–2; Copy of Reprieve, James B. Daniels Papers, Small Collections 1634 (1866), Montana Historical Society; Allen, 'Montana Vigilantes', p.9; Langford, *Vigilante Days*, pp.296–7.
24. Axline, 'Vigilante Justice', p.15.
25. Ibid, pp.14–15; Allen, 'Montana Vigilantes', p.9; Langford, *Vigilante Days*, pp.296–7.
26. Spence, *Territorial Politics*, pp.39–40; Athearn, *Thomas Francis Meagher*, p.152.
27. Thane, 'Thomas Francis Meagher', p.59; Malone, *Montana*, p.103; Spence, *Territorial Politics*, pp.43–4; Sanders, *History of Montana*, vol.1, pp.334–5.
28. Malone, *Montana*, p.103; Spence, *Territorial Politics*, pp.43–4; Sanders, *History of Montana*, vol.1, pp.334–5; Bruce, *Lectures*, p.52.
29. Spence, *Territorial Politics*, pp.43–5; Sanders, *History of Montana*, vol. 1, p.335; *Council Journal of the Third Session of the Legislative Assembly of the Territory of Montana*, (Helena, Montana: Wilkinson and Ronan, 1870).
30. For excellent accounts of the conflict on the Bozeman Trail see Dorothy M. Johnson, *The Bloody Bozeman* (New York: McGraw-Hill, 1971) and Susan Badger Doyle, *Journeys to the Land of Gold: Emigrant Diaries from the Bozeman Trail,1863–1866*, 2 vols (Helena, Montana: Montana Historical Society, 2000); Malone, *Montana*, pp.124–6; Burlingame, *Montana Frontier*, p.121.
31. Spence, *Territorial Politics*, p.51; Callaghan, 'Montana's Meagher'; Meagher to Honorable Speaker of the House of Representatives, 12 March 1866 , Meagher Papers, Short Collection 309, (Montana Historical Society); Malone, *Montana*, p.103; Athearn, *Thomas Francis Meagher*, p.157; Leeson, *History of Montana*, pp.118–19.
32. Spence, *Territorial Politics*, pp.52–3; Callaghan, 'Montana's Meagher'; Athearn, *Thomas Francis Meagher*, pp.157–8, 160; Lyon, *Brigadier-General*, pp.199–200; Bruce, *Lectures*, pp.65–73; Robert G. Athearn ,'The Montana Volunteers of 1867', *The Pacific Historical Review*, 19, 2 (1950), pp.127–9.
33. Leeson, *History of Montana*, p.119; Callaghan, 'Montana's Meagher'; Athearn, *Thomas Francis Meagher*, pp.157–8.
34. Leeson, *History of Montana*, p.119; Spence, *Territorial Politics*, pp.52–4; Callaghan, 'Montana's Meagher'; Athearn, *Thomas Francis Meagher*, pp.158–9; Malone, *Montana*, p.103; Athearn, 'Montana Volunteers', p.129; Bruce, *Lectures*, pp.62–4; John Barseness and William Dickinson, 'Minute Men of Montana', *Montana The Magazine of Western History*, 10, 2, (1960) p.3.
35. Athearn, *Thomas Francis Meagher*, pp.160–1; Spence, *Territorial Politics*, pp.53–4; Callaghan, 'Montana's Meagher'; Athearn, 'Montana Volunteers', pp.129–30.
36. Athearn, *Thomas Francis Meagher*, p.161.
37. *Ibid.*, pp.161–2; Malone, *Montana*, p.103; Spence, *Territorial Politics*, pp.52–3; Leeson, *History of Montana*, pp.118–20; Athearn, 'Montana Volunteers', pp.131–2.
38. Athearn, *Thomas Francis Meagher*, pp.162–4; Spence, *Territorial Politics*, pp.53–4; Callaghan, 'Montana's Meagher'; Malone, *Montana*, p.103; Athearn, 'Montana Volunteers',

p.132; Barseness and Dickinson, 'Minute Men', p.4.

39. Athearn, *Thomas Francis Meagher*, pp.163–4; Spence, *Territorial Politics*, p.53; Athearn, 'Montana Volunteers', p.132.
40. Leeson, *History of Montana*, p.259; Thomas Francis Meagher, 'Rides Through Montana', *Harper's New Monthly Magazine*, 25, 209, (1867), pp.568–85; Edith Toole Oberly, 'The Baron C. C. O'Keefe', *Montana The Magazine of Western History*, 23, 3, (1973), p.24.
41. *Montana Post*, April–June 1867 inc.; Athearn, *Thomas Francis Meagher*, pp.163–4; Malone, *Montana*, p.103; Spence, *Territorial Politics*, pp.53–4; Callaghan, 'Montana's Meagher'.
42. Athearn, *Thomas Francis Meagher*, pp.164–5; Lyons, *Brigadier-General*, p.204; Michael Cavanagh, *Memoirs of General Thomas Francis Meagher* (Worcester, MA: Messenger Press, 1892), Appendix One, p.12; 'Accident or Suicide?', *Eureka Journal*, 26 Feb. 1928; Sanders, 'How General Meagher Met His Death'; Joseph I.C. Clarke, 'Death of "Meagher of the Sword". A Mystery of Fifty Years', *New York Sun*, 8 June 1913; A.L. Stone, 'Baker Tells of Death of Gen. Meagher', unidentified newspaper on file at the Montana Historical Society, 20 June 1973.
43. Sanders, 'How General Meagher Met His Death'; Clarke, 'Death of "Meagher of the Sword"', *New York Sun*, 8 June 1913; Cavanagh, *Memoirs*, pp.11–12.
44. Sanders, 'How General Meagher Met His Death'.
45. Clarke, 'Death of "Meagher of the Sword"'; Lyons, *Brigadier-General*, pp.353–7; Athearn, *Thomas Francis Meagher*, pp.164–5.
46. Cavanagh, *Memoirs*, p.12; Malone, *Montana*, p.103; Clarke, 'Death of "Meagher of the Sword"'; Sanders, 'How General Meagher Met His Death'; Athearn, *Thomas Francis Meagher*, p.165; Lyons, *Brigadier-General*, pp.204–5, 353–4.
47. A conversation between Professor David Emmons of the University of Montana and the author revealed that a new argument has recently been made by an undergraduate student at the university that the general was, indeed, murdered by the Montana vigilantes. The student has indicated that Wilbur Fisk Sanders' presence in Fort Benton that day was no coincidence and that he had a hand in the murder of the Acting One. Cavanagh, *Memoirs*, pp.12–13; Lyons, *Brigadier-General*, pp.353–4; Lewis W. Hunt 'Thomas Francis Meagher: The 1913 Hoax', *Montana The Magazine of Western History*, 12: 1 (1962), pp.24–5, 28–9.
48. Athearn, *Thomas Francis Meagher*, p.166; Sanders, *History of Montana*, pp.336–7; Leeson, *History of Montana*, p.248; *Eureka Journal*, 26 Feb. 1928; Munson Proclamation, 3 July 1867, Meagher Papers, Short Collection, 309, Montana Historical Society; Bruce, *Lectures*, p.77; Sanders, 'How General Meagher Met His Death'.
49. Maginnis, 'Thomas Francis Meagher', p.118; Carroll Van West, 'Montana's Monuments: History in the Making', *Montana The Magazine of Western History*, 40, 4, (1990), p.15; David M. Emmons, 'The Orange and the Green in Montana: A Reconsideration of the Clark-Daly Feud', Robert R. Swartout and Harry W. Fritz (eds), *The Montana Heritage: An Anthology of Historical Essays* (Helena, Montana: Montana Historical Society, 1992), p.170n.

11

Thomas Francis Meagher in Love and War: A Narrative History

DAVID SMITH

I

'The love I bear my country'

T.F. Meagher

The extensive Meagher literature is permeated with references to Meagher's relationships with women. This present volume is no different. While there is a warmth and contentment characterizing these associations, it is also evident that these attractions were mutual and this provides an added dimension to an already complex life. Nonetheless, the fact that Thomas Francis Meagher married twice, and never saw either of his two children, has been used by some commentators to denigrate his character and, in so doing, cast aspersions on these relationships. However, there can be no doubt that women played an important role in Meagher's life but like his own life, they were also tinged with controversy and sadness. His mother died when he was just 4 years of age and his grandmother died in 1831, when he was only 9 years old. Consequently, he was reared by his aunts, the Quans, and it was to them and his grand-aunts that he returned during his school holidays from Clongowes and Stonyhurst. Although Meagher's schooling was in all male environments, females dominated his home life. This would account for Meagher's contentment in female company.

That Meagher was handsome is confirmed by the photographs of the time, and at his trial in Clonmel, October 1949 a *Times* of London reporter noted that he was (according to this reporter) a man 'of no occupation... five feet nine inches [tall], dark, nearly black hair, light blue eyes, pale face, high cheek bone, peculiar expression about the eyes, cocked nose, no whiskers; well dressed'.[1] Indeed, at the time of his transportation evidence suggests that Meagher was engaged to a young Clonmel woman, Mary O'Neill, who was the daughter of Edward O'Neill and Bridget Howley. The latter was an aunt of Bishop Howley of St John's, Newfoundland, thus making his fiancée a first cousin of the bishop.[2] Moreover, it seems that this was not his first female relationship. When he travelled to Dublin in 1844 to study at Queen's Inns, he stayed with the family of his school friend from Clongowes College, P.J. Smyth.[3] It was in the

Smyth family home at Mount Brown, Kilmainham, that Meagher renewed acquaintance with a young woman he had first met during his time at school. The young Miss Bruton, an aunt of Smyth, was acting as governess to the younger Smyth children and she was captivated by the dashing Meagher. They took long walks together near the Royal Hospital, cementing a friendship that would last for many years.[4] Whether they were linked romantically is a question that cannot be answered with certainty.

Meagher's main love, however, was at this time to Ireland itself, for he claimed that 'The love I bear my country; the proud love with which I recognise, assert, and worship, her ancient name, descent and glory; the jealous love with which I sit in sorrow by her tomb, awaiting the morning of her resurrection . . . ' was all-consuming.[5]

Following his conviction for treason and subsequent transportation, the well-educated Meagher was only 25 years old when he faced the prospect of rotting away in a penal colony.[6] Meagher and the other state prisoners, William Smith O'Brien, Terence Bellew McManus[7] and Patrick O'Donohoe[8] were sent to Van Diemen's Land on 9 July 1849 and as they passed by the coast of Waterford, Meagher bemoaned 'Will no one come out to hail me from Dunmore? . . . I pass by, and my own people know nothing of it.'[9] This *cri de coeur* was Meagher's first realization of the impending long isolation from the comfortable world in which he had lived. 'The Young Tribune' or, as Griffith dubbed him, the 'National Orator' was about to lose the very thing an orator requires most – his audience. He was also about to lose the security of a close-knit family. Although a political rupture had occurred between Meagher and his father, and reached its apogee when the Ballingarry affair exploded, nonetheless, Meagher's father remained loyal to his son, even to the point of financing his activities in Ireland as well as in Van Diemen's Land.[10]

VAN DIEMEN'S LAND

Meagher and his colleagues were offered 'tickets-of-leave' on their arrival in the penal colony, restricting them to designated areas under the jurisdiction of the local magistrate. A 'ticket-of-leave' granted a limited freedom to prisoners on the provision they gave their word of honour not to make an attempt to escape from the colony. There were between 3,000 and 4,000 such prisoners in the colony at that time, all of them convicts. These convicts had very liberal conditions attached to their 'tickets'– they could live where they pleased and they had to report only twice a year to the police. The Irish state prisoners were treated more harshly, however. They were restricted in their place of abode with only one person being allowed to live in a specified district and they were not allowed to associate with each other. They were also required to report twice a month, personally, to the police. All except O'Brien accepted these conditions.

Meagher was assigned to the district of Campbell Town in the island's midlands where crowds gathered daily to see the young rebel. This soon became irksome to Meagher and he moved to the village of Ross,

> a little apology of a town, seven miles nearer than Campbell Town to the seat of Government. The visit I paid it, short as it was, convinced me that Ross was a far more preferable place to take up my quarters than Campbell Town; the latter place has too much of the vulgar, upstart village in it; contains too much glaze, dust, and gossip, and it would be hard, I think, to do anything else than yawn, catch flies, and star-gaze in it. Here one can be more to himself; therefore, more free; consequently, more happy.[11]

After a while, he made the acquaintance of the most notable citizens of the district and was a welcome addition at evening gatherings in their homes, where his baritone voice was heard at its very best in his party-piece, *The Bells Of Shandon*. Despite these interludes, and his meetings with other Young Irelanders, Meagher was very lonely in Ross;

> Well, in this little cottage I manage to get through my solitary days cheerfully enough. It costs me an effort, however, to do so; for, I am sure, nature never intended me for an anchorite, and, often and often, I am as companionless and desolate here as Simon Stylites on the top of his pillar. Only one human being, for instance, has passed by my window today. He was a pedlar with fish and vegetables, from Launceston, and wished to know, as he was passing, if I wanted any fresh flounders for dinner.[12]

One of the most prominent citizens of Ross was the government medical superintendent, Dr Edward Hall, and it was through Dr Hall that Meagher met the young woman who was to become his wife. Hall was a zealous Catholic who was always on the lookout for the spiritual welfare of the Catholic inhabitants. 'On Sundays he walked to Mass at the head of his numerous family, with an illuminated volume of hymns and meditations, bound in brass and brown velvet, in one hand, and a black walking stick, embellished with the head of St Dunstan in ivory, in the other.'[13] The Halls, together with their six children and a governess, Catherine Bennett, had undertaken the journey to Ross where Dr Hall was to take up his employment. Their vehicle had broken down on the road and Meagher, taking one of his rambles in the hills, noticed the party in distress and hurried to their aid. After giving his assistance he made the acquaintance of Catherine, and learned that she already knew several of the Irish rebels. Indeed, O'Brien, McManus and O'Doherty had enjoyed her father's hospitality at his home in New Norfolk, a meeting place for the Irish of the area, including the Catholic clergy, where pleasant evenings were passed in an atmosphere of singing and story telling – mostly about Ireland. Meagher had told O'Brien that he would never marry in Van Diemen's Land – 'I shall never condescend so far to honour Van Diemen's Land as to make it the scene of my nuptials.'[14] He would soon change his mind.

II

'One of the beauties of this country'
Jenny Mitchel

CATHERINE BENNETT

Catherine was the daughter of Bryan and Mary Bennett of New Norfolk. Her father had an inauspicious beginning in the colony having been transported to Van Diemen's Land in 1818 for holding up a mail coach in Trim, Co. Meath.[15] Having worked out his sentence and become a free settler he had succeeded in building up a fine farm of over 100 acres in Stonefield, near New Norfolk. His daughter Catherine was 19 years old and beautiful, and Meagher became a regular caller to the Halls. By this time he had spent a year in Van Diemen's Land. His life was becoming more aimless by the day as he chafed at the restrictions imposed upon him and by the sheer boredom of the place. Meeting Bennie, as he affectionately called her, gave him a new lease of life. By Christmas, the young couple had intimated to Catherine's father that they wished to marry. Bryan Bennett assented immediately to the marriage, for this, surely, was confirmation of his rehabilitation into respectable society. Here was Meagher, the young Irish patriot, asking for his daughter's hand! The prospect was dazzling for the old man.[16] Meagher was clearly smitten by Bennie. Writing to O'Doherty thanking him for his congratulatory remarks regarding his imminent marriage, Meagher remarked that,

> In such matters... it is not... the flattering opinion of the World I seek for, but the sanction of my own heart and conscience, and the approval of those... I have reason to confide in and admire... I thank God that... an opportunity occurred to awaken in me the proud and generous nature that was sinking, coldly and dismally, into a stupid and sensual stagnation... I am myself again.[17]

If Meagher had sought the approval of his friends, he was to be sorely disappointed. O'Brien wrote that he could not envisage any advantage for Meagher from the union.[18] John Mitchel's wife, Jenny, wrote to a friend 'You will have heard before this of Mr Meagher's marriage to one of the beauties of this country. It is a pity on the whole (between ourselves). I feel his father will be very wroth with him.'[19] Her reaction was mild compared to that of John Martin's who wrote to O'Doherty that,

> You say you are struck dumb. I feel that I might better be struck dumb too... and the worst of all is that I am unable to discern any grounds of

> confident hope that any of his sanguine expectations from the marriage project will be realized…Notwithstanding…the social degradation to which the origin and present condition of his wife's family must subject him…it might turn out his salvation *if the woman of his choice were a paragon of perfection* and it might contribute to his happiness and his honour if she were a purely virtuous; amiable; high-spirited, intelligent and accomplished woman.[20]

Adelaide Dillon, wife of Meagher's friend and Young Ireland colleague, John Blake Dillon,[21] dismissed Catherine as unfit for Meagher because she was the daughter of 'a common English convict'.[22] The objections from Meagher's friends were because of Bennie's 'low birth' – she was not the daughter of a gentleman and was deemed, therefore, 'not suitable'. Most of the Young Irelanders were people of some wealth and position in society. Though they had shown by their actions that they were willing to die for the Irish peasant – God forbid that any of them should marry one!

The wedding took place on Saturday 22 February 1851, at the home of the Halls and was performed by Dr Willson, the first Catholic bishop of Hobart. The young couple (he was 27 years old, she was 19 years of age) went to live in a cottage that Meagher had built on the bank of Lake Sorell with the financial help of his father. Soon afterwards, Mitchel and Martin visited the newly married couple in their cottage. Mitchel described the scene in a letter to a friend in Ireland.

> A boat nears us slowly…a sunburnt man in a sailor's jacket stands in the stern-sheets, holding the tiller; by his side, on crimson cushions, sits a fair and graceful girl. The sun-burnt fellow is O'Meagher,[23] and that lady, so fair and graceful, is, who do you think? Why, Mrs O'Meagher! Martin and I spring into the boat, put the boat's head about, set the sail…and skim along under a tricolour flag (you know O'Meagher is great in flags), till we open a quiet bay, at the head of which bay, nestling under the shelter of untameable forest, stands a pretty cottage, with a verandah, and a gum-tree jetty stretching into the water. We step ashore, and are welcomed into our friend's newly-built house by his newly-wedded wife. They have elegant little rooms, books, horses, boats – why, it is almost like *living*.[24]

Martin, eventually became reconciled to the marriage and came to accept Bennie as a good-natured sensible woman.[25] Jenny Mitchel concurred and wrote to a friend 'I must say that his wife seems a handsome, nice, amiable girl.'[26] Meagher and Bennie were happy in their little idyll but Bennie was quite ill at times from chronic rheumatism as Meagher explained:

> Ever since that trip to Bothwell [at the beginning of July] Mrs O'Meagher has been laid up with a severe attack of rheumatism – the road (on our

> return from the Lakes) being excessively wet, and the weather very damp. Within the last ten days, however, she has made a delightful improvement, and will very shortly, I am confident, appear in the best of health.'[27]

There was, though, a dark side to their marriage – rumours of some impropriety on Meagher's part. Martin wrote to O'Doherty 'There is rather a serious quarrel between him (with Mrs O'M on his side) and the Halls, regarding some injurious representations made by Dr Hall and Mrs Hall about his conduct towards his wife. The best consideration is that his wife is quite on his side.'[28]

What were those 'injurious representations' to which Martin alluded? Was Meagher consorting with other women or was the ultra-conservative Dr Hall exaggerating some indiscretion of Meagher's? Bennie was the closest person to the allegations and she seems to have regarded the problem lightly, whatever its nature. However, similar allegations about Meagher, whether true or not, were to surface some years later during his tenure as secretary of Montana Territory.

Meagher and Bennie, nonetheless, seemed happy in each other's company. He wrote from his cottage to an old school friend, 'Whilst I am writing these few words... my wife is sitting, at the other end of the little table, the very picture of a fine Irish girl! Working away with her needle, in the brightest good humour.'[29] Nevertheless, despite his happiness with his wife, Meagher was becoming frustrated and bored with the inactivity and monotony of his life of farming and sailing. He became even more restless when he was made aware that efforts were being made to secure his liberation from exile. There was, though, one complication – Bennie was pregnant. She, nonetheless, encouraged Meagher in his quest for liberty and they agreed that should he escape, he would settle in America and Bennie would join him later. Being a free settler she could leave the island at a moment's notice and go wherever she pleased. The baby was due in February 1852 but the opportunity to escape came about in January. So with the blessing of Bennie and the help of friends, he was eventually taken on board an American ship and thus to freedom.

With Meagher gone, Bennie returned to her parent's home in New Norfolk to await the birth of her child. She received a pencilled note from Meagher just before he stepped onto the boat. She wrote to a friend, 'these few hurried lines... are dearer to me than a long letter would be at any other time... I have great hopes that he is far on the sea... I am in the best possible spirits at present and have kept them up well... our days of separation, I earnestly hope, will not be long'.[30] A month later, on 7 February 1852, Bennie was delivered of a son whom she named Henry Emmet Fitzgerald O'Meagher, in adherence to her husband's instructions.[31] Sadly, the boy lived only 4 months and he was buried at Richmond. Jenny Mitchel wrote 'Poor Mrs Meagher lost her baby... She has had a very pleasant letter from her father-in-law lately, the first time since her marriage. Also very handsome presents from Mr Harry O'Meagher.'[32]

Meagher arrived in New York City on 27 May 1852 to a tumultuous reception. He was described as being 'about 29 years of age, is very corpulent, and his exposure to a Southern sun gives him a dark, swarthy appearance. He has, we are informed, abundant means to enable him to live comfortably. His father is estimated to be worth £750,000…is a member of the British Parliament, and is also Chairman of the Waterford and Limerick Railway Company'.[33] Meagher was fêted as a rebel martyr, particularly among the Irish population, but he was also regarded by political figures as a symbol of resistance to Britain, at a time of heightened tensions between the two countries. He kept a low profile for a while but within a few short years his combative nature came to the fore and he became embroiled in controversy with the newspapers and his natural constituency, the Catholic Irish. There was unease, also, about the legitimacy of Meagher's surrender of his parole, delivered to the police in a letter and not personally. Mitchel and Martin in particular were unhappy but O'Brien defended Meagher. When this issue was highlighted in the American papers, Meagher offered to put himself on trial before a panel of American military men and agreed to return voluntarily to Van Diemen's Land, if the verdict went against him. He was, however, exonerated by the 'jury'.

BENNIE'S VISIT TO WATERFORD

It was arranged that Bennie would travel to Ireland before rejoining her husband in New York, where he now resided. She left Hobart on 5 February 1853 on the *Wellington* en route to London. A most-welcome fellow passenger was her friend and confidant Dr Willson, who was making his *ad limina* visit to Rome. Bennie arrived in Dublin and was met by her father-in-law, Thomas Meagher MP, and by Henry Meagher and Meagher's aunt, Miss Quan. They journeyed on to Waterford on 27 June and the *Waterford Mail* reported:

> Owing to that evening and the following day being exceedingly wet, no manifestations of joy could have taken place; but on Wednesday, at an early hour, hundreds were in waiting to catch one glimpse of Mrs. Meagher – and on her approach to the Franciscan Church, where she heard Mass, blessings were incessantly showered on her, in thousands, by the assembled crowd. After Mass the whole congregation assembled outside to bid her welcome…But it was the evening, which was the grand scene. The whole population literally turned out – a gigantic bonfire blazed on Ballybricken-hill, around which thousands assembled, with music and dancing; fireworks flashed away in several streets – two bands of music played through the City, accompanied by thousands – and at night-fall when they serenaded before *Mr. Meagher's* house, on the Mall, the scene was grand in the extreme…There could not be less than twenty thousand persons of all classes and ages there. By the expressed wish of the assemblage *Mrs. Meagher* presented herself at the window, and was received with the most deafening cheers. Peal upon peal resounded with

> the name of *Thomas Francis Meagher* – and you would think that the long pent-up love of the people rushed forth in one uncontrollable torrent. Mr. Henry Meagher returned thanks to the people… and all retired to their homes in the most decorous and happy manner. After the populace retired, a band of German Musicians serenaded *Mrs. Meagher* until after one o'clock at night.[34]

The welcome did not end there. The Mayor of Waterford, Laurence Strange, convened a meeting of the citizens at the City Hall, at the request of 106 of the most influential and respected inhabitants of all shades of politics, 'to pay a fitting tribute of respect to Mr. T. F. Meagher, in a manner which must be most gratifying and acceptable to him, namely to the person of Mrs. Meagher'.[35] A poem was composed in her honour and printed in the local press and the corporation of the city carried, unanimously, a vote of congratulations to Thomas Meagher Jr on the arrival of his daughter-in-law in the city. On the morning of her departure from Waterford to rejoin her husband, a deputation of sixty gentlemen proceeded to the Meagher residence on the Mall. They were ushered into the upstairs drawing room and were introduced, individually, to Mrs Meagher. The Waterford News wrote:

> Mrs. Meagher wore a rich green silk dress, made *à la mode*. She is well formed, rather slight, yet over the middle height – the outline of her nose is perfect – her lips are thin and finely formed – her hair is copious, dark, and glossy – from the effects of the climate her complexion partakes somewhat of the brunette – but her eyes are full and dark – in fact her whole appearance inclines in a marked degree to the Grecian type, which, according to most people's ideas, is the true standard of beauty.[36]

The greeting to Mrs Meagher was not, however, unanimous. There were dissenting voices especially among the conservative and unionist ranks. The *Waterford Mail* published a long letter from 'A Lover of Consistency'.

> SIR – I noticed in your paper of Saturday a requisition for a public meeting signed by individuals, 'anxious to avail themselves of the opportunity… of paying a tribute of respect (!!!) to their fellow-citizen, Thomas F. Meagher, in a manner which must be gratifying to his feelings.'… Many of the said requisionists were, in 1848, the avowed adherents of 'law and order'; as such were sworn and enrolled as special constables, and were, doubtless, prepared to oppose a bold front to the foe, if required. How like is the man who claims this 'tribute of respect'? The very man, whose machinations these requisionists sought in 1848 to crush – a man of talent, perhaps of genius, undoubtedly of eloquence; but alas! whose eloquence in that troublous year of '48 was directed to the one sole object of kindling the worst passions of the people and of goading them into rebellion. Had the

> revolt been permitted to ensue... many of these now busying themselves about the concocting of a maudlin address would long since have been mouldering in their bloody graves, the victims of civil massacre, their houses the prey of the incendiary, their property ransacked, and the fate of their families too awful to contemplate, and who would have been among the chief authors of such woes? Thos. F. Meagher!! Happy for them and for us all that he speedily ceased to be their *fellow-citizen*... I do not say that Mr. Meagher thirsted for blood. On the contrary, I believe that personally he was, and is, generous and humane; but like a wizard he sought to summon into life a demon which no spell might afterwards subdue.[37]

In its next issue, the *Mail* published, from 'A Friend Of Order', another letter condemnatory of the objects of the public meeting,

> SIR – Allow me to thank your correspondent 'A Lover of Consistency', for his truly admirable letter, contained in the *Waterford Mail* of this day... The rebels of '48 have had, for themselves, a most fortunate escape from an ignominious death. Her most gracious Majesty displayed a benevolence which I venture to assert no foreign potentate would have shown to the concoctors of such foul treason; and they had far better let time wash out the prints of their footsteps during that eventful year, than be forever reminding the loyal citizens of Waterford who were the parties that prepared arms for their destruction.[38]

These letters would have made uncomfortable reading for those requisionists, including many of Waterford City's merchants – repealers all – who had flocked to the police stations in 1848, itching to become special constables ready to defend the country against Meagher and his friends. Indeed, Meagher's father was reputed to be the third special constable sworn in at Waterford City.[39]

Shortly after the reception, Bennie left with her father-in-law to travel to Liverpool where they boarded the *Arctic*, arriving in New York on Saturday, 6 August 1853. They joined Meagher in his residence at the Metropolitan Hotel and there received many visitors including the Archbishop of New York, John Hughes.[40] Meagher then began a round of speechmaking, accompanied by his wife and father, travelling all over the north-eastern United States. But Bennie, her health delicate at the best of times, was pregnant again and the steaming heat and humidity of August and September would only have aggravated her already chronic and debilitating rheumatism. Having almost circumnavigated the globe in the previous six months and, after a stay of only four months in the United States, she was on the move once more, on the journey back to Waterford.

There has been much speculation as to why Bennie did not stay in America with her husband. Some commentators believe that a rift had occurred between Meagher and his wife and that the young girl from the Australian wilderness did not fit into his new lifestyle in metropolitan New York City. Perhaps this was so, but Meagher argued that he had been offered free passage to San Francisco and that he needed to seize this opportunity of making some money as lecture fees were his only means of income. Meagher was heavily criticized for this decision, but there was merit in it. A free passage to California was something he could not spurn lightly, at a time before the transcontinental railway was built, when the cost of the passage from New York to San Francisco was over $1,000. There was also the prospect of additional lucrative lecture fees to be garnered. Meagher also argued that, out of consideration for her own health and that of her unborn child, it would be the best for Bennie to return to Waterford and there live out her confinement. When the baby was born, both would rejoin Meagher in New York. But husband and wife were fated to never meet again.

SEPARATION AND DEATH

While Meagher was touring the western states, Bennie and her father-in-law returned to Waterford via Liverpool by the steamship *America*, arriving in Liverpool on 22 October and then proceeding to Waterford where she was to await the birth of her second son. A month later Meagher wrote to the Mayor of Waterford, acknowledging the welcome afforded his wife on her arrival in the city;

> My Dear Mr. Mayor
> ...To me...the cordial greetings, the golden offerings...with which you received the companion of my exile, were sources of the happiest interest and reflection...For what you said and did in my regard, I heartily thank you. For what you said and did in regard of her, whom I love to see honoured above myself, I know not how to thank you...I leave you with the assurance, that as you have not forgotten me, neither have I forgotten you...your warmly attached friend,
> Thomas Francis Meagher[41]

At the beginning of May 1854 a son, Thomas Francis Meagher II, was born in Waterford. But Bennie, already weakened by the birth, succumbed to typhoid fever and died in the Meagher family home on 9 May, aged just 22 years. She was buried in the Meagher family vault at Faithlegge just a few miles to the east of the city. The sorrow in Waterford was sincere and widespread and the local newspapers reflected those feelings in their obituaries.

> It is with deep and heartfelt sorrow we announce the death of this amiable and beautiful young lady...She has...lived among us; and we have witnessed the gentle innocence and sweetness of character that endeared

> her to all who had the happiness of knowing her, and which now wrings many a sorrowing pang for her loss from the hearts of all to whom her name is familiar... Deeply and sincerely do we lament for her... Deeply do we sorrow for her adopted relatives; theirs is a grief as unbounded, and their affections for her were unboundable... Deeply do we grieve for that dear baby boy, whose infant prattle can never be blessed with a mother's love... But more than all, we grieve for the poor stricken exile, far away in a strange land, without one sustaining element except his own soul to rest on.[42]

In the months immediately after his wife's death, Meagher's depression was clearly evident, and in July, all that pent-up anger, frustration and guilt exploded in a shocking street scene in New York City. Meagher had been writing a series of articles for John Mitchel's newspaper, the *Citizen*, wherein he excoriated the sycophantic Catholic press. These had led to angry articles in return. One editor, James McMaster of the *Freeman's Journal*, published an article that contained imputations against Meagher's honour and manhood; he also charged Meagher with violating his parole in Van Diemen's Land. This latter charge was one that had haunted Meagher ever since his arrival in New York. To seek redress, Meagher, accompanied by a friend, Edward Boyle, proceeded to McMaster's home at East 6th Street. As McMaster had not yet arrived home Meagher, Boyle and an old friend of Meagher's, Mr Collender of Cappoquin, County Waterford, repaired to a drinking saloon to await McMaster's return. Meagher was reading a newspaper when Collender spied McMaster approaching. They immediately left the saloon and Meagher, after instructing his friends not to interfere in any way, passed McMaster and, in the words of the *New York Times*

> ... turned round and directly facing Mr. McMaster, sprang upon him, and seizing him by the back of the collar, commenced using his whip about the back and shoulders of his antagonist... The latter was carrying... a heavily loaded walking-cane... The collision between the parties continued for four or five minutes... Finally Mr. Meagher succeeded in wresting the cane from the hands of Mr. McMaster, and having severely used his whip for some seconds compelled the latter... to take flight. Mr. Meagher pursued him and having gained upon him... Mr. McMaster drew out a revolver, and... prepared to fire... Mr. Meagher... sprang upon him, and throwing his right arm around Mr. McMaster's back, seized the upper part of the pistol arm of the latter. A violent struggle took place during which Mr. McMaster... fired. The ball grazed Mr. Meagher's forehead, the powder covering the upper part of his face, and wounding both eyes... Mr. McMaster, having disengaged himself from Mr. Meagher, who had been considerably stunned by the grazing of the ball, prepared to discharge a second shot... The crowd having now closed round the parties, the pistol was wrested from Mr. McMaster by a young lad from Jersey City. Mr.

> Meagher then felled Mr. McMaster to the ground with a blow of his clenched hand. The police immediately arriving, took both parties into custody.[43]

Both men were bound over to keep the peace in the sum of $500 each. Clearly, Meagher was in need of someone to take him in hand and soothe his tortured spirit. Fortunately, his salvation was near at hand, for within a few months he had met the woman who was to become his second wife.

III

> 'A Fifth Avenue lass and nothing more'
>
> John Blake Dillon

ELIZABETH TOWNSEND

Bennie's family had come from the Irish peasantry but Elizabeth Townsend was of a different class. She was born on 20 September 1830 into the wealthy and influential Townsend family of Southfield, Orange County, New York and could trace her ancestry over eleven generations to Robert (Townsend) Townshend (1512–1556), of Ludlow, Shropshire, England. Thomas Townsend (1594–1613), Robert's great-grandson, immigrated to Massachusetts and started the American branch of the family – a family that had impeccable credentials during the American War of Independence. Peter Townsend (Elizabeth's great-grandfather and Thomas Townsend's great-great-grandson) took the Revolutionary Association oath at Goshen, New York in June 1775. Furthermore, Townsend owned the Sterling Ironworks, which was commissioned in 1778 to build and erect a massive chain boom across the River Hudson at West Point Military Academy. This giant undertaking was successfully completed and for five years, until the end of the Revolutionary War, it prevented the English from ascending the Hudson River and thereby detaching New England from the other new-born United States and undoubtedly played an essential role in winning the war.[44]

Elizabeth, or 'Libby' as Meagher came to know her, was 24 years old when they first met. Meagher had risen to fame as a lecturer and he and Libby were introduced to one another at one such lecture when, by his own admission, he had fallen hopelessly in love with her. On 2 January 1855, he wrote of that first meeting to 'My dear, dear, Miss Townsend' in a long, somewhat prolix, love letter.[45] In this letter Meagher wrote,

> I know not whether you observed it or not, but the moment I was introduced to you, I was overcome with this consciousness – with this belief. And until I met you again – until, indeed, I revealed to you the secret with which my heart was throbbing, almost breaking, this

> consciousness, this belief, was to me a torture. I could not – dare not – hope for such a wife... But when I heard from you, that 'you could deeply love me', there passed through me a wild delight which made my pulse beat quick, and my brain reel, and... felt the heart, that had been bruised and wounded, filled with a fresh and glowing life.[46]

Although Meagher and Libby had professed their love for each other and were unofficially engaged, there were several major obstacles to be overcome; his religion, his status in society and his lack of employment. Although Meagher was the scion of a wealthy family and was not 'Potato Famine' Irish, his union with Libby would cause unease in her 'Blue-Blood' family circles. Meagher envisaged the objections that would result from his proposal:

> I should have to meet no slight contradictions and rebuke. For, I have no fortune – at least, nothing that I know of. I never asked my father a single question on the subject. I have fought my own way through the world, and will fight it to the end. I am... a homeless exile – dependant on my own good name and labour for a fortune. I am not yet an American citizen, and have not, therefore, a recognized standing in this country. I am here alone.[47]

SECOND MARRIAGE

Religion was a major obstacle in his second marriage, for Libby was an Episcopalian. Notwithstanding this, they were married on 14 November 1855. Meagher's witnesses were Bartholomew O'Connor and Richard S. Emmet; Libby's were her sister Alice Townsend Barlow and Caroline Townsend.[48] A society marriage such as this would normally have taken place in St Patrick's Cathedral but, because Elizabeth was not yet a Catholic, canon law decreed that it should take place in private, so the couple were married at the Madison Avenue residence of Archbishop Hughes. Libby would later convert and become a devout Catholic.

After their marriage the couple moved into Peter Townsend's Fifth Avenue mansion and Meagher looked forward, with some optimism, to a good and lucrative career at the bar with the help of the Townsend's Tammany Hall connections. Before Meagher met Libby he had thought of settling in California but decided, ultimately, to practice law in New York City, where he was admitted, by special dispensation to the New York bar in September 1855.

> To win distinction in this profession, shall be my study and ambition – that so, I may, to some extent, reflect honour on the noble girl, who, in giving her hand and heart to one so humble and so downcast, conferred upon him a dignity higher and more precious than even the citizenship to which it has been his glory to aspire.[49]

The Townsend Family Tree – American Branch

The first record of the Townsend family was in England with Robert Townsend, born Ludlow, Shropshire in 1512. His great-grandson, Thomas, immigrated to America where he died in 1677 at Lynn, Essex, Massachusetts. Thomas's son, Henry, started the American branch of the family tree (see below)

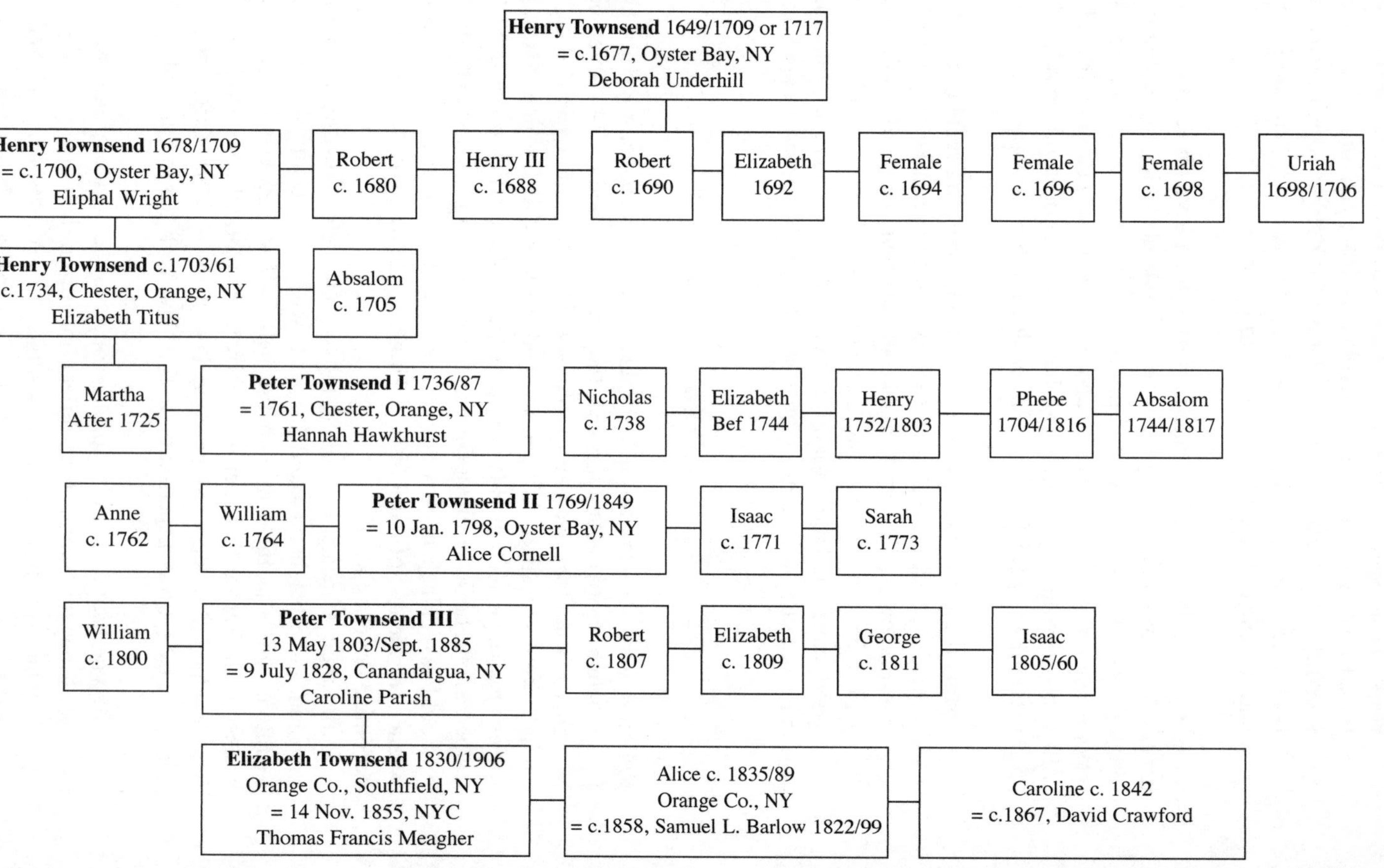

Briefs were slow in coming, however, and in desperation Meagher decided on a course that several prominent Irishmen had pursued before him; he established a newspaper. The *Irish News* was founded on 12 April 1856 and was published from the same building as his law offices. In foreign matters Meagher's paper advocated 'filibustering' – armed intrusions, mostly by American adventurers, undertaken during the nineteenth century against countries then at peace with the United States, especially in Central America; domestically it supported Democratic Party policies and also set out to be the voice of the New York Irish. Meagher's paper quickly achieved a circulation of 50,000 readers compared to the 25,000 of the *New York Times*, founded five years earlier.[50]

In September 1857, it was decided that Libby would travel to Waterford to meet her father-in-law and Meagher's three-year-old son, whilst he would tour the southern states to examine slavery and the southern way of life; an issue he had written about somewhat favourably in the *Irish News*. Of Libby's visit to Waterford there is, strangely, no mention in the Waterford newspapers of the time, except to say that she left the city on 9 June 1858, to return to New York.[51] This was in stark contrast to the media interest shown in Bennie's visit.

Meagher was becoming restless again. His ventures heretofore had met with only limited success and, now that he was married, he desperately needed to find a meaningful role that would find favour with his wife and her family. He had become infatuated with Central America where he and Libby took long trips and, whilst there, wrote a series of articles for *Harper's New Monthly Magazine* entitled 'Holidays in Costa Rica'. Meagher was, however, unsuccessful in seeking a diplomatic post in the region. In 1859 Meagher severed his connection with the *Irish News* and, shortly afterwards, he was retained as lawyer by a shipping line owner who had investments in Panama. As a result, Libby, Meagher and a servant set sail for the Isthmus where he hoped to revive his fortunes; but that venture also failed. It seemed that his life, which had blazed like a meteor across the American sky on his arrival as an escaped prisoner, would die out in a whimper. Then came the American Civil War.

CIVIL WAR

At the outbreak of the American Civil War Meagher was perhaps one of the best-known Irishmen in America and would become an important figure in the recruitment of Irish soldiers in the cause of the Union. While Meagher's role in the American Civil War has been well documented, the part played by his wife, Elizabeth, has received little attention. Elizabeth Meagher played an important role in the formation of the Irish Brigade. When the Brigade was finally established, a group of patriotic ladies from New York formed a committee to provide a set of colours for each of the Irish Brigade's New York regiments, the 63rd, 69th and 88th New York Infantry. The flags were made by Tiffany of New York and were of the richest silk and each regiment received a national and a regimental flag, and a pair of guidons. The national colours were fringed with saffron silk, with the name of the regiment embroidered in the centre on a crimson stripe. The regimental colours were of a deep green with a richly embroidered Irish harp in the centre. Above the harp was a sunburst with a wreath of shamrock beneath. Underneath, on a crimson scroll, was the motto 'Fág an Bealach'.[52] On 18 November 1861, watched by thousands of spectators, the Irish Brigade received its new colours in a glittering ceremony outside the residence of Archbishop Hughes at 198 Madison Avenue. The *New York Times* singled out Libby for special mention, noting that 'among the ladies [was] Mrs. Thomas Francis Meagher charming all around her by her graceful courtesy and joyousness'.[53] On that occasion Libby personally presented to the 88th regiment the colours she herself had embroidered and this regiment became known subsequently as 'Mrs Meagher's Own'. The 88th was comprised largely (75 per cent) of men from the Irish province of Connacht and a large proportion of them had served in the British army. When the brigade was required to take part in the universal numbering system, the unit took the number of the 88th Connaught Rangers. The language of the regiment was Gaelic (Irish).

It was not unusual for the wives of officers to visit the military camps during the winter when there was, usually, little action. In 1862, Libby visited her husband at camp with the Irish Brigade. The brigade's celebrated chaplain Fr Corby wrote of her thus;

> I had the pleasure of meeting the wife of Gen. Thomas Francis Meagher, a lady of marked character and possessed of more than an ordinary degree of refinement and excellent social virtues. She was a devout convert to the Catholic Church, and was highly respected by the army officers, many of whom had known her and her family in New York long before the war.[54]

Fr Corby was also very impressed with General Meagher and reported that,

> Gen. Meagher was more than an ordinary gentleman. He possessed high-toned sentiments and manners, and the bearing of a prince. He had a superior intellect, a liberal education, was a fine classical writer, and a born orator. He was very witty, but more inclined to humour; was fond of witty or humorous persons, and admired those who possessed such gifts. He was a great lover of his native land, and passionately opposed to its enemies; strong in his faith, which he never concealed, but, on the contrary, published it above-board; and, wherever he went he made himself known as a Catholic and an Irishman . . . It is to be regretted that, at times, especially when no fighting was going on, and time grew heavy on his hands, his convivial spirit would lead him too far. But by no means must it be concluded from this that he was a drunkard. It was not for love of liquor, but for the love of sport and joviality that he thus gave way, and these occasions were few and far between.[55]

The Irish Brigade fought with distinction and great bravery in all the major battles of the war but the final two battles under Meagher's leadership – Fredericksburg and Chancellorsville – proved almost fatal to the brigade.[56] A month after Fredericksburg, in January 1863, in a packed St Patrick's Cathedral, New York City, Meagher and Libby attended a solemn Requiem High Mass celebrated for all the dead of the brigade since the start of the war. The *New York Times* reported that 'Brig. Gen. Meagher, accompanied by many officers of the brigade, occupied prominent seats, and the General, particularly, was the object of much observation, as he was in the course of the sermon addressed several times from the pulpit.' After the religious ceremonies were concluded Meagher hosted a dinner at Delmonico's restaurant on 5th Avenue for about a hundred officers of the brigade.[57] After Chancellorsville, Meagher was refused permission to take home the remains of his regiments to refit and recruit so he resigned his commission. Though re-instated in December 1863, he ended the war commanding a few thousand convalescent soldiers, transporting them from Tennessee to New Bern, North Carolina. He remained in the army until 12 May 1865 when, along with all civilian generals, he resigned, although he continued to feature prominently in the brigade's non-military activities.

On 9 May Washington, D.C. was *en fête* with thousands of people assembled to see the 'Grand Review' of the Grand Army of the Republic when it would march for the last time. After the 'Review' the 400 New York soldiers arrived home on 4 July and marched through cheering crowds to Irving Hall, where they partook of a sumptuous banquet provided for them by a number of citizen friends in conjunction with several ex-officers of the brigade, including Meagher. At the end of the banquet 'Brevet Brigadier General Nugent brought them to attention and marched them out into the rest of their lives and history'.[58]

The war had ended and Meagher had not found a meaningful role for himself in his new country. His stay with his father-in-law at the Townsend mansion had been an uneasy one, and he and Libby moved to the fashionable East 23rd Street in midtown Manhattan. He was still a lodger, however, for the 23rd Street house belonged to Samuel Barlow who was married to Alice Townsend, Libby's sister. This home was a double brownstone house filled with paintings, engravings, *objets d'art* and a library that was richer than any other private library in America – the collection of early American history was one of the most extensive in existence. Barlow's wealth was estimated at $8 million, all earned from his profession as a lawyer,[59] thus making Meagher's lack of business success even more conspicuous.

MONTANA

During the presidential campaign of 1864, Meagher had alienated thousands of Irish voters all over the eastern states by declaring for the Republican Party candidates Lincoln and Johnson. He had been denounced in the influential *Irish*

American and accused as being a deserter from the Democratic cause. In a letter to his old friend, Tipperary-born Colonel Guiney, 9th Massachusetts Volunteers, dated 7 October 1863, Meagher wrote,

> as for the great bulk of Irishmen in this country, I frankly confess to an utter disregard, if not a thorough contempt, of what they think or say of me in my relations to the questions and movements that are supported or designed to affect the fortunes of this nation...I have discarded with the haughtiest insensibility and disdain the 'Irish opinion' of this country, having come to the conclusion that it was passed [*sic*] redemption, and, therefore, passed [*sic*] consideration or respect.[60]

All Meagher's ventures in the East and in Central America had come to naught and, like thousands of other Americans, he would turn his attention to the West. Perhaps there he could revive his fortunes! With the war over, the West was being opened up for development and thousands followed the exhortation of Meagher's friend Horace Greeley to 'Go West, Young Man'![61] However, in August 1865, Meagher was rewarded for his support of Lincoln in the 1864 presidential election with the secretaryship of Montana Territory, a post he accepted with alacrity. But within a few short months he had clashed with every faction in Montana politics, and accusations about drinking and womanizing surfaced again. He had, initially, travelled alone to Montana, but Libby rejoined him in the spring of 1866.[62] Both were very happy together and Meagher's friend Johnny Doran wrote that the general had spoken to him 'in the most tender and affectionate terms of his wife, residing at Helena', saying that in their mountain home they were 'as happy as two thrushes in a bush'.[63] Meagher wrote to his friend, Captain Lyons, that he had contemplated resigning his official position since he had become weary of his lack of success. However, with Libby now at his side he was 'strengthened by her presence, the burden of his public duties would be lightened...and the prospect of carving out a fortune for himself ...would be all the brighter because she was there to cheer and encourage him'.[64]

On the day of his death, 1 July 1867, he was very ill when he arrived in Fort Benton. Dehydrated and suffering from dysentery, he retired to the back room of I.G. Baker's log store to rest and write some letters. One of those letters revealed the extraordinary fact that Meagher was practically penniless at the time. Despite the fact that he had occupied the highest office in the territory for almost two years, he had still not been remunerated. There is therefore a certain poignancy attached to his letter of 1 July 1867 to John H. Ming, the Territorial Auditor requesting his back pay.

> My Dear Friend Ming:
> As I believe you have decided on giving me the pay, authorized by the Bannack statute touching the same, due me as acting governor for nearly

two years, I beg, as a personal favour which shall be most gratefully remembered, that you will send the amount due (in whatever amount of greenbacks you can obtain for it) and direct the enclosure to this great seaport for me, to the care of I.G. Baker Esq.
I am utterly – utterly – out of funds and it is absolutely necessary I should have some. So, my dear fellow, do what I ask, and that as soon as you can possibly do it, and you will gratefully oblige and serve,
Yours most faithfully
T. F. MEAGHER.[65]

After Meagher's death, Libby was a pitiable figure as she roamed the banks of the Missouri river near Fort Benton in a fruitless search for her husband's body. After several months, she left the area and retired to her family home in New York State where she outlived the general by thirty-nine years. During that time she led a quiet life, caring for her invalid sister and rarely venturing far from her home, but she did attend some of the reunions of the Irish Brigade. Meagher had wanted his son to come and live in the United States with himself and Libby, but his death prevented that happy outcome. Libby, however, sent for her stepson and he joined her in New York in the early 1870s.

THOMAS BENNETT MEAGHER

Thomas Francis Meagher II (known in the USA as Thomas Bennett Meagher) was born in Waterford, Ireland in April 1854, the only one of Meagher's two children to grow to manhood. After his mother's death, when he was just an infant, he lived in the family home at the Mall, with his grandfather and maiden aunts.[66] Nothing more is known of him until the early 1870s when his stepmother, Elizabeth Townsend Meagher, took him to New York City, where they lived at East 23rd Street in the house she had shared with Meagher prior to her husband's departure for Montana.

Thomas Bennett Meagher entered West Point Military Academy on 1 September 1872. On entry he was 18 years old and looked forward to a military career. While he resembled his father in face, feature and physique to a remarkable degree, and was very intelligent, he lacked application and his tastes were not military. His medical examination at West Point indicates that he was 5′ 8$^1/_8$″ tall (a little over the average), had 20/20 vision, his vaccination was bad and he was an occasional smoker. His academic record shows that he had little aptitude for French and Mathematics and, though he was very studious, he was not attentive to regulations, being awarded twenty-eight demerits. It was no surprise when he was discharged from the academy just over four months later, for being deficient in French and Mathematics. It was not unusual for students to be discharged for out of ninety-five cadets who entered the academy in 1872, twenty-four were discharged and five resigned.[67]

After he left West Point, he lived in New York City for some years and was a familiar figure at gatherings of Irish nationalists. He inherited his father's political opinions, became a member of the Napper Tandy Club of Clan-na-Gael, and his associations were all Irish.[68] He was a young man of fine presence and good manners, but was of a retiring disposition. His resemblance to his father was so striking that many of the veterans of 1848 and of the Civil War knew him, on sight, for a son of the general.

Young Meagher, after remaining some years in New York, had a falling-out with his stepmother, Elizabeth Meagher, and they parted company. There were rumours that Thomas Bennett contemplated an acting career but that was short-lived. Libby remained in New York City sharing her widowed father's mansion on 5th Avenue with her father, her widowed sister, Caroline, and her four young daughters and eight servants. Thomas Bennett remained in New York where he met and married Mary Lavinia Carpenter, a native of Sacramento, on 6 February 1884. At the end of that year their son, Thomas Francis Meagher III, was born in Manhattan. The young family eventually moved to San Francisco where Thomas Bennett was employed in the San Fancisco Mint as a civil servant. Another son, Gerard Clarence Meagher, was born in San Francisco but lived only one year.[69]

Thomas Bennett Meagher had married well. His wife was a member of one of San Francisco's most respectable and respected families, the Badlams, and they lived with his wife's sister, Sarah Badlam Winans, at 926 Clay Street, San Francisco.[70] Through his wife's connections Thomas Bennett gained an entrée into San Francisco high society. An entry in the 1888 *San Francisco Society Directory* shows that he was a member of the Pacific Yacht Club.[71] This very elite and exclusive club was comprised of top society members in San Francisco, and was organized on 1 July 1878, for the purpose of encouraging and fostering an interest in yachting in the bay. It had its headquarters in Sausalito, California, across the bay from San Francisco, and Thomas Bennett sailed across by private boat as there were no bridges at that time.

Following his wife's death in 1893, he continued living at this address as a boarder with his wife's aunt, Sarah Winans.[72] He was employed later in some capacity with the Fellowship of Eagles, of which he was a member, and worked for that group in Manila, Philippine Islands, where he died on 29 November 1909. Irishmen in the East who knew him had lost all knowledge of him and the news of his death from pneumonia, following an attempted suicide, came as a complete surprise.[73] The funeral in Manila was a tribute worthy of the respect in which he was held in the American community of the Philippines. Present were representatives of the United States Army, the Insular Constabulary, Representatives of the Philippine Assembly, the Manila Lodge of Eagles with their members and regalia, the local branch of the Knights of Columbus and the Municipality of the City of Manila. The American business community was also represented. The residents paid evident respect to the remains as the cortege passed through the streets of the old historic Spanish city. Numerous wreaths adorned the casket of the deceased and among the most prominent and significant was a wreath depicting an Irish Harp, worked in flowers with the figures '48', with a simple card attached bearing the words 'from the Clan-na-Gael'.[74]

He was buried in the Cemetario del Norte in Manila and, in December 1910, a monument to his memory was unveiled in the cemetery. A letter to the *Waterford News* of 17 February 1911, on behalf of the monument committee, reported

> Irish-Americans and other friends in Manila erected a beautiful Celtic cross as a fitting mark of respect to a good Irishman, a good American, and a worthy and loving friend. All of the participants in this brotherly and kindly sentiment to Mr. Meagher were mainly actuated by the merits of the deceased gentleman; his kindliness, his patriotism, and his means, were in evidence whenever the occasion called for it in his lifetime. The children of the great very often bask in the sunshine reflected from their parents, but in the case of the late T.F. Meagher it was the exception. It was a long time before the writer, and many others, too, were aware that he was the only son of one of the great Irish heroes of history...The unveiling of the monument took place on Thursday, December 15th, 1910. Most Rev. Dr. Harty, Roman Catholic Archbishop of Manila...dedicated the cross and made a...touching address to those assembled.[75]

THE GRIEVING WIDOW

With the departure of young Thomas Bennett to California, Libby was alone again. She visited Helena in the summer of 1877 and attended the annual meeting of the society of Montana Pioneers. Shortly afterwards she presented to that society a large and life-like oil portrait of General Meagher – one of two portraits painted by the Waterford-born artist Mr T. Gallagher. A letter from Libby, indicative of her modest and retiring character, was read at the presentation:

> Elsinore[76]
> Glen Cove
> Long Island
> May 30
>
> Dear Friends – I regret my unavoidable absence from the city will prevent my attending the ceremonial of tomorrow evening.
> We were obliged to bring my invalid sister to the country. I will not be missed and my absence need not be known. There will be a crowd, and everybody will suppose I am among them.
> Hoping it will prove all your anticipation. I am very truly yours,
> Elizabeth M. J. Meagher

In New York, in 1886, Libby presented to the City of Waterford the second of the two portraits of Meagher painted by Gallagher, together with two of the Irish Brigade battle flags and a 'sprig of green' found nearest the Confederate works at Fredericksburg.[77] These relics of Meagher were sent to the Young Ireland Society in Waterford where they were welcomed by a crowd of over 60,000 people from all parts of Ireland.

On May 3 1886, US Congressman Woodburn introduced a bill (H.R. 8463) in the Second Session of the 49th Congress to award Libby Townsend a pension of $50 a month as the widow of General Meagher. The original bill was for a pension of $100 per month from the time of death of Meagher but for some reason the pension was amended by the Committee of the Whole House to $50 per month, dated from its enactment on 14 January 1887. A double tragedy befell Libby in 1889 when her sister Alice and Alice's husband, Samuel L. Barlow, both died within a few months of each other. Libby was now utterly alone. She had not forgotten Thomas Bennett, however, and had maintained contact with him, albeit cursory and infrequent. Shortly after the death of Thomas Bennett's wife in 1893, Libby wrote and offered to adopt her husband's grandson, Thomas Francis Meagher III who was now 8 years old. However, the boy's father refused his consent and the young boy was also not amenable to a move. Libby then took up with a young man named Thomas Durkin and adopted him, changing his name to Meagher.[78]

Libby died at her home in Rye, New York on 5 July 1906, and two days later her relatives brought her body from Rye to St Francis Xavier's church on 16th Street. Her funeral was held after a solemn Requiem Mass, celebrated by Fr Thomas Campbell, SJ. The honorary pallbearers were Meagher's subordinates and his old friends in the Irish Brigade, Dr John Dwyer, Col. James Quinlan, Thomas J. Byrne, Col. James W. Meagher, Col. Denis McCarthy and Capt. Michael McGuire. Libby was interred in Greenwood Cemetery, Brooklyn, in the Townsend family plot.[79] Her simple gravestone reads 'ELIZABETH TOWNSEND MEAGHER/BORN SOUTHFIELDS N.Y./SEPTEMBER 20 1830/DIED RYE N.Y./JULY 5 1906.

In her will dated 15 June 1901, at Rye NY, Libby bequeathed some articles to three nieces and named Thomas Meagher Durkin as her executor and main beneficiary, but a sword and bloodstained sash (from the Civil War) and the general's papers were sent to Thomas Francis Meagher III. On the latter's death in 1943, his wife, Edna, burned the papers.[80]

EPILOGUE

Many commentators have criticized Meagher's treatment of his first wife, especially when she rejoined him in New York after her voyage from Van Diemen's Land.[81] The general opinion is that he rejected her as being his inferior in class and education. Yet, when some of his patriot friends questioned his decision to marry

Bennie he rejected their advice and wrote that his love for Bennie had awoken in him 'the proud and generous nature that was sinking, coldly and dismally, into a stupid and sensual stagnation... I am myself again.'[82] Even the most sceptical of them were soon won-over by the happiness that was evident in their marriage. All of Meagher's subsequent writings about Bennie show that he was very affectionate towards her. He and Bennie had, also, made plans to start their married life anew as soon as their second child was born and was old enough to travel.

Meagher corresponded frequently with his son, Thomas Bennett, in Waterford, yet it is strange that he never saw him and apparently made little effort to see him. Meagher could not set foot in Ireland or any part of the United Kingdom without fear of arrest, but he could have arranged to meet him at some other place. Paris was an obvious choice: it was the favoured meeting place for most Irishmen banished from their native land; it was also familiar to Meagher and his father and was a relatively short trip from Ireland. Meagher was aware of this when he wrote to his father in August 1865 that, all going well, he looked forward to seeing him (and his son, no doubt) in France later that year. He also planned to have his son join him in America. In the letter to Elizabeth Townsend of January 1855 (after Bennie's death and when his son was only a baby) he wrote that he looked forward to the day when she would be 'my noble wife and the mother of my little boy'.[83]

In Meagher's short life he gained the love and admiration of most people he met and, there can be no doubt, that he was loved deeply by Bennie and Libby. All who befriended him and who were, in turn, befriended by him, remained his friends until his death; and they mourned him as a brother. While Meagher's life contained many of the elements of 'Grand Opera' – larger than life characters, great adventures and high drama – it also descended, at times, to 'Opera Buffa'. However, it exhibited great moral and physical courage, love of country and fidelity to a cause. When the sacrifices he made in the early part of his life are remembered, his later failings may well be forgotten and his name, placed high in the pantheon of Irish patriots, will justify for him the proud title of 'the best-beloved Waterford-man of his generation'.[84]

Meagher's family is scattered to the four winds. His first son lies in Richmond, Tasmania; his second son in Manila, Philippine Islands. His first wife is buried amidst the sylvan beauty of Faithlegge, Waterford and his second wife in Brooklyn, New York – but Meagher himself has no resting-place where his admirers might pay their respects. We can but echo the thoughts of the poet –

Ah, would to God his grave had been,
On mountain side, in glen or plain,
Beneath the turf kept soft and green
By wind and sunshine, dew and rain;
That men and maids, in after years,
Might come where sleep the true and brave,
And plant, and wet with flooding tears,
The Irish shamrock on his grave.[85]

MEAGHER FAMILY PEDIGREE

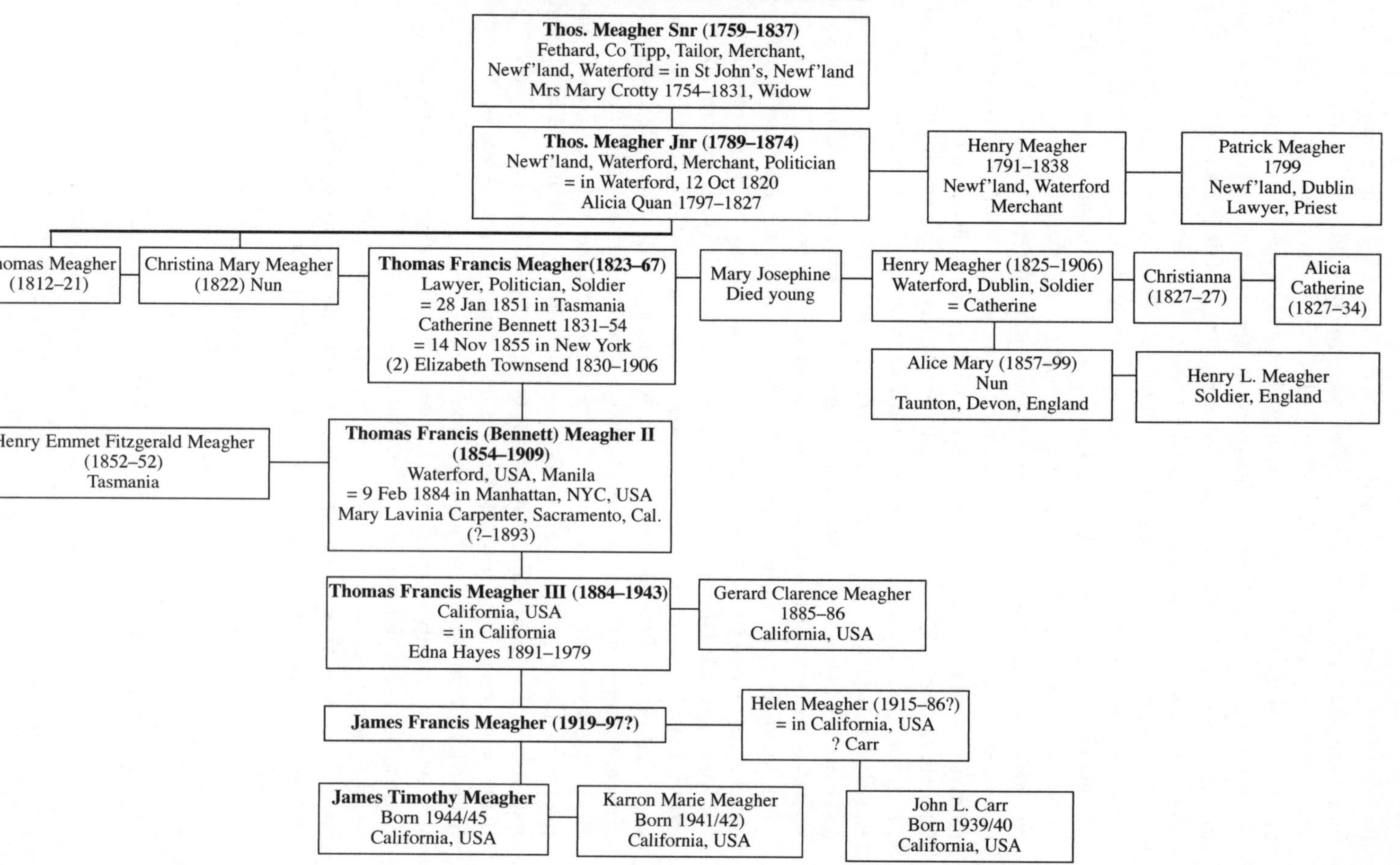

NOTES

1. *The Times of London*, 4 Aug. 1848.
2. I am indebted to Professor John Mannion, for this information.
3. Patrick James Smyth (1823–85), went to the USA after 1848 and planned the escape of John Mitchel from Van Diemen's Land, 1854. Returned to Ireland in 1856 and was called to the bar. Became MP for Tipperary in 1880. Opposed the Land League and resigned his seat in 1882. He died in poverty, 1885.
4. Reg. A. Watson, *The Life And Times Of Thomas Francis Meagher* (Tasmania: Southern Holdings, 2001), p.10.
5. T.F. Meagher, 'A Personal Narrative of 1848', in Arthur Griffith (ed.), *Meagher of the Sword*, (Dublin: M.H. Gill & Son, 1915), p.229.
6. Meagher's education in Waterford was, initially, at the Misses Quan's Academy, The Mall – a school for young ladies conducted by his aunts in the building beside his home. He later was a pupil at the Sisters of Charity school, see S.A., *Mary Aikenhead: Her Life, Her Work and Her Friends: Being a history of the foundation of the Congregation of the Irish Sisters of Charity* (Dublin: M.H. Gill & Son, Ltd., 1896), p.292. 'Thomas Francis, afterwards of Young Ireland celebrity, General of Brigade in the United States army, and Governor of Montana Territory, used to go to the convent when a little fellow to learn his letters and his catechism.' There is a Waterford tradition that Meagher attended Mount Sion Schools but this cannot be verified as no records are extant. Meagher certainly knew and revered Br Rice, the founder of Mount Sion. He delivered an oration in 1845, extolling the virtues of Br Rice, at a dinner to celebrate the gift, from the people of Waterford, of a chapel and classroom. This was to commemorate Br Rice, who had died the previous year.
7. McManus (1823–60) was born in Tempo, Co., Fermanagh into a middle-class family. He went to Liverpool where he became a prosperous shipping agent. He died in poverty following the collapse of his business.
8. At the time of his arrest he was a law clerk who was earning £200–£300 a year. He died in America in 1854.
9. Michael Cavanagh, *Memoirs Of General Thomas Francis Meagher* (Worcester, MA: The Messenger Press, 1892), p.299.
10. As an example of this largesse, see letter from Meagher to O'Doherty, June 18 1851, O'Doherty Papers, microfilm no. 1396; National Library of Ireland (hereafter NLI), where Meagher mentions that his father had paid a debt of £550 on his behalf. This debt was for the attempted rescue of Smith O'Brien from Van Diemen's Land. Meagher's father paid his son's (Meagher's) expenses for clothing, et cetera, for his transportation, amounting to a total of £9.18s.0d. (Ms. 7410, NLI). He also paid the full expenses of his son's trial, £488.10s.0d (see *Waterford News Supplement*, 23 Feb. 1895) and Meagher himself paid, out of his own resources, the full expenses of O'Donohoe's trial. See *Waterford Chronicle*, 1 Nov. 1848).
11. Waterford City Archives (WCA), Ms. P11/03, *Letter from Meagher to Gavan Duffy*, 16 Feb. 1850, p.37.
12. *Ibid.*, p.43.
13. Rev. J.H. Cullen, *Young Ireland in Exile* (Dublin and Cork: The Talbot Press, 1928), p.76.
14. Meagher to O'Brien, 21 Feb. 1850, O'Brien Papers, NLI.
15. Thomas Keneally, *The Great Shame. A Story of the Irish in the Old World and the New* (London: Vintage, 1998), p.233.
16. Bryan (sometimes spelt Brian) Bennett was born in 1776 and was 74 years old at Bennie's marriage to Meagher. He died on 8 June 1874 aged 98 years, a resident of New Norfolk Mental Hospital. His wife, Mary Bennett, died on 24 May 1871, aged 86 years at the Bridge Inn, Bridge Street, Richmond, the residence of her daughter Bridget, wife of Daniel Murphy. The above information is courtesy of Reg. A. Watson, Tasmania, who helped with the Tasmanian references and pictures.
17. O'Doherty Papers, NLI, microfilm no. 1396, Meagher to O'Doherty, 2 Jan. 1851.
18. Keneally, *Great Shame*, p.235.

19. *Ibid.*, pp.239–40. Jenny Mitchel [wife of John Mitchel] to Miss Mary Thompson, 1851.
20. O'Doherty Papers, NLI, microfilm no. 1396; Martin to O'Doherty, Bothwell, 27 Jan. 1851.
21. John Blake Dillon (1816–66), lawyer, born in Ballaghadereen, Co. Roscommon. After 1848, he escaped to the USA. He was amnestied in 1855, returned to Ireland and became MP for Tipperary in 1865. He died of cholera in 1866.
22. Brendan Ó Cathaoir, *John Blake Dillon, Young Irelander* (Dublin: Irish Academic Press, 1990), p.138.
23. Cullen, *Young Ireland in Exile*, p.64, noting that O'Donohoe wrote in his diary of 20 July 1849, 'Mr. Meagher, on this day announced the 'O' as a prefix to his name'.
24. *Ibid.*, pp.46–7. The italics are Mitchel's. See also, Meagher to Sir Colman O'Loughlin, 27 Aug. 1851, microfilm no. 8419, NLI. Symbols were important to Meagher. He had a greyhound, Brian, named after King Brian Boru. His boat, *Speranza*, was named in honour of Miss Jane Elgee (the future Lady Wilde and mother of Oscar), one of the poets of the *Nation* whose pen name was *Speranza*. The flags that flew from its masthead were, variously, the Stars and Stripes (the symbol of liberty) and Meagher's tricolour. It was Meagher, as president of the Waterford City Wolfe Tone Confederate Club, who first flew the Irish tricolour from a public building in Ireland. This occurred on 1 March 1848, at the club's headquarters, 33 The Mall, Waterford, during Meagher's unsuccessful Waterford city election campaign.
25. O'Doherty Papers, Martin to O'Doherty, undated, microfilm no.1396, NLI.
26. Keneally, *Great Shame*, p.245
27. The Connell Papers, Meagher to Mrs Connell, 15 Aug. 1851, Ms. 3224, NLI.
28. Hickey Collection, Martin to O'Doherty, 13 Aug. 1851, Ms. 3226, NLI.
29. Meagher Papers, Meagher to his school-friend Stephen Curtis (a barrister in Waterford), 20 Oct. 1851, Ms. 3900, NLI.
30. 11 Jan. 1852, Ms. 3224, NLI.
31. Meagher wished his son to be named Henry (a family name), Emmet for Robert Emmet and Fitzgerald for Lord Edward Fitzgerald, thus baptizing him into the Meagher family and Ireland's struggle for freedom.
32. Keneally, *Great Shame*, pp.254–5, Jenny Mitchel to her friend Miss Thompson. Harry O'Meagher was Meagher's brother, Henry.
33. *New York Times*, 29 May 1852. The father's fortune would be worth, today, about $40,000,000 (£23,000,000).
34. *Waterford Chronicle*, 2 July 1853.
35. *Ibid.*, 2 July 1853.
36. *Waterford News*, 8 July 1853.
37. *Waterford Mail*, 6 July 1853.
38. *Ibid.*, 9 July 1853.
39. K. Theodore Hoppen, 'National Politics and Local Realities in Mid-Nineteenth Century Ireland', in Art Cosgrove and Donal McCartney (eds), *Studies in Irish History: Presented to R. Dudley Edwards* (Dublin: University College Dublin, 1979), p.196. See also editorial in *Waterford Chronicle*, 2 Aug. 1848, 'The swearing in of constables is fast progressing. Poor men, they would be of little use as a National Guard. Some of the most feeble old men in the City have been sworn in. But what they are to be called on to do is still a mystery, surely it cannot be to fight, it would be perfectly ridiculous.'
40. John Joseph Hughes, born in Co. Tyrone, Ireland in 1797, became the fourth bishop (1842) and first Catholic Archbishop of New York (1850). His enemies gave him the soubriquet 'Dagger John', a reference to the cross that preceded his signature and to his pugnacious character. He clashed with Meagher over the latter's liberal Catholicism and support for Mazzini, the anti-clerical Italian revolutionary. The row was healed when Meagher sent him a conciliatory letter (1853). Curiously, this letter was drafted, not by Meagher, but by John Blake Dillon. Hughes died in 1864.
41. *Waterford News*, 4 Nov. 1853, Letter from Meagher to the Mayor of Waterford, 10 Oct. 1853.
42. *Ibid.*, 12 May 1854.
43. *New York Times*, 1 July 1854.
44. Lincoln Diamant, *Chaining the Hudson* (New York: Citadel Press, 1994), Preface p.ix. I am

indebted to Dr Rory Cornish for providing me with a copy of this book.

45. Meagher Papers, Small Collection 309, Folder 2, Ac 83–4, Montana Historical Society (hereafter MHS). I am very grateful to Lenore Puhek, Montana, for her invaluable help with the Montana references.
46. *Ibid.*
47. *Ibid.*
48. Marriage register is courtesy of Joann Rodriguez, St Patrick's Old Cathedral, Mulberry Street, New York. O'Connor was a lawyer friend of Meagher. Richard Stockton Emmet (1821–97), son of Thomas Addis Emmet, had been a nephew of the Irish patriot Robert Emmet who was executed in 1803.
49. Meagher Papers, Small Collection 309, (MHS).
50. This information was carried on the paper's masthead.
51. *Waterford Chronicle*, 12 June 1858.
52. 'Leave the Gap' or 'Clear the way'.
53. *New York Times*, 19 Nov. 1861.
54. See Lawrence Frederick Kohl (ed.), *Memoirs Of Chaplain Life, Three Years with the Irish Brigade in the Army of the Potomac* by William Corby CSC (New York: Fordham University Press, 1992), p.118.
55. *Ibid.*, pp.28–30.
56. Geoffrey C. Ward, *The Civil War* (New York: Alfred A. Knopf, Inc., 1990), p.171.
57. *New York Times*, 17 Jan. 1863.
58. *Irish American*, 15 July 1865, quoted in Joseph Bilby, *The Irish Brigade in the Civil War* (Conshohocken, PA: Combined Publishing, 2000), p.127.
59. *New York Times*, 11 July 1889.
60. *Irish American*, 15 Oct. 1863.
61. Horace Greeley (1811–72) was editor of the *New York Tribune*, the nation's most influential and widely-read newspaper. He stood for election to the presidency in 1872 but was defeated badly by the incumbent, Grant. Greeley died less than a month after the defeat.
62. In the spring of 1867 Meagher honoured his wife by naming one of Montana's frontier forts 'Fort Elizabeth Meagher'. This was established near the present-day town of Bozeman. The town of Libby, Montana, was also named in her honour.
63. Capt. W.F. Lyons, *Brigadier General Thomas Francis Meagher: His Political and Military Career* (London: Burns Oates & Washburn Ltd., 1869), p.184, Doran to Lyons, 16 Dec. 1869.
64. *Ibid.*, p.107.
65. Meagher Papers, Small Collection 309, (MHS).
66. *Waterford News*, 16 July 1910. In an article by John P. Sutton, editor of the *Chicago Citizen*, he reminisces about his life in Waterford before he went to America. Remembering the old Cathedral in Barronstrand Street he wrote 'We can see in the pew next to the one we used to occupy, old Tom Meagher, the General's father; the Misses Quan, and young Tom, the General's son'.
67. From *The National Archives and Records Administration of the United States*, Washington, DC, and *Official Register of the U.S. Military Academy, West Point*, New York, June 1873. My thanks to Elaine McConnell, Ms. Librarian at the Academy for her help in this matter.
68. Clan-na-Gael was a secret, oath-bound organization founded in New York in 1867 and dedicated to achieving Ireland's independence from Britain. Thomas Bennett Meagher was a member of the Brooklyn Napper Tandy Club of Clan-na-Gael.
69. Vital Records for 1875/84, microfilm M-3140 in the *San Francisco Call* newspaper, 'Meagher, Thomas F., married in 1884 to Carpenter, Mamie L.' Mary Lavinia died on 18 January 1893. TFM II had two sons, Thomas Francis Meagher III and Gerard Meagher. TFM III married Edna Hayes and they had two children: James Francis Meagher of Napa City, CA and Helen Meagher Carr of Vallejo, CA. The above James Francis had at least two children, James Timothy Meagher (born 1944/45) and Karron (sic) Marie Meagher (born 1942/43) of Napa CA. The above Helen Meagher Carr had at least one child, John L. Carr (born 1939/40) of Vallejo, CA – see letter dated 30 June 1946 from Edna Meagher to Professor Robert G. Athearn of the University of Minnesota. John L. Carr is the current owner of the grave in

which TFM III is buried. TFM III bought this plot in 1913 and had the bodies of his wife's relatives exhumed from two other sites and re-interred there. This grave is at Saint Helena Cemetery, 2461 Spring Street, St Helena, California, 94574. TFM III is buried in lot 19, block 22. Cemetery records indicate that he died 2 March 1943, at age 58. The cause of death was pneumonia and residence at time of death is recorded as Vallejo, CA. He is buried next to Edna Hayes Meagher (1891–1979). Only one other Meagher, Gerard Meagher, is included in this grave. All attempts to find living descendants of the general have failed. I wish to thank Joe Myers, Hilton Head Island, SC, USA, for his most generous help in tracing the Meagher family in America.

70. History of prominent families in *San Francisco Blue Book*, 1889 and 1890, Sutro Library, San Francisco.
71. *San Francisco: Our Society Directory 1888.*
72. *San Francisco Blue Book*, 1894, Sutro Library, San Francisco.
73. '29 November 1909, Thomas Meagher, son of the Irish patriot, died today of pneumonia following an attempt at suicide.' Extract from the obituary of T.F. Meagher II in the *California Information File* and the *San Francisco News Index 1904–59*, cited in *The Nugget* (Journal of the California Genealogical Society), Vol. 3 No. 2.
74. *Waterford News*, 12 Feb. 1910.
75. *Ibid.*, 17 Feb. 1911. Letter from Dominick Twomey, Monument Committee, to the Mayor of Waterford, Cllr James Hackett.
76. 'Elsinore' was the summer home of Libby's sister, Alice Townsend Barlow.
77. *Irish American*, 3 Jan. 1863. Letter from John Donovan, First Lieutenant Company D, 69th Regiment, Irish Brigade, 'The Irish Brigade was drawn up in line of battle at ordered arms and a *parade rest*. A green sprig was ordered by General Meagher to be placed in the caps of both officers and men, himself first setting the example.'
78. Edna Meagher to Robert G. Athearn, 30 June 1946 and 17 July 1946.
79. *New York Times*, 8 July 1906.
80. Edna Meagher to Robert G. Athearn, 30 June 1946 and July 17 1946. Meagher Papers, Small Collection 309, (MHS).
81. *The War of the Rebellion: a Compilation of the Official Records of the Union and Confederate Armies (1880–1901)*, Government Printing Office, Washington, Series 4, Volume 3, p.4. This criticism was there from the start. He was considered to be vulnerable on this point and his enemies made much of it. S.C. Hayes of the Confederate States Register's Office wrote, in a letter to C.S. President Jefferson Davis of 6 January 1864, 'After the first battle of Manassas, T.F. Meagher came to Philadelphia to drum up recruits for his Irish Brigade. He made a capital speech; I feared a telling one. I worked night and day to neutralize his speech. His treatment of the Irish [*sic*] girl who aided him in making his escape from Australia, and his subsequent marriage with a Yankee girl, was an admirable argument against him, which I failed not to use on every occasion. The result was he obtained but few recruits in Philadelphia – not more than a corporal's guard.'
82. See note 17.
83. Meagher Papers, Small Collection 309, (MHS).
84. *Waterford News*, 17 May 1935 (Mathew Butler).
85. T.D. Sullivan, 'Lines On The Death Of Thomas Francis Meagher', from *Green Leaves, A Volume of Irish Verses* (Dublin: T. D. Sullivan, 1885), p.101.

The Strange Death of Thomas Francis Meagher: Tribal Politics in Territorial Montana

David Emmons

Thomas Francis Meagher's life was dramatic, colourful and bordered almost on the mythical. His unexpected death, however, was strangely inappropriate and almost unbecoming for the valiant commander of the famed Irish Brigade. Few Victorian romances contained so many elements of dash and passion as the life of Meagher of the Sword. He strutted his way through a rebellious Ireland, became a noted young orator, was sentenced to death, spent time in and escaped from the British penal colony of Van Diemen's Land, dodged Confederate bullets in the American Civil War and served as acting territorial governor of Montana. This last official posting also seems incongruous as the résumé compiled by Meagher would have usually led to more prestigious postings than that of governor of a remote western territory. His death by drowning in remote Montana struck his friends as a miserable end for such a figure as Meagher. His fellow Young Irelander, Richard O'Gorman, lamented in his eulogy at Meagher's memorial service 'would that he had died on the battlefield'. Similarly, Martin Maginnis bemoaned the fact that it had not been Meagher's fate to 'perish by the gibbet of his country's tyrants... nor by the murderous volleys of their hireling sentinels'. It would have been useful if Maginnis had actually identified which had been Meagher's country and who would have hired the sentinels and, of course, for what purpose.[1]

THEORIES

Although the details of Meagher's ignoble death by drowning on 1 July 1867 have been discussed at some length by other historians, there remains some controversy regarding the event itself. The conventional interpretation has suggested that Meagher was ill, possibly drunk, and that he tripped over a coiled rope left on the upper deck outside his cabin. In other words, he fell off the boat, the *G.A. Thompson*. The Missouri was twelve feet deep and running at nine miles per hour, about what could be expected after a typical Montana winter. His body was never recovered; it was probably washed ashore miles down steam from Fort Benton and was eaten by marauding wolves or bears. The best that can be said of his death was that it might serve as a coda, a cautionary tale on what can befall those of careless and/or intemperate habits.[2]

It is not the intention in this essay to argue that Meagher's death was of great historical importance as this would be revisionism unrestrained by good judgement. While a distinguished and gallant death would have filled out the historical record more fittingly, one cannot assign Meagher such a death simply to put an epic end to an epic life. That would be romanticism unrestrained by common sense; Meagher was not the only nineteenth-century swashbuckler to die an unheroic death. There is, however, the possibility that his death was not an accident and, if so, this in itself may be historically significant. A new and further analysis of how he died may also illustrate the tribal nature of Montana and American politics after the Civil War. This, perhaps, is reason enough to inquire again into how he came to fall off the *G.A. Thompson.*

The historian Robert Winks has suggested that all historians are really detectives, or at least they should be.[3] It is not necessary to take Winks' point literally but here it may benefit the analysis to restate, detective-like, the obvious facts of the case: there are only five possible alternatives for what happened to Meagher on 1 July 1867. Firstly, he committed suicide or, secondly, he accidentally fell, whether drunk or sober into the Missouri River. A third alternative should not be taken too seriously, that he jumped from the boat, swam ashore, and escaped into the wilderness to take up a new identity far from Montana. There remains a possibility that he was killed in a personal quarrel, or by a robber or homicidal psychopath. There also remains the last possibility, that Meagher, a controversial figure, was assassinated and murdered for political or quasi-political reasons.

The possibility of suicide arose from the single uncorroborated account by Wilbur Fisk Sanders, one of the territory's best known and most important leaders, who happened to be in Fort Benton on the night of Meagher's death. In his 1902 account of the events of that night Saunders stated that Meagher was 'deranged' and that, totally without cause, felt his life was in danger. Sanders insisted that he did not intend this to sound mean-spirited but he wanted to counter the growing rumour that Meagher was inebriated on the night of his death. Drink had nothing to do with Meagher's possible paranoia, Sanders suggested, as he had been uncharacteristically abstemious that day. This led Sanders to conclude that Meagher's suspicions and fears were the result of a 'disturbed mental condition' brought on, Sanders further reported, by a feud between Meagher and the Blackfeet Indian agent over the distribution of whiskey. It was perhaps this state of mind that led Meagher, according to the ship's 'negro' barber, to jump into the river and be carried down stream.[4] Although Sanders noted in his account that his and Meagher's relationship had always been cordial, this was far from the truth, as the two men had become bitter political enemies. This brings into question Sanders' own reliability as a witness, and his account may have been intended to suggest that Meagher was not only a bad Irishman, but also a worse Catholic. Meagher had killed himself over a trivial quarrel involving liquor and Indians. Catholics, of course, have committed suicide and Meagher's own Catholicism was not as devout as some of his contemporary supporters have suggested.

Nonetheless, the vigour with which Meagher had lived, and enjoyed life, would militate against suicide. Indeed, he had written a letter on the day of his death outlining a grand future for himself. While the experiences of the Civil War had left its mark on Meagher, none of his contemporaries ever suggested that he was permanently morose or depressed.[5]

The second alternative explanation regarding Meagher's death, that it was accidental, has enjoyed the greatest favour. Meagher had travelled more than 200 miles from the territorial capital in Virginia City to Fort Benton and the trip, by horseback, had involved numerous river crossings, making it an arduous journey for one even in the best of health. On the last few days of the trip, however, Meagher was clearly seriously ill and he had to rest for six days at the Sun River in an effort to gather the strength to continue to Fort Benton. Nineteenth-century physicians would have probably identified his condition as dysentery, but that generic label is too imprecise to be of much use as dysentery was used to describe any ailment that caused or was accompanied by extreme diarrhoea. It was 'commonly known', said P.J. Condon, one of Meagher's 'most esteemed and trusted friends' as 'the summer complaint' and it caused serious dehydration in its victim.[6] Meagher clearly exhibited such symptoms on the trip and a number of historians have attributed Meagher's fall from the *G.A. Thompson* as accidental while he attempted to relieve himself from the violence of his disorder.[7] Other medical factors support this hypothesis and Meagher's 'dysentery' may well have been cholera or, because no other members of his party were stricken, typhoid fever, possibly caused by drinking contaminated water from buffalo wallows and mud holes. Whether he was feverish is unknown, but by the time his party reached Fort Benton, Meagher was displaying anxiety and delusionary fears, symptoms of the dehydration typically associated with typhoid. As typhoid fever can kill quickly it is possible that Meagher was dead or nearly so before he ever hit the water; witnesses recalled no shout for help, only low 'agonizing' cries. Meagher was able to swim thus it is highly likely that, at best, he was too disoriented and weak to have made any but the feeblest effort to swim to safety.[8]

Given available evidence, it is clear that Meagher was a drinker and, it seems, on occasion was prone to drinking to excess. The possibility that he was intoxicated had an understandable attraction at the time of his death. Nativists in the United States presumed all Irishmen drank a lot and Meagher tended to correspond to this nativist stereotype.[9] However, there is little evidence to suggest that Meagher was drunk on the night of his death and there is even less evidence that a wandering homicidal psychopath may have murdered Meagher. It remains a possibility that a cold sober Meagher tripped and fell into the river but a healthy Meagher should have been able to swim ashore, or at least cried out loudly and lustily for help. While the evidence that Meagher was sick when he fell to his death is persuasive, the little explored alternative that he was murdered, assassinated by political enemies, remains a possibility. For this explanation to be plausible, and to play detective, there has to be motive, opportunity and, in this instance at least, a historical pattern. This alternative is an attractive alternative and what follows is the creation of its plausibility, not a definite or final judgement. Historians, in the end, have wider latitude than detectives or even prosecuting attorneys for they do not have to prove their case beyond a reasonable doubt. To raise important questions about a previous thesis is often worthwhile in itself and a further investigation into the circumstances of Meagher's death can throw a useful light on one aspect of his world that needs to be explored more, the area of religion and ethnic conflict in nineteenth-century America.

VIGILANTES

Previous historians have ably demonstrated that the Montana that Meagher travelled to in 1865 was a dangerous and often violent frontier society, a society that was still divided along sectional and political lines. Its mining communities that had settled along the Beaverhead River were dominated by young, single men and were without any effective form of law enforcement. The 'better' elements in Montana soon borrowed tactics that had been used earlier in the mining camps of California and Nevada and formed themselves into vigilance committees. Beginning in 1864, they began the summary execution of those whose behaviour was thought excessively rambunctious even by the loose standards of the time. One of the leading vigilantes was Wilbur Fisk Sanders. Sanders was like many of his fellow vigilantes who undoubtedly saw themselves as righteous men, paladins who would save the fledgling commonwealth from the worst excesses of evil and rapacious men.[10] This was not a time for coddled sensibilities – or procedural obstructions such as trials. There were no federal marshals, no police departments of internal affairs, no one who could have brought official charges against the alleged marauders. Consequently, justice was swift and, when bad men were caught, they were hanged, often with a note pinned to them with the numbers 3-7-77 scrawled upon it. This was presumed, then and later, to be the dimensions of a grave and Montanans were so taken by the essential justice of the vigilantes' actions that they have adorned the shields of the state's Highway Patrol cars with those portentous numbers as fair warning to any who would mess with the law. This, perhaps, remains as clear an expression of Western life imitating bad Western art as could be imagined.[11]

This vision of vigilante virtue, like a great deal of the history of the West, is a myth and many of their victims were innocent of any serious wrongdoing. The notion that the 'respectable' elements of Montana could not afford to wait for the civil authorities to deal with purported depredations is not only flimsy, but also absurd. Most of those killed by the vigilantes were identified by one Red Yeager, but the vigilantes could not even agree on whose name should be on Yeager's list. In fact, it seems indisputable that the list was put together after the hangings not before. The evidence against the vigilantes' victims was not just sketchy or circumstantial, it was often non-existent. Whatever the appeal of this brand of frontier retribution, and one particularly frenzied champion of the vigilantes wrote that their methods, like those of their models in California, represented the 'Anglo-Saxon' love of justice at its best, there can be little justifiable defence of their violent actions. In short, the vigilantes were little more than sanctimonious thugs.[12]

MASONIC ORDER

There is more to the vigilante story, however, than simple frontier justice. In the first place, they were motivated by political partisanship as they all appear to have been Republicans and many of them were members of the Union Leagues. These were quasi-political organizations whose assigned role was to ensure that Confederate sympathizers, for which read Democrat, would not dominate the post-Civil War era in Montana or anywhere else in the West. The pre-war clash between the Republicans and Democrats over the future of the West had turned on the question of the expansion of slavery. Although the Union victory had led to the abolition of slavery, there were serious concerns that the Republicans may have won the war but still may lose the West to the Democrats.[13] Another interesting point is that many of the vigilantes were members of the Masonic Order and, like the California Committees of Vigilance, they were anti-Catholic to the core. Many of the Montana vigilantes had spent time in California and had borrowed freely from its mining and civil codes. There can be little doubt that they also shared with their Californian brothers the doctrine suggested in the *Morals and Dogma... of Freemasonry*, that a society content to merely follow the ideas of their priests is in danger of falling into servitude, a condition that will induce a trance-like state which occasionally will be interrupted by furious fits of frenzy. The Masons saw themselves as preventative agents who would defend the West against such developments, God's agents who would protect the region against religious subversion.[14]

The two earliest and largely sympathetic accounts of Montana vigilantism were written by Thomas Dimsdale and Nathaniel Langford, both of whom were Republicans, vigilantes and Masons. Dimsdale was editor of the *Montana Post* and he divided Montana into 'patriots and traitors', with the territory being a battleground in which good and evil, right and wrong, civilization and savagery were the combatants. Langford, a president of the Montana Union League as well as a Mason, was of the same mind:

> All the worst crimes of the Decalogue stained [Montana's]... annals, until... the sober minded and resolute population visited in their might with condign punishment the organized bands of ruffians which had preyed upon their lives and property... Equal in degree to the sacrifices

> made by the brave soldiers of the war who saved our Republic, were the deeds of those who saved the Territory from rapine and slaughter.

His reference was to the 'Masonic fraternity' and the vigilante movement itself; it is possible that the numbers 3-7-77 may not have been the dimensions of a grave but a Masonic symbol.[15] Both men were close associates of Wilbur Fisk Sanders, the Grand Master of Montana's Masonic Lodge, and, not surprisingly, they despised the Catholic Meagher. To the partisan and fraternal aspects of vigilantism in Montana must be added the sometime rabid anti-Catholicism that often attended both. The Republican Party arose in the 1850s from the still live ashes of the nativist Know-Nothing Party and its anti-Catholicism, though usually muted, marked it as surely as anti-slavery had. As for Masonry, anti-Catholicism was one of its best-known features. The nativist American Protective Association actively recruited in Masonic Lodges in the 1890s, as the Ku Klux Klan also did in the 1910s and1920s. In sum, to say that the Montana vigilantes who dominated the territory from 1863 to at least 1867 were simply champions of public order is to miss the point; they were also Republican Union Leaguers and Masons who were hostile towards Catholics as well as to Confederate sympathizers, Democrats and alleged highwaymen.[16]

MEAGHER IN MONTANA

This was the Montana that Meagher would come to in September 1865, hoping to both find adventure and resurrect his military and public career. He became the acting territorial governor within days of his arrival and he learned quickly enough that making his way through the territory's partisan, sectional and religious minefields would require all of his political agility. To say that he was not perhaps up to the task is not to condemn Meagher for he was not only an ambitious Irish Catholic Democrat, but also an appointee of President Andrew Johnson, whose own notions of how to reconstruct his native South were rapidly alienating Radical Republicans. Given the cross currents within Montana's own political and social development it is doubtful whether Meagher could have avoided controversy even if he had wanted to. His wartime support for Lincoln and his military record initially recommended Meagher to the territory's Radical Republicans led by Wilbur Fisk Sanders, but Meagher's changing political outlook and his religious background would cast doubts on his reliability. In Republican eyes, the topics of Montana's chance of accelerated statehood and the growing number of Irish Democrats in the mining communities, would focus their attention on Meagher's policies as acting governor.[17]

The bitter political fights between Meagher and the territory's Republicans have been often and well discussed elsewhere and there is little reason to revisit this topic here. One aspect of this feud, however, the cultural, that is, the tribal and religious, has received scant attention in the past by historians and this aspect of the feud partially arose from Meagher's expressed intention of making Montana a haven for Irish immigrants trapped in the eastern American cities. Prior to his arrival in Bannack, Meagher had discussed his plans with bishops Thomas Grace and John Ireland of St Paul, Minnesota. There was nothing new or original in Meagher's plan, for General James Shields, the Irish-born soldier who had been elected Senator for Minnesota in 1858, had actively supported such a western plan, and Bishop Ireland himself was engaged in a number of ambitious schemes to colonize Minnesota with both Irish and Irish-American settlers. Some of the past-proposed Irish colonies, though not those of Bishop Ireland, had a faintly military aspect to them; they were intended to serve as staging grounds for Irish-American nationalist organizations, particularly Fenians, attacks on British North America. There would later be Fenian raids in 1867 and 1871 into Canada involving John O'Neil, the founder of an Irish colony bearing his name in Nebraska.[18]

In Montana, Fenians took a very lively interest in the activities of Louis Riel, the rebellious Métis leader in neighbouring Alberta, Canada, and a delegation from the Fenian Brotherhood (by then known as the Clan-na-Gael) visited Riel in 1868. One of the leading Montana Fenians was Andrew O'Connell of Helena, a close friend of Meagher's. O'Connell, together with Martin Hogan, then stationed at Fort Shaw, had developed plans for supporting Riel by dispatching armed Montana Irishmen from Fort Benton. It cannot be known with certainty that Meagher was a party to any of these plans. His political opponents, however, accused him of being a Fenian and certainly his well-known involvement with the more advanced forms of Irish nationalism and his time in a British penal colony lent credibility to the charges. His position as acting governor and his political ambitions made Fenian membership indiscreet if not impossible, but he was sympathetic to its goals.[19]

Whether Meagher was an active Fenian is open to debate but his intention to attract more Irish to Montana would be of great concern to his Republican enemies. A substantial percentage of the American people still considered Meagher's countrymen as besotted and at best only semi-civilized. There were more than a few Montanans who thought the same of Meagher. Whether it was their Catholicism or their 'racial' deformities that were thought to ill fit the Irish to a democratic republic is unclear and unimportant; few, in fact, bothered to distinguish between the two. But quite apart from the Irish religion and genome, no politically aware Montanan would need to have been reminded of the fact that the vast majority of the Irish Catholic vote went to the Democratic Party. Democrats were, in the eyes of the Republicans, often no better than Confederate rebels, and no more easily reconstructed. The majority of Montana's territorial populations were Democrats and Meagher's intention to recruit the Irish to settle Montana would seriously endanger continued Republican domination of the territory. Meagher cannot have been unaware of these feelings and, given the increasing hostility towards him from the Republicans, perhaps he was audacious enough to believe that implementation of his plan would overwhelm his enemies.[20]

The link between Montana Republicans, vigilantes and the Masons has already been made in this article, yet it should be stressed that in the second half of the nineteenth-century notions of supposed Anglo-Saxon superiority were dominant and a significant number of Americans were of the mind that the West was the special playground and preserve of Anglo-Saxon Protestants; God had not given America a frontier to provide shanty space for the Irish. Meagher was of different mind. What Montana needed, he told a friend in 1866, was 'a strong infusion of... Celtic blood to counteract the acidity and poverty' of the territory's non-Irish and non-Catholic elements. If Montana was to be truly civilized it would not be through the agency of Anglo-American Protestants but by the 'heart', the 'genius' of the 'true Irish Celt'. But it was not just 'the bounty of the Celtic sceptre' that was at issue. As important was 'the aspiring piety of the Celtic mitre'. Montana, in other words, needed the Irishmen's faith as well as their mind and muscle. As for Meagher's Protestant fellow-countrymen, he told them that the spirit of St Patrick 'would convert "every mother's sowl of them" with that miraculous crozier of his, should he ever get among them'.[21] While these remarks were made playfully as part of Meagher's St Patrick's Day address in Virginia City, the idea of converting Protestants to Catholicism was not something one joked about in nineteenth-century Montana. Even more to the point, Meagher's comments came only five days after the vigilantes in Helena had lynched James Daniels, the Irishman whom Meagher had pardoned.

THE HANGING OF JAMES DANIELS

In his private correspondence Meagher made no reference to the Daniels affair or the threat the vigilantes made against him personally, yet there was no public apology either. He was, however, clearly affected by this most recent example of vigilante terrorism. From this point forward Meagher's speeches were filled with ill-disguised anger and contempt for the vigilantes. For example, after extolling the Celtic mitre and sceptre, he described the followers of Oliver Cromwell as 'the canting scoundrels of this copper-nosed disseminator of the Gospel' to which his Irish audience responded with 'loud laughter'. Some of the non-Irish who read his remarks the next day and who had their own view of the Daniels' killing were doubtless less amused. Meagher plainly did not care. Though his reference to the 'acidity and poverty' of the non-Celts in Montana was made in a private letter, from this point forward he was never shy about, nor politic, in describing his enemies.[22] In a remarkable address in Diamond City, August 1866, he made clear and quite public his feelings. Even in the over-heated political atmosphere of post-war nineteenth-century American politics, Meagher's language can only be described as incendiary. He spoke of 'the scurrility of the blackguards who had assailed him' and of 'their depraved and distempered natures' and the viciousness with which they were 'malignantly diseased'. His enemies were jack-rabbits, skunks, vermin, pimps, lame poltroons, despotic radicals, palsied politicians and crumbling fossils who 'stood, or rather cowered, with quivering legs and palpitating heart, their marrow less back-bones to the transitory storm they had raised'.[23]

His reference to despotic radicals, probably the gentlest of his descriptions, was to the point of the partisan rancour of the times and partisanship in Montana tended toward the deadly. The summary executions by the vigilantes, including their most recent one, were a form of recall or impeachment. As an individual who came near to being hanged by the British judicial system and as one openly threatened with lynching, Meagher cannot have looked with any tolerance on the vigilantes. The fact that they had only hanged his political allies must also have seemed eerily reminiscent of Ireland. Even before the Daniels affair, Meagher had condemned what he called 'midnight executions', ordering the vigilant ones, whom he must have known by then were Masons and Republicans, as well as self-appointed dispensers of justice, to 'stand at ease'. When Meagher told the legislature that he had called them into session because he had found Montana in a state 'of imbecility and stagnation' he meant to include the vigilantes among the imbecilic and stagnant.[24] Meagher saved particular invective for Wilbur Fisk Sanders who replied in kind that Meagher was a 'played out' fool who 'is dead beyond hope of resurrection'. Sanders' main complaint against Meagher was that he talked of reconciliation with those who had supported the Confederacy and he warned that 'Meagher and the other villains must never be permitted to assemble... we must put a quietus on the doings of this pretender'.[25]

MEAGHER AND EDUCATION

The Meagher/Republican feud did not just exist in the realm of the political abstract; it also concerned the most divisive issue in American politics, public education. One of the first acts of the Montana Territorial Assembly under Governor Edgerton had been the passage of a common school bill. The schools would be under the direction of a territorial superintendent of schools, a position held by the vigilante and later chronicler and champion of vigilante justice, Thomas Dimsdale. Like all such schools nation-wide, Montana's would be heavily sectarian in both curriculum and pedagogy. They would, Sanders hoped, be agents of reconstruction, making the children of alien cultures, particularly Catholics, into good Americans.[26] Sectarian education had been opposed in Ireland by Meagher's own political mentor, Thomas Davis, and it is clear that Meagher saw schools in a different light than Sanders. For him, as for many Irish Catholics, they were all too often agents of cultural imperialism. Whether they reminded him of the British schools in Ireland cannot be known but he acted as if they did. First he fired the English-born Dimsdale, replacing him as superintendent with Peter Ronan, an Irish Catholic. Then he vetoed the bill appropriating money for the schools, not because he opposed education generally but

> for the reason that [the bill] does not authorize the Superintendent...to exclude from the public schools of this Territory any sectarian tracts or other publications [that]...excite discord upon religious subjects. Nor does it empower him to prevent and suppress sectarian instruction, in which the world knows, teachers of every religious denomination are apt and prone to indulge.[27]

This was as near a declaration of cultural war as could be imagined and Meagher must have been aware of this.

The veto of the school bill was not the only instance when Meagher raised the sectarian issue. His reference to the Cromwellians as 'canting scoundrels' may have been an example of Meagher's 'sunburstery', Irish rhetorical excess, but Meagher was not afraid to address accusations that he was becoming pro-southern. He rejected Republican claims that he was disloyal to the Union by reference to his war record and he reminded his enemies that the war was over and that former Confederates were as loyal and civic-minded as Republicans. It was time, he believed, that the Republicans and the Union Leagues accept this fact and accept that the West should be dedicated to 'the consolidation of liberty with law, the crushing of the malevolence of faction, nationality against sectionalism and the foundation of an enlightened civilization, where religion may flourish without bigotry and loyalty without humiliation'.[28] The reference to religion and bigotry is particularly interesting as Meagher was not speaking about southern loyalty at that point in his speech but Irish Catholic Democrats. Meagher in Montana was beginning to undertake his own policy of reconstruction and his support for the construction of a new Catholic church in Virginia City must have convinced many Masonic vigilantes that Meagher was becoming their own worst nightmare.

Meagher remained unmoved by Republican attacks and he answered his critics directly when he told an astonished audience that it was the American who 'has no thought beyond putting a mighty dollar out at mighty interest' and who 'hates the Irish for their generous qualities, their infallible religion and their inveterate democracy'. Implying that many Americans may be sanctimonious hypocrites he intemperately asked his audience if loyalty to Ireland was, as his critics had suggested, incompatible with loyalty to the United States? Such a view, he suggested, was little more than cant from bigots with small brains and even smaller hearts. To a cheering crowd Meagher proclaimed 'Out upon the bastard Americanism, that spews this imputation' this type of American who 'regards with cod-liver eye, a nutmeg nose, a Maine-Liquor-Law howl, and a Cromwellian depreciation, the love of Ireland'. These remarks were greeted by 'loud and long continued cheering' from Meagher's overwhelmingly Irish audience, but what truly aroused the crowd was his final peroration:

> Let the marrow less bigot...carp and deprecate; let the hungry Puritan with his nasal music importune the God of Blue Laws to save the Yankee

> nation from the witch-craft of St. Patrick's daughters and the deviltry of St. Patrick's sons...the Irish people in America will not, and can not, forget the land of their birth, their sufferings, their dearest memories, and proudest hopes.[29]

There had to have been vigilantes in Meagher's audience and one can only wonder at their reaction to Meagher, the Irish orator in full flow. Meagher's speech was an announcement that in this cultural war for the future of Montana there would be at least no limits on rhetoric. Whether it would be waged without limits on violence is less easily determined.

MEAGHER'S DEATH AND THE HELENA MONUMENT

As stated at the beginning of this chapter, it is important to perhaps just raise questions regarding Meagher's death and there is no intention here of trying to prove anything regarding that death. Montana politics were furious and abusive and the vigilantes did often kill their political enemies. This does not prove that they were always murderous or that they killed Meagher in July 1867. That Meagher was no longer acting governor and was something of a spent force in Montana politics is irrelevant, as he was not going to leave the territory. In fact, he intended to pursue with even greater fervour his dream of filling Montana with Irish Catholics and thus Meagher was possibly a greater threat to the vigilantes as a private citizen than he had been as governor. Granted, this does not mean they killed Meagher, but certainly his leaving public office was no reason for them not to and Sanders, one of their most important leaders, hated Meagher, a fact he attempted to disguise in his 1902 testimony. Sanders was also in Fort Benton the night of Meagher's death and while this does not mean he killed Meagher or conspired to have him killed, in 1913 a drifter named Frank Diamond confessed that the vigilantes paid him $8,000 to kill Meagher. Diamond later withdrew his testimony and, consequently, little credibility has been afforded to the Diamond story.[30] However, a careful detective should pay some attention to the circumstantial, what historians would call the contextual, evidence and this raises the question of how to interpret the reflections of Fr Hugh Quigley.

In 1878 Quigley, an Irish-born priest, compiled a large book on *The Irish Race in California and on the Pacific Coast.* Quigley appended a chapter on the Irish in Montana and in this he wrote that Meagher had 'set his face, like a globe of steel, against the vigilance men' and it was for this reason Meagher's life had been threatened 'by a murderous banditti'. That much was clear in 1867, but Quigley went on to record that 'it is the general opinion now, formed from reliable data, that poor Meagher was dogged day and night by the agents of the vigilantes, who, in the dark hour of midnight, assassinated the hero...by stabbing him and flinging his body into the muddy waters of the Missouri'.

Meagher was the victim of a malicious 'gang of conspirators, who, under the name of "Vigilance Men", set the laws at defiance and attempted to make peace by committing crimes of murder and banishment of obnoxious individuals'.[31] Quigley did not mention Sanders by name and, unfortunately, he did not identify either his sources or what he described as 'reliable data'. He did, however, introduce his comments about Meagher with a critical discussion of the California 'vigilance committees' and there is a strong indication that Quigley knew many Irishmen who had been in Montana for years, including a number who had been there in 1867.

While it cannot be proved that Meagher was murdered, the historian should not only concern himself/herself with what actually happened, but also with what people thought true and Quigley concluded that it was 'the general opinion' in Montana that vigilantes had assassinated Meagher. He was right about that, particularly if 'Irish' is added to 'general'. The notion that Meagher had been murdered gained credence in the years 1894 to 1905 as events in Montana recreated and replayed the turbulent post-Civil War years. The impressive statue to Meagher outside the Capitol Building in Helena is a testimony to these events.

MEAGHER MONUMENT AND DALY–CLARK FEUD

The Montana State Capitol is an imposing and stately building and apart from some interior murals it could have been built, generically, anywhere in the United States. However, there is an important link between the building and Montana history for, its whole north side is dominated by a monument, a colossal equestrian statue of Thomas Francis Meagher as a Union general. Upon first reflection, the statue may seem somewhat incongruous, for why would Montanans build a statue to an Irish rebel who died more than two decades before Montana achieved statehood and who had resided in the state for less than three years? The official explanation at the time of its unveiling, 4 July 1905, was that as Meagher had been an acting governor it was fitting that it should be erected on the State Capitol grounds. Its dedication, however, reflected the final arrival of the Irish voice in Montana, a voice that had for a long period been both angry and recriminatory. If the monument is treated as historical text, it speaks volumes regarding the people and place.[32]

The idea of building a monument to Meagher was first proposed by Montana's Fenian Brotherhood in 1869. Nothing came of that plan but in the mid-1890s, however, a couple of related events resurrected the idea. Firstly, the American Protective Association (APA), a nativist, anti-Catholic organization formed nationally in 1887, began operations in Montana. It published its own newspaper, *The Examiner*, and in general tried to make life difficult for Catholics, whether immigrant or American-born. On 4 July 1894 there was an APA riot in Butte, Montana that resulted in two deaths and considerable property damage. Like the vigilantes thirty years earlier, the APA actively recruited from the Masonic Lodges and, secondly, the Association involved itself very directly in the state-wide vote on the location of Montana's permanent capital. The finalists were Helena, the seat of government since the 1870s, and Anaconda, scarcely a decade old and a city founded by Marcus Daly, the owner of the giant Anaconda Copper Mining Company. Born in Ireland, and a Catholic who was a proud member of two Irish nationalist associations, Daly had championed the case of Anaconda as had, not surprisingly, the Irishmen who worked in his Butte mines. Helena's principal advocate was the equally wealthy William Andrews Clark, a descendant of Scots-Irish Presbyterians, a 33rd degree Mason, good friend of Wilbur Fisk Sanders, and a man whose hatred of Daly reflected Sanders' own hatred of Meagher. Daly and Clark's estrangement had been caused by Clark's insensitivity, if not overt bigotry, toward Irish Catholics and in the competition *The Examiner* identified Helena as a Protestant town and Anaconda as Catholic. The capital fight, in other words, was an example of Montana tribal politics at its most venomous.

In an extremely tight election, Helena defeated Anaconda and within months of the vote, Daly formed and assumed the chairmanship of the Thomas Francis Meagher Memorial Association. To raise money Daly even allowed members of the Association to go underground and solicit money from miners while they were at work, not a usual practice among multi-million dollar American companies. The monument was placed directly in front of the new capitol building and there can be absolutely no doubt that it was intended not just to honour Meagher, but also as an open act of Irish defiance. As one member of the Memorial Association put it, placing the statue on the capitol grounds meant that members of the American Protective Association, and all other Montana nativists, would have to look in his (Meagher's) face and salute his glorious memory for all ages. There were rumours that Clark was an Association member, that he had also once been a vigilante and that only his profligate spending, together with some well-practised calumny against Irish Catholics, had made Helena the state capital. The Meagher statue was, therefore, an Irish testament to their participation in the creation and development of Montana.

Nearly thirty years after Meagher's death the unpublished proceedings of the Meagher Memorial Association also tell a compelling story. The Memorial Association members estimated in 1898 that they would need at least $20,000 to create a proper tribute to Meagher and they agreed, privately, that no subscription would be refused with one exception, Wilbur Fisk Sanders. To quote the Association's minutes, 'if (a) subscription be received from Wilbur Fisk Sanders it is to be returned... through the public press'.[33] Contemporaries did not know how Meagher died and neither do historians, but there is contextual evidence that he was murdered and many members of the Memorial Association candidly thought this. This suspicion has strong roots in Montana popular culture.[34] Montana's vigilantes had killed others for 'offences' significantly less serious than those of Meagher's but his veto of the school bill, his pardon of Daniels, his plans to turn Montana into an Irish colony, his sympathy for Democrats and his astonishingly inflammatory language each singly may have been enough to move the vigilantes to action. Taken together, they made him a marked man, a situation only compounded by his foreign Catholicism.

CONCLUSION

The unexplained circumstances of his death and the hatred Meagher generated during his short time in Montana at least makes the possibility of assassination plausible. Irishmen in Butte and elsewhere knew, or thought they knew, exactly how Meagher came to meet his death and at whose hands. Many of them had long and accurate memories and they believed that Meagher was a victim of tribal politics between North and South, Republican and Democrat, native and immigrant, Protestant and Catholic. In this scenario Sanders was uniquely implicated, but in more general terms, nativism and religious prejudice in the malignant form of vigilantism had killed Meagher, and for precisely the same reasons it had killed, by some counts, 102 others. Meagher was of the wrong party, the wrong church and was far too vocal in his opposition to the status quo in Montana.

While P.J. Condon may have been right in that Meagher was 'assailed' by diarrhoea and fell off a boat while trying to relieve himself, one has to wonder if the Catholic Irishmen who raised money for the Meagher statue were simply being petulant over the loss of the situation of the capital . The vast majority of them were miners whose wage was $3.50 per day. If they could not afford self-indulgence, they would certainly have not subscribed to the Meagher monument just to make Marcus Daly feel better over his defeat regarding the site of the new capital. Perhaps, and just perhaps, Fr Hugh Quigley had got it right and the Butte Irish knew how Meagher really died. Their statue to Thomas Francis Meagher undoubtedly reminds us of the past ferocity of Montana's tribal politics, not to mention clearing up how that large and unlikely statue came to stand guard over Montana's capital.

NOTES

1. O'Gorman's eulogy is in Michael Cavanagh, *Memoirs of General Thomas F. Meagher* (Worcester, MA: The Messenger Press, 1892), Appendix, pp.3–10. For Maginnis, see his 'Thomas Francis Meagher', *Contributions to the Historical Society of Montana*, 6, (1907), p.117.
2. On the depth and speed of the Missouri River see the testimony of the captain of the *G.A.Thompson* in W.F. Lyons, *Brigadier General Thomas Francis Meagher: his Political and Military Career* (New York: D. and J. Sadlier, 1870), p.356.

3. See Robin Winks, *The Historian as Detective: Essays on Evidence* (New York: Harpers, 1970).
4. Helen F. Sanders, *A History of Montana*, 2 vols (Chicago, IL: Lewis Publishing, 1913), vol. 2, pp.338–41.
5. *Ibid.*, p.339. For the letter Meagher wrote on the day of his death regarding his future see Cavanagh, *Memoirs*, Appendix, p.10. Isaac G. Baker was also with Meagher on that day and thought he was fine. See Baker, 'Account of the Drowning of General Thomas Francis Meagher', *Contributions to the Historical Society of Montana*, 8, (1917), p.131. The Catholic Church did not consider Meagher had committed suicide as a Requiem Mass was held for him at St Francis Xavier Church in New York City. See Cavanagh, Memoirs, Appendix, pp.1–11.
6. Condon's comments are in Cavanagh, *Memoirs*, Appendix, pp.11–13. On Meagher's trip to Fort Benton see Robert Athearn, *Thomas Francis Meagher: An Irish Revolutionary in America* (Boulder, CO: University of Colorado Press, 1949), pp.163–5.
7. Condon's letter in Cavanagh, *Memoirs*, pp.11–13.
8. Information on dysentery, cholera and typhoid fever from an interview with Dr Sean Callan, Missoula, Montana, 16 Oct. 2003. Notes in possession of the author. See also, Thomas Keneally, *The Great Shame and the Triumph of the Irish in the English Speaking World* (New York: Doubleday, 1998), p.453 and Lyons, *Brigadier General*, p.356.
9. On nativist assumptions that the Irish immigrants drank to excess, see Dale T. Knobel, *Paddy and the Republic: Ethnicity and Nationality in Antebellum America* (Middletown, CT: Wesleyan University Press, 1986), pp.165–82; Ray Billington, *The Protestant Crusade, 1800–1860* (New York: Rinehart & Co., 1938), pp.195, 238; John Higham, *Strangers in the Land; Patterns of American Nativism, 1860–1925* (New York: Atheneum, 1981), pp.25, 41, 60, 267–9.
10. The connection between Californian and Montana vigilantism is made by Hoffman Birney, *Vigilantes* (Philadelphia, PA: The Penn Publishing Company, 1929). For vigilantes in general see Richard Maxwell Brown, *Strain of Violence: Historical Studies of American Violence and Vigilantism* (New York: Oxford University Press, 1975) and Roger McGrath, *Gunfighters, Highwaymen, and Vigilantes: Violence on the Frontier* (Berkeley, CA: University of California Press, 1984).
11. The earliest and best-known accounts of Montana vigilantes are Thomas Dimsdale, *The Vigilantes of Montana or Popular Justice in the Rocky Mountains* (originally published in 1864–65; Butte, MT: W.F. Bartlett, 1915) and Nathaniel P. Langford, *Vigilante Days and Ways* (originally published in 1892; Missoula, Montana State University Press, 1957). For a semi-fictional account of the Montana Vigilantes, see Frank Bird Linderman, *Henry Plummer; A Novel* (Lincoln, NA: University of Nebraska Press, 2000).
12. For the quote on Anglo-Saxon superior notions of law see W.F.Sanders, II, and Robert T. Taylor, *Biscuits and Badmen: The Sanders Story in Their Own Words* (Butte, MT: Editorial Review, 1983), p.72. The idea that vigilante justice was a contradiction in terms and that the Montana vigilantes were amongst the worst of a bad bunch see R.E. Mather and F.E. Boswell, *Vigilante Victims: Montana's 1864 Hanging Spree* (San Jose, CA: History West Pub. Co., 1991).
13. For Republican Party affiliation of the vigilantes, see Clark Spence, *Territorial Politics and Government in Montana, 1864–1889* (Urbana, IL: University of Illinois Press, 1975), pp.22–5. This connection is also made in Mather and Boswell, *Vigilante Victims*, pp.161–77. For the antebellum struggle over the future of the West, see Michael A. Morrison, *Slavery and the American West: The Eclipse of Manifest Destiny and the Coming of the Civil War* (Chapel Hill, NC: University of North Carolina Press, 1997). Langford was the president of the Montana Union League. See his *Vigilante Days*, p.175.
14. On the California origins of Montana laws, see Spence, *Territorial Politics*, pp.28, 203–4. That many of the by-laws and constitutions of the miners were also linked to California precedent, see Richard Lingenfelter, *The Hardrock Miners; A History of the Mining Labor Movement in the American West, 1863–1893* (Berkeley, CA: University of California Press, 1974), pp.45, 130ff., 148,165, 183,198 and 221. On Masonic hostility to Catholicism and the principles of Masonic justice, see *Morals and Dogma of the Ancient and Accepted Scottish*

rite of Freemasonry (originally published 1871; Washington, D.C., House of the Temple, 1966), pp.33, 75.

15. Dimsdale may not have been aware that he had been admitted to the Masons. He died at the age of 35 and the evidence that he was a Mason is sketchy. See, Mather and Boswell, *Vigilante Victims*, pp.174–5. Langford was avowedly Masonic and a vigilante; see *Vigilante Days*, pp.142, 446–7. Linderman in his novel illustrates the Masonic/vigilante link, see Henry Plummer. Linderman was a devout Mason. That the figures 3-7-77 had Masonic significance is discussed in Rex Myers, 'The Fateful Numbers: 3-7-77: A Re-examination', *Montana the Magazine of Western History*, 14, (1974), pp.67–70. Also see, Frederick Allen, 'Montana Vigilantes and the Origins of 3-7-77', *Montana the Magazine of Western History*, 41, (2001), pp.2–19.
16. For Sanders' leadership of the Montana Masons, see *Progressive Men of the State of Montana*, Anonymous, 3 vols (Chicago, IL: A.W. Bowen, 1912), vol. I, p.34. For the Republican Party/ Know-Nothing nexus, see Philip Bagenal, *The American Irish and Their Influence on Irish Politics* (London: Kegan Paul, Trench & Co., 1882), p.41; Tyler Anbinder, *Nativism and Slavery: The Northern Know-Nothings and the Politics of the 1850*'s (New York: Oxford University Press, 1992); William Gienapp, *The Origins of the Republican Party* (New York: Oxford University Press, 1987) and Eric Foner, *Free Soil, Free Labor: The Ideology of the Republican Party Before the Civil War* (New York: Oxford University Press, 1995). For the equation of Catholicism with slavery see the comments of Thomas Whitney in 1856 in Jon Gjerde, *Mines of the West: Ethnocultural Evolution in the Rural Middle West, 1830–1917* (Chapel Hill, NC: University of North Carolina Press, 1997), p.36. For American Protective Association and Klan recruiting, see John Higham, *Strangers in the Land*, pp.80, 287–9. On the idea that Masons were themselves a threat to American institutions, see Dale T. Knobel, *Paddy and the Republic*, pp.19, 30 and 168; also see, David Brion Davis, 'Some Themes of Counter-Subversion: An Analysis of Anti-Masonic, Anti-Catholic and Anti-Mormon Literature', *Mississippi Valley Historical Review*, 47, (1960), pp.186–215.
17. See, Spence, *Territorial Politics*, pp.4–73. For reference to southerners in the mining camps, see Margaret Ronan, *Frontier Woman: The Story of Mary Ronan.* edited by H.G. Merriam (Missoula, MT: University of Montana Publications in History, 1973), pp.30–1.
18. See, Athearn, *Thomas Francis Meagher*, pp.143–71 and his 'The Great War Muddies the Mountain Waters: The Civil War and Montana Gold', *Montana the Magazine of Western History*, 2, (1962), pp.62–73. See also, Meagher to Con O'Keefe, 26 Sept. 1866, Thomas Francis Meagher Papers, Montana Historical Society, Helena. Reference to an Irish Colony in California can be found in Walter Nugent, *Into the West: The Story of its People* (New York: Knopf, 1999), p.52. The standard account of the Minnesota experiments are James P. Shannon, *Catholic Colonization on the Western Frontier* (New Haven, CT: Yale University Press, 1957); Mary Evangela Henthorne, *The Irish Catholic Colonization Association of the United States* (Urbana, IL: University of Illinois Press, 1932) and Mary Gilbert Kelly, *Catholic Immigrant Colonization Projects in the United States, 1815–1860* (New York: Catholic University Press, 1939). On Bishop Ireland, see Marvin O'Connell, *John Ireland and the American Catholic Church* (St Paul: Minnesota Historical Society, 1988), pp.136–62. On Fenian activity, see Keneally, *The Great Shame*, pp.440–2, 500–1.
19. Joseph Kinsey Howard, *Strange Empire: A Narrative of the Northwest* (New York: William Morrow, 1952), pp.74, 93, 102, 133, 137, 216–29 and 354. Martin Hogan to Andrew O'Connell, 21 July, 25 Aug., 17 Sept. 1866; 6 Jan. 1867, Martin Hogan Papers, Montana Historical Society, Helena.
20. On the relationship between the Catholic vote and the Democrat Party, see Paul Kleppner, *The Cross of Culture: A Social Analysis of Midwestern Politics, 1850–1900* (New York: Free Press, 1970), pp.31–70. Also see, Paul Kleppner, *The Third Electoral System, 1853–1892: Parties, Voters, and Political Cultures* (Chapel Hill, NC: University of North Carolina Press, 1979) and his ' Voters and Parties in the Western States, 1876–1900', Western Historical Quarterly, 14 (1983), pp.49–68.
21. Meagher to Rev. George Pepper, 20 Jan. 1866, cited in Spence, *Territorial Politics,* p.36. Meagher's comments on the mitre and sceptre are in his 'Recollections of Ireland. An Address

of Thomas Francis Meagher at the Fenian Library, 30 Dec. 1865', in John Bruce (comp.), *Lectures of Governor Thomas Francis Meagher in Montana* (Helena, MT: Bruce and Wright, 1867), p.35. For Meagher's St Patrick's Day speech in Virginia City, 17 March 1866, see *Lectures*, p.22.

22. Meagher, 'Recollections of Ireland', *Lectures*, p.33.
23. 'An Address by General Thomas Francis Meagher, 5 August 1866', *Lectures*, pp.50–5.
24. An Address by General Thomas Francis Meagher, 13 April 1866, *House Journal*, Second Session, (Helena, MT: Ronan and Wilkinson, 1867), p.125. Also, see Spence, *Territorial Politics*, p.219.
25. Sanders to James B. Fergus, 14 Feb. 1866, in James B. Fergus Papers, Montana Historical Society, Helena. See, Spence, *Territorial Politics*, pp.37–8.
26. *Montana Post*, 9 Sept. 1865. The original legislation in the Edgerton period can be found in *Acts, Resolutions, and Memorials... Passed by the First Legislative Assembly* (Virginia City, MA: D.W. Tilton, 1864), pp.443–8.
27. Meagher, Executive Office, Territory of Montana, April 1866, Meagher Papers, Montana Historical Society, Helena. Ronan is listed as superintendent in *House Journal*, Second Session, 1866. Ronan's printing company was also given the contract for publishing the proceedings of the Territorial legislature.
28. Cited in Maginnis, 'Thomas Francis Meagher', p.105. See also, Spence, *Territorial Politics*, pp.37–8; Col. Finerty, 'Oration by Col. Finerty, Dedication of the Meagher Memorial, 4 July 1905', *Contributions to the Historical Society of Montana*, 6, (1907), p.139 and R. A. Watson, *The Life and Times of Thomas Francis Meagher* (Sandy Bay, Tasmania: Anglo-Saxon-Keltic Society, 1989), p.84.
29. Meagher, 'Recollections of Ireland', *Lectures*, pp.28–30
30. For the Diamond story, see Lewis W. Hunt, 'Thomas Francis Meagher; The 1913 Hoax', *Montana the Magazine of Western History*, 12, (1962), pp.26–35.
31. Fr. Hugh Quigley, *The Irish Race in California and on the Pacific Coast* (San Francisco, CA: A. Roman & Co., 1878), pp.167–8, 543.
32. *Helena Independent*, 5 July 1905. Interestingly, members of The Grand Army of the Republic showed up in force to celebrate Meagher's memory,
33. Cited in David Emmons 'The Orange and the Green in Montana: A Reconsideration of the Clark-Daly Feud', *Arizona and the West*, 28 (1986), pp.225–45. Also, see David Emmons, *The Butte Irish: Class and Ethnicity in an American Mining Town* (Urbana, IL: University of Illinois Press, 1989), pp.118–19.

13

Meagher Memorabilia on Display at Waterford Museum of Treasures

Eamonn McEneaney and John M. Hearne

It is indeed appropriate that the permanent exhibitions of memorabilia pertaining to both Thomas Meagher Jr and his son, Thomas Francis Meagher should take place in Waterford Museum of Treasures, a renovated granary once owned by the Meagher family. The difficult work of converting the granary began in 1997 and was executed with a fastidious attention to detail, ensuring that the integrity of this eighteenth-century building was retained. When completed in 1999 this dedication was rewarded with a number of prestigious national and international awards. In 1999, it won Irish Museum of the Year Award and, one year later, won the Irish American Cultural Institute Award. It was finally designated a museum in 2002 and, in 2003 was one of six European museums to receive a special commendation in the European Museum of the Year Awards.

MEMORABILIA, THOMAS MEAGHER JR

There are a number of items on display relating to Thomas Meagher Jr. Although the latter part of his political career was overshadowed by his son, Thomas Francis, his reputation for good and fair governance was well known as was his benevolence towards the less well off. A generous benefactor of the many charities and religious orders in Waterford City, a chalice and paten gifted by him to the Sisters of Charity is displayed in the museum. This chalice, the bowl internally gilded, is inscribed: 'The gift of Thomas Meagher Esqre to God and Our Lady of Charity. Pray for him.' The maker's initials, I.S., and the hallmarks show that it was made in Dublin.

When, in 1853, he accompanied his son's wife Catherine, to America to join her husband, he was the recipient of a gold-topped walking stick from a group of Irish exiles resident in Cincinnati, Ohio. Cut from a tree growing on the grave of George Washington, this walking stick was presented as a mark of recognition that Meagher Jr was the father of 'a gallant and gifted son'. It was also given in recognition of his character as an Irish gentleman and a representative in the British House of Commons where, in the midst of treachery and corruption, he was always found the 'earnest friend of the people'.

Perhaps unusually, the museum is home to portraits of both father and son. The portrait of Thomas Meagher Jr in his mayoral robes was executed by W. Lawrence, Dublin. It was most likely painted during Meagher's mayoralty 1843–44. This portrait was acquired in 1883 from an antique shop in Dublin, by one of his mayoral and parliamentary successors, John A. Blake. Recently conserved, it is now displayed in Waterford Museum of Treasures, giving due recognition to this distinguished man.

THOMAS FRANCIS MEAGHER

One of the more impressive displays in the museum is that honouring Thomas Francis Meagher. One of the earliest of Meagher's possessions displayed is his clarinet. Meagher was an accomplished tenor and musician; it was this clarinet that propelled him into the limelight of nationalist politics when, in his first months at Stonyhurst College, he refused, as first clarinettist in the orchestra to play his instrument in celebration of the Battle of Waterloo. This led to the cancellation of the concert and established his republican credentials. He brought this clarinet to Van Diemen's Land with him and used it to entertain his fellow exiles. This particular clarinet was made by Dalmaine & Co., (late Golding & Dalmaine), Soho Square, London.

In 1845 Meagher helped establish a new '82 Club to commemorate the achievement of legislative independence in 1782. Members had special green uniforms embroidered with gold, which they wore to meetings. Later, Meagher urged that the '82 Club be used to propagate the ideology of Young Ireland. Displayed in the museum is Meagher's original coatee, part of his uniform. It was donated to Waterford Corporation by a Mr Donegan of Cork in 1886.

Most of the memorabilia pertaining to Meagher displayed in the museum relate to his time in the United States, 1852–67; and in particular to his involvement in the American Civil War. As brigadier general of the Irish Brigade, Meagher was involved in the most significant battles of the war. But following Chancellorsville in May 1863, he resigned his commission. Later in the summer of 1863, the Napper Tandy Light Artillery, Brooklyn presented Meagher with a specially commissioned sword in recognition of his contribution to the war. This sword is an ornate 1850 staff officer's sword with decorative engraving and a panel containing a spread wing eagle and another panel with a large US etched into the blade. It has an engraved silver grip and the pommel is topped with a large eagle. The sword was made by the Ames Manufacturing Company, Chicopee, Massachusetts. It bears the inscription 'Presented to Thomas Francis O'Meagher by the members of the Napper Tandy Light Artillery, as a small token of their high admiration of his sterling devotion to the cause of Ireland and Liberty'. The silver-plated steel scabbard has mounts of heavy cast brass with stands of arms and acorns with oak leaves on the drag. A second, less ornate, and lighter 1860 sword bearing the inscription 'Tiffany's

& Co. New York', is decorated with the emblem of an eagle with, on either side, three flags. The brass scabbard is plain. Although adopted in 1860, this sword did not become standard until after the heavier 1850 model was discontinued in 1872. It was this particular sword that Meagher's widow, Elizabeth, gifted to Waterford Corporation in 1886. Both swords, modelled on French originals, are displayed in the museum.

During the presentation ceremony in August 1886, Elizabeth Meagher donated a number of other valuable possessions of her late husband to the city of his birth. Two of these treasures, The Kearney Cross and the Sumter Medal, had been presented to Meagher in 1863. The Kearney Cross was named in honour of General Philip Kearney, killed during the Battle of Chantilly, 1862. Kearney, a veteran of the Mexican and Italian wars, won the French Legion of Honour for bravery at Solforino. Following his death he was succeeded by General David B. Birney. On 13 March 1863, Birney authoriszed the decoration in Kearney's honour. Designed as a 'cross of valour' it is inscribed with the words 'Kearney Cross' on one side and 'Birney's Division' on the obverse. Thomas Francis Meagher was its first recipient and the decoration was conferred on him in New York's Astor House by Alderman Farley in June 1863.

Meagher was also the recipient of the Sumter Medal later in 1863. Unlike the Kearney Cross which was a divisional decoration, the Sumter Medal (also known as the Gillmore Medal) was a decoration for gallantry and meritorious conduct. It was commissioned in 1863 by Major General Quincey Gillmore to reward valour in the Union Army, in operations before Charleston. Designed by James Pollock, Director of the Mint, it was crafted by the artist Christian Schuller. Both decorations are displayed in Waterford Museum of Treasures.

Elizabeth Meagher also presented Waterford Corporation with a 'sprig of green' similar to that worn in the caps of the Irish Brigade soldiers during the Battle of Fredericksburg. It was this 'sprig of green' that helped identify the brigade's dead. A US army general officer's buff coloured silk net sash belonging to Meagher was also donated and is also on display. Mrs Meagher also donated two regimental flags. One, a double pointed pennon, the top half red and the bottom white is inscribed '5th Regt. Irish Brigade'. This seems to correspond to the flag of the 28th Massachusetts that the Confederate Army claim to have taken (a large red and white flag with the number 1 in the centre) after the Battle of Fredericksburg. The second flag is a blue square of eighteen inches and is embroidered with thirty-four white stars. There were thirty-four states in the Union at the outbreak of the Civil War. This flag would almost certainly seem to be the Union canton from a national flag. These are currently in possession of Waterford Museum of Treasures and are awaiting conservation.

In August 1886 a crowd of over 60,000 lined the streets of Waterford to welcome the American party who had come to gift the city the memorabilia of one of its famous sons. One of the more interesting items at this ceremony was a large oil on canvas portrait of Meagher in the uniform of a brigadier general. Painted by T. F. Gallagher of New York, a native of Waterford, the artist was himself there to present the gift to the mayor, Richard Power. This portrait of Meagher, was one of two similar paintings of the general by Gallagher and both were probably painted in 1865, prior to Meagher leaving New York for the West. The other portrait was presented by Mrs Meagher to the Society of Montana Pioneers in 1887, and now adorns the offices of the Bank of the Rockies, White Sulphur Springs, Montana.[1]

NOTE

1. All references to the above items can be found in E. McEneaney (ed.) with R. Ryan, *Waterford Treasures. A Guide to the Historical and Archaeological Treasures of Waterford City* (Waterford: Waterford Museum of Treasures, 2004), pp.198–208.

Index

[Throughout this index 'Meagher' refers to Thomas Francis Meagher, except as otherwise shown, while 'aunt', 'uncle' and other such relationships are those of the people named to Thomas Francis Meagher.]